# SPECTRUM 2

### • Junior Certificate English •

**John Moriarty**
SERIES EDITOR

First published in 1999 by

MENTOR Publications
43 Furze Road
Sandyford Industrial Estate
Dublin 18

Tel: 01-2952112/3   Fax: 01-2952114
e-mail: mentor1@indigo.ie

All Rights Reserved

Text by Paul Gannon, John Moriarty & Brian Murphy,
Artwork by Ann O'Connell, Heather McKay, Nicola Sedgwick &
Christine Warner
Edited by Claire Haugh, John McCormack & Una Whelan
Designed by Erin Price

© John Moriarty 1999

ISBN: 1-902586-55-7

Printed by ColourBooks Ltd., Dublin

# Contents

Basic Writing Skills . . . . . . . . . . . . . . . . . . . . . . . . . . . . . . . . . . 1
Sentences — Using Capitals and Full Stops Correctly . . . . . . . . . . . . . . . . . . . . . 17

## POETRY

| | | |
|---|---|---|
| Choosing Shoes | Ffrida Wolfe | 29 |
| The Dustbin Men | Gregory Harrison | 30 |
| Parrot | Alan Brownjohn | 32 |
| The Battery Hen | Pam Ayres | 34 |
| The Pied Piper of Hamelin | Robert Browning | 36 |
| Spancil Hill | Traditional | 45 |
| Missing You | Jimmy McCarthy | 46 |
| The Boys of Barr na Sráide | Sigerson Clifford | 48 |
| Back in the Playground Blues | Adrian Mitchell | 50 |
| Who Killed Davey Moore? | Bob Dylan | 52 |
| Nora | G. W. Johnston | 54 |
| Holly | Seamus Heaney | 56 |
| The Witnesses | Clive Sansom | 58 |
| The Band Played Waltzing Matilda | Eric Bogle | 60 |
| Evacuee | Edith Pickthall | 63 |
| The Green Fields of France | Eric Bogle | 64 |
| Reported Missing | John Bayliss | 66 |
| Love Letters of the Dead | Douglas Street | 67 |
| The Identification | Roger McGough | 68 |
| Dover Beach | Matthew Arnold | 70 |
| They Will Say | Carl Sandberg | 71 |
| Happiness | Carl Sandberg | 71 |
| The Harbour | Carl Sandberg | 72 |
| Streets of London | Ralph McTell | 74 |
| Lion | Leonard Clark | 76 |
| The Caged Bird in Springtime | James Kirkup | 77 |
| The Encounter | Clifford Dyment | 78 |
| Hedgehog | Chu Chen Po | 78 |
| The Defence | Geoffrey Summerfield | 79 |
| Bats | Randall Jarrell | 80 |
| The Intruder | James Reeves | 82 |
| My Animals | Elizabeth Jennings | 83 |

## SHORT STORIES

| | | |
|---|---|---|
| Too Many Rabbits | *Paul Jennings* | 85 |
| Smart Ice-Cream | *Paul Jennings* | 99 |
| The Haunting | *Mary Fitzgerald (adapted)* | 103 |
| A Break for 3G | *Shane Lee* | 115 |
| The Greatest Gift | *Philip Van Doren Stern* | 133 |
| Strangers | *Karel Capek (adapted)* | 147 |
| The Anniversary | *Anon* | 153 |
| Night Train | *Nuala Lavin* | 159 |
| The Goalkeeper's Revenge | *Bill Naughton* | 167 |
| Spit Nolan | *Bill Naughton* | 173 |
| The Boy Judge | *John Turvey* | 181 |
| On My Mother's Life | *Eamonn Burke* | 189 |
| Spoil the Child | *Howard Fast* | 193 |
| The Witch's Fire | *Anon* | 205 |

## NOVELS

| | | |
|---|---|---|
| Danny the Champion of the World | *Roald Dahl* | 209 |
| Buddy | *Nigel Hinton* | 210 |
| The Runaways | *Victor Canning* | 214 |
| Roll of Thunder, Hear My Cry | *Mildred D. Taylor* | 215 |

## DRAMA

| | | |
|---|---|---|
| Our Day Out | *Willy Russell* | 219 |
| Film Studies | *To Kill a Mockingbird* | 255 |

## READING & MEDIA

| | |
|---|---|
| Reading | 263 |
| Newspapers | 297 |
| Advertising | 323 |

| | |
|---|---|
| *Index* | 345 |
| *Alphabetical List of Poems & Short Stories* | 346 |

# Acknowledgements

The author and publisher would like to thank the following for their kind permission to reproduce the following information:

POETRY Jimmy McCarthy for *Missing You*; Faber and Faber for *Holly* by Seamus Heaney; Eric Bogle for the lyrics of *No Man's Land* (alternative title *The Green Fields of France*) and *The Band Played Waltzing Matilda* with the kind permission of Roberton, Brown and Associates, London; Peters, Fraser and Dunlop for *The Identification* by Robert McGough; James Kirkup for *The Caged Bird in Springtime*; The Orien Publishing Group for *The Encounter* by Clifford Dyment.

SHORT STORIES Puffin for *Too Many Rabbits* and *Smart Ice-cream* by Paul Jennings; Mary Fitzgerald for the short story *The Haunting* with the kind permission of Lissadell Books; Shane Lee for *A Break for 3G*; Catbird Press for *Strangers* by Karel Capek; Nuala Lavin and Trident Publications Limited for the short story *Night Train*; Erna Naughton for *Spit Nolan* and *The Goalkeeper's Revenge* from "The Goalkeeper's Revenge and Other Stories" by Bill Naughton published by Heinemann New Windmills; Longman Group, UK for *The Boy Judge* by John Turvey; Eamonn Burke and Quarry Publications for the short story *On My Mother's Life*.

PLAY Willy Russell for the play *Our Day Out* from the Stanley Thornes edition with the kind permission of Casarotto Ramsay Limited. All rights whatsoever in this play are strictly reserved and application for performance etc., should be made before rehearsal to Casarotto Ramsay Ltd., National House, 60-66 Wardour Street, London W1V 3HP. No performance may be given unless a licence has been obtained.

Considerable effort has been made to locate all of the copyright holders of the material used in this book. In the event of any copyright holders having been overlooked, the publisher will be pleased to come to a suitable arrangement at their earliest convenience.

# Introduction

*Spectrum 2* meets the requirements of the Junior Certificate English programme and is principally aimed at Second and Third Year students preparing for the Ordinary Level. With features on Reading (Non-fiction), Personal and Functional Writing, Media, Fiction, Elements of Grammar, Poetry, Drama and Film it provides a wide selection of material and offers teachers much scope in devising a variety of work to suit the needs of their particular classes. The views and advice of many experienced teachers and examiners of Junior Certificate English were taken into consideration in selecting and devising the material in this book.

### Questions & Assignments

The Questions and Assignments which follow all items provide opportunities for both written and oral work. The written responses will provide students with a record of the literature they have studied and their responses to it. This in turn will clearly be a useful examination aid.

### Points to Note

These follow most items and aim to highlight important features relating to style and technique. Literary terms are clearly explained in the context of the short stories, poems, plays and extracts in which they arise. A knowledge of these literary terms provides students with the technical language for discussing and writing about all forms of literature as well as a solid foundation for the new Leaving Certificate programme. An Index of key terms is also provided at the back of the book.

### [Answer Guidelines]

The Answer Guidelines use the following formats:
- Useful words, phrases and sentence starters from which students can construct answers.
- 'Exploration'-type questions which direct students towards appropriate responses to assignments.

The purpose of the answer guidelines is not to provide pupils with an outline 'answer' but rather to 'spark off' ideas to complement those of their own. For this reason the significance of an odd word or phrase in an answer guideline may not be immediately obvious. They should be regarded as a 'fall-back' answering strategy rather than a substitute for the students' own original responses.

### Word Games

The book contains a selection of word games – matching words to meanings, spell checks, cryptic puzzles, anagrams etc – which are designed to improve spelling, vocabulary, syntax and other literacy skills. These word games are intentionally demanding and some pupils may encounter difficulties. Should this occur, teachers can provide additional clues, such as the initial letters of the solutions. Answers to all word games are included in the Teacher's Handbook.

# BASIC WRITING SKILLS

Essays in which capital letters and punctuation marks are omitted or used incorrectly confuse the reader and lose their impact. Throughout this book you will find twenty one *Spot the Errors*. These are aimed at sharpening your basic writing skills. Each exercise consists of a passage containing twenty errors of the types frequently found in students' work. Before attempting these you should read carefully over the guidelines in this section. As you do each *Spot the Errors* you should refer back to these guidelines whenever you are in doubt. Included also in the *Spot the Errors* are spelling mistakes.

## Basic Writing Skills – Guidelines

1. Using Capital Letters Correctly — Eleven Simple Rules

2. Laying out Dialogue — Quotation Marks

3. Spelling Plurals Correctly — Six Basic Rules

4. Using Commas Correctly — Two Simple Rules

5. Adjectives — Six Spelling Guidelines

6. Forming the Past Tense of Verbs — Two Spelling Rules

7. Prepositions — Some Common Errors

8. Using the Apostrophe Correctly — Two Simple Rules

9. Words that Sound the Same — Which One to Use?

## Guideline 1: Using Capital Letters Correctly – Eleven Simple Rules

The following two sentences contain examples of Rules 1 – 5 for capitals.

**When Paula Redmond was interviewed on BBC on St. Patrick's Day she spoke about her life on the Aran Islands.**

**When Tom Roberts left UCD on Friday he drove to the Wicklow Mountains.**

### Rules

1. Capitals are used to begin — A sentence

2. Capitals are used to begin — People's names

3. Capitals are used to begin — Days of the week, months and holidays. (Note: the seasons — spring, winter, autumn and summer — do not get capitals.)

4. Capitals are used to begin — Names of places. (Note: the word 'Islands' is part of the name of the Aran Islands and so it is given a capital letter.)

5. All letters in initials are capital letters.

### Important Note on Rule 4

**When she was interviewed on television today she spoke about her life on the islands.**

**The man left the college yesterday and drove to the mountains.**

The first sentence here — similar in meaning to the first sentence above — shows where confusion sometimes arises between small letters and capitals. When place names such as 'Island', 'Park', 'Street', 'College' and 'Lake' are part of the name of a specific place they begin with a capital letter.

The following sentence contains examples of Rules 6 – 8.

**She bought a Pepsi in Burgerland and read *The Examiner*.**

### Rules

**6**    Capitals are used for — Brand names.

**7**    Capitals are used for — Names of restaurants, clubs, ships etc.

**8**    Capitals are used for — Titles of newspapers, books, films, songs etc.

The following passage contains examples of Rules 9 – 11.

**At midnight Doctor Flynn's phone rang.**
**"Can you come to the harbour?" said a voice. "A Spanish trawler has just docked and Captain Alvarez is very ill."**

### Rules

**9**    Capitals are used to begin; — Titles that are used as part of a name.

**10**    Capitals are used to begin; — The first word of direct speech.

**11**    Capitals are used to begin; — Adjectives that are formed from proper nouns — Irish, British, American etc.

#### Important Note on Rule 9

**At midnight the doctor's phone rang.**
**"Can you come to the harbour?" said a voice. "A trawler has just docked and the captain is very ill."**

Note that in this example the words 'doctor' and 'captain' do not begin with a capital because they are not part of a name.

## Guideline 2: Laying Out Dialogue — Quotation Marks

> "Oh no! I left the money at home," shouted Tom.
> 
> "Oh no!" shouted Tom, "I left the money at home."
> 
> Tom shouted, "Oh no! I left the money at home."

These are the three ways in which to write this piece of dialogue. The first one is most commonly used.

> "Hello!" said Jane.

Remember that <u>only</u> the spoken words are enclosed in quotation marks (sometimes referred to as speech marks). In some novels and stories single quotation marks are used.

> 'Hello!' said Jane.

We recommend that you use double quotation marks in your work.

Begin a new line for each speaker. Like this —

> "I paid two hundred pounds for the piano," said Anna.
> 
> "Who did you buy it from?" asked Matt.
> 
> "A relative of Jane's," replied Anna.

Not like this —

> "I paid two hundred pounds for the piano," said Anna. "Who did you buy it from?" asked Matt. "A relative of Jane's," replied Anna.

. . . as it can make the page layout crowded and cause difficulties for the reader.

If there are only two speakers you do not need to continue naming the speaker after each speech. For example —

> The next day Ali and Hussein took the matter to the judge.
> "Did anyone see you put the gold in the jar?" the judge asked Ali.
> "No, I was alone. I have no wife or family."
> "Did you tell anybody about putting the gold in the jar?"
> "No, I did not want anybody to know."
> "What did you tell Hussein was in the jar?"
> "Olives."
> Then the judge turned to Hussein. "Did anyone tell you there was gold in the jar?"
> "No."
> "Did you at any time open the jar?"
> "No."

(from *The Boy Judge*)

## Dialogue in Drama

All dialogue used in essays should be laid out like the above example. However, in the case of drama scripts dialogue is laid out differently. No quotation marks are used and the speaker's name comes before each speech. For example —

> **Judge:** Did anyone see you put the gold in the jar?
> **Ali:** No, I was alone. I have no wife or family.
> **Judge:** Did you tell anybody about putting the gold in the jar?
> **Ali:** No, I did not want anybody to know.
> **Judge:** What did you tell Hussein was in the jar?
> **Ali:** Olives.
> **Judge (turning to Hussein):** Did anyone tell you there was gold in the jar?
> **Hussein:** No.
> **Judge:** Did you at any time open the jar?
> **Hussein:** No.

## Guideline 3: Spelling Plurals Correctly — Six Basic Rules

### Rules

1. The first rule is obvious. Add 's'.
   — **One cat. Two cats.**

2. Words that end in s, ss, x, sh, ch. Add 'es'.
   — **Buses; Classes; Foxes; Marshes; Perches.**

3. Words that end in 'y' which is preceeded by a consonant. Change the 'y' to 'i' and add 'es'.
   — **One army. Two armies. One lady. Two ladies.**

4. Words ending with a 'y' which is preceeded by a vowel. Rule 1 applies. Add 's'.
   — **One toy. Two toys. One replay. Three replays.**

5. Words ending with 'f'. Change the 'f' to 'ves'.
   — **One wolf. Two wolves.**
   (Note: There are some exceptions to this rule such as **chief, gulf, proof, roof, reef.** — Simply add an 's'.)

6. Words ending in 'o' add 'es'. **One hero. Two heroes.**
   (Note: There are some exceptions to this rule such as **solo, piano, Eskimo.** Simply add an 's'.)

### Unusual plurals

Compound words. Change the principal word to the plural.
— **One father-in-law. Two fathers-in-law.**

Words that change completely in the plural form.
— **One mouse. Two mice.**

Words that are identical in both singular and plural.
— **One sheep. Two sheep.**

Foreign words now used in English. The plurals are formed according to the rules of the original language.
— **One radius. Two radii. One crisis. Two crises.**

Basic Writing Skills

## Guideline 4: Using Commas Correctly – Two Simple Rules

### Rule 1

To mark short pauses in sentences and to make longer sentences easy to understand by dividing them up with commas.
(Note: There is no hard and fast rule here. If you would pause while speaking then insert a comma.)

*Peter, who is six, plays the piano.*

*If I decide to go, I will let you know tomorrow.*

### Rule 2

To separate items on a list.
(Note: The last item on a list is separated from the rest by the word 'and'.)

*We visited London, Paris, Amsterdam, Rome and Vienna.*

*When Andrew went to town he saw a film, had a meal, bought shoes and collected a jacket from the cleaners.*

## Guideline 5: Adjectives – Six Spelling Guidelines

All adjectives have three forms, for example — late, later, latest. Spelling the latter two forms correctly — the comparative form ('later') and the superlative form ('latest') sometimes causes problems.

**Guideline 1**
In the case of most adjectives, simply add -er or -est.
For example: fast, faster, fastest.

**Guideline 2**
If the adjective ends in an 'e', drop the 'e' before adding -er or -est.
For example: large, larger, largest.

**Guideline 3**
If the adjective ends in 'y' this letter should be changed to 'i' before adding -er or -est.
For example: lucky, luckier, luckiest.

**Guideline 4**
If the adjective ends in a consonant sound, preceded by a single vowel, the consonant is doubled before adding -er or -est.
For example: big, bigger, biggest.

**Guideline 5**
Adjectives of three or more syllables do not use -er or -est. Instead the words 'more' or 'most' are used. This rule also applies to some two-syllable adjectives. You will know what sounds right and what doesn't.
For example: adventurous, more adventurous, most adventurous.

**Guideline 6**
Some adjectives change completely to form the comparative and superlative forms. For example —
little, less, least
many, more, most
much, more, most
good, better, best
bad, worse, worst.

## Guideline 6: Forming the Past Tense of Verbs – Two Spelling Rules

The tense of a verb tells us when the action took place. The three most common tenses used are:

The past tense (He **sang** a song)
The present tense (He **sings** a song)
The future tense (He **will sing** a song)

### Rules

**1** If the present tense ends in a 'y' change it to an 'i' before adding 'ed'.
— **cry/cried; terrify/terrified.**

**2** If the present tense ends in a consonant which is immediately preceded by a single vowel, double the last consonant before adding 'ed'.
— **drip/dripped; stop/stopped.**

### Participles

A participle is a word that can be used either as part of a verb (He is **running** home) or an adjective (The **running** water is safe to drink).

The word 'running' is an example of the present participle. Using the present participle will not give you problems. However, students frequently get confused between the past tense of a verb and the past participle.

✓ *Having beaten Kerry by a goal, the Leitrim team decided to celebrate.*

Here the words 'having beaten' are used as a verb. The word 'beaten' is the participle.
✗ It would be incorrect to write '**Having beat Kerry . . .**'

✓ *The beaten team was very disappointed.*

Here the word 'beaten' is used as an adjective.
✗ It would be incorrect to write '**The beat team . . .**'

| Right | Wrong |
|---|---|
| Having broken a window, we ran away. | Having broke the window, we ran away. |
| The sunken boat was recovered. | The sunk boat was recovered. |
| He went out after he did his homework. | He went out after he done his homework. |
| When he had spoken he left the meeting. | When he had spoke he left the meeting. |

## Guideline 7: Prepositions – Some Common Errors

✓ The bus went past the stop.
✗ The bus went passed the stop.

'Past' is a preposition. 'Passed' is a verb.

✓ He fell into the river from the boat.
✗ He fell in the river from the boat.

'Into' refers to movement from one place to another. 'In' shows position.

✓ That dog is different from ours.
✗ That dog is different to ours.
✗ That dog is different than ours.

'From' always follows 'different'.

✓ Two teachers were there besides the principal.

'Besides' means in addition to.

✓ Two teachers were there beside the principal.

'Beside' refers to a position.

✓ The sweets were shared among the class.

There are more than two people.

✓ The sweets were shared between the twins.

There are only two people.

## Guideline 8: Using the Apostrophe Correctly – Two Simple Rules

### Rule 1

**Ownership**
The apostrophe is used to denote ownership. When there is one owner, keep the singular form of the noun and add –'s.

*My brother's keys, Jane's ring, the man's watch.*

When there is more than one owner, use the plural form of the noun if it ends in 's' or 'es' and simply add –'.

*The ladies' club, the dogs' kennels, the boys' room*

However, in a small number of cases the plural form of the noun does not end in 's' or 'es'. In these cases simply add –'s.

*The men's tent, the women's room, the children's present.*

### Rule 2

**Missing Letters**
The apostrophe is used also to show that one or more letters have been omitted from a word. In conversation people say, "It's early" instead of "It <u>is</u> early" and "I'd like to go" instead of "I <u>would</u> like to go".

## Guideline 9: Words that Sound the Same — Which One to Use?

### Which One to Use — There; Their; They're

**There** refers to a situation or position.

> There is one sweet left.
> Tom found the ball over there.

**Their** means belonging to them or owned by them.

> The Ryans returned to their home.

**They're** is a short way of saying **they are**. The apostrophe is in place of the letter 'a'.

> They're late again!

### Assignment

Attempt the following six exercises, using **there**, **their** or **they're** to fill in the gaps.

1. _____ was no one _____ when we got to the station.
2. _____ house was sold.
3. The boys say that _____ not going to the match.
4. _____ dog was found over _____ .
5. _____ are too many passengers travelling on the bus.
6. We saw _____ car in town.

## Which One to Use — Whose; Who's

**Who's** is a short way of saying '**Who is** . . .'. The apostrophe is in place of the letter 'i'.

> Who's going to the match?
> Look who's running towards us.
> Do you know who's playing in goal?

**Whose** indicates or questions ownership.

> Whose coat is this?
> I don't know whose pen it is.

## Which One to Use — To; Two; Too

**To** — Opposite of 'from'

> I walk to school.
> I am going to my piano lesson.
> I am sailing to France.

**Too** — Use instead of 'also' or 'more than required'.

> Will you come too?
> Too many drivers speed on our roads.
> My socks are too small.

**Two** — The number 2.

> The lion had two cubs.
> David will be back in two or three minutes.

## Which One to Use??? — There's; Theirs

**Theirs** — Indicates ownership.

> That dalmation is theirs.
> Is the red car theirs?

**There's** — A short way of saying '**There is** . . .' The apostrophe is in place of the letter 'i'.

> There's a big crowd gathering.
> There's little point in going any further.

## Which One to Use — We're; Were

**We're** — A short way of saying '**We are** . . .' The apostrophe is in place of the letter 'a'. If 'we are' won't replace it, don't use 'we're'.

> We're late again.
> When we're early the teacher is surprised.

**Were** — Past tense of 'are'.
If uncertain, test the sentence by putting in 'are'. If it makes sense then use 'were'.

> Were you playing in the match?
> The dogs were barking all night.

(In each of these cases 'are' can be inserted instead of 'were'.)

## Which One to Use — Its; It's

<u>Its</u> — denotes ownership, i.e. belonging to 'it'.

(Note: While an apostrophe is normally used to indicate ownership, e.g. the dog's kennel, in case of something being owned by 'it' an apostrophe is <u>not</u> used.)

> The dog is in its kennel.
>
> John has a new bike. Its handlebars are straight.

<u>It's</u> — short for **it is**. The apostrophe is in place of the letter 'i'.

(Note: Avoid using **it's** except when including the word in dialogue.)

> "It's very late."
>
> "It's a great book."
>
> "Egypt! It's an amazing country."

### Assignment

Attempt the following four exercises, using **its** or **it's** to fill in the gaps.

1. "_____ too early for the daffodils to flower."
2. Sharon has a new tennis racquet. _____ handle is made of graphite.
3. "Pass the salt, please. _____ behind the ketchup."
4. "The rainbow is very clear. Look at _____ colours. _____ the best rainbow I've seen in a long time."

# Sentence Building

> The exercise below contains ten sentences. The sentences have been broken up into a number of parts and the parts have been mixed up. Rearrange the sentences correctly and write them out again, adding the necessary punctuation.

## HENRY FORD (1863 - 1947)
## FOUNDER OF FORD MOTORS

1. gave his name to the car
   the word 'Ford' means an automobile
   the man who
   the modern automobile industry
   led the way in creating
   because
   To almost everyone
   and this is not surprising,

2. his imagination was stirred
   when he saw
   When Henry Ford was twelve
   a steam-driven traction engine and
   from then on,
   engines were his chief interest

3. When he was older
   so he spent every day
   Ford trained
   working with engines
   as a machinist,

4. were then the most common
   but Ford was interested in
   the newly invented gasoline internal combustion engine
   type of engine,
   Steam engines

5. his own version
   and drove out in his first automobile
   of the engine
   In 1896 he put
   in a four-wheel carriage body

6. the main means of transportation
   Ford dreamed of
   that anyone could afford
   producing a cheap automobile
   because he believed the automobile
   would some day become

7. started the Ford Motor Company
   In 1903,
   Ford and a few partners

8. he achieved this goal
   In 1908
   when the Model T,
   of the Ford plant
   selling for $550,
   rolled out

9. as the 'Tin Lizzie',
   in automobile history
   The Model T,
   popularly known
   became the most famous car

10. and the Ford Motor Company
    were sold
    was well on its way to becoming
    it is today
    the industrial giant
    Over 15,000,000 Model T's

# Sentences
## – Using capitals and full stops correctly

> A sentence is a group of words that expresses a complete statement or asks a question.

Sentences are the basic building blocks of all writing. Capital letters are used to begin sentences and full stops are used to mark the end of sentences.

Using capital letters and full stops correctly is one of the most important basic writing skills. Do we really need capital letters and full stops? See for yourself. We have reproduced these two paragraphs with all the full stops and capitals omitted.

> sentences are the basic building blocks of all writing capital letters are used to begin sentences and full stops are used to mark the end of sentences using capital letters and full stops correctly is one of the most important basic writing skills do we really need capital letters and full stops see for yourself we have reproduced this paragraph with all the full stops and capitals omitted — *Confused?*

The following guidelines and assignments aim to help you master this important writing skill. We will start with two simple sentences.

> ✔ A helicopter flew over our house. Our dog barked.

In the case of sentences that are questions, a question mark (?) is used instead of the full stop.

> ✔ Why did the dog bark?

Provided it is complete, a statement need not be true — or even make sense — in order to be a sentence.

> ✔ A dog flew over our house. Our helicopter barked.

Two pieces of information can also be linked together to form a sentence. **And, but, if, when, where, although, why** and **because** are some of the link words used to connect two or more statements.

> ✔ A plane flew over our house and our dog barked.

> ✘ A plane flew over our house and.

— The second example is not a sentence because it is not complete. If someone said this to you, you would reply "And what?"

> ✘ And our dog barked.

— Likewise this is not a sentence because the word 'And' at the beginning suggests that some information has been left out. If someone said this to you, you might ask "Why did the dog bark?"

### IMPORTANT NOTE ON LINK WORDS

Statements beginning or ending with other link words do not form sentences.

> ✘ When a helicopter flew over our house.
> ✘ If a helicopter flew over our house.
> ✘ Because a helicopter flew over our house.
> ✘ Our dog barked when.
> ✘ Our dog barked because.
> ✘ Our dog barked but.

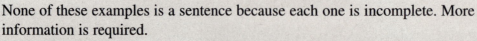

None of these examples is a sentence because each one is incomplete. More information is required.

Here are some more examples of two pieces of linked information that form single sentences.

> ✔ The dog barked because the postman knocked.
> ✔ Tom played the match although he was injured.
> ✔ Paul would go to Cork if he had the train fare.
> ✔ The crowd cheered when they saw the seal.
> ✔ Mary built a snowman but within hours it had melted.

Take out the 'link' words and you have two sentences in each case.

> ✔ The dog barked. The postman knocked.
> ✔ Tom played the match. He was injured.
> ✔ Paul would go to Cork. He had the train fare.
> ✔ The crowd cheered. They saw the seal.
> ✔ Mary built a snowman. Within hours it had melted.

Some sentences, containing many pieces of linked information, can be quite lengthy.

> The young boy cycled frantically up to a bus stop where there was a huddle of people, threw the bike aside and knelt down in front of them.
> "Help me! I'm being kidnapped," he wailed to the bewildered onlookers.

You should vary your writing by using both short and long sentences.

### Assignment – Full Stops and Sentences 1

Here are twenty groups of words. Write out the numbers of those that form complete sentences. In the case of the remainder make them into sentences by adding a few suitable words.

1. One morning in June.
2. The girls went to the beach.
3. Into the river and watched it sink.
4. In the centre of the city.
5. The moon is rising and the countryside is silent.
6. Before the dawn broke.
7. The Beatles are probably the most famous band of all.
8. John Delaney brought a hamster to school.
9. Would you like some tea?
10. When Tom arrives.
11. From Limerick to Galway.
12. When did Tom arrive?
13. He will play.
14. If it stops raining.
15. When evening comes and the crowds begin to gather.
16. What do you want?
17. Look it up in the telephone directory.
18. Peter sang.
19. If I pay for the ticket will you go?
20. Tomorrow never comes.

### Assignment – Full Stops and Sentences 2

The following pages contain five tests consisting of fifty facts about the world of nature. Each fact **either** consists of a complete single sentence **or** two sentences combined with the full stop and the capital omitted. Identify the numbers of those facts that are single complete sentences. In the case of those facts that are two sentences, rewrite them by inserting the full stop and the capital in the correct place. For example, in Test A fact number 1 is two sentences while fact number 9 is a single sentence.

# animal facts
## TEST A

1. Tortoises are the longest living animals some live to be over 150 years old.

2. Because they face many dangers, wild animals don't usually live as long as pets or zoo animals big animals, generally, live longer than small ones like insects.

3. Animal intelligence is hard to measure, but most experts think that chimpanzees and dolphins come top of the class.

4. Chimpanzees can use simple tools dolphins can talk to one another under water, using a musical language of their own.

5. Very few types of shark will attack swimmers the deadliest animals are much smaller.

6. Some snakes, spiders and jellyfish have poisonous bites or stings which can kill a person in minutes.

7. As many as forty thousand people a year are killed as a result of snake bites most of these deaths are caused by the Indian cobra.

8. Birds are the record-holders for speed in a dive, a peregrine falcon can reach 320km/h when diving.

9. In level flight the Asian spine-tailed swift can fly at speeds of more than 160km/h.

10. The champion sprinter of all the land animals is the cheetah who can reach speeds of 110km/h for short periods.

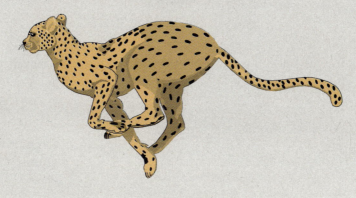

# animal facts
## TEST B

*Sentences – Using capitals and full stops correctly*

1. Animals like hawks which hunt and kill other animals for food are called predators.
2. The kestrel hovers as it hunts wings beating and tail spread, it waits in the sky the albatross has the biggest wingspan of all birds — nearly 4 metres across.
3. Not all birds can fly flightless birds include the ostrich and the emu.
4. Kiwis are shy flightless birds which live in New Zealand they wander about on the ground at night, hunting for a juicy meal of insects and worms.
5. Penguins can't fly, but they can swim well.
6. The smallest bird is the bee hummingbird it is less than 60 millimetres long.
7. Hummingbirds' tiny wings beat too fast to see, at up to 50 times a second.
8. Bats fly by flapping their wings, just like birds do bats are mammals, however, not birds.
9. Bats sleep in the day, roosting upside down in trees or caves they wake at dusk.
10. Bats cluster together for winter, sleeping upside down in caves and old buildings.

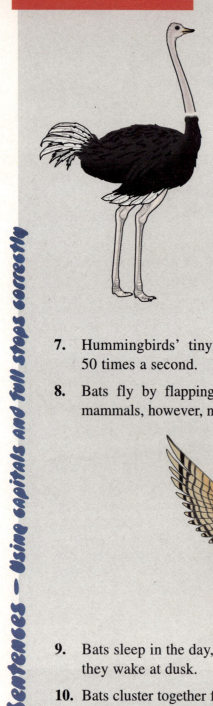

# animal facts
## TEST C

1. Whales are the largest animals on Earth the biggest whale is the blue whale, which can be up to 30 metres long and weigh as much as 150 tonnes.

2. The largest land animal is the African elephant, which is twice as tall as a person and can weigh 6 tonnes.

3. Hibernation is like a deep sleep, which some animals go into when food is scarce.

4. In late summer the dormouse crams itself with fruit and nuts until it is very fat then it curls up inside its nest and goes to sleep.

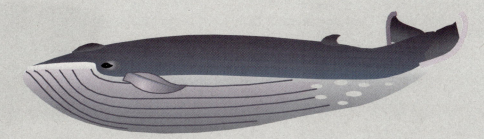

5. The dormouse lives off its body fat throughout the winter and wakes up in spring, very thin and very hungry.

6. Snakes become sluggish in cold weather they begin to stir only when it gets warmer.

7. A chameleon is a type of lizard whose skin changes slowly to match the colours of its surroundings.

8. The largest lizard is Indonesia's Komodo dragon which has a length of around 3 metres.

9. Most lizards can shed their tails when they want to they often do this to get away from enemies, who are left clutching a wriggling bit of tail while the lizard escapes.

10. The lizard's tail grows back again, but it is slightly shorter than before.

# animal facts
## TEST D

1. Most bats can see quite well, but their large ears help them to track insects when hunting at night.

2. The fin on top of a fish's back is called its dorsal fin the fish uses this fin to help it change direction.

3. The seahorse swims slowly in an upright position, by fanning its small dorsal fin so quickly that it looks like a boat's propeller.

4. Few snakes are poisonous some snakes kill animals for food by crushing them in their jaws while others coil their long bodies around their victims and squeeze them to death.

5. The python grows to 10 metres and is the world's longest snake it uses its powerful body to squeeze its victims to death, and it can even kill pigs and deer.

6. Rattlesnakes are very poisonous they rattle the ends of their tails as a warning signal.

7. Snakes are expert hunters, even though they don't see or hear well they hunt mainly by smell.

8. There is very little difference between most frogs and toads and it is often difficult to tell them apart.

9. Frogs tend to hop and leap about on land, while toads generally have shorter back legs and prefer to crawl.

10. The Goliath frog of Africa is the world's largest frog it can grow to 30 centimetres.

*Sentences – using capitals and full stops correctly*

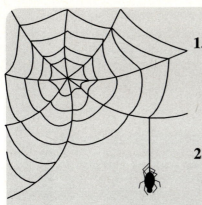

1. The caterpillar spends most of its time eating it crawls around, chewing on leaves, and grows quickly.

2. The Bolas spider of South America spins a single thread of silk with a sticky blob at the end, and swings it to catch flying insects.

3. Dragonflies are fast fliers they have been recorded reaching speeds of 80 km/h.

4. Bees make honey from pollen and nectar, which they collect from flowers in summer.

5. Back at their hive, the bees put the mixture into little wax 'rooms' called cells the cells are six-sided and join to make the shape we call a honeycomb.

6. The bees make a special substance in their bodies which they add to the mixture this turns it into honey for them to eat in winter.

7. Flies can walk up windows and across ceilings because they have special hooks and sucker pads on their feet instead of toes.

8. The buzzing that a fly makes is the sound of its wings beating at over a hundred times a second.

9. One of the main reasons why animals become extinct is because a major change takes place in their habitat weather patterns change or the food they need becomes hard to get.

10. More than three hundred animal species have become extinct in the last three hundred years thousands more are on the danger list including the African elephant and the blue whale.

# SPOT THE ERRORS

The following **Spot the Errors** exercise is aimed at sharpening your basic writing skills. Spot the 20 errors in the Sample Passage below and rewrite the passage correctly. In this example the location of each error is marked by a number. (Note: Refer to the Guidelines on pages 1—15.)

## Sample Passage

Robin of Locksley was nicknamed Robin Hood. The band of Outlaws① grew quickly. Sum② were from Locksley, like Will Stutely③ others④ were tradesmen, like arthur⑤ Bland, a tanner from nottingham⑥. He was outlawed because he had beaten a norman⑦ merchant who had cheated him over some leather.

One day.⑧ Robin called the men together.

"There are almost forty of us now," he said. "We are all wanted men. So we must be ready to fight for our freedom. We must also fight to defend the poor⑨ the weak and the helpless."

"But how can we fight⑩" asked Nic. "Were⑪ not warriors and we have no weapons?⑫"

⑬Then you must learn," said Robin. "First you will learn how to fight with quarterstaves. We have a champoin⑭ in our midst — right, Mutch?'

"I one⑮ a prize at Nottingham Fair," Mutch confessed⑯ blushing. "But thats⑰ only sport."

"Your⑱ a good fighter," said Will Stutely. "I seen⑲ you fight at the fare⑳."

— *from Robin Hood*

(Note: Error 3 is an omission — a full stop omitted at the end of a sentence. Error 4 is an omission — a capital omitted at the beginning of the next sentence. Error 8 is a full stop inserted incorrectly. Error 9 is a comma omitted in a list. Error 13 is an omission of opening speech marks.)

## Corrected Passage

Robin of Locksley was nicknamed Robin Hood. The band of outlaws grew quickly. Some were men of Locksley, like Will Stutely. Others were tradesmen, like Arthur Bland, a tanner from Nottingham. He was outlawed because he had beaten a Norman merchant who had cheated him over some leather.

One day Robin called the men together.

"There are almost forty of us now," he said. "We are all wanted men. So we must be ready to fight for our freedom. We must also fight to defend the poor, the weak and the helpless."

"But how can we fight?" asked Nic. "We're not warriors and we have no weapons."

"Then you must learn," said Robin. "First you will learn how to fight with quarterstaves. We have a champion in our midst — right, Mutch?"

"I did win a prize at Nottingham Fair," Mutch confessed, blushing. "But that's only sport."

"You're a good fighter," said Will Stutely. "I saw you fight at the fair."

# Spot the errors

Sentences — Using Capitals and Full Stops Correctly

The following **Spot the Errors** exercise is aimed at sharpening your basic writing skills. Spot the 20 errors in the Passage below and rewrite the passage correctly. (Note: Refer to the Guidelines on pages 1—15.)

## 1    A Holiday in Jamaica

My room in the hotel had a little balcony, and from there I could step strait down on to the beech. There were tall coconut palms growing all around, and every so often an enormous green nut the size of a football would fall out of the sky and dropped with a thud on the sand. It was considered foolish to linger underneat a coconut palm because if one of those things landed on your head, it would smash your skull.

The Jamaican Girl who came in to tidy my room told me that a wealthy american called Mr. Wasserman had met his end in presicely this manner only too months before.

"Your joking," I said to her.

"No sir!" she cried. "I saw it hapening with my very own eyes!"

So she told me the story. Mr. Wasserman was standing right underneath a tall tree on the beach he had got his camera out and was pointing it at the sunset. It was a red sunset that evening and very pretty. Then all at once, down came a big green nut that landed with a smack on top of his bald head.

"And that," she added with a touch of relish, "was the very last sunset Mr. Wasserman ever did see."

"You mean it killed him instantly?" i asked.

I don't know about instantly, she said. "I remember the next thing that happened was that the camera fell out of his hands on to the sand. His arm's dropped down to his sides and hung there. Then he started swaying. He swayed backwards and forwards several times ever so gently. I was standing their watching him and I taught that maybe he would faint any moment. then very, very slowly he keeled right over and down he went."

"Was he dead"

"Dead as a doornail," she said.

# Sentence Building

*Spectrum 2*

The exercise below contains ten sentences. The sentences have been broken up into a number of parts and the parts have been mixed up. Rearrange the sentences correctly and write them out again, adding the necessary punctuation.

## FINGERPRINTING

1. impressions / Fingerprints are the / an exact and practical / identification / the fingertips / of the ridges of / It is / means of

2. because no two people / have the same fingerprints / in the world, / It is exact / not even identical twins,

3. ink and paper / It is practical / because it is / simple and inexpensive, / requiring only

4. for the purpose of identification / Although fingerprinting / early man knew something / the 19th century, / about the value of prints / on a large scale until / did not start

5. and seals / Print marks have / been found on / ancient clay tablets

6. types of fingerprint records, / The files of / civil and criminal / the FBI include two

7. victims of loss of memory, / of identifying missing persons, / involved in accidents / serves as a means / The civil file / or people

8. who have police records and sometimes / It is used to identify offenders / to identify suspects / is a record of / The second file / the fingerprints of criminals

9. babies are taken / the footprints of / shortly after birth / In many hospitals

10. like fingerprints, / never change, / provided with / a permanent means of identification / the baby is in this way / Since footprints,

# Poetry

### Choosing Shoes

New shoes, new shoes,
Red and pink and blue shoes,
Tell me what would *you* choose
If they'd let us buy?

Buckle shoes, bow shoes,
Pretty pointy-toe shoes,
Strappy, cappy low shoes;
Let's have some to try.

Bright shoes, white shoes,
Dandy dance-by-night shoes,
Perhaps-a-little-tight shoes;
Like some? So would I.
BUT
Flat shoes, fat shoes,
Stump-along-like-that shoes,
Wipe-them-on-the-mat shoes
O that's the sort they'll buy.
— *Ffrida Wolfe*

## Points to Note — RHYTHM

If you recite this poem aloud you will see that it could be accompanied by a regular drumbeat as in a 'rap'. We could say that this poem has a regular rhythm pattern. The rhythm is fast and lively. It adds to the light-hearted mood of the poem. A slow rhythm usually helps to create a more serious or sad mood in a poem. Some poems have no rhythm pattern.

If you are asked about the sound effects in a poem or the musical quality of the poem, you should comment on the rhythm pattern.

### Questions & Assignments

1. What kind of person is speaking in this poem?
2. Who are *'they'* as referred to in the first and last verses?
3. Describe the kind of shoes the poet would like to buy.
4. (a) There is a phrase in the third verse that we might occasionally hear in a shoe shop. Who might use this phrase and why?
   (b) Make a list of other phrases that are used when shoes are being bought.
5. What is the difference between the shoes referred to in the first three verses and the shoes referred to in the last verse?

# The Dustbin Men

The older ones have gone to school,
My breakfast's on the plate,
But I can't leave the window-pane,
I might be just too late.

I've heard the clatter down the street,
I know they're creeping near,
The team of gruff-voiced, burly men
Who keep our dustbins clear.

And I must watch and see them clang
The dustbins on the road,
And stand in pairs to heave up high
The double-handled load.

Yes, there they come, the lorry growls
And grinds in bottom gear;
The dustman knees the garden gate
As, high up by his ear,
Firmly he balances the bin,
Head tilted to one side;
The great mouth of the rubbish cart
Is yawning very wide;
To me the mouth looks like a beast's
A dragon's hungry jaws
That snap the refuse out of sight
Behind those sliding doors.

The lorry-dragon every day
Is in a ravenous mood,
And cardboard boxes, bottles, jars
Are all part of his food.

He gobbles up old magazines,
Saucepans and broken jugs
Pieces of red linoleum,
And dirty, tufted rugs.
He crunches shattered pictures,
Old bicycles and tyres,
A bird-cage with its seed-tray,
Its bell and rusty wires;

And fractured clocks and mirrors,
A rocking-chair and broom,
A mattress and an iron bed;
Where does he find the room?
And like a dragon sated,
His great maw crammed quite tight,
He lifts his head and swallows
His breakfast out of sight.

What would the careless people
Who clutter up the street
Do without hungry dragons
To keep our houses neat?

— *Gregory Harrison*

## Questions & Assignments

1. Who is the speaker in this poem? Refer to the poem to support your answer.
2. How do we know that the poet looks forward to the arrival of the dustbin men?
3. What sounds signal the arrival of the dustbin men?
4. (a) To what is the dustbin lorry compared?
   (b) Do you think this is a suitable comparison? Give a reason for your answer.
5. List, in alphabetical order, all the items of rubbish left for the dustbin men.
6. Find words in the poem to match the following meanings: strong, broken, very hungry, cracked, packed tightly.
7. This poem has many vivid images. Choose one that appeals to you and explain why you chose it.
8. Describe the rhyming pattern of the poem.
9. 'What I want to be when I grow up.' Write about your dreams and ambitions when you were four or five years old. Have they changed? Why?

## Points to Note — SIMILES AND METAPHORS

We make a comparison when we say that one thing is similar to another. Similes and metaphors are two types of comparisons that are frequently used in poetry.

**A simile says that something is like something else.**

A simile uses the words 'like', 'as', or 'than'. For example: He fought like a tiger. There are two similes in the poem *The Dustbin Men*. Can you spot them?

However, while a simile is a comparison which uses the words 'like' or 'as', a metaphor is more difficult to spot.

**A metaphor says that something is something else.**

We use metaphors a lot in conversation. For example: 'He was a tiger in the ring.'

Look at the third stanza of *The Dustbin Men*. If the poet had written 'the back of the rubbish cart looked like a great mouth yawning', it would have the same meaning but would be more long-winded. Instead the poet uses a metaphor. He suggests that the rubbish cart has a mouth and was yawning. The poet goes on to develop the metaphor over the remainder of the poem. Can you see how?

You should be able to understand now what a metaphor is. If you are still not sure, here are a few common metaphors for you to extend into similes.

- The boy raced up the stairs.
- The car screeched to a halt.
- That singer shot to fame overnight.
- Pearls of dew lay on the grass.

You will see also from this exercise that metaphors and similes make language – both spoken and written – more colourful and descriptive. They give us a clearer impression of something and help us to imagine it more easily.

## Parrot

Sometimes I sit with both eyes closed.
But all the same, I've heard!
They're saying. "He won't talk because
He is a *thinking* bird."

I'm olive-green and sulky, and
The family say, "Oh yes,
He's silent, but he's *listening*,
He *thinks* more than he *says*!"

"He ponders on the things he hears,
Preferring not to chatter."
— And this is true, but *why* it's true
Is quite another matter.

I'm working out some shocking things
In order to surprise them,
And when my thoughts are ready I'll
Certainly *not* disguise them!

I'll wait, and see, and choose a time
When everyone is present.
And clear my throat and raise my beak
And give a squawk and start to speak
And go on for about a week
*And it will not be pleasant!*
— *Alan Brownjohn*

### Questions & Assignments

1. Who is the speaker in this poem?
2. Is the parrot in the poem a *'thinking'* bird?
3. Does the parrot like the family? Give a reason for your answer.
4. When will the parrot speak?
5. 'The thoughts of your family pet.' Write a paragraph *or* a poem on this subject.

The following **Spot the Errors** exercise is aimed at sharpening your basic writing skills. Spot the 20 errors in the Passage below and rewrite the passage correctly. (Note: Refer to the Guidelines on pages 1—15.)

## 2  Alligators

Alligators are members of the crocodile family. They have broad, flatt and rounded snouts, as opposed to the longer, sharper snouts of other crocodiles. Also, unlike other crocodiles, their lower teeth cant be seen when they're mouths are closed. Alligators feed on all types of animal's. In North america they are also known to attack humans ocassionally.

Alligators breed mainly in spring. When the eggs are ready to hatch, in about sixty days, the young begin to croak softly within the egg. The female may then assist the young in excaping from the nest and may even carry them in her mouth to the water's edge. The female may remain near her young for a year or more, while the male occupies his own territory A young alligator in distress will give a few sharp croaks that may quickly bring the female to investigate.

Only too species of alligator exist – the chinese alligator and the American alligator. the Chinese alligator makes it's home in the Yangtze river in China. It is more timid and much more smaller than the American alligator and is considered little threat to humans. The American alligator lives mainly in freshwater swamps and lakes in the southeastern united states. It is larger, reaching up two about six metres in length, and is potentially dangerous to humans. Attacks are occasional and usually happen when humans have strayed onto an alligators territory. The American alligator was a popular hunting target for many years and was declared an endangered species in 1967 because of falling populations. Under this protection it maid a strong comeback and, little more than ten years later, hunting of the American alligator was again aloud in some states.

### The Battery Hen

Oh, I am a battery hen,
On me back there's not a germ,
I never scratched a farmyard,
And I never pecked a worm,
I never had the sunshine,
To warm me feathers through,
Eggs I lay. Every day.
For the likes of you.

When you has them scrambled,
Piled up on your plate,
It's me what you should thank for that
I never lays them late,
I always lays them reg'lar,
I always lays them right,
I never lays them brown,
I always lays them white.

But it's no life, for a battery hen,
In me box I'm sat,
A funnel stuck out from the side,
Me pellets comes down that,
I gets a squirt of water,
Every half a day,
Watchin' with me beady eye,
Me eggs, roll away.

I lays them in a funnel,
Strategically placed,
So that I don't kick 'em,
And let them go to waste,
They rolls off down the tubing,
And up the gangway quick,
Sometimes I gets to thinkin'
"That could have been a chick!"

I might have been a farmyard hen,
Scratchin' in the sun,
There might have been a crowd of chicks,
After me to run,
There might have been a cockerel fine,
To pay us his respects,
Instead of sittin' here,
Till someone comes and wrings our necks.

I see the Time and Motion clock,
Is sayin' nearly noon,
I 'spec me squirt of water,
Will come flyin' at me soon,
And then me spray of pellets,
Will nearly break me leg,
And I'll bite the wire nettin'
And lay one more bloody egg.

— *Pam Ayres*

## Questions & Assignments

1. (a) Who is the narrator of this poem?
   (b) Is she happy or sad with her life? Give reasons for your answer.
2. Describe a day in the life of a battery hen.
3. (a) What other type of life does she imagine for herself?
   (b) Outline the advantages and disadvantages of each lifestyle.
4. Why, according to the battery hen, should we be grateful to her?
5. Describe the rhyming pattern of this poem.
6. What features of the poem amused you?
7. Write a poem, similar in style to *The Battery Hen*, about your own life.

## [Answer Guidelines]

5. There are six verses in the poem. There are eight lines in each verse. The rhyming pattern of each verse is identical. The second line rhymes with the fourth line and the sixth line rhymes with the eighth line. There are no rhymes between the first, third, fifth and seventh lines of any verse.

## Points to Note — RHYME

Rhyme is the repetition of similar sounds at the end of lines and is a feature of most poetry. Rhyme, like rhythm, is another **device** that gives poetry a musical quality.

In *The Battery Hen* each verse or stanza consists of eight lines where the second line **rhymes** with the fourth, and the sixth line **rhymes** with the eighth. For example, in stanza two 'plate' rhymes with 'late' and 'right' rhymes with 'white'.

The **rhyming pattern** or **rhyming scheme** of any stanza of this poem could be expressed as follows **o, a, o, a, o, b, o, b**. (Note: **o** denotes a line which does not rhyme).

It is important to note that, while the words **rhythm** and **rhyme** look very alike, they refer to two very different things.

# The Pied Piper of Hamelin

**I**
Hamelin Town's in Brunswick,
By famous Hanover city;
The river Weser, deep and wide,
Washes its wall on the southern side;
A pleasanter spot you never spied;
But, when begins my ditty,
Almost five hundred years ago,
To see the townsfolk suffer so
From vermin, was a pity.

**II**
Rats!
They fought the dogs, and killed the cats,
And bit the babies in the cradles,
And ate the cheeses out of the vats,
And licked the soup from the cook's own ladles.
Split open the kegs of salted sprats,
Made nests inside men's Sunday hats,
And even spoiled the women's chats,
By drowning their speaking
With shrieking and squeaking
In fifty different sharps and flats.

**III**
At last the people in a body
To the Town Hall came flocking:
''Tis clear,' cried they, 'our Mayor's a noddy;
And as for our Corporation — shocking!
To think we buy gowns lined with ermine
For dolts that can't or won't determine
What's best to rid us of our vermin!
You hope, because you're old and obese,
To find in the furry civic robe ease?
Rouse up, Sirs! Give your brains a racking
To find the remedy we're lacking,
Or, sure as fate, we'll send you packing!'
At this the Mayor and Corporation
Quaked with a mighty consternation.

**IV**
An hour they sat in council,
At length the Mayor broke silence:
'For a guilder I'd my ermine gown sell —
I wish I were a mile hence!

It's easy to bid one rack one's brain —
I'm sure my poor head aches again,
I've scratched it so, and all in vain.
Oh for a trap, a trap, a trap!'
Just as he said this, what should hap
At the chamber door, but a gentle tap?
'Bless us,' cried the Mayor, 'what's that?'
(With the Corporation as he sat,
Looking little though wondrous fat;
Nor brighter was his eye, nor moister
Than a too-long-opened oyster,
Save when at noon his paunch grew mutinous
For a plate of turtle green and glutinous.)
'Only a scraping of shoes on the mat!
Anything like the sound of a rat
Makes my heart go pit-a-pat!'

V

'Come in!' — the Mayor cried, looking bigger:
And in did come the strangest figure!
His queer long coat from heel to head
Was half of yellow and half of red;
And he himself was tall and thin,
With sharp blue eyes, each like a pin,
And light loose hair, yet swarthy skin,
No tuft on cheek nor beard on chin,
But lips where smiles went out and in —
There was no guessing his kith and kin!
And nobody could enough admire
The tall man and his quaint attire:
Quoth one: 'It's as my great-grandsire,
Starting up at the Trump of Doom's tone,
Had walked this way from his painted tombstone!'

VI

He advanced to the council-table:
And, 'Please your honours,' said he, 'I'm able
By means of a secret charm to draw
All creatures living beneath the sun,
That creep or swim or fly or run,
After me so as you never saw!
And I chiefly use my charm
On creatures that do people harm,
The mole and toad and newt and viper;
And people call me the Pied Piper.'
(And here they noticed round his neck
A scarf of red and yellow stripe,
To match with his coat of the self-same check;
And at the scarf's end hung a pipe;

And his fingers, they noticed, were ever straying
As if impatient to be playing
Upon his pipe, as low it dangled
Over his vesture so old-fangled.)
'Yet,' said he, 'poor piper as I am,
In Tartary I freed the Cham,
Last June, from his huge swarms of gnats;
I eased in Asia the Nizam
Of a monstrous brood of vampire-bats:
And as for what your brain bewilders,
If I can rid your town of rats
Will you give me a thousand guilders?'
'One? fifty thousand!' — was the exclamation
Of the astonished Mayor and Corporation.

**VII**
Into the street the Piper stept,
Smiling first a little smile,
As if he knew what magic slept
In his quiet pipe the while;
Then, like a musical adept,
To blow the pipe his lips he wrinkled,
And green and blue his sharp eyes twinkled
Like a candle-flame where salt is sprinkled;
And ere three shrill notes the pipe uttered,
You heard as if an army muttered;
And the grumbling grew to a mighty rumbling;
And out of the houses the rats came tumbling.
Great rats, small rats, lean rats, brawny rats,
Brown rats, black rats, grey rats, tawny rats,
Grave old plodders, gay young friskers,
Fathers, mothers, uncles, cousins,
Cocking tails and pricking whiskers,
Families by tens and dozens,
Brothers, sisters, husbands, wives —
Followed the Piper for their lives.
From street to street he piped advancing,
And step for step they followed dancing,
Until they came to the river Weser
Wherein all plunged and perished!
— Save one who, stout as Julius Caesar,
Swam across and lived to carry
(As he the manuscript he cherished)
To Rat-land home his commentary:
Which was, 'At the first shrill notes of the pipe,
I heard a sound as of scraping tripe,
And putting apples, wondrous ripe,
Into a cider-press's gripe:

And a moving away of pickle-tub boards
And a leaving ajar of conserve-cupboards,
And a drawing the corks of train-oil flasks,
And a breaking the hoops of butter-casks;
And it seemed as if a voice
(Sweeter far than by harp or by psaltery
Is breathed) called out, Oh rats, rejoice!
The world is grown to one vast dry-saltery!
So, munch on, crunch on, take your nuncheon,
Breakfast, supper, dinner, luncheon!
And just as bulky sugar-puncheon,
All ready staved, like a great sun shone
Glorious scarce an inch before me,
Just as methought it said, Come, bore me!
— I found the Weser rolling o'er me.'

**VIII**
You should have heard the Hamelin people
Ringing the bells till they rocked the steeple.
'Go,' cried the Mayor, 'and get long poles!
Poke out the nest and block up the holes!
Consult with carpenters and builders,
And leave in our town not even a trace
Of the rats' — when suddenly, up the face
Of the Piper perked in the market-place,
With a 'First, if you please, my thousand guilders!'

**IX**
A thousand guilders! The Mayor looked blue;
So did the Corporation too.
For council dinners made rare havoc
With Claret, Moselle, Vin-de-Grave, Hock;
And half the money would replenish
Their cellar's biggest butt with Rhenish.
To pay this sum to a wandering fellow
With a gipsy coat of red and yellow!
'Beside,' quoth the Mayor with a knowing wink,
'Our business was done at the river's brink;
We saw with our eyes the vermin sink,
And what's dead can't come to life, I think.
So, friend, we're not the folks to shrink
From the duty of giving you something to drink,
And a matter of money to put in your poke;
But as for the guilders, what we spoke
Of them, as you very well know, was in joke.
Besides, our losses have made us thrifty.
A thousand guilders! Come, take fifty!'

**X**

The Piper's face fell, and he cried,
No trifling! I can't wait. Beside,
I've promised to visit by dinner time
Bagdad, and accept the prime
Of the Head-Cook's pottage, all he's rich in,
For having left, in the Caliph's kitchen,
Of a nest of scorpions no survivor —
With him I proved no bargain-driver,
With you, don't think I'll bate a stiver!
And folks who put me in a passion
May find me pipe to another fashion!'

**XI**

'How?' cried the Mayor, 'd'ye think I'll brook
Being worse treated than a Cook?
Insulted by a lazy ribald
With idle pipe and vesture piebald?
You threaten us fellow? Do your worst,
Blow your pipe there till you burst?'

**XII**

Once more he stept into the street;
And to his lips again
Laid his long pipe of smooth straight cane;
And ere he blew three notes (such sweet
Soft notes as yet musician's cunning
Never gave the enraptured air)
There was a rustling, that seemed like a bustling
Of merry crowds justling at pitching and hustling,
Small feet were pattering, wooden shoes clattering,
Little hands clapping and little tongues chattering,
And, like fowls in a farm-yard when barley is scattering,
Out came the children running.
All the little boys and girls,
With rosy cheeks and flaxen curls,
And sparkling eyes and teeth like pearls,
Tripping and skipping, ran merrily after
The wonderful music with shouting and laughter.

**XIII**

The Mayor was dumb, and the Council stood
As if they were changed into blocks of wood,
Unable to move a step, or cry
To the children merrily skipping by —
And could only follow with the eye
That joyous crowd at the Piper's back.
And how the Mayor was on the rack,

And the wretched Council's bosoms beat,
As the Piper turned from the High Street
To where the Weser rolled its waters
Right in the way of their sons and daughters!
However he turned from South to West,
And to Koppelberg Hill his steps addressed,
And after him the children pressed;
Great was the joy in every breast.
'He never can cross that mighty top!
He's forced to let the piping drop,
And we shall see our children stop!'
When, lo, as they reached the mountain's side,
A wondrous portal opened wide,
As if a cavern was suddenly hollowed;
And the Piper advanced and the children followed,
And when all were in to the very last
The door in the mountain-side shut fast.
Did I say, all? No! One was lame,
And could not dance the whole of the way;
And in after years, if you would blame
His sadness, he was used to say, —
'It's dull in our town since my playmates left!
I can't forget that I'm bereft
Of all the pleasant sights they see,
Which the Piper also promised me.
For he led us, he said, to a joyous land,
Joining the town and just at hand,
Where waters gushed and fruit-trees grew,
And flowers put forth a fairer hue,
And everything was strange and new;
The sparrows were brighter than peacocks here,
And their dogs outran our fallow deer,
And honey-bees had lost their stings,
And horses were born with eagles' wings:
And just as I became assured
My lame foot would be speedily cured,
The music stopped and I stood still,
And found myself outside the Hill,
Left alone against my will,
To go now limping as before,
And never hear of that country more!'

**XIV**
Alas, alas for Hamelin!
There came into many a burgher's pate
A text which says, that Heaven's Gate
Opes to the Rich at as easy rate
As the needle's eye takes a camel in!

The Mayor sent East, West, North and South,
To offer the Piper, by word of mouth,
Wherever it was men's lot to find him,
Silver and gold to his heart's content,
If he'd only return the way he went,
And bring the children behind him.
But when they saw 'twas a lost endeavour,
And Piper and dancers were gone for ever,
They made a decree that lawyers never
Should think their records dated duly
If, after the day of the month and year,
These words did not as well appear,
'And so long after what happened here
On the Twenty-second of July,
Thirteen-hundred and seventy-six:'
And the better in memory to fix
The place of the children's last retreat,
They called it, the Pied Piper's Street —
Where anyone playing on pipe or tabor
Was sure for the future to lose his labour;
Nor suffered they hostelry or tavern
To shock with mirth a street so solemn;
But opposite the place of the cavern
They wrote the story on a column,
And on the great Church-Window painted
The same, to make the world acquainted
How their children were stolen away;
And there it stands to this very day.
And I must not omit to say
That in Transylvania there's a tribe
Of alien people that ascribe
The outlandish ways and dress
On which their neighbours lay such stress
To their fathers and mothers having risen
Out of some subterraneous prison
Into which they were trepanned
Long time ago in a mighty band
Out of Hamelin town in Brunswick land,
But how or why, they don't understand.

XV
So, Willy, let you and me be wipers
Of scores out with all men, — especially pipers!
And, whether they pipe us free from rats or from mice,
If we've promised them aught, let us keep our promise!
— *Robert Browning*

The Pied Piper of Hamelin was written by Robert Browning who lived in the 19th century. Some of the words and phrases in the poem are no longer used in everyday conversation and may present you with difficulties here and there in the poem. With a little thought and imagination (and the use of a dictionary) you will be able to overcome these. However, it is not necessary to understand every word to enjoy the poem.

**Stanzas I – VI**
1. What do we learn about the town of Hamelin in the first stanza?
2. Explain in detail how, according to the poem, the rats affected the lives of the people of the town.
3. Who did the people of the town ask to remedy the problem of the rats? What did they threaten if the problem was not solved?
4. What was unusual about the appearance of the piper?
5. (a) What powers did the piper claim to have?
   (b) What kind of things did he claim to have achieved with his powers?
6. What line suggests that he mainly uses his powers for the benefit of people?
7. (a) What offer did the piper make?
   (b) How did the Mayor and Corporation react?

**Stanzas VII – XI**
1. (a) What happened when the piper stepped into the street?
   (b) What words and phrases suggest that a very large number of rats responded to the piper's tune?
2. One rat survived to tell the tale. What do we learn from him about the way the music of the piper affected the rats?
3. What did the people of the town do after the rats were drowned?
4. 'The Mayor looked blue;' What does this line suggest?
5. Why did the mayor feel safe refusing to pay the agreed fee to the piper?
6. (a) What did the piper threaten to do?
   (b) How did the mayor respond to the piper's threat?
7. Where in stanza X is there a suggestion that the piper has unnatural powers?

**Stanzas XII – XVI**
1. What happened when the piper stepped into the street for a second time?
2. What evidence is there that the children were happy following the piper?
3. Explain how the piper used his strange powers on the adults of the town as he led the children away.
4. (a) What did the adults fear the piper would do when he left the town?
   (b) Why were they relieved when he turned to the Koppelberg hill?
5. What happened when the piper and the children reached the mountainside?
6. What do we learn about the effect of the piper's music on the children? From whom do we learn this?
7. What did the mayor and corporation do after the children disappeared?
8. Were the children ever heard of again? Explain your answer.

**General Questions**
1. Who was to blame for the disappearance of the children?
2. The poet uses a number of comparisons (in this case similes). Pick out four that you liked.
3. There are many groups of rhyming words in the poem. Pick out ten sets of rhyming words. Do you think that these rhyming words add to the pleasure of reading the poem or not? Give a reason for your answer.
4. Select your favourite stanza and give a reason for your choice.

## PERSONAL WRITING

# ASSIGNMENTS

1. Rewrite the story of *The Pied Piper of Hamelin* in story form suitable for including in a book aimed at 7 to 9-year-old children.

2. Change another 'fairytale' of your choice from story to verse. (It needn't be as long as *The Pied Piper of Hamelin*!)

## Points to Note

### END-STOPPED LINES AND RUN-ON LINES

A line of poetry can either be an end-stopped line or a run-on line. An **end-stopped** line is complete in terms of meaning and its ending usually has a punctuation mark.

A **run-on** line of poetry is one where the next line must also be read to get a clear meaning. There are no punctuation marks at the end of run-on lines.

As a general rule end-stopped lines sound firm and finished and a series of them will usually produce the effect of a slow and steady pace. Run-on lines, on the other hand, can quicken the pace by creating a sense of suspense, of expectation and of breathlessness.

### PAUSES

A pause within a line of poetry may be located by some form of punctuation mark (a full-stop, comma, semi-colon, question mark, exclamation mark or a dash), though this is not always the case. Pauses can also be located by paying particular attention to the meaning of a line and how it should be read aloud.

Being unaware where pauses should be located in a poem will make it more difficult to understand. In speech, when we pause, we give the impression that we are searching for the perfect words to express an idea. A pause in a line of poetry will also achieve this effect. It gives the impression of deep thought and of care in the choice of words that follow the pause.

Practice reading *The Pied Piper of Hamelin* bearing these points in mind.

# Spancil Hill

## poems about emigration

Last night as I lay dreaming of pleasant days gone by,
My mind bein' bent on rambling to Ireland I did fly,
I stepped aboard a vision and I followed with my will,
Till next I came to anchor at the cross near Spancil Hill.

It being the 23rd June the day before the fair,
When Ireland's sons and daughters in crowds assembled there,
The young, the old, the brave and the bold they came for sport and kill,
There were jovial conversations at the cross of Spancil Hill.

I went to see my neighbours to hear what they might say,
The old ones were all dead and gone, the others turning grey,
I met with the tailor Quigley, he's as bold as ever still,
Sure he used to make my britches when I lived in Spancil Hill.

I paid a flying visit to my first and only love,
She's as white as any lily and as gentle as a dove.
She threw her arms around me saying "Johnny I love you still."
Oh she's Mag the farmer's daughter and the pride of Spancil Hill.

I dreamt I stooped and kissed her as in the days of yore,
She said, "Johnny you're only joking like many's the time before."
The cock crew in the morning, he crew both loud and shrill,
And I woke in California, many miles from Spancil Hill.

(Spancil Hill is in Co. Clare)

## Questions & Assignments

1. These are the words of an old ballad. Give reasons why the words are suitable for setting to music. Should the song be sung to a slow or a lively rhythm? Explain your answer.
2. Did the narrator actually return to Spancil Hill? Explain your answer.
3. What changes did he find there?
4. Explain the phrase – *'the days of yore'*.
5. What do we learn about the character of the narrator?
6. What details in the ballad suggest that the narrator missed his homeland?

# poems about emigration

## ASSIGNMENT

1. Write a similar ballad about your own neighbourhood or town. Try to follow the structure of *Spancil Hill* — four line verses and a similar rhyming scheme.

### Missing You

In nineteen hundred and eighty six,
Not much work for a chippie or swinging the pick.
And you can't live on love and on love alone,
So you sail o'er the ocean, away 'cross the foam.

To where you're a Paddy and where you're a Mick,
Not much use at all but for stacking the brick.
And your mate was a spade and he carried the hod.
Two old heavy horses heavily shod.

*Oh I'm missing you. I'd give all for the price of the flight.*
*Oh I'm missing you under Piccadilly's\* neon*

Who did you murder and are you a spy?
I'm just fond of the drink; helps me laugh, helps me cry.
And I took to the port for a permanent high,
Now I laugh and lot less and I'll cry till I die.

Now the summer is fine, but the winter's a fridge,
Wrapped up in old cardboard under Charing Cross Bridge.
And I'll never go home, it's because of the shame,
Of misfit's reflection in a shop window pane.

*Oh I'm missing you. I'd give all for the price of the flight.*
*Oh I'm missing you under Piccadilly's neon*

So you young people take an advice,
Before crossing the ocean you'd better think twice.
'Cause you can't live without love and without love alone.
Here's proof round the West End in the nobody zone.

— *Jimmy McCarthy*

\*Piccadilly is in Central London

From the time of the Great Famine up to quite recently, many Irish people were forced to emigrate in search of work. Emigration touched almost every family in Ireland. Many songs have been written about emigration. Missing You was written in the mid-eighties when Ireland was in the depths of an economic recession and work was hard to find. During that time also the IRA were planting bombs in England and many Irish people living there were suspected of being terrorists.

# poems about emigration

## Questions & Assignments

1. What lines in the first stanza tell us that jobs were scarce in 1986?
2. Why did the writer use the word *'cross'* in the fourth line?
3. What does the second stanza suggest about how Irish emigrants were regarded in Britain? Refer to phrases in the stanza to support your answer.
4. Do you think the *'you'* in the first two stanzas and the *'you'* in the chorus is the same person? Explain your answer.
5. Who do you think could be the speaker in the first line of the third stanza?
6. Explain the meaning of the other three lines of the third stanza.
7. Identify the comparison in the fourth stanza. Is it a simile or a metaphor? Do you think it is a good comparison? Explain your answer.
8. Explain the final line of the fourth stanza.
9. What advice is being offered in the final stanza?
10. There is a line in the final stanza that is similar to another line in the poem. Write out both lines and say how they are similar and how they differ.
11. What do you think the writer means by *'the nobody zone'*?
12. What is the mood of this song — angry? sad? bitter? Give reasons for your choice.
13. What is your response to the song?

## WORD PUZZLE

Solve each of the word puzzles below. Some clues are provided to help you. The clues are not in the same order as the anagrams. For example, the first clue 'Old saying' refers to puzzle 6 — 'BRROPEV'. Can you spot a **similarity** in the spelling patterns of each word?

| | | |
|---|---|---|
| 1. OPEPYLRR | 5. RMOEGAMPR | 9. GRROSSEP |
| 2. IPETCOTNOR | 6. BRROPEV | 10. MPROPT |
| 3. ROBEMPL | 7. ERCDUPO | 11. SIRSNOFPEO |
| 4. ABPLBEOR | 8. RPOYPRTE | 12. OVIPDRE |

- Old saying
- Somebody's job
- Something owned
- Make
- Correctly
- TV Show
- Improvement
- Supply
- Most likely
- Defence
- Unsettled question
- To suggest an answer

## poems about emigration

### The Boys of Barr na Sráide

Oh, the town, it climbs the mountains and looks upon the sea
At sleeping time or waking time, it's there I'd like to be.
To walk again those kindly streets, the place where life began,
With the Boys of Barr na Sráide who hunted for the wren.

With cudgels stout they roamed about to hunt for the dreólín*
We searched for birds in every furze from Litir to Dooneen.
We danced for joy beneath the sky, life held no print nor plan
When the Boys of Barr na Sráide went hunting for the wren.

And when the hills were bleedin' and the rifles were aflame
To the rebel homes of Kerry the Saxon strangers came,
But the men who dared the Auxies and fought the Black-and-Tan
Were the Boys of Barr na Sráide who hunted for the wren.

But now they toil in foreign soil where they have made their way
Deep in the heart of London or over on Broadway,
And I am left to sing their deeds and praise them while I can
Those Boys of Barr na Sráide who hunted for the wren.

And here's a health to them tonight wherever they may be.
By the groves of Carham River or the slope of Bean a' Tí
John Daly and Batt Andy and the Sheehans, Con and Dan,
The Boys of Barr na Sráide who hunted for the wren.

When the wheel of life runs out and peace comes over me
Just take me back to that old town between the hills and sea.
I'll take my rest in those green fields, the place where life began,
With those Boys of Barr na Sráide who hunted for the wren.

— *Sigerson Clifford*

* Dreólín is the Irish word for wren.

The Wren Boys, and hunting the wren on St. Stephens' Day are very old Irish customs. Christy Moore has made recordings of Spancil Hill, Missing You and The Boys of Barr na Sráide. On Christy Moore's recording of Missing You, some of Jimmy McCarthy's lyrics have been changed slightly.

# poems about emigration

**Questions & Assignments**

1. What do we learn about the town in the first line?
2. What are the writer's feelings for the town? Refer to words in the song in your answer.
3. Did they enjoy hunting for the wren? Give a reason for your answer.
4. Explain the phrase *'life held no print nor plan'*.
5. Explain the opening line in the third stanza.
6. Would you agree that the song deals with various stages in the lives of the boys of Barr na Sráide? Explain.
7. In the fifth stanza a number of names are mentioned. Explain why.
8. What do we learn about the song from these lines?
9. What is the mood of this song?
10. Which of the three emigrant songs did you prefer? Give a reason for your choice.

## Back in the Playground Blues

Dreamed I was in a school playground, I was about four feet high
Yes dreamed I was back in the playground, and standing about four feet high
The playground was three miles long and the playground was five miles wide

It was broken black tarmac with a high fence all around
Broken black dusty tarmac with a high fence running all around
And it had a special name to it, they called it the Killing Ground.

Got a mother and a father, they're a thousand miles away
The Rulers of the Killing Ground are coming out to play
Everyone thinking: who they going to play with today?

You get it for being Jewish
Get it for being black
Get it for being chicken
Get it for fighting back
You get it for being big and fat
Get it for being small
O those who get it get it and get it
For any damn thing at all

Sometimes they take a beetle, tear off its six legs one by one
Beetle on its black back rocking in the lunchtime sun
But a beetle can't beg for mercy, a beetle's not half the fun

Heard a deep voice talking, it had that iceberg sound;
"It prepares them for Life" — but I have never found
Any place in my life that's worse than the Killing Ground.

— *Adrian Mitchell* (b. 1932)

### Questions & Assignments

1. Who is the narrator in the poem?
2. Would you agree that the poet exaggerates in line three? Can you suggest why? Identify another exaggeration in the poem and explain why it is there.
4. Who are the rulers of the *Killing Ground*?
5. *'Everyone thinking: who they going to play with today?'* What do you understand this line to mean?
6. (a) What is the *'it'* mentioned in the short lines?
   (b) What type of people get *'it'*?
7. What do we learn about the rulers of the *Killing Ground* from the second last stanza?
8. (a) Who is the owner of the *'deep voice'*?
   (b) Why did the poet describe it as having an *'iceberg sound'*?
9. *'It prepares them for Life.'* Who is speaking here and what is meant?
10. Do you think the poet's school days were happy days? Refer to the last line to support your answer.
11. Do you think that this is a good poem about bullies? Say why you think so.

## Points to Note

### ADJECTIVES

Adjectives go with nouns — we say that they 'qualify' nouns. Adjectives describe nouns clearly and more fully.

> broken black dusty tarmac
> a high fence
> a deep voice

Adjectives help our imagination to experience an image more sharply.

### HYPERBOLE

When we exaggerate our aim is to deceive. Hyperbole occurs when a poet deliberately exaggerates in order to emphasise the importance or something, rather than to deceive. Hyperbole is a useful device to express strong feelings or emphasise a particular point. Can you find examples of hyperbole in the poem *Back in the Playground Blues?*

## WORD PUZZLE

Solve each of the word puzzles below. Some clues are provided to help you. The clues are not in the same order as the anagrams. For example, the first clue 'Break during a show' refers to puzzle 9 — 'NALTRIVE'. Can you spot a **similarity** in the spelling patterns of each word?

1. ERNTERIFE
2. TIPNEUTRR
3. RENETTAIGOR
4. ERCTETIPN
5. ELRNIAATINNOT
6. EOIRRITN
7. INTWEEVIR
8. RSTEIENT
9. NALTRIVE
10. TECERITSN

- Break during a show
- Butt in on
- Cut off
- Inside
- Between countries
- Question
- Curiosity
- Reporters do this
- Cut across
- Meddle

### Who Killed Davey Moore?

Who killed Davey Moore,
Why an' what's the reason for?

"Not I," says the referee,
"Don't point your finger at me.
I could've stopped it in the eighth
An' maybe kept him from his fate,
But the crowd would've booed, I'm sure,
At not gettin' their money's worth.
It's too bad he had to go,
But there was a pressure on me too, you know.
It wasn't me that made him fall.
No, you can't blame me at all."

Who killed Davey Moore,
Why an' what's the reason for?

"Not us," says the angry crowd,
Whose screams filled the arena loud.
"It's too bad he died that night
But we just like to see a fight.
We didn't mean for him t' meet his death,
We just meant to see some sweat,
There ain't nothing wrong in that.
It wasn't us that made him fall.
No, you can't blame us at all."

Who killed Davey Moore,
Why an' what's the reason for?

"Not me," says his manager,
Puffing on a big cigar.
"It's hard to say, it's hard to tell,
I always thought that he was well.
It's too bad for his wife an' kids he's dead,

But if he was sick, he should've said.
It wasn't me that made him fall.
No, you can't blame me at all."

Who killed Davey Moore,
Why an' what's the reason for?
"Not me," says the gambling man,
With his ticket stub in his hand.
"It wasn't me that knocked him down

My hands never touched him none.
I didn't commit no ugly sin,
Anyway, I put money on him to win.
It wasn't me that made him fall.
No, you can't blame me at all."

Who killed Davey Moore,
Why an' what's the reason for?

"Not me," says the boxing writer,
Pounding print on his old typewriter,
Sayin' "Boxing ain't to blame,
There's just as much danger in a football game."
Sayin', "Fist fighting is here to stay,
It's just the old American way.
It wasn't me that made him fall.
No, you can't blame me at all."

Who killed Davey Moore,
Why an' what's the reason for?

"Not me," says the man whose fist
Laid him low in a cloud of mist,
Who came here from Cuba's door
Where boxing ain't allowed no more.
"I hit him, yes, it's true,
But that's what I am paid to do.
Don't say 'murder,' don't say 'kill.'
It was destiny, it was God's will."

Who killed Davey Moore,
Why an' what's the reason for?
— *Bob Dylan*

## Questions & Assignments

1. How did the referee excuse himself?
2. Why did the people in the crowd not think they were to blame?
3. How did Davey Moore's manager explain that he was innocent?
4. Why did the gambling man not consider himself responsible for Davey Moore's death?
5. Describe the boxing writer's attitude to boxing?
6. How did Davey Moore's opponent see his position?
7. Who do you think was responsible for Davey Moore's death? Give reasons for your answer.

# Nora

The violets were scenting the woods, Nora;
Displaying their charms to the bees
When I first said I loved only you, Nora;
And you said you loved only me.

The chestnut's bloom gleams through the glade, Nora;
The robin sang out from every tree
When I first said I loved only you, Nora;
And you said you loved only me.

The golden-dewed daffodils shone, Nora;
And danced in the breeze on the lea
When I first said I loved only you, Nora;
And you said you loved only me.

The birds in the trees sang their songs, Nora;
Of happier transports to be,
When I first said I loved only you, Nora;
And you said you loved only me.

Our hopes they have never come true, Nora;
Our dreams they were never to be
Since I first said I loved only you, Nora;
And you said you loved only me.

— *G. W. Johnston*

## Questions & Assignments

1. These are the lyrics of a very popular song. To whom is this song addressed?
2. *'displaying their charms'*. Explain what the words *'their'* and *'charms'* refer to in this phrase.
3. (a) What pictures of nature do we get in the first four verses?
   (b) Which words help to make these pictures vivid?
   (c) Which of these word pictures do you prefer? Why?
   (d) Would you agree that these pictures of nature help to establish a happy mood? Explain your answer.
   (e) How, in your opinion, are the pictures linked to the mood of the poet?
4. How does the final verse differ from the rest of the poem?
5. Give reasons why this poem is suitable for setting to music.

## [Answer Guidelines]

3. (d) I agree that these pictures of nature help to establish a happy mood. They describe nature at its best. The flowers are in bloom and the birds are singing. It is spring, when the world of nature comes to life again after the dreary winter.
   (e) The poet is very happy because he is in love. This makes him more aware of the beauty of the world around him. He seems to be suggesting that the birds and the flowers are happy for him.

The following Spot the Errors exercise is aimed at sharpening your basic writing skills. Spot the 20 errors in the Passage below and rewrite the passage correctly. (Note: Refer to the Guidelines on pages 1—15.)

### 3  Picking Blackberries

Saturday was gloriously warm and sunny and matthew took little persauding to go picking blackberrys.

"And bring back enough for a pie for dinner," said his mother, handing him a bowl. Don't eat all you pick. The rest of us want some too.

He knew where the best berrys were to be found, hanging in clusters. Like grapes almost. He sauntered along the lane to the bushes he knew. He picked slowly and casually, eating every third berry he picked. That he thought, was a fare reward for his labour. His lips were soon coloured a deep purple from the juce and his bowl was filling slowly.

He stoped as he saw one branch, almost hidden in the thicket, hanging heavy with fruit. He put his bowl down on the grassy bank and reached up to the branch the fruit was higher than he had thought. It was out of reach, but he was determined, now that he had seen it, to gather it in. He climed further up the hedge, hardly aware of the thorns scratching at his arms and catching his clothing. He reached up and forward and grabbed at the swinging branch he could just reach it. He held it between two fingers and pulled it gently towards him. The fruit was so ripe and ready for picking that a sudden movement wood set it falling, lost, into the tangle of grass and weeds below.

He inched his finger's carefully along, stretching out further from the edge. A bramble, spiny with thorns, caught at his cheek and he turned sharply away, let go of the branch. He twisted awkwardly to regain his balance and fell through the thicket of brambles into a ditch beyond.

# Holly

It rained when it should have snowed.
When we went to gather holly

the ditches were swimming, we were wet
to the knees, our hands were all jags

and water ran up our sleeves.
There should have been berries

but the sprigs we brought into the house
gleamed like smashed bottle-glass.

Now here I am, in a room that is decked
with the red-berried, waxy-leafed stuff,

and I almost forget what it's like
to be wet to the skin or longing for snow.

I reach for a book like a doubter
and want it to flare round my hand,

a black-letter bush, a glittering shield-wall
cutting as holly and ice.
— *Seamus Heaney*

## Questions & Assignments

1. What point is the poet making in the first line of this poem?
2. What sensations does the poet recall about gathering holly?
3. *'like smashed bottle-glass'*. Do you think this is a good comparison (in this case a simile)? Give a reason for your answer.
4. Would you agree that this poem deals with two separate stages in the poet's life? Explain your answer by referring to the poem.
5. Explain why you did *or* did not enjoy reading this poem.
6. Write an essay — 'Christmas when I was young and Christmas now'.

# Points to Note

## IMAGE

**An image is a word or a phrase used to create a mental picture.**

When we talk about the images in a poem we use the term imagery. All poems have imagery — words and phrases which help us to 'see' something in our imagination, e.g. 'the ditches were swimming'.

However, imagery can also help us to 'hear' or 'feel', 'taste' or 'touch' in our imagination, e.g. 'water ran up our sleeves'. Images are built from nouns — words that name things. When we read the name of something we instinctively create a mental picture of the object.

## SIMILES

**A simile says that something is like something else.**

We often use similes in our everyday conversation to describe things more vividly.

- He ran like a hare.
- The dress was as white as snow.

These are examples of similes in everyday use. We usually put little thought into the similes we use in conversation. These three expressions are used again and again.

- as cold as ice
- as black as coal
- went out like a light

One mark of a good writer is his/her ability to give the reader a clear and vivid impression of a situation. One way of doing this is to use similes that are imaginative and original. An example of such a simile is in the fourth stanza of *Holly*. The simile compares the sprigs of holly lights to 'smashed bottle-glass'. Think of a green wine bottle smashed and think of holly leaves — can you see the similarity?

## WORD PUZZLE

Solve each of the word puzzles below. Some clues are provided to help you. The clues are not in the same order as the anagrams. For example, the first clue 'Big animal' refers to puzzle 7 — 'ANEHPTEL'. Can you spot a **similarity** in the spelling patterns of each word?

1. AOGUTHAPR
2. OGRPAHEGY
3. SEHNPAAT
4. HPMISEHEER
5. UHMPTIR
6. HAPNOR
7. ANEHPTEL
8. ELPEHOTNE
9. RPOHENOIMC
10. WEPEHN
11. REEHPS
12. ABTPHEAL

- Big animal
- Long-tailed bird
- Singers use it
- Subject involving rivers, mountains etc
- For speaking to people far away
- All the letters
- Ball
- Half of the earth
- Victory
- Child without parents
- Signature
- Your sister's son

## The Witnesses

It was a night in winter.
Our house was full, tight-packed as salted herrings -
So full, they said, we had to hold our breaths
To close the door and shut the night-air out!
And then two travellers came. They stood outside
Across the threshold, half in the ring of light
And half beyond it. I would have let them in
Despite the crowding - the woman was past her time -
But I'd no mind to argue with my husband,
The flagon in my hand and half the inn
Still clamouring for wine. But when trade slackened,
And all our guests had sung themselves to bed
Or told the floor their troubles, I came out here
Where he had lodged them. The man was standing
As you are now, his hand smoothing that board.
He was a carpenter, I heard them say.
She rested on the straw, and on her arm
A child was lying. None of your creased-faced brats
Squalling their lungs out. Just lying there
As calm as a new-dropped calf - his eyes wide open,
And gazing round as if the world he saw
In the chaff-strewn light of the stable lantern
Was something beautiful and new and strange.

— *Clive Sansom*

## Questions & Assignments

1. What event is being described in this poem? What evidence is there in the poem to support your answer?
2. Who is speaking in this poem? Refer to the poem to support your answer.
3. How does the poem show us that the house was very crowded?
4. Is there evidence in the poem to suggest that there was a disagreement about whether the two travellers should be let in? Support your answer by referring to the poem.
5. Choose some lines that describe the atmosphere of the inn.
6. *'Or told the floor their troubles'*. What do you understand by this line?
7. Explain what was different about the child.
8. Select one feature of this poem that impressed you.

## [Answer Guidelines]

2. The speaker in this poem is the wife of the innkeeper who let Mary and Joseph rest in a stable. The speaker says that *'our house was full'* and tells us that she had *'no mind to argue with my husband'*.
5. Lines two, three and four tell us that the inn was so crowded that there was hardly room to move. '. . . *half the inn still clamouring for wine'* gives us an impression of a very noisy place. Lines twelve and thirteen - *'And all our guests . . . their troubles'* suggest that plenty of singing and drinking took place.

## Points to Note — VERBS

**Verbs are words that describe actions and movement.**

Verbs bring life to a poem. A carefully chosen verb can help us to imagine an action clearly. For example, in the poem *The Witnesses* the words 'clamouring' and 'gazed' could be substituted with the words 'shouting' and 'looked' but they would not convey the same level of meaning.

# The Band Played Waltzing Matilda

When I was a young man I carried a pack,
I lived the free life of a rover;
From the Murray's green basin to the dusty outback,
I waltzed my Matilda all over.
Then in Nineteen-fifteen, the country said, "Son,
It's time you stopped roving, there's work to be done."
So they gave me a tin hat and they gave me a gun,
And sent me away to the war.

*And the band played Waltzing Matilda,*
*As the ship pulled away from the quay,*
*And midst all the cheers, flag-waving and tears,*
*We sailed off to Gallipoli.*

How well I remember that terrible day,
How our blood stained the sand and the water.
And how in that hell that they called Suvla Bay,
We were butchered like lambs at the slaughter.
Johnny Turk he was ready, he'd primed himself well,
He showered us with bullets and he rained us with shell,
And in five minutes flat he'd blown us all to hell,
Nearly blew us right back to Australia.

*And the band played Waltzing Matilda,*
*When we stopped to bury the slain;*
*We buried ours, the Turks buried theirs,*
*Then we started all over again.*

And those that were left, we tried to survive,
In a sad world of blood, death and fire.
And for ten weary weeks I kept myself alive,
Though around me the corpses piled higher.
Then a big Turkish shell knocked me heels over head,
And when I woke up in my hospital bed,
I saw what it had done and I wished I was dead,
Never knew there were worse things than dying.

*For I'll go no more Waltzing Matilda,*
*All round the green bush far and free.*
*To hump tent and pegs, a man needs both legs,*
*No more Waltzing Matilda for me.*

So they gathered the crippled and wounded and maimed,
And they shipped us back home to Australia.
The legless, the armless, the blind and insane.
The brave wounded heroes of Suvla.
And when our ship pulled into Circular Quay,
I looked at the place where my legs used to be,
And thanked Christ there was nobody waiting for me,
To grieve, to mourn and to pity.

*But the band played Waltzing Matilda,*
*As they carried us down the gangway,*
*But nobody cared, they just stood and stared,*
*And they turned their faces away.*

So now every April I sit on my porch,
And I watch the parade pass before me.
And I see my old comrades, how proudly they march
Reviving old dreams and past glory.
The old men march slowly, old bones stiff and sore,
Tired old men from a forgotten war,
And the young people ask, "What are they marching for?"
I ask myself the same question.

*But the band plays Waltzing Matilda*
*And the old men they answer the call.*
*But as year follows year, they get fewer and fewer*
*Someday no-one will march there at all.*

— Eric Bogle (b. 1950)

## Questions & Assignments

1. What put a stop to the poet's rovings?
2. What details capture the horror of the battlefield?
3. *'Never knew there were worse things than dying'.* What point is being made in this line?
4. Write out the line which tells us what the shell did to the narrator.
5. What words and phrases does the poet use to give us an idea of the injuries which war inflicts on soldiers?
6. Explain how the scene of their departure from Australia was different from the scene of their return.
7. What message do you get from the final verse and chorus?
8. Do you think that this is a good anti-war song? Explain why.
9. In the words of the song a soldier looks back on his life. Retell his lifestory in your own words.

## Points to Note — TONE

In our everyday speech we use many tones of voice. We can speak in a cheerful tone; an angry tone; a weary tone. Our words, in turn, reflect our moods.

Identifying the particular tone of spoken words is easy; we know when somebody is angry or bitter or weary from the sound of their voice.

Identifying the mood or tone of the written word can be a little harder — particularly in the case of poetry. It is important to remember that every poem, like every word we speak, has a certain tone, reflecting a particular mood.

In dealing with questions on attitude, tone and mood you should be clear on the following points:
- What is the poet's attitude towards the topic of the poem?
- Where is this attitude evident? Look out for words or phrases that reflect this attitude.
- What mood was the poet in when he was inspired to write the poem?
- Does the poet's mood change over the course of the poem? Where does this happen? Why?

The answers to these questions will also give you an insight into the poet's character.

## WORD PUZZLE

Solve each of the word puzzles below. Some clues are provided to help you. The clues are not in the same order as the anagrams. For example, the first clue 'To be owned' refers to puzzle 2 — 'NLGEOB'. Can you spot a **similarity** in the spelling patterns of each word?

| 1. EHNAEBT | 5. IEGSEBE | 9. EIDBSE |
| 2. NLGEOB | 6. AERTBY | 10. EBEILVE |
| 3. WEEEDILRBD | 7. INEHBD | 11. ECBEOM |
| 4. REINEFBD | 8. BUHOREAIV | 12. LEAHBF |

- To be owned
- To change into
- Puzzled
- At the back of
- To make friends with
- To think something is true
- Conduct
- In the place of
- At the side of
- Under
- To be disloyal
- To surround

## poems about war

### Evacuee

The slum had been his home since he was born;
And then war came, and he was rudely torn
From all he'd ever known; and with his case
Of mean* necessities, brought to a place
Of silences and space; just boom of sea
And sigh of wind; small wonder then that he
Crept out one night to seek his sordid slum,
And thought to find his way. By dawn he'd come
A few short miles; and cattle in their herds
Gazed limpidly as he trudged by, and birds
Just stirring in first light, awoke to hear
His lonely sobbing, born of abject fear
Of sea and hills and sky; of silent night
Unbroken by the sound of shout and fight.
— *Edith Pickthall*

*mean — cheap

### Questions & Assignments

1. What do we learn about the evacuee's background in the first line?
2. Do you think the phrase *'rudely torn'* is a good phrase to describe the way the boy was evacuated to the countryside? Explain your answer.
3. What did the boy bring with him?
4. (a) He was brought to *'a place/of silences and space'*. Is this a good description of the countryside?
   (b) How does this description make us aware of the slum that the boy left behind?
   (c) Are there any other details in the poem that help form an impression of the slum from which the boy had been taken.
5. What kind of sounds was he aware of in the countryside?
6. What did the boy attempt to do?
7. What frightened him most about the countryside?
8. What does this poem tell us about the nature of war?

# The Green Fields of France

### I
Well how do you do young Willie McBride,
Do you mind if I sit here down by your graveside?
And rest for a while 'neath the warm Summer sun
I've been working all day and I'm nearly done
I see by your gravestone you were only nineteen
When you joined the great fallen in nineteen sixteen.
I hope you died well, and I hope you died clean,
Or young Willie McBride was it slow and obscene?

**Chorus**
*Did they beat the drum slowly, did they sound the fife lowly,*
*Did they sound the dead march as they lowered you down?*
*And did the band play the last post and chorus,*
*Did the pipes play the Flowers of the Forest?*

### II
And did you leave a wife or sweetheart behind,
In some faithful heart is your memory enshrined?
Although you died back in nineteen sixteen
In that faithful heart are you forever nineteen?
Or are you a stranger without even a name,
Enclosed and forever behind the glass frame
In an old photograph, torn and battered and stained
And faded to yellow in a brown leather frame?

### III
The sun now it shines on the green fields of France
There's a warm summer breeze, it makes the red poppies dance
And look how the sun shines from under the clouds
There's no gas, no barbed-wire, there's no guns firing now.
But here in this graveyard it's still no man's land
The countless white crosses stand mute in the sand
To man's blind indifference to his fellow man
To a whole generation that were butchered and damned.

### IV
Now young Willie McBride, I can't help but wonder why
Do all those who lie here know why they died
And did they believe when they answered the Cause
Did they really believe that this war would end wars?
Well the sorrows, the suffering, the glory, the pain
The killing and dying was all done in vain
For Willie McBride, it all happened again
And again, and again, and again, and again.

— *Eric Bogle*

Poetry

**Questions & Assignments**

poems about war

1. This famous anti-war song is in the form of a one-sided conversation.
   (a) Identify some conversational expressions used.
   (b) Explain why the conversation is 'one-sided'.
2. (a) What do we know about Willie McBride from the song?
   (b) What details of Willie McBride's life does the poet wonder about?
3. *'In that faithful heart are you forever nineteen?'* What do you understand this line to mean?
4. What point is the writer making in the last four lines of the second verse? (*'Or are you . . . leather frame.'*)
5. The third verse contains a contrast. Identify this contrast and suggest how it contributes to the message of the poem.
6. *'It's still no man's land'*. Comment on the effectiveness of this phrase.
7. (a) Outline, in your own words, the questions posed in the final verse.
   (b) Who responds to these questions?
   (c) Outline, in your own words, the response.
8. Referring to the chorus, list the military honours that may have accompanied Willie McBride's burial.
9. What features of these verses make them suitable for setting to music?
10. Outline, briefly, the mood of the speaker in these lyrics. Support your answer by referring to the poem.
11. Explain how the poem affected you.

[Answer Guidelines]

10. In the first two stanzas the speaker's mood is sorrowful as he thinks of Willie McBride's short life and tragic death. By the end of the third verse the mood is one of anger as he thinks of *'man's blind indifference to his fellow man'* and a *'whole generation'* killed in the trenches. The poem ends on a bitter note with the speaker thinking that all the sufferings were *'in vain'* and that men have learned nothing from the war.

### Reported Missing

With broken wing they limped across the sky
caught in late sunlight, with their gunner dead,
one engine gone, – the type was out-of-date,
blood on the fuselage turning brown from red:

knew it was finished, looking at the sea
which shone back patterns in kaleidoscope
knew that their shadow would meet them on the way,
close and catch at them, drown their single hope:

sat in this tattered scarecrow of the sky
hearing it cough, the great plane catching
now the first dark clouds upon her wing-base,
patching the great tear in evening mockery.

So two men waited, saw the third dead face,
and wondered when the wind would let them die.

—*John Bayliss*

### Questions & Assignments

1. What details in the first stanza outline the hopeless plight of the air crew?
2. Explain the final two lines of the second stanza.
3. Do you think the phrase *'tattered scarecrow'* is a good phrase to describe the plane? Explain your answer.
4. Why did the poet use the word *'cough'*?
5. Explain the final two lines.

# Love Letters of the Dead
## A Commando Intelligence Briefing

"Go through the pockets of the enemy wounded,
Go through the pockets of the enemy dead.
There's a lot of good stuff to be found there —
That's of course if you've time," I said.
"Love Letters are specially useful,
It's amazing what couples let slip —
The effects of our bombs for example,
The size and type of a ship.
These'll all give us bits of our jigsaw.
Any questions?" I asked as per rule-book.
A close-cropped sergeant from Glasgow,
With an obstinate jut to his jaw,
Got up, and at me he pointed.
Then very slowly he said:
"So you think it right, well I don't,
For any bloody stranger to snitch
What's special and sacred and secret,
Love letters of the dead?"

— *Douglas Street*

## Questions & Assignments

1. Who is speaking in the first ten lines of this poem?
2. What does he mean by *'good stuff'*?
3. *'That's of course if you've time,'* What did he mean by this?
4. Why are the commandoes being asked to search the pockets of the dead and wounded?
5. *'. . . as per rule-book'*. Explain this phrase.
6. Was the narrator acting on his own initiative in giving these orders?
7. What physical details of the sergeant are given? Do they reflect his personality? Explain your answer.
8. Do you agree with the sergeant? Explain your answer.

## The Identification

So you think it's Stephen?
Then I'd best make sure
Be on the safe side as it were.
Ah, there's been a mistake. The hair
you see, it's black, now Stephen's fair . . . .
What's that? The explosion?
Of course, burnt black. Silly of me.
I should have known. Then let's get on.

The face, is that the face I ask?
That mask of charred wood
blistered, scarred, could
that have been a child's face?
The sweater, where intact, looks
in fact all too familiar.
But one must be sure.

The scoutbelt. Yes that's his.
I recognise the studs he hammered in
not a week ago. At the age
when boys get clothes-conscious
now you know. It's almost
certainly Stephen. But one must
be sure. Remove all trace of doubt.
Pull out every splinter of hope.

Pockets. Empty the pockets.
Handkerchief? Could be any schoolboy's.
Dirty enough. Cigarettes?
Oh this can't be Stephen.
I don't allow him to smoke you see.
He wouldn't disobey me. Not his father.

But that's his penknife. That's his alright.
And that's his key on the keyring
Gran gave him just the other night.
So this must be him.

I think I know what happened
. . . . . . . . about the cigarettes
No doubt he was minding them
for one of the older boys.
Yes that's it.
That's him.
That's our Stephen.
— *Roger McGough*

> **Questions & Assignments**
>
> 1. Describe briefly what this poem is about.
> 2. Who is the speaker in this poem? Refer to the poem to support your answer.
> 3. What details suggest that the victim (a) may not be Stephen (b) is probably Stephen?
> 4. From your reading of the poem describe the kind of boy Stephen was.
> 5. Would you agree that this poem presents a very real picture of the result of a terrorist bomb?
> 6. What feelings did this poem arouse in you?

## WORD PUZZLE

Solve each of the word puzzles below. Some clues are provided to help you. The clues are not in the same order as the anagrams. For example, the first clue 'Measure of heat' refers to puzzle 1 — 'EEGEDR'. Can you spot a **similarity** in the spelling patterns of each word?

| | | |
|---|---|---|
| 1. EEGEDR | 6. GDHIELT | 11. ERVLEDI |
| 2. IETLECAD | 7. TAEDRP | 12. LIEUSDOIC |
| 3. ETAFDE | 8. ELYAD | 13. ECDSNDE |
| 4. DOSREYT | 9. ELEVDPO | 14. EDESVER |
| 5. CIEEDD | 10. MDEADN | 15. BIDRECES |

- Measure of heat
- To insist on
- Hold up
- To ruin
- Tastes beautiful
- To become clearer gradually
- Make up your mind
- To leave
- Beat
- To take somewhere
- Very dainty and light
- To give account of
- Happiness
- Come down
- To be worthy of

## Dover Beach

The sea is calm tonight.
The tide is full, the moon lies fair
Upon the straits; — on the French coast the light
Gleams and is gone; the cliffs of England stand
Glimmering and vast, out in the tranquil bay.
Come to the window, sweet is the night-air!
Only, from the long line of spray
Where the sea meets the moon-blanched land,
Listen! You hear the grating roar
Of pebbles which the waves draw back, and fling,
At their return, up the high strand,
Begin, and cease, and then again begin,
With tremulous cadence slow, and bring
The eternal note of sadness in.
— *Matthew Arnold*

### Questions & Assignments

1. (a) Describe in your own words the scene pictured in the first five lines of this poem.
   (b) In your view is it a pleasant scene? Give reasons for your answer.
2. Is the poet speaking to someone in this poem? Explain.
3. Select at least two lines or phrases which you found particularly descriptive. In each case explain your choice.
4. What is *'the long line of spray'* to which the poet refers?
5. Why does the poet describe the land as *'moon-blanched'*?
6. Why do the pebbles make a *'grating roar'*?
7. Do you think that the poet was in a cheerful mood at the time of writing this poem? Give one reason for your answer.

## They Will Say

OF my city the worst that men will ever say is this:
You took little children away from the sun and the dew,
And the glimmers that played in the grass under the great sky,
And the reckless rain; you put them between walls
To work, broken and smothered, for bread and wages,
To eat dust in their throats and die empty-hearted
For a little handful of pay on a few Saturday nights.
— *Carl Sandburg*

### Questions & Assignments

1. The word *'you'* is used twice in the poem. To whom does it refer?
2. What point is the poet making in lines 2 and 3 and part of line 4? *('You took . . .' to 'reckless rain')*
3. What point is the poet making in the remainder of the poem?
4. Choose one phrase or image from the final four lines that describes something well and say why you chose it.
5. The poet uses alliteration in the poem. Identify some examples and show how it is effective.

## Happiness

I ASKED the professors who teach the meaning of life to tell
   me what is happiness.
And I went to famous executives who boss the work of
   thousands of men.
They all shook their heads and gave me a smile as though
   I was trying to fool with them
And then one Sunday afternoon I wandered out along
   the Desplaines River
And I saw a crowd of Hungarians under the trees with
   their women and children and a keg of beer and an
   accordion.
— *Carl Sandburg*

### Questions & Assignments

1. What point is being made in this short poem?
2. Consider the three poems by Carl Sandberg. In what ways are they similar?

## The Harbour

PASSING through huddled and ugly walls
By doorways where women
Looked from their hunger-deep eyes,
Haunted with shadows of hunger-hands,
Out from the huddled and ugly walls,
I came sudden, at the city's edge,
On a blue burst of lake,
Long lake waves breaking under the sun
On a spray-flung curve of shore;
And a fluttering storm of gulls,
Masses of great gray wings
And flying white bellies
Veering and wheeling free in the open.
— *Carl Sandburg*

### Questions & Assignments

1. The poet uses two descriptive words in the first line. Identify these and say why you did or did not think they are suitable.
2. Some words are repeated in the first five lines. Suggest why.
3. What is the poet describing in the first five lines?
4. Does the remainder of the poem present a contrasting picture? Explain.
5. What images does the poet use to describe the lake? Which one did you prefer most? Give a reason.
6. There is a comparison somewhere in the final four lines. Identify the comparison and say if the comparison is a simile or a metaphor. Do you think it is a good comparison? Explain.
7. Why do you think that the poet drew our attention to the gulls?

### Assignment

**Personal Writing**

Write two paragraphs (or poems) describing your favourite and least favourite part of your town.

# Poetry

## Points to Note

### ALLITERATION

As well as rhyme and rhythm, another device used to gain a musical effect in poetry is alliteration. Alliteration occurs when two or more wods in the same line begin with the same sound. Examples from *The Harbour* include 'blue burst' and 'Long lake'. Can you find other examples in the poem?

We often use alliteration in our every day conversation to make a phrase stand out. Advertisers also frequently use alliteration to make a phrase or a slogan more punchy and memorable, e.g. memorable, mouth-watering mint.

### ASSONANCE

Assonance is another device that adds music to language. We can say that assonance is present in a phrase when a certain sound, usually a vowel sound, is repeated. For example, assonance is present in the first line of *The Harbour* in the words 'huddled' and 'ugly'. It is present again in the phrase 'waves breaking' where the long 'a' sound is repeated. There are other examples of assonance in the poem. How many can you find?

## WORD PUZZLE

Solve each of the word puzzles below. Some clues are provided to help you. The clues are not in the same order as the anagrams. For example, the first clue 'To blow up' refers to puzzle 12 — 'NFIATLE'. Can you spot a **similarity** in the spelling patterns of each word?

| | | |
|---|---|---|
| 1. TDNASEI | 5. IETSNEGAVTI | 9. NSTTCIRU |
| 2. NECMIO | 6. RNTDEIU | 10. UDROCNTIE |
| 3. VENIONINT | 7. EIESNACR | 11. ERNHTII |
| 4. DNUAIVLIDI | 8. ITNBHIA | 12. NFIATLE |

- To blow up
- Check out
- Live in
- To bring in for the first time

- To give directions on how to do something
- To receive in a will
- In place of
- To butt in on

- To make bigger
- One person
- Creation
- Earnings

## Streets Of London

Have you seen the old man in the closed down market,
Kicking out the papers with his worn out shoes?
In his eyes you see no pride, hands held closely by his side,
Yesterday's paper telling yesterday's news.

### Chorus
*So how can you tell me you're lonely,*
*And say for you that the sun don't shine?*
*Let me take you by the hand and lead you through the streets of London,*
*I'll show you something that'll make you change your mind.*

Have you seen the old girl who walks the streets of London?
Dirt in her hair and her clothes in rags.
She's no time for talking, she just keeps right on walking,
Carrying her home in two carrier bags.

In the all night café at a quarter past eleven,
Same old man sitting there on his own.
Looking at the world over the rim of his tea cup,
Each tea lasts an hour, then he wanders home alone.

Have you seen the old man outside the Seamen's Mission*?
Memory fading with the medal ribbons he wears.
In our winter city the rain cries a little pity,
For one more forgotten hero in a world that doesn't care.

— *Ralph McTell*

*Seamen's Mission — a hostel for homeless men.

### Questions & Assignments

1. What details in the first verse tell us that the man was poor and unhappy.
2. In the chorus the writer speaks to somebody. What do we learn about this person from the first two lines of the chorus?
3. Why does the writer believe that leading this person through the streets of London will change his (or her) mind?
4. What do lines 2, 3 and 4 of the second verse tell us about the *'old girl'*? Deal with each line separately.
5. The same *'old man'* is pictured again in the third verse. What do we learn about his life from this verse?
6. Explain the line — *'Memory fading with the medal ribbons he wears'* from the final verse. How does this line link to the phrase *'one more forgotten hero'* in the final line.
7. Do you think that the mood of the final verse is angry or sad? Give a reason for your choice.
8. What is your response to this song?

## Points to Note — SYMBOLS

Taken literally, the word 'white' describes a colour and nothing more. However, over the centuries white is a colour that is associated with qualities such as purity, innocence and goodness. When the word 'white' is used in a poem to evoke these ideas then we can say it is a **symbol**.

Other traditional symbols include:
- Autumn as a symbol for growing old
- Sunrise symbolising a new beginning
- Sunshine symbolising happiness, rain and clouds symbolising unhappinness and hard times
- A rose symbolising beauty and grace
- Night symbolising death

Traditional symbols are fairly easy to identify and are frequently used by modern poets.

## PERSONAL WRITING — ASSIGNMENT

Imagine what it is like to be homeless in Ireland today and write a page or two on a homeless person talking about his or her life.

## Lion

Poor prisoner in a cage,
I understand your rage
And why you loudly roar
Walking that stony floor.

Your forest eyes are sad
As wearily you pad
A few yards up and down,
A king without a crown.

Up and down all day,
A wild beast for display,
Or lying in the heat
With sawdust, smells and meat,

Remembering how you chased
Your jungle prey, and raced,
Leaping upon their backs
Along the grassy tracks.

But you are here instead,
Better, perhaps, be dead
Than locked in this dark den;
Forgive us, lion, then,
Who did not ever choose,
Our circuses and zoos.
— *Leonard Clark*

### Questions & Assignments

1. To whom is the poet speaking?
2. What words and phrases in the first stanza show us how the poet felt towards the lion?
3. How does the lion spend his day?
4. Why does the poet speak of the lion as *'A king without a crown'*?
5. (a) What words in the poem suggest that the cage is not a nice place?
   (b) What does each of the words you have chosen suggest to you about the cage?
6. For whom does the poet ask forgiveness in the last three lines?
7. What do you understand the last two lines of the poem to mean?
8. List (a) four reasons for and (b) four reasons against having circuses and zoos.
9. (a) What message do you think the poet is trying to get across in this poem?
   (b) Is there a similar message to be found in the poem *A Caged Bird in Springtime*? Explain your answer.
10. Do you think that birds and animals should be kept in captivity? Give reasons for your answer.

# The Caged Bird in Springtime

What can it be,
This curious anxiety?
It is as if I wanted
To fly away from here.

But how absurd!
I have never flown in my life,
And I do not know
What flying means, though I have heard,
Of course, something about it.

Why do I peck the wires of this little cage?
It is the only nest I have ever known.
But I want to build my own,
High in the secret branches of the air.

I cannot quite remember how
It is done, but I know
That what I want to do
Cannot be done here.

I have all I need -
Seed and water, air and light,
Why, then, do I weep with anguish,
And beat my head and my wings
Against those sharp wires, while the children
Smile at each other, saying: 'Hark how he sings'?
— *James Kirkup*

## Questions & Assignments

1. Explain who is speaking in this poem.
2. In the first two lines the bird seems to be puzzled and anxious about something. What do you think it is?
3. *'But how absurd!'* Why does the bird say this?
4. *'It is the only nest I have ever known.'* What do we learn from this line?
5. The bird says that what she wants to do *'cannot be done here'*. Why not?
6. The final part of the poem begins with the line *'I have all I need'*. Do you agree that the bird has all she needs? Explain your answer.
7. Why do the children smile?

## The Encounter

Over the grass a hedgehog came
Questing the air for scents of food
And the cracked twig of danger.
He shuffled near in the gloom. Then stopped.
He was sure aware of me. I went up,
Bent low to look at him, and saw
His coat of lances pointing to my hand.
What could I do
To show I was no enemy?
I turned him over, inspected his small clenched paws,
His eyes expressionless as glass,
And did not know how I could speak,
By touch or tongue, the language of a friend.

It was a grief to be a friend
Yet to be dumb; to offer peace
And bring the soldiers out …
— *Clifford Dyment*

### Questions & Assignments

1. What was the hedgehog *'questing'* (watching out for)?
2. How do we know that the meeting took place in late evening?
3. What word does the poet use to describe the movement of the hedgehog? Do you think that it is a good word? Explain your answer.
4. What happened when the poet went to look closely at the hedgehog?
5. Explain the poet's problem in your own words.
6. Describe, in your own words, how the hedgehog behaved when the poet turned him over.
7. If you were writing to the poet about this poem, what would you say to him? Compose a short letter you might write.

## Hedgehog

He ambles along like a walking pincushion,
Stops and curls up like a chestnut burr.
He's not worried because he's so little.
Nobody is going to slap him around.
— *Chu Chen Po*

### Questions & Assignments

1. There are two comparisons (in this case similes) in this poem. Give your opinion on each of them.
2. Find a word in the poem that has a similar meaning to the word 'walks'.

## The Defence

A silent murderer,
A kestrel came today,
Canny marauder
In search of prey.

He scanned the ground for signs,
Hovered on the lifting air,
His claws poised ready to snatch
Some victim off to his lair.

But swallows gathered fast,
Closed in from all around,
Sounding a shrill alarm,
Filling the sky with furious sound.

They soared into the sky,
And peeled off to attack,
Jabbing with dagger beak and needling cry
To drive the killer back.
The kestrel wavered once,
Then, like a useless glove
Thrown down, he tumbled on the wind
And fled from the birds above.

And we who sat and watched,
We too had been afeared,
Had held our bated breath.
But now we stood up and cheered.
— *Geoffrey Summerfield*

### Questions & Assignments

1. Why is the kestrel described as a silent murderer?
2. Select three words from the second stanza which describe the actions of the kestrel. What do each of these words tell us about the nature of the kestrel?
3. Describe clearly what the swallows did when the kestrel appeared.
4. Why does the poet compare the kestrel to a useless glove?
5. Who else witnessed the event?

## Bats

A bat is born
Naked and blind and pale.
His mother makes a pocket of her tail
And catches him. He clings to her long fur
By his thumbs and toes and teeth.
And then the mother dances through the night
Doubling and looping, soaring, somersaulting -
Her baby hangs on underneath.
All night, in happiness, she hunts and flies.
Her high sharp cries
Like shining needlepoints of sound
Go out into the night and, echoing back,
Tell her what they have touched.
She hears how far it is, how big it is,
Which way it's going:
She lives by hearing.
The mother eats the moths and gnats she catches
In full flight; in full flight
The mother drinks the water of the pond
She skims across. Her baby hangs on tight.
Her baby drinks the milk she makes him
In moonlight or starlight, in mid-air.
Their single shadow, printed on the moon
Or fluttering across the stars,
Whirls on all night; at daybreak
The tired mother flaps home to her rafter.
The others all are there.
They hang themselves up by their toes,
They wrap themselves in their brown wings.
Bunched upside-down, they sleep in air.
Their sharp ears, their sharp teeth, their quick sharp faces
Are dull and slow and mild.
All the bright day, as the mother sleeps,
She folds her wings about her sleeping child.

— *Randall Jarrell*

# Poetry

## Questions & Assignments

1. What do we learn about young bats in the first five lines?
2. *'And then the mother dances through the night'*. What idea is the poet trying to get across in this line?
3. List the words used by the poet to describe the flight of the bat. Are they good descriptive words? Explain your answer in each case.
4. *'She lives by hearing.'* How does the poem help us to understand this?
5. What other unusual powers does the bat possess? In answering you should note the phrase *'In full flight'*.
6. The poet also uses the word *'flaps'* to describe the movement of the bat. Why do you think he chose this word?
7. Describe how bats spend the day.
8. Poets sometimes help us to see things in a different way or to change our attitude to something. Has this poem shown you something in a new light or changed your attitude in any way? Explain how.

## WORD PUZZLE

Solve each of the word puzzles below. Some clues are provided to help you. The clues are not in the same order as the anagrams. For example, the first clue 'Can't be done' refers to puzzle 8 — 'MLPESOISIB'. Can you spot a **similarity** in the spelling patterns of each word?

| | | |
|---|---|---|
| 1. YIPLM | 5. MOPVIRE | 9. IESMSPR |
| 2. TMOPIR | 6. EMLPENITM | 10. ITREFMECP |
| 3. ORPATINMT | 7. IAITLMARP | 11. PIOMIELT |
| 4. TINPEMNEIRT | 8. MLPESOISIB | 12. ILSASMEBPA |

- Can't be done
- Not quite correct
- Not to be ignored
- Can't be travelled on
- Rude
- Neutral
- Make an impression
- Tool
- Hint at
- Cheeky
- To get better
- To bring into a country

## The Intruder

Two-boots in the forest walks,
Pushing through the bracken stalks.

Vanishing like a puff of smoke,
Nimbletail flies up the oak.

Longears helter-skelter shoots
Into his house among the roots.

At work upon the highest bark,
Tapperbill knocks off to hark.

Painted-wings through sun and shade
Flounces off along the glade.

Not a creature lingers by,
When clumping Two-boots comes to pry.

— *James Reeves*

### Questions & Assignments

1. Write a paragraph describing the event that takes place in this poem.
2. (a) What creatures are referred to in the poem?
   (b) Do you think the names given by the poet to these creatures are suitable? Give reasons for your answer.
3. *'like a puff of smoke'*. Do you think this is a good comparison (in this case simile)? Explain your answer.
4. Give your opinion of the poet's choice of the following words : *'shoots'; 'knocks off'; 'pry'; 'clumping'*.
5. Describe the rhyming scheme of this poem.

### Points to Note — VERBS

Verbs are words that describe movement and actions — walked; talked; sang; ran; kissed; thought — are a few simple examples. Writers take care in choosing verbs in order to express ideas accurately. In the poem *The Intruder*, the writer uses 'flies' instead of 'runs'; 'lingers' instead of 'waits' and 'pry' instead of 'look'. We could say that these verbs are apt (suitable).

In your own writing you should take care to choose your verbs carefully. Verbs such as 'went' and 'said' appear too frequently in the writing of many students.

## My Animals

My animals are made of wool and glass,
Also of wood. Table and mantelpiece
Are thickly covered with them. It's because
You cannot keep real cats or dogs in these

High-up new flats. I really want to have
A huge, soft marmalade or, if not that,
Some animal that *seems* at least to love.
Hamsters? A dog? No, what I need's a cat.

I hate a word like 'pets'; it sounds so much
Like something with no living of its own.
And yet each time that I caress and touch
My wool or glass ones, I feel quite alone.

No kittens in our flat, no dogs to bark
Each time the bell rings. Everything is still;
Often I want a zoo, a whole Noah's ark.
Nothing is born here, nothing tries to kill.

— *Elizabeth Jennings*

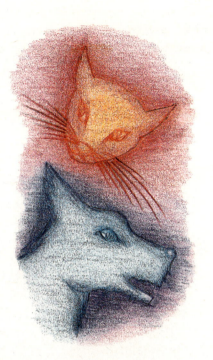

### Questions & Assignments

1. (a) Why can't the poet keep a pet?
   (b) What does she have instead?
2. Why, according to the poet, are the *'wool and glass'* ones not as good as a living animal?
3. What is the mood of the poet in this poem?
4. Describe the rhyming pattern of the poem.

### [Answer Guidelines]

3. The poet seems to be in a discontented mood here. The reason for this is that she wants to have a cat but, because she lives in a flat, she cannot. Instead she has animals made from glass, wool and wood but she is discontented with these.

**PERSONAL WRITING**

## ASSIGNMENT

Write a paragraph on the best toy you ever had.

**The following Spot the Errors exercise is aimed at sharpening your basic writing skills. Spot the 20 errors in the Passage below and rewrite the passage correctly. (Note: Refer to the Guidelines on pages 1—15.)**

## 4  The Party

The party was not what Mrs. McDonald would have called a great sucess. Usualy when she had visitors she liked to sum the evening up afterwards, classify it under various headings, such as lively, a bit slow and so fourth. This evening would require a heading all of it's own. To begin with Herbert did not drink coffee after nine o'clock in the evening as it kept him awake Mrs. McDonald paused, coffee pot suspended over his cup, and tried to cope with this inexpected refusal.

People were usually thrilled to get reel coffee rather than instant coffee Jenny quickly offered to make herbert a cup of tea but he did not want anyone to be troubled on his behalf; half a cup of cold milk would do him nicely.

Cold milk, said Mrs. McDonald bleakly. Jenny poured it.

"A piece of cake, Herbert?" He hesitated. "Its chocolate cake."

"Oh! Does cake keep you awake too" asked Jenny.

Herbert answered that it didn't, exactly, but it did made him dream. What was wrong with that? Jenny was astonished by the idea that anyone mite dislike dreaming.

"Please don't eat it if you don't want to, Herbert. Pass Herbert the salami sandwiches please, Jenny."

"Salami," stammered Herbert.

"Salami on rye," said Jenny, passing the plate. "Delicous. Or does it make you dream too" Herbert said that he did not know.

"We'll do an experement then, shall we?" cried Jenny, refusing to meet her mother's eye, which she knew was telling her to behave.

"Don't you like salami, Herbert? if so, please don't eat it if you don't want to," said Mrs. McDonald.

He admitted that he only liked plane food.

# Short Stories

## Too Many Rabbits
*Paul Jennings*

### PART 1

Sex is not talked about in our place. No one has told me anything. I have worked out quite a few things myself though. I keep my ears open and my eyes to the ground.

I know the main bits. I see things. Like when Sky's dog had pups. One day Sandy was fat and there were no puppies and the next day she was thin and there they were. You don't have to be too smart to work out where they came from.

How they got in there, I even know that too.

Sandy is a great dog. And the puppies are beautiful. I would like one of them more than anything in the world. But I just can't talk Dad around. He will not have any pets at all.

"Can I have a pet, Dad?" I asked him.

"What sort of pet?" he said.

"A dog?"

"Nah, they bark too much. And they dig holes and annoy the neighbours."

"A cat?" I said.

"Nah, they leave fur everywhere."

"A bird?"

"Nah, it's cruel to keep them in cages."

"A mouse?" I begged.

"Nah, they breed like rabbits."

"An elephant," I yelled.

Dad grinned at this. "If you can find one you can have it," he said.

I raced out and grabbed Saturday's paper. Before he changed his mind. You have to strike while the lion is hot. I looked and looked but there were no elephants for sale. Not one. I bet that Dad knew this all along. Parents can be so sneaky sometimes.

After this I was sent to my room for throwing the paper on the floor and yelling.

We live in a bookshop in the main street. Upstairs is Mum and Dad's room. Under that is the shop. Down the bottom is the storeroom and my bedroom. There are no windows in my room. It's like a jail. I am always getting sent to my room. It's not fair.

If I was to dig a hole in the wall I could make a tunnel. I could escape. Like prisoners of war do.

It would be great to have an escape tunnel. Even if it took me twenty years to dig, I would have a way out when I was sent to my room. It would be worth it in the long run.

Anyway, there I was lying on my bed and not allowed out. I just stared at the wall. It was made out of wooden panels. There was nothing else to do so I decided to pull a panel off and start to dig into the wall behind it. I started pushing at the wood with an old screwdriver. I put the blade in a crack and levered.

Bingo. Kerpow. Wow. The panel just swung open. Just like that. It was a door. A secret door. I couldn't believe it. I didn't have to dig a tunnel. There was already something there.

I stared into the hole but I couldn't see a thing. It was dark. And musty. It smelled all stale. I wanted to go straight in and explore. But I didn't have a torch. It might be dangerous.

No, this would take a bit of thinking about. I wouldn't go in until I could get a torch. There could be horrible things lying around. I could hurt myself in the dark. It's important to look before you weep.

I shut the door and waited for my time in solitary confinement to be over.

## Questions & Assignments — PART 1

1. What pets did the narrator (Philip is his name) ask to have? In each case, say why his father refused.
2. Why did his father grin when he asked if he could have an elephant?
3. Write a short description, in your own words, of the house where Philip lived.
4. (a) What did Philip discover in his room? (b) Why did he not go in and explore?
5. When we speak we use certain phrases over and over again. For example, the phrase 'raining cats and dogs' is frequently used in everyday chat. In this section of the story the writer uses some well-worn phrases but doesn't get them quite right. Find three examples in this part of the story. List other examples from the other sections of the story as you read on.
6. What makes you want to read on at this point in the story?

## [Answer Guidelines]

6. I want to find out what . . . I also want to see if he talks his father into . . .

## Word power!

Find the words in the story which have similar meanings to each of the words and phrases below. The number in brackets after each one indicates the number of letters in the answer. The words appear in the story in the same order as the meanings given below.

### CLUES

1. clever (5)
2. people who live nearby (10)
3. shouting (7)
4. alone; no one else there (8)

## PART 2

The following day I went next door to see Sky. She owned a junk shop and I knew she would have an old torch somewhere. You could find wonderful things in that shop.

Sky grinned when I asked her. "A torch? I don't know, love. There might be one in the corner over there."

I rummaged around for ages. Beads, candles, bits of broken bikes, one thong, hats, a cracked toilet seat, a knife with no handle, a rabbit in a cage.

A rabbit in a cage.

A beautiful, lovely, pink-eyed rabbit with a black patch on its white back. "Wow," I said. "This is the most beautiful rabbit in the world. I wish it was mine." I pressed its warm fur up to my face.

"Ten dollars," said Sky. "You can have it for ten dollars. That's what I paid for it."

I shook my head. "Dad will never let me have it," I said. "Anyway, I haven't got ten dollars."

She smiled at me kindly. "You can have it for eight," she said. "I can't say fairer than that. But you'll have to be quick. I had six yesterday and this is the last one left."

I spent ages stroking the rabbit. "Pinky," I said. "Her name is Pinky and she loves me."

"I've only got ten cents on me," I said. "But I've got eight dollars at home." I knew that Dad wouldn't let me keep the rabbit but I had an idea. I would hide Pinky. Dad would never know.

But where? Where could I hide her?

Of course. The space behind the wall. You could keep a rabbit in there and no one would know. But first I would need a torch.

"What about this?" said Sky. She had a torch in her hand. Not a bad one either. And it had batteries that worked.

"How much?" I asked.

Sky was wearing about a hundred strings of bright beads around her neck. She always fiddled with them when she was with a customer. "Ten cents," she said.

"Gee thanks," I said. I put Pinky

down and ran back into our bookshop. I was in such a hurry that I bumped straight into Dad. Oh no, he was going to ask me what I wanted a torch for.

"Where'd you get that?" said Dad. "It's a nice-looking torch."

"I bought it from Sky," I said. "Ten cents."

"Ten cents," said Dad. "It's worth at least ten dollars. No wonder she's going broke."

"What?" I said.

"She's got no money. She's behind with the rent. She feels sorry for people and sells everything for less than she bought it for. They'll kick her out soon for sure."

"Who will?" I said.

"The bank. The bank owns all these shops along here."

The bank was right next door. "They can't kick her out," I yelled. "She's my friend."

"We're not doing so well ourselves," said Dad.

I ran down to my room and slammed the door. I was very upset about Sky. I looked at the torch. The torch. The tunnel. I had forgotten all about them.

I switched on the torch and stepped through the wall.

## Questions & Assignments — PART 2

1. What kind of things did Sky have in her shop?
2. Why was Philip upset about Sky?
3. What kind of person do you think Sky is? Give reasons for your answer.
4. What do you hope will happen to Sky at the end of the story?

## [Answer Guidelines]

3. Try to think of at least two qualities — She is . . . sly? lazy? generous? mean? disorganised? businesslike? Remember that you can also describe a person in terms of what they are not — She is not . . . selfish?

## Word Power!

Find the words in the story which have similar meanings to each of the words and phrases below. The number in brackets after each one indicates the number of letters in the answer. The words appear in the story in the same order as the meanings given below.

### CLUES

1. items that are no longer used (4)
2. searched (8)
3. closed with a bang (7)

## PART 3

It was a big, dark cellar. The floor and three of the walls were concrete. The wall at the back was just dirt and stones. There was nothing there except cobwebs, dust and an old bookshelf with two ancient bird books in it.

Books. My heart sank. I had been hoping for treasure or jewels. I snooped around for a bit but there was nothing to be found. There was a light switch and I turned it on. No, there was nothing to see. Just a cold, gloomy cellar. Still, it would be great for a rabbit. I wouldn't even have to build a cage.

I looked up. Over the top was our shop. On one side was Sky's junk shop. And on the other was the bank. I just stood there thinking. That's when I got the idea. That's when it popped into my head. I could dig a tunnel.

And rob the bank.

Like Robbing Hood. You take from the rich and give to the poor. The bank was rich. Sky was poor. I would take some money and give it to Sky. I wouldn't keep any for myself. Not even eight dollars for a Rabbit. I would give it all to Sky. Then she could give it back to the bank and they wouldn't kick her out of her shop. They would get their money back and everybody would be happy.

I smuggled Pinky in and she sniffed around her new home. I could tell that she liked it.

It was a good plan and I made a start straight away. I borrowed Dad's spade and started to dig at the wall. The spade was heavy and the wall was hard. All rocks and stones. After about an hour I stopped. My hands were blistered and sore. I was sweaty and tired. And I had hardly made a scratch on the wall.

Digging tunnels is hard work.

I picked up Pinky and gave her a cuddle. She was very, very fat. She nibbled at my hand. "She wants food," I said to myself. I went upstairs and raided the fridge. Two carrots. Pinky finished them off in no time at all. Talk about hungry. And fat. "Your thighs are bigger than your stomach," I said.

### Questions & Assignments — PART 3

1. What did Philip find in the cellar?
2. (a) What plan did Philip come up with?
   (b) In your view, is this plan likely to work? Explain your answer.
3. What sentences in the passage tell us that Philip was not very successful at digging the tunnel.

### Word Power!

Find the words in the story which have similar meanings to each of the words and phrases below. The number in brackets after each one indicates the number of letters in the answer. The words appear in the story in the same order as the meanings given below.

CLUES
1. very old (7)
2. almost dark; dull (6)
3. brought in illegally (8)
4. a friendly squeeze (6)

## PART 4

The next day I took the eight dollars in to Sky. "Thanks," she said. "It's my only sale for the day." She was down in the dumps. Just sitting there munching on an apple.

"Don't worry," I said. "They won't kick you out. I've got a plan."

"What's that, love?" said Sky.

"I'm digging a tunnel into the bank. I'm going to get you some money."

Sky shook her head. "No, no, no," she said. "You can't do that."

"Why not? They've got plenty of money."

"Yes, but it's not ours. It belongs to other people. It wouldn't be right. And anyway, tunnels are dangerous. It might fall in and kill you. If you dig a tunnel I'll have to tell your dad."

I couldn't believe it. Sky didn't want me to dig a tunnel. I made up my mind not to tell her anything about the secret cellar. Just in case.

"It was a sweet idea, love," she said. "But don't worry. Something will turn up. You shouldn't worry yourself too much about money." She took a big bite out of her apple.

"Yeah," I said. "Money is the fruit of all evil."

I went home and got some straw and rags for Pinky. The floor of the cellar was cold. I also took her another three carrots. She gobbled them down like crazy. Rabbits sure do eat a lot. Especially big fat ones like Pinky.

That night Mum had a few words to say at tea-time. "Nearly all the carrots have gone," she said. "Have you taken them, Philip?"

I nodded my head.

"I'm glad to see you eating vegetables," she said. "But please ask first. Yours isn't the only mouth around here."

She was right about that. When I got down to the cellar there were another eight mouths. Pinky had given birth to eight of the cutest little bunnies you have ever seen. They were pink and hairless and blind and they sucked away at Pinky's teats like crazy. No wonder she was hungry.

I rushed upstairs and took a bunch of celery out of the fridge. Pinky finished it off in ten minutes flat.

There was one thing I knew for sure. Feeding my family was going to be a problem.

### Questions & Assignments  PART 4

1. What did Sky think of Philip's plan?
2. What sentence tells us that business was not going well for Sky?
3. What was the attitude of Philip's mother towards the missing carrots?

> **word power!**
>
> Find the words in the story which have similar meanings to each of the words and phrases below. The number in brackets after each one indicates the number of letters in the answer. The words appear in the story in the same order as the meanings given below.
>
> <u>CLUES</u>
> 1. eating (8)
> 2. ate quickly (7)
> 3. went quickly (6)

## PART 5

I named the new bunnies One, Two, Three, Four, Five, Six, Seven and Eight. I couldn't give them real names because I didn't know what sex they were. I found out after a bit that all of them except poor little Eight were females.

Days passed. Weeks passed. Months passed. My little bunnies became big bunnies.

I had four big problems:

1. Sky was going broke and the bank people were talking about tossing her out of her shop.

2. The rabbits were eating more and more and food was hard to find.

3. What goes in one end comes out the other.

4. One, Two, Three, Four, Five, Six and Seven were all getting very fat indeed.

"Times are hard," said Sky. "People aren't throwing out their old things. I just haven't got enough stock to sell. The rent costs more than I make."

I nodded wisely. I was short of money myself. I was spending it all on vegetables for my rabbits. "It's hard to make lends meet," I said.

Mum was watching the fridge like a hawk. She counted every carrot. Every leaf of lettuce. She even knew how many peas were in there. "I think he must have a lack of Vitamin C," said Mum. "All he does is eat vegetables and fruit."

"At least he'll be regular," said Dad.

Well, things went on like this for quite a bit. Every day I searched for grass, thistles, old cabbage leaves. Anything for my rabbits to eat.

Twice a day I would pull back the secret panel and feed my rabbits. Then I would sweep up the poo and put it out in our tiny backyard.

Dad was starting to get suspicious. "This is crazy," said Dad. "Why are all these rabbits coming into our yard? There are droppings everywhere. Why our place? Why not next door's?"

That night he sat up all night waiting for rabbits. He sat out there in the yard shivering behind some old boxes, waiting and waiting for the rabbits. But none came. "Something's going on," he said. "And I'm going to find out what it is."

I knew that if he discovered my secret he would give the rabbits away. Or let them go. Or even worse.

Rabbit pie.

That night I found something else. More rabbits. Five had had six babies. Wonderful, hairless little babies. Still blind with their eyes closed. My little bunnies. It was up to me to look after them. Protect them. Stop Dad finding them.

Two nights later One gave birth. Then Two, Three, Four, Six and Seven followed. My family had grown to thirty-nine wonderful rabbits.

It was great having so many. But going in with the food and out with the poo left no time for anything else. It took over an hour to find grass and thistles and stuff. Mr Griggs from the greengrocer's gave me rotten vegetables but I couldn't take too much. He might tell Dad.

And the poo was becoming a big problem. There was nowhere to put it in the middle of the main street.

One night I watched this movie about prisoners of war digging an escape tunnel. They had to hide the dirt that they dug out. What they did was put the soil in old socks and hide them in their trouser legs. When they pulled on a string the soil would fall out while they were walking along. No one noticed it.

Brainwave. I rubbed my hands together. Truth is stranger than friction.

I filled up two socks with rabbit poo and walked into the street. As I went along the footpath I let a little poo fall to the ground. It worked like a charm. No one noticed.

Well, not at first. "I can't believe it," said Dad. "The whole footpath is covered in rabbit droppings. But you never see a rabbit. Where are they coming from? I'm going to call a meeting of the other shop owners. Something has to be done."

Two nights later Dad and five of the other shopkeepers sat up watching for the rabbits. Sky told me all about it. "We waited and waited," she said. "In the freezing rain. But not so much as a single rabbit showed up."

I smiled and shuffled out onto the street to spread a bit more joy around. I was only a kid but I could make things happen. I liked pulling strings.

## Questions & Assignments — PART 5

1. Philip had four big problems. Explain clearly what problems 3 and 4 were.
2. 'Or even worse.' What does this phrase suggest?
3. (a) How did Philip solve problem 3? (b) From where did he get the idea?
4. 'I liked pulling strings.' What, in your opinion, is meant by this sentence?

## word power!

Find the words in the story which have similar meanings to each of the words and phrases below. The number in brackets after each one indicates the number of letters in the answer. The words appear in the story in the same order as the meanings given below.

### CLUES

1. bird of prey with good eyesight (4)
2. shortage (4)
3. curious; puzzled (10)
4. shaking with cold (9)
5. found out (10)
6. keep safe (7)
7. thorny weeds (8)

## PART 6

More months went by. My whole life was spent looking after the rabbits. Dirt and sand for the floor. Straw for them to sleep on. Old vegetables and grass for food. Then carting out the poo and dirt and sand and spreading it along the street. It took hours and hours. I had to sneak out at night. In out, in out. The responsibility was getting too much for me.

Then it happened. The next batch of babies. Before I knew it I had one hundred and fifteen rabbits. I couldn't remember their names. I was so tired from carting poo and grass that I could hardly keep my eyes open. The whole thing was turning into a nightmare.

I had to do something.

I sat down and had a good think about my situation. They were all pet rabbits. I couldn't let any go. Foxes and cats would eat them. They didn't know how to look after themselves in the wild. I tried to give a few away at school but the kids' mothers just sent them back. Dad would find out if I kept on with that. But I couldn't let them keep breeding.

How could I stop them?

There was only one way. Keep the males and females apart.

Sky had a second-hand roll of chicken wire. "You can have it for two dollars," she said. "It doesn't matter any more. The bank is closing me down." Her lips were trembling and her voice was all croaky. I looked at the window. There was a big sign saying: CLOSING DOWN SALE – EVERYTHING CHEAP.

"No," I yelled. "You can't leave, Sky. You're my best friend."

She just shuffled off into the back of the shop so that I wouldn't see her crying.

That afternoon I went into the bank when they were busy and spread some rabbit poo around on the floor. Everyone started sniffing and saying how disgusting it was. As I left I thought I heard someone say something about making a deposit.

After tea I sneaked into the rabbit cellar and built a fence. I put all the males on one side and all the females and babies on the other. It was a good fence. Now there wouldn't be any more babies. "You are a genius, Philip," I said to myself.

That night, after feeding the rabbits, I lay down to sleep. All was quiet. For a little while. Then suddenly I heard a terrible squealing noise coming from behind the wall. It grew louder and louder. Squealing and thumping and rustling. It would wake Dad for sure.

"Quiet in there," I whispered.

The noise grew louder. Oh no. If Dad came down – rabbit pie.

I opened the secret door. A terrible sight met my eyes. The male rabbits were fighting each other. Others were flinging themselves at the fence. Some of the bigger ones were jumping up in the air trying to get over. "Stop it," I whispered. "Stop it."

But they didn't stop it. More and more male rabbits threw themselves against the fence. They were crazy. They were wild. The fence began to sag. Wham. Down it came. The rabbits poured across like water from a broken dam. Then they started jumping all over each other.

I shut the pane. "Disgusting," I said to myself. "Sex sure is a powerful merge."

More powerful than I thought. In no time at all I had about four hundred and fifty rabbits.

Things were getting out of hand. The smell was so bad that I could hardly bear to go into the cellar. And it was starting to seep through into my bedroom.

"What's that smell?" said Dad. He sniffed around trying to find something. He looked under the bed and in the cupboard but he didn't find the secret panel. My rabbits were safe. For the time being.

"Make sure you change your socks every day," Dad said. "This room smells terrible."

## Questions & Assignments — PART 6

1. What problems had Philip as his rabbit population grew?
2. Explain why he could not let them go?
3. Why did Philip visit the bank?
4. Describe Philip's plan to prevent the rabbits from continuing to breed.

## word power!

Find the words in the story which have similar meanings to each of the words and phrases below. The number in brackets after each one indicates the number of letters in the answer. The words appear in the story in the same order as the meanings given below.

CLUES
1. food plants (10)
2. go without being seen (5)
3. duty (14)
4. group (5)
5. bad dream (9)
6. position (9)
7. shaking (9)

## PART 7

Everything was going wrong. I was facing a mid-wife crisis. I sat down and had a little talk to myself. "Philip," I said. "You can't keep this up. You can't get enough food for the rabbits. You can't keep up with the poo pile. You can't give the rabbits away and you can't keep them. You can't let them go or the foxes will get them. You can't tell Dad and he is going to discover them any day. Sky is getting kicked out of her shop. You are just a kid. You are out of your depth. The rabbits are too much for you. You are too big for your brutes." My eyes started to water.

There was worse to come. Dad sat next to me on the bed. He saw that I was crying. He took my hand and smiled kindly. "You've heard then?" he said.

"Heard what?"

"We have to leave the shop. It's not just Sky who can't afford the rent. We've been behind for months. The bank is throwing us out."

"No," I screamed. "No, no, no." My heart was in my shoes. I didn't want to leave. And I would have to show Dad the rabbits. I couldn't leave them there to starve.

Rabbit pie.

Dad started sniffing around. "There must be a dead possum in the walls," he said. "That smell is disgusting." He started to tap on the walls, listening and sniffing. He was going to find the rabbits. I just knew he was.

I couldn't bear to watch. I ran up the stairs and into the sunlight. I ran and ran and ran. In the end I was out of breath. I just dropped down onto the footpath and hung my head in my hands.

I couldn't say how long I stayed there. It was a long time. Finally I was driven home by hunger.

When I arrived back I knew straight away that something was wrong. No one was in the shop. Mum and Dad were both downstairs. In my room.

I crept down the stairs. The panel was open. Mum and Dad were inside the cellar. And the rabbits were gone.

"Murderers," I yelled.

"What?" said Dad.

"You've killed my rabbits."

"No," said Dad. He pulled the old bookshelf away. "Look at this."

I couldn't believe it. Amazing. A tunnel. The rabbits had made a break for freedom. They were all gone. Every last one.

"The foxes," I screamed. "The foxes will get them."

I pelted up the stairs.

I looked up the street. I looked down the street. Nothing. Not a rabbit in sight.

Then I looked at Sky's window. The closing-down sign had gone. There was a new one in its place. It said: RABBITS FOR SALE – $15.00 EACH.

The junk shop was full of rabbits. Sky was smiling. There were rabbits everywhere. She even had one on her head. "I told you something would turn up," she said. "They just came out of a hole in the floor. I've sold fifteen already. I'll make a fortune. And I won't have to leave."

I didn't say anything. There wasn't anything to say. I was happy for Sky. And happy for the rabbits. I smiled and walked slowly back to my room.

"Don't look so gloomy," said Dad.

"I don't want to leave," I said. "I like it here."

Dad was waving one of the old books I

had found.

"We don't have to go," he yelped. "You've saved the day, Philip."

"What?" I mumbled.

"This book. It's a John Gould original. Worth a fortune. We can pay off the bank now, no worries."

I grinned. I was so happy.

"There's more good news," said Mum. "I'm going to have a baby – babies. I'm having twins."

Geeze, I was happy. Fancy that. Twins. I know why she's having them, too. Mum and Dad own a bookshop. Well, it's obvious, isn't it?

They read like rabbits.

## Questions & Assignments — PART 7

1. What bad news does Philip hear from his Dad?
2. Why did Philip run out of the house?
3. When Philip returns all the problems are solved. Explain how this happened.
4. Describe in your own words two scenes from this story that you found particularly amusing.
5. Tell the story in your own words in around ten sentences.

## [Answer Guidelines]

5. Philip lives with his parents in . . .
   He wants . . . but . . .
   He discovers a . . .
   Sky, the lady who has a . . . gives Philip . . .
   The rabbit soon has . . . and gradually . . .
   Philip's problem is . . .
   Philip is not the only one with . . .
   The bank . . .
   One day the problem becomes too much for Philip and . . .
   When he returns . . .

## word power!

Find the words in the story which have similar meanings to each of the words and phrases below. The number in brackets after each one indicates the number of letters in the answer. The words appear in the story in the same order as the meanings given below.

**CLUES**
1. problem (6)
2. very unpleasant (10)
3. first of a kind (8)
4. large amount of money (7)

## ASSIGNMENTS

1. Your grandparent – or some other old person that you know – talks about some part of his or her youth. The topic could be school, toys, street games, life at home or any other feature of his or her younger days. Write it as if the person is speaking.

   *The best game of all, if you could call it a game, was getting chased by a grown-up. It was easy getting a chase but you needed a good hiding place because if they caught you, you'd remember it. I remember a coal delivery man who came up our street every Friday. His real name was Jimmy Frawley but we called him ...*

2. 'Making Friends.' Use this title to write about a time when you had to try to make new friends or when somebody you know had to try to make new friends as a result of moving to a different school or a new house.

   *I could feel twenty pairs of eyes staring at me when I walked into that strange classroom.*

3. Describe somebody in your neighbourhood who doesn't 'fit in' and explain why. Is it the fault of the person themselves or the other people in the neighbourhood?

   *'Mad Maggie Sullivan who lived in No. 37 was an odd character. She wore a tattered old coat and went everywhere with a plastic bag full of bits and pieces.*

4. 'My Best Friend.' Write about your best friend and explain the importance of the friendship to you. Tell what you get from the friendship and what you put in.

   *"I've got twenty pounds saved and you're welcome to it. It should be enough to get you out of this mess you're in."*

   *"No, Peter," I replied. "I couldn't take your money".*

   *"Pay me back when you can. I'll drop it down to you later," Peter went on, taking no notice of what I said. "That's what friends are for ..."*

**PERSONAL WRITING**

## REMEMBER
When you're writing non-fiction essays be sincere. It adds depth and interest to your writing.

## Points to Note — COMEDY

We all like funny stories but the proverb "One man's meat is another man's poison" is one that can be applied to comedy. Not everybody finds the same situation funny. All comic writing though will have at least one of the following elements in it:

### Funny Situations

This type of comedy arises from a series of misunderstandings and mishaps, leading to characters ending up in odd or ridiculous situations.

### Odd Characters

People with an eccentric or an odd side to their personality are a source of humour, especially in their efforts to carry out everyday tasks or deal with minor problems. Often such people do things to extremes. They are over-polite; over-shy; over-rude. They pursue hobbies and ambitions to unusual extremes.

### Funny Dialogue

The two elements above – situation comedy and odd characters – invariably result in a humorous exchange of words. All comic drama on film and stage is largely made up of these three elements. However, the writer who is aiming for a humorous effect has some further scope.

### The Way It's Told

The writer can use phrases and expressions that are funny in themselves.

### Let The Joke Be On You

Also, the narrator can choose to become the main source of the humour, by directing the laughter at herself or himself. When this is happening the narrator will pretend not to see the joke. Readers like to discover the funny side of a story for themselves rather than having the narrator point it out.

## About Paul Jennings

Paul Jennings' amazing success as a writer began in December 1985 when his first book of stories Unreal! was published. Within months it was on the bestseller lists. It's been the same with every book that followed.

Spooky, funny, wacky and always with a surprise ending, Paul's stories are devoured by readers of all ages. Every year his books top the lists of nominations for the Australian state awards chosen by children.

In 1990, a thirteen-part television series based on Paul's early stories was screened in Australia and in the UK. Round the Twist, the series and the book, received much praise. A few years later, the second series of Round the Twist was screened in Australia and the UK where it was one of the top-rated young people's programs. Both series have since been screened in over forty countries throughout the world.

Paul Jennings has written over eighty stories and has sold more than two million copies of his books. He receives thousands of fan letters every year and claims to reply to them all.

# Smart Ice-Cream
## Paul Jennings

Well, I came top of the class again. One hundred out of one hundred for Maths. And one hundred out of one hundred for English. I'm just a natural brain, the best there is. There isn't one kid in the class who can come near me. Next to me they are all dumb.

Even when I was a baby I was smart. The day that I was born my mother started tickling me. "Bub, bub, bub," she said.

"Cut it out, Mum," I told her. "That tickles." She nearly fell out of bed when I said that. I was very advanced for my age.

Every year I win a lot of prizes: top of the class, top of the school, stuff like that. I won a prize for spelling when I was only three years old. I am a terrific speller. If you can say it, I can spell it. Nobody can trick me on spelling. I can spell every word there is.

Some kids don't like me; I know that for a fact. They say I'm a show off. I don't care. They are just jealous because they are not as clever as me. I'm good looking too. That's another reason why they are jealous.

Last week something bad happened. Another kid got one hundred out of one hundred for Maths too. That never happened before — no one has ever done as well as me. I am always first on my own. A kid called Jerome Dadian beat me. He must have cheated. I was sure he cheated. It had something to do with that ice-cream. I was sure of it. I decided to find out what was going on; I wasn't going to let anyone pull a fast one on me.

It all started with the ice-cream man. Mr Peppi. The old fool had a van which he parked outside the school. He sold ice-cream, all different types. He had every flavour there is, and some that I had never heard of before.

He didn't like me very much. He told me off once. "Go to the back of the queue," he said. "You pushed in."

"Mind your own business, Pop," I told him. "Just hand over the ice-cream."

"No," he said. "I won't serve you unless you go to the back."

I went round to the back of the van, but I didn't get in the queue. I took out a nail and made a long scratch on his rotten old van. He had just had it painted. Peppi came and had a look. Tears came into his eyes. "You are a bad boy," he said. "One day you will get into trouble. You think you are smart. One day you will be too smart."

I just laughed and walked off. I knew he wouldn't do anything. He was too soft-hearted. He was always giving free ice-creams to kids that had no money. He felt sorry for poor people. The silly fool.

There were a lot of stories going round about that ice-cream. People said that it was good for you. Some kids said that it made you better when you were sick. One of the teachers called it 'Happy Ice-Cream'. I didn't believe it; it never made me happy.

All the same, there was something strange about it. Take Pimples Peterson for example. That wasn't his real name — I just called him that because he had a lot of pimples. Anyway, Peppi heard me calling Peterson 'Pimples'. "You are a real mean boy," he said. "You are always picking on someone else, just because they are not like you."

"Get lost, Peppi," I said. "Go and flog your ice-cream somewhere else."

Peppi didn't answer me. Instead he spoke to Pimples. "Here, eat this," he told him. He handed Peterson an ice-cream. It was the biggest ice-cream I had ever seen. It was coloured purple. Peterson wasn't too sure about it. He didn't think he had enough money for such a big ice-cream.

"Go on," said Mr Peppi. "Eat it. I am giving it to you for nothing. It will get rid of your pimples."

I laughed and laughed. Ice-cream doesn't get rid of pimples, it gives you pimples. Anyway, the next day when Peterson came to school he had no pimples. Not one. I couldn't believe it. The ice-cream had cured his pimples.

There were some other strange things that happened too. There was a kid at the school who had a long nose. Boy, was it long. He looked like Pinocchio. When he blew it you could hear it a mile away. I called him 'Snozzle'. He didn't like being called Snozzle. He used to go red in the face when I said it, and that was every time that I saw him. He didn't say anything back — he was scared that I would punch him up.

Peppi felt sorry for Snozzle too. He gave him a small green ice-cream every morning, for nothing. What a jerk. He never gave me a free ice-cream.

You wouldn't believe what happened but I swear it's true. Snozzle's nose began to grow smaller. Every day it grew a bit smaller. In the end it was just a normal nose. When it was the right size Peppi stopped giving him the green ice-creams.

I made up my mind to put a stop to this ice-cream business. Jerome Dadian had been eating ice-cream the day he got one hundred for Maths. It must have been the ice-cream making him smart. I wasn't going to have anyone doing as well as me. I was the smartest kid in the school, and that's the way I wanted it to stay. I wanted to get a look inside that ice-cream van to find out what was going on.

I knew where Peppi kept his van at night — he left it in a small lane behind his house. I waited until about eleven o'clock at night. Then I crept out of the house and down to Peppi's van. I took a crowbar, a bucket of sand, a torch and some bolt cutters with me.

There was no one around when I reached the van. I sprang the door open with the crowbar and shone my torch around inside. I had never seen so many

tubs of ice-cream before. There was every flavour you could think of: there was apple and banana, cherry and mango, blackberry and watermelon and about fifty other flavours. Right at the end of the van were four bins with locks on them. I went over and had a look. It was just as I thought — these were his special flavours. Each one had writing on the top. This is what they said:

> HAPPY ICE-CREAM for cheering people up.
> NOSE ICE-CREAM for long noses.
> PIMPLE ICE-CREAM for removing pimples.
> SMART ICE-CREAM for smart alecs.

Now I knew his secret. That rat Dadian had been eating Smart Ice-Cream; that's how he got one hundred for Maths. I knew there couldn't be anyone as clever as me. I decided to fix Peppi up once and for all. I took out the bolt cutters and cut the locks off the four bins; then I put sand into every bin in the van. Except for the Smart Ice-Cream. I didn't put any sand in that.

I laughed to myself. Peppi wouldn't sell much ice-cream now. Not unless he started a new flavour — Sand Ice-Cream. I looked at the Smart Ice-Cream. I decided to eat some; it couldn't do any harm. Not that I needed it — I was already about as smart as you could get. Anyway, I gave it a try. I ate the lot. Once I started I couldn't stop. It tasted good. It was delicious.

I left the van and went home to bed, but I couldn't sleep. To tell the truth, I didn't feel too good. So I decided to write this. Then if any funny business has been going on you people will know what happened. I think I made a mistake. I don't think Dadian did get any Smart Ice-Cream.

\* \* \* \* \*

It iz the nekst day now. Somefing iz hapening to me. I don't feel quite az smart. I have bean trying to do a reel hard sum. It iz wun and wun. Wot duz wun and wun make? Iz it free or iz it for?

## Questions & Assignments

1. Is there any evidence that the narrator exaggerates in the story? Give a reason for your answer.
2. Explain the phrase 'pull a fast one'.
3. What is the narrator's view of himself?
4. What are your feelings towards the narrator? Refer to this part of the story to support your points.
5. What do you expect will happen to the narrator by the end of the story?
6. What evidence is there that 'there was something strange about the ice-cream'?
7. What kind of a person is Mr. Peppi?
8. What evidence is there that the narrator is a bully?
9. Why did the narrator break into the ice-cream van?
10. What do you understand by the phrase 'smart alec'?
11. Explain what happens in the final paragraph.

Spectrum 2

**Word power!**

Find the words in the story which have similar meanings to each of the words and phrases below. The number in brackets after each one indicates the number of letters in the answer. The words appear in the story in the same order as the meanings given below.

CLUES
1. excellent (8)
2. acted dishonestly (7)
3. made up his mind (7)
4. taste (7)
5. line of people (5)
6. unusual (7)
7. went quietly (5)
8. pleasant to the taste (9)
9. occurred (8)
10. error (7)

## PERSONAL WRITING

### ASSIGNMENT

We can see from this story that the author and the narrator are not the same. We are told about the events of this story by one of the people in it – a twelve year-old boy whose name is never revealed. We call him the narrator. The author, on the other hand, is the person who made up the story.

Retell the story with (a) Mr. Peppi or (b) Snozzle as the narrator.

### REMEMBER
Always use the capital form when using the word 'I'.

## Points to Note — POINT OF VIEW

There are two main points of view — the **first person** point of view and the **omniscient** point of view. It is easy to identify the first person point of view. The word 'I' is continually used — I remember the first time I met . . . I was scared . . . etc. The omniscient point of view uses **He, She, They**.

Stories narrated (told) from the first person point of view allow the readers, to feel very **close** to the events of the story. **Someone who was there** is telling us what happened. This enables us to feel the fears and hopes of the narrator, who is usually a central character.

The author can have the narrator say and do things which may not meet our approval. We must judge the character of the narrator and assess how reliable he or she is. This requires us to ask what attitude the writer wants us to take towards the narrator: approval? disapproval? pity?

# THE HAUNTING
## Mary Fitzgerald

I had a choice. I could either face Fennessy and McNiff. Or I could face the Vampire. I decided to take my chances with the Vampire.

It had all started with a school raffle to raise funds for something or other. There was a prize of ten pounds for the person who sold the most tickets in each year. I won the prize in the Second Years. During morning break, Fennessy and McNiff came over to me, smiling like reptiles.

"See you after school, Billy," said Fennessy. "We'll be home along with you just in case someone tries to nick your prize. We'll protect you."

"Yeah, we'll protect you," said McNiff. McNiff always repeats what Fennessy says.

My heart sank. I didn't need the kind of protecting that Fennessy and McNiff were offering. To look at them, they wouldn't strike you as protective, caring types. Fennessy, with his Doc Martens and shaved head, looked like a relative of Desperate Dan. McNiff had a thin snakelike body — with a face to match. His nickname was 'McSniff' but nobody called it to his face.

The pair had first got into the protection business in sixth class in primary school. Their method was simple – mainly due to the fact that they were both bigger than anyone else in the class. McNiff came along and asked you for a loan of twenty pence. If you didn't give it to him, Fennessy came along and bullied you. These were the pair who wanted to protect me and my ten pounds!

That's why I nipped out of school quickly that day and headed towards home on a different route. As I hurried along Ballindoon Road I was sure I had given them the slip. Then, as I passed by Ballindoon House, I spotted them in the distance. They were on bikes.

Ballindoon House is an old derelict house. It's said to be haunted by a vampire. All the kids in our neighbourhood called him 'The Vampire' and none of them ever wandered near the house. Still, when you get to my age you don't take talk of ghosts and vampires too seriously. There are worse horrors such as Fennessy and McNiff.

And they were the reason why I darted through the broken fence and into the garden of Ballindoon House. The garden was full of broken glass, tin cans and old prams, partly hidden by a jungle of tall weeds. The walls of the house were covered in ivy and the dark empty windows looked gloomy.

I heard the loud voices of Fennessy and McNiff on the other side of the fence.

"Where can he be?"

"He must be around here. I'm certain I saw him."

"Maybe he's hiding in there in the haunted house . . . "

I wasted no more time and scarpered into the house through a door in the basement.

When I was inside I wasn't exactly scared, even though I didn't feel like laughing. It was pretty weird. The windows were boarded over and it was very dark. Most of the floorboards were rotten and it was a tricky job to avoid falling down one of the many holes. There was a smell like old cupboards, and a creaking noise that might have been caused by me treading on the broken boards – or by rats; a nasty thought when you hadn't got anything to throw at them. After a while the voices of Fennessy and McNiff faded away.

I should have gone straight back to the safety of the outside world, but I was feeling pleased with the old house for helping me to escape from Fennessy and McNiff and I suddenly realised that I had never really explored it thoroughly. So, treading carefully, I made my way out of the basement and up the rickety stairs to the ground floor. I found myself in a big squarish hall but I couldn't make out many details because very little light came through the boarded-up windows. From the hall a door led into what was, I supposed, the front room. I pushed it open and went in. The door swung to behind me, closing with a little bang. The room was empty except for some rubbish in one corner, great pieces of wallpaper hanging from the walls and a huge fireplace which looked as though it might fall down at any moment.

Then, for no reason that I could think of, I went all hot and cold. My throat tightened and my heart started to pump away like mad. There's nothing to be afraid of, I told myself, hoping that I was telling myself the truth and, just to prove it, I began to whistle. The next moment I would have been out of that room like a scalded cat if the floor had been safe, for my whistling was interrupted by a voice. "Hush, boy," it said, "I can't abide that tiresome noise."

It wasn't an angry or threatening voice, but my hair was suddenly standing on end, and I must have looked pretty scared with my mouth open and my eyes popping out.

"There's no need to be frightened, child," the voice went on.

Child! I may be only fourteen – nearly – but I'm tall for my age, and "child" made me feel as though I were back in a sailor suit. "I'm *not* frightened," I lied, and my voice sounded like a transistor radio when the battery is running out. "I just didn't see you, that's all." I turned round and still didn't see anyone, and a cold shiver attacked me from head to toe.

"No," said the voice, almost in my ear, "not many people do – but here I am."

I tried to say "Where?" but it was not easy to talk with my teeth chattering. In any case, there wasn't any need. She was there, right in front of me – a little old woman not much taller than me, wearing a dark dress down to her ankles. There was just enough light for me to see her wispy white hair and pale wrinkled face, and I stopped trembling because it was a *kind* face, though anxious. I didn't know what to say next, but she kept the conversation going.

"I am so pleased that you have come," she said, just as if she had been expecting me. "It is not often I can get through and when I do manage it, there is never anyone here."

"Get through where?" I asked, thinking that she meant on the telephone.

"Oh, just through – but never mind that. You wouldn't understand, child."

Here we go again, I thought. "I'm *not* a child," I retorted, and then it was her turn to get flustered.

"Of course you're not – you're a big boy, I can see that now. So big and clever that I know you will do something for me."

"I will if I can," I said, "but who are you and what are you doing here?"

"My name is Mrs. Carroll," she said after a pause, "and this is my house."

"But surely you don't live here," I said, in a matter-of-fact voice.

She hesitated. "For many years I—"

## The Haunting

she began, then changed the subject. "If you are going to help me, you must do so at once – there is no time to lose."

"What is it?" I asked quickly, because it had just occurred to me that if this *was* her house she might think of asking me what I was doing there.

"I want you to take something to the authorities for me – the gardaí, the parish priest, the doctor – it does not matter which – so that Seán may be helped before it is too late."

"OK," I said, then, in case she didn't like slang, I added, "Very well. What do you want me to take?"

"My jewels, boy! They said that Seán had stolen them after he had frightened me to death, but he did no such thing! They also accused him of manslaughter, but fortunately he was acquitted."

I gave a little laugh just to show that I had a sense of humour and knew that she couldn't have been manslaughtered when she was standing there before my eyes. *She* didn't laugh, though, so I changed mine into a cough.

"Seán would never steal my jewels," the old lady went on sternly, "and they could find no proof that he had. But the stigma of thief was on him, and within a short time he went out of his mind."

"You mean he went mad and was innocent all the time?" I asked, trying to sort out all this rigmarole in my mind.

"Exactly. For a long time I have tried to prove his innocence but nobody has stayed here long enough to give me the help that you have kindly offered."

I puffed out my chest, feeling pretty smug. Then I had a worrying thought. "But why haven't you gone to the gardaí, Mrs. Carroll?"

"I cannot go beyond these four walls," she said abruptly. I waited to hear why, but she didn't seem inclined to tell me. "Come, boy, I will show you where the

jewels are hidden, then you can take the information to whomever you choose."

She made for the door with a sort of skater's glide. I started to follow her, and then suddenly my whole world turned upside down. The door was closed – and she had passed right through it!

I'm not clear about the next few minutes. I know my head was spinning like a roulette wheel, and my heart was trying to force its way through my throat. I must have tugged the door open and stumbled down the stairs into the basement and then out into the garden. In the open air my legs gave way and I collapsed into a clump of rose-bay willow herb in a dead faint.

I don't know how long I lay there and when I came to I wasn't clear about what had happened, but felt very frightened. I staggered through the gate, still groggy, and straight into the arms of Mr. McMahon, who lives next door but one to me in the flats.

"Steady on, Billy," he said "What's the matter with you? You're white as a sheet

– have you seen a ghost or something?"

Then it all came back to me. "Yes, I have," I blurted out and promptly fainted again, almost pulling Mr. McMahon to the ground with me.

The next thing I remember was my mum coming into the bedroom with a bowl of soup. "You did give us a fright, love," she said as she plumped the pillow for me to sit up. "Drink this and you'll soon feel better."

I insisted that there was nothing wrong with me, but *she* insisted that I had caught a chill through some complaint she always called "outgrowing your strength". Mind you, the best way to pacify a worried mother is not to say, as I did, "I haven't got a chill – I've seen a ghost." All that did was to send her rushing downstairs for Dad. I tried to tell them everything, but it was no use. "Take it easy, son, you'll feel better in the morning," was Dad's reaction, and they went away, shaking their heads and clucking about sending for a doctor.

I had two big worries myself. The first was why I had been stupid enough to be frightened of little Mrs. Carroll, ghost or no ghost, when it was obvious that she wouldn't have hurt a fly. The other was how to tell the gardaí about the jewels if I didn't know where they were. I called myself all sorts of names for getting panicky at the wrong moment. After all, why *should* ghosts open doors if they don't need to? Then there was poor old Seán. How could I help him – whoever he was – without more information? And Mrs. Carroll had said it was urgent . . . I spent the next half-hour making plans.

In the morning I hurried down to breakfast and flashed my biggest smile at Mum and Dad. I didn't give them a chance to tut-tut about my so-called chill. I left them in no doubt that I was fit enough to run the 1,500 metres before eating a single cornflake. What convinced them that I was brimming over with good health was my offer to dry up before going to school. What's more, I did it! After I had put the last plate away I called good-bye to Mum and set off for school – or, to be more accurate, for the derelict house.

I felt more than a bit silly stumbling about the old house calling "Mrs. Carroll – where are you?" But she must have decided that I was no use to her after all, for she didn't appear. I went to the back of the house and had a look round to see if I could locate any possible hiding-places for the jewels, but I might have saved my time. The rooms were in almost total darkness and there could have been a score of places. Reluctantly I decided I had better go to school.

The day was an awful drag, but I got through it somehow. After school I went back to the house. Still no sign of Mrs. Carroll. So I went to the police station.

The gardaí were all right but they treated the whole thing as a joke and told me to lay off cheese last thing at night and to remember that they were busy men. They also suggested that it would be better if I kept away from empty houses unless I wanted to get into trouble.

The parish priest was more understanding and listened patiently without making any jokes. He said something about exercising the ghost, but I told him that Mrs. Carroll was pretty old and didn't need much exercise. Then he explained that he'd said 'exorcising', and that it was a kind of religious way of getting rid of ghosts. Anyway, we had a look at the parish registers for many years back and there wasn't a single Carroll mentioned. That could mean, the priest said, that she had probably been a Methodist or something. So I said good-bye to him and thank you, and went home none the wiser.

After tea I went to the library, and there I found somebody with some sense. It was Mr. Collins, the Librarian, and if I'd been the Lord Mayor himself I couldn't have been better treated. I asked him how I could find out about a Mrs. Carroll of Ballindoon House, and he went to work just as if a starting-gun had gone off in his ear. In a couple of minutes he produced the electoral registers of people entitled to vote going back for years and years and left me to plough through them while he went off to attend to other people, though whenever he had a spare moment he would come back and give me a hand.

I began to get a bit fed-up after a time. It was a dreary job, not made any better by having to keep dead quiet because of all the people sitting around with their heads buried in books. It was rather like trying to do your homework in church.

Then suddenly the silence was broken by a loud, high-pitched cry, and everybody looked up and frowned and Mr. Collins went as red as a tomato. It was he who had made the noise, you see. He coughed, straightened his tie, and whispered hoarsely, "Diligence rewarded at last, old son."

He pointed to a list of names on the sheet he was holding. There were dozens of names and numbers on it, but one of them almost jumped off the page and hit me. "Carroll, Elizabeth".

"You see!" I said. "There *was* a Mrs. Carroll! But what does this mean?"

"It means," said Mr. Collins, "that your Mrs. Carroll was living at Ballindoon House in 1935, but not —" He looked up another list and went on, "Not in 1936."

"So she must have died in 1935," I said, catching on quickly, "or early in 1936."

"Or else she moved out of the district."

"No, she didn't move. I – I know that." Mr. Collins didn't ask me why I was so sure, thank goodness, because I didn't feel like telling him the story in whispers. "Is there any way of finding out whether she did die about this time?" I asked.

"Wait here," Mr. Collins said, as though I'd got up to go, and hurried away himself. In a couple of minutes he had returned with two enormous bound books which he put on the table in front of me. "Copies of the local paper for 1935 and 1936," he murmured. "I should try the later one if I were you." Then he dashed away to answer the telephone.

I didn't much like the idea of going through all those newspapers. It would take hours and the library was due to close in forty-five minutes. But I opened the 1936 volume at random, somewhere near the beginning. Looking back, what happened seemed too good to be true and a bit mad, but at the time it didn't surprise me very much. I believe now that Mrs. Carroll was helping me, because the very first item I saw was a headline: "Adopted son cleared of manslaughter charge." It was followed by: "Seán Carroll, adopted son of Mrs. Elizabeth Carroll, a widow, of Ballindoon House, was acquitted yesterday . . ."

But there's no need to give you the rest of it. To cut a long story short, this is what had happened. Mrs. Carroll had lived alone in the house, apart from a woman who came in daily to do the cleaning. Seán, whom she and her husband had adopted when he was a baby, worked in an office at Castletown and didn't live at home. He gambled a lot and had got into debt. He daren't ask Mrs. Carroll for money because she was opposed to gambling in any shape or form and wouldn't even buy raffle tickets for charity, and he had planned to sneak into the house when she was asleep and steal some of her jewellery. He actually broke into the house to make it look like an ordinary burglary, but Mrs. Carroll heard a noise and waited for the intruder with a poker. According to Seán, when she saw who the 'burglar' was she must have had a heart attack, for she fell and hit her head on the marble fireplace. He panicked, left her lying there and ran out of the house – straight into the arms of a passing garda. The doctor who was called confirmed that Mrs. Carroll had had a heart attack. There was no proof that Seán had actually stolen anything, so he got off, and that was about all.

I thanked Mr. Collins and went home, trying to find the answers to all sorts of questions. Why had the house been empty all these years? If Seán had inherited it, why hadn't he sold it? Why hadn't he found the jewels afterwards if his story at the trial had been true? Had he really gone mad, as Mrs. Carroll had said? Was he alive or dead? If alive, he must be about sixty-six or -seven now. Most important of all, where was he now?

It was hard work trying to be my usual cheerful self when I got home, but I had to try, otherwise it would have meant soup in bed again. Fortunately, Mum and Dad didn't suspect a thing.

I had been in bed about a couple of hours, tossing and turning all over the place, and at last faced up to the fact that I wasn't going to get to sleep. I knew that I had to go to the old house, and the sooner the better. She might be there, or if not, I might find a clue to some of the problems that were worrying me.

I slipped out of bed and dressed by the light of the moon. It must have been nearly midnight when I crept past my parents' room, tip-toed downstairs and let myself out of the front door. When I reached the old house and slipped through into the garden I felt a sudden stab of fear and wished like anything that

I hadn't come. The front of the house looked like a hideous face, the two upper windows its sightless eyes, and the wooden slats of the lower ones were like mis-shapen teeth in a grinning mouth. I think I would have slunk away if there had not been a scuttering sound behind me. I ran for the basement door before I realised that it was only a cat, probably more scared of me than I was of it.

I took a deep breath and went in. I wondered what would happen if I disturbed a sleeping tramp, or fell and broke an ankle and had to spend the night with the mice and rats . . . Then I remembered how Mrs. Carroll had trusted me – how she had been sure that I would help her – and some of my courage came back. She would see that I didn't come to any harm – so I went straight to the front room. There was no tramp there – that was one problem out of the way.

"Mrs. Carroll," I called softly, "are you here?" The only answer was my own voice bouncing back from the dead wood. I called again and again, but nothing happened. Then I said, "I want to help Seán. I've found out what happened in 1936, but I don't know where he is. Won't you help me, Mrs. Carroll?"

I was just about to give up and go when there was something that I can't describe – a change in the feel of the room. It was as though a breeze had blown through it very lightly without there having been an actual breeze. At the same time my scalp began to prickle. Then I heard a voice. It was very faint and seemed to be struggling against something. "I can't come through," it said.

"Where are you?" I turned round and round, hoping to see the old lady.

"It's no use," the voice said, even more faintly.

I spoke loudly, as you do when you're trying to attract the attention of someone who is walking away. "Where is Seán?"

From Mrs. Carroll came two words. They sounded like "Say day", but they were so muffled that I wasn't sure whether I had heard them properly.

"Please say that again," I said, but this time there was no reply. For a minute or two I waited, straining my ears into the silence, but something told me that it was useless and there was nothing to do but give up and go home.

"Say day, Say day," I kept on saying to myself on the way back, and I must have gone to sleep with the words on my lips.

The next night I went to the library again. I thought Mr. Collins would groan when he saw me but in fact he greeted me like his prodigal son. "Ah," he said, then gave his little cough. "I'm glad you've come. I've found out something about your Mrs. Carroll. There was a piece in another issue of the local paper about her will. She left everything – house and contents, and her jewels – to her adopted son. It seems, though, that after the trial Seán Carroll had a breakdown and never actually lived in the house."

"I wondered about that," I said, trying to make my voice sound as grown-up as possible. "I suppose it didn't say in the paper where he did go?"

"As a matter of fact, it did. He went to Saint David's."

You've read about people hitting the roof – I didn't exactly do that but it was a near thing. "Say day!" I shouted. "Say day – that's it – that's what she was trying to say!"

About a hundred and twenty people said "Shush!" and Mr. Collins grabbed me and propelled me into the passage outside. "My dear boy," he said, breathing hard, "you must *never* do that again."

"I'm sorry," I said, and I was, because I wouldn't have done anything to annoy Mr. Collins after what he had done for us – Mrs. Carroll and me, that is. "But what is this Saint David's?"

"It's a hospital for the – er – mentally sick. I fear that if Seán Carroll went there, he must have been very ill."

"Would they let me see him?" I asked.

"I couldn't say – it would depend on how ill he is. Are you a relative?"

"No, it's just that I've promised his mother that I would try to help him."

"His mother – you mean Mrs. Carroll?"

"That's right," I answered, lost in thought.

"But – but she died in 1936 . . ."

"That's right," I said again, smiled, thanked him, and hurried off, just in case he decided that I was due for a spell in Saint David's.

I had enough information now to convince anyone that my story was worth looking into. But somehow I knew that no one would listen. Mum and Dad would put everything down to growing pains, the police would be too busy catching present-day criminals to bother about clearing someone wrongly accused over thirty years ago. If I went to the hospital they'd be sure to turn me away. I thought I would try the parish priest again . . .

He was just as friendly as he had been before. He gave me a cup of tea and a biscuit and I told him every single thing that had happened. "All I want to know," I said, "is whether there is a Seán Carroll at Saint David's, and I've come to you because a priest can usually get in anywhere."

"I'm flattered," he said, smiling. Then he began to puff at a foul old pipe. "As it happens, I do go to Saint David's occasionally, to visit one of my parishioners. I think I am well enough known there to be able to find out what you want to know. Wait here while I telephone."

When he returned he said very thoughtfully, "It is quite extraordinary."

"Do you mean he *is* there?" I asked, jumping to my feet.

"*Was* there, Billy. I'm afraid that Seán Carroll died about half past twelve this morning."

I don't care who knows this but I sat down again and burst into tears. Who was I crying for? I don't know – perhaps it was for myself because the whole story had suddenly collapsed about my ears; or for Mrs. Carroll who would never get her wish for Seán to be cleared; or for Seán who had never known how she felt about him. Later on I realised why Mrs. Carroll's voice had faded away. It must have been about half past twelve when I had said, "Where is Seán?" — and at that moment she had met him again after more than thirty years.

And that was the end of the story as I wrote it a year ago. I put it away, and the details had begun to grow a bit dim in my mind, though I never forgot I had seen the old lady's ghost. Then, a few days ago, a long stretch of Ballindoon was knocked down to make way for new houses, and Ballindoon House was one of the first houses to go. For the first time since 1936 it hit the headlines again. "Workman finds treasure in derelict house," the local paper said.

I don't know what happened to the treasure and, since Seán is dead, I don't care. I daren't think what might have happened if Mrs. Carroll had been able to show me where it was hidden, but I'm pretty sure that no one would have believed that I'd been guided by a ghost.

*Mary Fitzgerald (Adapted)*

# The Haunting

## Questions & Assignments

1. Explain clearly the events that forced Billy to hide in Ballindoon House.
2. (a) What does Mrs. Carroll tell Billy about Seán?
   (b) What does she want Billy to do?
3. (a) What hints are there in the story that Mrs. Carroll is a ghost?
   (b) At what point in the story is it clear that she is a ghost?
4. Write, in dialogue form, the conversation that took place between Billy and the gardaí at the garda station.
5. (a) Describe how Billy set about the task of finding Seán.
   (b) At what point, in his search, was he particularly lucky?
6. (a) In most ghost stories, ghosts return for one of the following reasons: to seek revenge; to warn of danger; to right some wrong. Identify the reason why the ghost of Mrs. Carroll returned.
   (b) Was she successful in her efforts? Explain your answer.
7. Suggest an alternative ending to the story.
8. Explain why you did *or* did not enjoy reading *The Haunting*.

## Word Power!

Find the words in the story which have similar meanings to each of the words and phrases below. The number in brackets after each one indicates the number of letters in the answer. The words appear in the story in the same order as the meanings given below.

### CLUES

1. cold-blooded creature (7)
2. a plan of a journey (5)
3. in bad repair; abandoned (8)
4. walking (8)
5. room below ground level (8)
6. lined (from old age) (8)
7. shaking with fear (9)
8. a brief stop in conversation (5)
9. people in charge (11)
10. walked in an unsteady manner (8)
11. fell down (9)
12. needing immediate attention (6)
13. went quickly to be on time (7)
14. books with lists of names (9)
15. dull (6)
16. very big (8)
17. moved quickly (6)
18. received (property) in a will (9)
19. luckily (11)
20. skin covering top of skull (5)

## Points to Note — CHARACTERS

When we talk about people in stories we refer to them as **characters.** When we read a story we get to know the characters in it. Getting to know characters in stories is like getting to know people in real life.

- We get to know characters by noting what the author or narrator tells us about them, i.e. their appearance, occupation and background.
- We get to know characters by noting what they say about themselves and others. Of course in stories — just as in life — people do not always mean what they say. Therefore when characters talk about themselves and others we have to think carefully about whether they really mean what they actually say.
- We get to know characters by noting what kind of things they do — especially when they are under pressure.
- We get to know characters by noting what their attitudes and opinions are on different matters.

Characters often change over the course of the story. For example, a character may change from being a greedy person to a generous person as a result of an event in the story.

### Writing about Characters

When you are required to write about a character in a story or play, you should bear in mind all the points above. Here are some words that will be useful when writing about characters in stories, plays and films.

| kind | lazy | foolish | poor | bad-tempered | spiteful |
|---|---|---|---|---|---|
| generous | cunning | impatient | daring | confident | cautious |
| brave | loyal | friendly | reliable | eccentric | fussy |
| nervous | dishonest | modest | rude | bitter | sarcastic |
| sly | insincere | boastful | scornful | timid | polite |
| caring | arrogant | | | | |

When using these types of words to describe people, be sure to refer to a particular part of the story or play to back up your view.

**Example**

> 'Andrew was a brave man. This can be seen from the way he refused to . . .'
> 'Jane's kindness is shown when she . . .'

Remember that people can have a number of qualities or characteristics. A person can be both brave and cunning; lazy and generous; confident and rude etc.

## Points to Note — POINT OF VIEW

What have the two stories *The Haunting* and *Spoil the Child* in common? Both are told from a similar point of view. In both cases, they were told by a character in the story, i.e. the author decides to 'be' the character telling the story.

When an author decides to tell a story from the point of view of the character in the story, there can only be a certain amount that we can be told – what that character experiences, sees and thinks. Everything we learn comes from the character who is 'narrating' (telling) the story. Stories of this kind are called the **first-person** narrative. The vast majority of stories that are written, are told either from the **omniscient** point of view or else the point of view of a character in the story. Both techniques have advantages and drawbacks.

## ASSIGNMENT

**Personal Writing**

### Apostrophe

Rewrite each of the following sentences correctly by inserting apostrophes where necessary.

1. She said shell come to Kerry with us if its not raining.
2. Dads going to be mad when he finds out were going to visit Mums Aunt Jill tomorrow.
3. Shes got Peters coat and hes left with Joans.
4. If theyre winning shell be very happy.
5. Ive got to go because its time for Marys piano lesson.
6. Well never win – theyre too good.
7. I cant go to Brians party because Im going on holidays on the same day.
8. It isnt a good film. Ive seen it and theres no action.
9. Thats where were going to stay – in Freds house.
10. Its too late. Theres no turning back now.

The following **Spot the Errors** exercise is aimed at sharpening your basic writing skills. Spot the 20 errors in the Passage below and rewrite the passage correctly. (Note: Refer to the Guidelines on pages 1—15.)

## 5   A bad year for tourism

Its proving to be a gloomy year for tourism. Such was the gloom brought on by the wet and overcast whether one evening last week that Michael cahill, who runs a pub, restaurant and guesthouse in rossbeigh, in Kerry, though it could have been the middle of winter.

He blames the rain for the dramatic slump in tourism numbers in the Ring of Kerry and throughout the rest of the Country.

"On a sunny Sunday last may, their were about five thousand people on the beech here. Now on any Sunday there wood be about fifty, he says. "The bad weather is putting people off."

He contrasts the slump with last summer, when his pub and restaurant where doing good buisness and his guesthouse was busy with holidaymakers and day-trippers.

The story is the same all over Ireland some of the large hotels are doing well because of the pre-booked foreign visitors, but the numbers of Irish holidaying at home has fallen sharply.

Small hotels guesthouses, pubs and restaurants are suffering most, mainly in scenic rural areas and in resorts which usually attract visitors in large numbers.

A spokeswoman for Dublin Tourism said that while the number of forieng tourists visiting it's offices was marginally up on last year, their was a definite decrease in dubliners booking holidays in Ireland.

She said that visitor attractions outside the city area were experiencing a drop in numbers because the bad weather was discouraging visitors from making day-trips.

# A Break for 3G
*Shane Lee*

## PART 1

Charlie Murray was a teacher at Kilmoone Community School. He would have been the first to admit that he was not a good teacher.

Charlie wanted to be a good teacher. He tried very hard to be a good teacher. He tried to do the things that he had been told to do when he was training to be a teacher. He corrected homework very carefully. He spent many hours preparing classes in order to make them interesting for the students. He gave book tokens as prizes for the best essay. He treated his students with respect and was never sarcastic towards them. He wanted to bring them for educational trips but the principal, Mr. Bacon, would not let him.

He only shouted at the students when they made so much noise that he had to shout at them to make himself heard. Charlie, therefore, spent a good deal of time shouting.

"Please be quiet and listen!"

"Get out your books!"

"Stop banging the desks off the floor!"

"Stop kicking the waste-paper bin around the room!"

"WILL YOU ALL SHUT UP!!!"

On his first day in school Charlie had met the principal, Mr. Bacon. Mr. Bacon was a short but very stout man. He had a pink face, pudgy lips and very, very small eyes.

"Do you enjoy a challenge Charlie?" asked Mr. Bacon.

"Eh . . . yes," said Charlie, who was eager to impress his new boss.

"Good!" exclaimed Mr. Bacon. "You'll be taking Class 3G for English, Religion and Irish. That certainly will be a big challenge. Good day Charlie and best of luck."

"But . . . I didn't train as an Irish teacher . . . nor a Religion teacher . . . nor as an English teacher. My subjects are Maths and Computers. I'm particularly interested in teaching computers . . ."

"Like I said Charlie, it will be a big challenge . . . and I wouldn't worry about Irish, English or Religion. You won't need to know much Irish or English to teach that shower . . . er . . . I mean that class."

Mr. Bacon nodded and smiled. Charlie noticed that the smile never reached his eyes.

On the first day Charlie went in to 3G and said "Good morning boys and girls. My name is Mr. Murray and I'm your new English and Religion and . . . eh . . . Irish teacher. We'll start by finding out who is who."

He nodded at a boy in the back row. "What's your name?"

"Are you a bog man?" came the reply.

"I . . . I beg your pardon," stammered Charlie, unprepared for this.

"He means are you a culchie, you know, a muck savage, a munchie, a redneck," said a girl in the front row.

"That's none of your business and your manners need . . ."

"We won't tell you our names unless you tell us where you're from. That's only fair!"

"Well . . . er . . . OK. I'm from Borrisokane in County Tipperary. Now answer your names when I ask . . . "

"Borrisokane!" said a boy in the front row with stud in his nose. "I don't believe it. You're making it up. Borrisokane. Never heard of it. What a weird name for a place."

"I know a fella called Peter O'Kane," said a girl in the back row.

"Is he any relation?" shouted someone else.

"Boris. Is he Russian? Sounds like a Russian name," another voice chimed in.

"Are you from Russia?" the boy with the nose stud asked.

"He's not. He's a bogman from Borris . . . what is it?"

Charlie sighed. "I'll say it again. I'm from Borrisokane in County Tipperary."

They could not believe it.

"Borrisokane."

"Borrisokane."

"Borrisokane."

The name of Charlie's hometown echoed around the room.

They shouted it again and again, as if it was the best joke they had ever heard. Their laughter became uncontrollable. They clutched their sides. They rocked in their desks. Some fell on the floor with mirth. They giggled and chuckled over and over again. They slapped each other on the backs. They waved their hands in the air.

"Borrisokane!" they echoed, again and again.

"SHUT UP!" roared Charlie and a brief lull followed. "Settle down all of you! Be quiet and answer your names!"

"Hiya Boris!"

"Yahoo Boris!"

"Yo Boris!"

"How's she cutting, Boris?"

"It's so lonely round the fields of Borrisokane," they sang to the tune of *The Fields of Athenry*.

That was the first day. After that things began to go downhill.

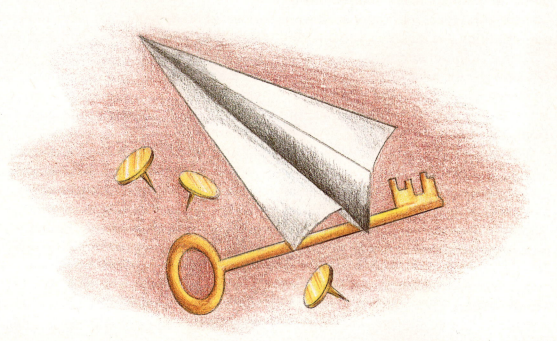

Next morning they locked him out of the classroom. They were inside, making faces and waving out at him through the glass panel in the door. Charlie had to get the vice-principal, Mrs. Bacon, to open the door. She looked very annoyed. The class explained politely to her that the lock had jammed and that they had tried to open it but they couldn't.

Then in the afternoon, just before they went home, they locked him in the storeroom, when he was putting away the exercise books.

"Open the door someone. I'm locked in," Charlie shouted over and over.

After a half an hour Mr. Bacon came along. He looked very annoyed as he let Charlie out.

The next morning Mr. Bacon came back to visit 3G. He wanted to know who was responsible for locking Mr. Murray in the storeroom. The pupils explained that they had no idea he was locked in the storeroom. They said that they were so busy working at their Irish that they didn't even notice that he had gone in to the storeroom.

"He probably leaned against the door by mistake and it locked," one girl said in a helpful voice.

After break Charlie came back into the classroom and noticed a strange warbling sound coming from his briefcase. When he opened it a pigeon flew out and circled around room, high above the heads of the pupils. Uproar followed. Then Mr. Bacon arrived. He looked extremely angry. He wanted the person who brought in the pigeon to own up. They explained that they were so busy studying their Religion that they didn't notice anything.

"He probably came in the window by mistake, Sir," one boy said.

"Indeed!" snapped Mr. Bacon.

The next day a bag of crisps hit Charlie on the back of the head as he was writing on the blackboard. When he turned round the pupils were all writing in their copies, their heads down. During the remainder of the week they made very rude noises, put thumbtacks on his chair, slipped chewing gum into his jacket pocket and hid his briefcase behind the press.

During some classes they chatted among themselves and ignored any request he made. They occasionally amused themselves by throwing paper aeroplanes, making noises and calling him names like 'mucksavage', 'redneck' and, of course, 'Boris'.

He gave them poems to copy out as punishment, but they didn't do them. He gave them detentions, but they didn't turn up.

Charlie continued to try and interest them. When they refused to do any work he warned that he would send them to the principal.

They laughed. "Mr. Piggy. All he will do is have a friendly chat with us and tell us to have a bit of pride in ourselves".

" . . . and ask us if we think that you're a good teacher," added a boy in the back row.

"What did you call him?" asked Charlie.

"Mr. Piggy. You know, like Miss Piggy on *The Muppets*. He kind of looks like her brother. Don't you think so, Boris?"

Though he didn't say so, Charlie had to agree that there was a certain resemblance.

Sometimes, when things got completely out of hand, Charlie sent for the principal, who would come and have a friendly chat with them and tell them to take pride in their work and their school.

Charlie tried writing to some of their parents. He got back one letter. It said that he could hit Darren a clatter any time that he got cheeky. "A good clatter is the only language that he understands," the letter-writer said.

The other classes that Charlie taught were not so bad. They had their good days and their bad days and he felt that the pupils were beginning to trust and respect him. But 3G had him beaten. They treated him with contempt, they mocked him and made him look like a fool.

At night Charlie sat in his flat, feeling miserable. He remembered his days in college and how he wanted to be a teacher. He wanted to make school interesting and enjoyable for his students. He wanted them to be happy and to do well in their exams and go out into the world and get good jobs. He felt miserable. He felt a failure.

One morning, as Charlie sat in the staffroom correcting copies, Mr. Bacon came in.

"Ah Charlie, the very man! I wonder could you step into my office for a moment. I'd like a word with you."

Charlie's heart sank, but Mr. Bacon was very friendly. Too friendly.

"Come in Charlie. Have a seat. Relax." Mr. Bacon smiled.

Charlie felt uneasy.

"Charlie, I won't beat around the bush. I know that things have not been going very well for you, particularly with class 3G."

Charlie nodded sadly.

"They're a challenging class to teach. A lively bunch of kids. They enjoy a bit of crack a lot better than the ol' books. Ha-ha. Ho-ho." Mr. Bacon laughed at his little joke.

Charlie smiled weakly.

"Charlie, I want to help you. I care. Kilmoone Community School is a caring school. As principal I care about the pupils — all the pupils, even those in 3G, ha-ha. As principal I also care about myself . . . er . . . I mean my staff — all my staff, including you Charlie."

"That's very kind of you, Mr. Bacon," murmured Charlie.

"That's why I want to help you. We are a caring school, Charlie. A school that cares."

"Of course," said Charlie politely, although he felt that Mr. Bacon was being less than sincere. Charlie was beginning to dislike Mr. Bacon.

"Charlie, you need a break from here."

Charlie looked shocked. Was he going to be sacked he wondered.

"No need to look so shocked," said the principal. "I'm not going to sack you. I just want you to take a break. The school has the use of a hostel down in Wicklow near Glencree. Take a day or two down there. How about heading off on Wednesday next and coming back on Thursday?"

The idea appealed to Charlie. Anything for a bit of peace and quiet. A chance to go for a few walks, read a book, relax. It would be nice to get away from the city, away from Kilmoone Community School and 3G — especially 3G!

"Fine," said Charlie, "That's very kind of you, Mr. Bacon."

"Not at all, Charlie," smiled Mr. Bacon. "I believe that once you leave the school behind, you and your class can build up a new friendship. A fresh start so to speak. New feelings of trust and

# A Break for 3G

respect for each other . . . "

An alarm bell was beginning to ring in Charlie's mind. He felt the blood drain from his face. Had he heard right? What did Bacon mean about him *and his class* building up a new relationship. Surely Mr. Bacon wasn't suggesting that 3G were also going to Wicklow with him?

"What do you mean — me and my class . . . ?" gasped Charlie.

"Why, you and class 3G of course," smiled Mr. Bacon.

"3G?"

"Yes, 3G. You didn't think you could have two days off on your own, did you, Charlie? No, you'll have to take some students with you, and this will be a fine chance for you and your class to get to know one another outside of the classroom."

"But I don't want to get to know them outside the classroom. It's bad enough knowing them inside the classroom . . . "

"Rubbish! You'll have a grand time, Charlie — hill-walking, fishing, sing-songs and ghost-stories at night. A grand time! Now Charlie, if you'll excuse me but I have an appointment with the treasurer of the Parents' Committee. Pull the door after you."

Mr. Bacon then waved impatiently, dismissing Charlie from his office and from his mind.

In the staffroom that afternoon, Miss Donovan, the Home Economics teacher, leaned over and said to Charlie.

"Isn't it ever so exciting, Charlie?"

"What is so exciting?"

"The Minister for Education, Mrs. Chawke, is coming here to this school."

"When? Nobody told me about it."

"Mr. Bacon told me this morning. The Minister for Education is visiting this school next Thursday. She will be coming by helicopter. Isn't it so exciting! I'm just dying to meet the Minister. If she is impressed by the school we will be getting a roomful of new computers. And Mr. Bacon is arranging that some pupils from class 3A paint a message of welcome on the roof of the school. The Minister will see it from her helicopter. Isn't it just so exciting!"

So that was his trick! Charlie's jaw dropped open. He understood the whole thing now! He was going to be in the wilds of Wicklow with the worst class in the school, stuck in a cold hostel, eating crisps and burnt fish fingers in order that class 3G would not get within forty miles of the visiting Minister for Education.

Charlie returned to the principal's office to try and get him to change his mind.

"What about the parents? You'll need to let them know."

"I have already phoned them. Without exception they are delighted. They're looking forward to a few days peace and quiet with their little darlings out of the way."

"But what about me? I can't go through with it. They'll be impossible to manage in the open countryside. They'll cause a forest fire, a flood or an earthquake or some other major disaster. I know it!"

"Now, Charlie, be sensible. Out there in the wilds of Wicklow they can't do much. And remember they're city kids. They're not used to the countryside, while you are. You grew up in the country. They will be on your territory so to speak!"

Charlie tried to sound firm. "No, Mr. Bacon. I definitely can't do it and that's final."

Mr. Bacon stared coldly at Charlie. He no longer smiled.

"Now listen, Charlie. It's time for a bit of straight talking. As a teacher, you have not been very successful here. In fact you have been very unsuccessful. And you are still on probation. You're still on trial. Your job here next year depends on my recommendation. Now this visit by the Minister for Education is very important to this school. Extremely important to the staff. Very important to me. It is important that we make a good impression. And we will not make a good impression if that 3G class comes anyway close to Mrs. Chawke. They must be kept well out of the way and you are the person I have chosen to keep them out of the way. If you refuse you won't be back here next year. Do you understand me, Charlie?"

Charlie nodded miserably.

"Of course if you don't refuse I think we can say that there will be a job here for you next year. Do you understand?"

Charlie knew he was trapped. He nodded again.

Mr. Bacon smiled. "That's settled then."

When Charlie got back to his class, they had already heard the news. To his surprise they were not pleased.

"Two bleedin' days."

"Nothing to do except walk around fields."

"Boring."

"And bulls everywhere. We could be savaged by bulls."

"It wasn't my idea," Charlie told them.

"And the rest of the school are getting off early on Thursday because the Minister for Education is coming"

"Yeah, that's why that fat redneck Mister Bleedin' Piggy wants us out of the place, I bet."

"Afraid we'll nick her bleedin' helicopter or something."

"Look at her. She has a face like a hawk!" said Wayne Byrne, inspecting a picture of the Minister on a letter that Mr. Bacon had sent around to all students.

"Like I said, it wasn't my idea," said Charlie miserably.

Charlie glanced at the picture. Wayne is right, he thought to himself. With her long crooked nose and stern look, Mrs. Chawke's face bore a certain resemblance to a hawk.

## Questions & Assignments

### PART 1

1. In what ways did Charlie try to be a good teacher?
2. Why did Charlie tell Mr. Bacon that he enjoyed a challenge?
3. Would you agree that the class were rude to Charlie on his first day? Give reasons for your answer.
4. What kind of things did the class do to make life difficult for Charlie?
5. Do you think that they were justified in behaving as they did? Explain your answer.
6. When Charlie was told by Mr. Bacon that he needed a break in Wicklow he was (a) shocked (b) then happy and (c) dismayed. Explain why he experienced each of these feelings.
7. Explain why Mr. Bacon wanted Charlie to take his class to Wicklow.
8. How did the class react when they heard that they were going to Wicklow?

## PART 2

**W**ednesday started badly for Charlie.

As 3G left the school in a hired bus, they made up a song. It had only two lines but they sang it with gusto for at least a half hour.

*Mister Piggy is a bogman.*
*Ee-I-ee-I-Oh.*

After a while they began putting in other words instead of 'bogman'. The group in the back seat gave the usual finger signs to cars behind. Someone poured a can of 7-up down someone else's back. When Darren Hosford threw an empty cola can out of the window the bus pulled in suddenly and stopped.

The bus driver turned to Charlie and shouted, "Have you any control over them lot?" He was really angry.

Charlie looked up miserably and shook his head.

"Well, can you control this lot?" the driver roared again.

The bus went silent.

"No," said Charlie, "I can't control them."

He said it in a matter-of-fact voice as if he was talking about a herd of wild buffalos. The bus remained silent. It was as if the class were ashamed of themselves, thought Charlie.

"You!" said the driver pointing at Darren. "Out and pick up that can."

Reluctantly Darren left the bus. The driver followed. A minute or so later the driver returned, carrying the can in one hand and dragging Darren by the collar with the other hand. Darren was clutching his stomach and looking very pale.

"Right, you lot!" roared the driver. "Listen to me. Anymore messing and you're out."

There was no more messing.

An hour later they left the main Dublin–Wexford road and headed for the mountains. The bus trundled along a windy mountain road in a valley. 3G were looking glum.

At a crossroads in the middle of nowhere the bus came to a halt. In every direction tree-covered hillsides stretched upwards. In the distance a few farmhouses were dotted on the hills.

"Well this is where we part company," shouted the driver. "You have about a half hour's walk to the hostel up that way." He pointed to a narrow road. "Too narrow for buses," he added by way of explanation.

He winked at Charlie and whispered, "I could drive up no problem but the walk will do them good. Calm them down a bit and tire them out. And it's a bit longer than half an hour!"

Two hours later a weary group of teenagers arrived at a sign that read 'Avonbeg Hostel'. It pointed in the direction of a path that crossed a field to a big stone house. In a distant corner of the field a half-dozen cattle grazed quietly.

"Here at last," announced Charlie, who had kept ahead of the others and had actually enjoyed the walk.

"What a kip," muttered someone, but the others seemed to be too tired to complain.

As they made their way across the field, Tracey Coyle noticed that the cattle were wandering in their direction. Now anybody brought up in the country will know that when cattle spot a human coming into a field they wander over to have a look. They are curious animals but are rarely dangerous. Of course 3G didn't know this.

"Bulls!" she screamed. "The bulls are after us!"

"Run for the house!" someone else shouted in panic.

And of course, as anyone raised on a farm will know, if you run towards a herd of cattle they will run away. If you stand still, they will wander closer for a look before going back to their main business which is eating grass. On the other hand, if you run away from them, they tend to follow you. And the faster you run the faster the cattle run after you.

Which was why 3G sprinted the last fifty metres of their journey with a small herd of curious cattle trotting after them. They rushed through the little gate of the small garden surrounding the hostel and slammed it behind them. Charlie strolled along in a leisurely fashion. As he approached the gate he was amused to see 3G gazing over the wall, their faces pale with fear. Outside the wall stood a half dozen cattle, gazing over the hedge.

"The bulls!" they shouted. "They could have killed us!"

"Watch out, Sir, bulls!"

"Run, Sir!"

Then it suddenly dawned on Charlie. A herd of cattle had succeeded in doing something that Mr. Bacon and he himself had failed to do. They had scared the living daylights out of 3G!

And 3G had called him 'Sir'. Charlie felt a surge of delight. There they were, all of 3G, trapped in the front garden of a youth hostel. The hostel was in the middle of a field. And in the field, roamed a herd of harmless cattle, hoping that someone had come to throw them a few bales of hay. Except that 3G thought that they were a herd of raging bulls. And 3G were scared.

Charlie strolled up to the herd of cattle and slapped one or two of them on the sides with his hand. They in turn stood back respectfully, sensing the hand of experience. Then he ambled through them and into the garden, closing the gate behind him.

"Are you not afraid of the bulls, Sir?" Jason Blake asked.

Charlie gazed at him for a few moments. "I know how to handle them," he said simply.

He sensed that for the first time 3G were impressed by him.

"They chased us, Sir."

# A Break for 3G

"They could have killed one of us."

"Indeed they could," agreed Charlie.

"Are they dangerous, Sir?" asked another.

"Yes," lied Charlie, "they're extremely dangerous. The brown ones are particularly dangerous. Once they get going they can run as fast as a train. One belt of their head and you're down. Then they simply trample on you — and that's the end of you!"

"How will we get out of here?"

"We're trapped."

"Let's go in, sit down, have something to eat and then we'll work something out," said Charlie. "The key should be under the stone by the door."

For the first time he felt he had total control of 3G.

\* \* \* \* \*

It was twilight. Charlie was alone, walking along a path that twisted up the side of a mountain. He had been walking for about an hour. The setting sun had filled the sky with a soft orange glow that was fading fast. Other than the soft chirping of birds and the distant barking of a dog, all was still.

He had left 3G back in the hostel. After the meal some of them settled down to listen to some CDs, a few more tapped a ball around the garden, taking care not to venture into the field where the cattle grazed peacefully. Another group were half-asleep.

"We're knackered, Sir. We had a lot of art homework to do last night," one of them said.

For some reason the others found this very funny. Charlie couldn't see the joke. He was not very interested in finding out what was so funny. He just wanted a bit of peace and quiet. And that's why he went on the walk. As he crossed the field he could feel the eyes of 3G on him. The cattle, too, had spotted him strolling across the field and they wandered towards him. He didn't quicken his pace. As the herd drew close Charlie stopped and looked at them. They stopped. Charlie took a few steps towards them and they moved back. He turned and continued his journey and again they followed him, but slowly and keeping a distance from him. He reached the end

of the field, leaped over the gate and disappeared up the road.

3G had watched his progress, their mouths hanging open in admiration.

Dusk was beginning to fall as Charlie decided to turn around and make his way back to the hostel. On one side of the path the mountainside fell steeply away to his left. In the distant valley far below the odd glimmer of light from the few scattered farmhouses began to appear. Charlie noted that a full moon was rising. He would have no problem making his way back to the hostel in the moonlight. He wouldn't need to use the torch that he carried in his pocket.

Just as he began to make his way back downwards he thought that he heard a faint shout. He stood still and listened. There it was again. Very faint, but definitely the sound of a man's voice.

Charlie took a deep breath, cupped his hands around his mouth and shouted.

"Is anyone there?"

The reply came immediately.

"Aaah!" It was faint and it seemed to come from further up the mountain.

Charlie hurried upwards along the path. After fifty metres he stopped, took a deep breath, cupped his hands and shouted again.

"Is there anybody there?"

This time the reply was a little louder. It was also more clear.

"Help. Please help."

He's up further, Charlie thought to himself. He tried to trot but the pathway was getting steeper.

"Where are you?" roared Charlie when he had scrambled up a little further.

"Here. Here on a ledge." The voice was closer now and seemed to be coming from below.

Dusk was rapidly giving way to darkness. Charlie looked down but couldn't see anything. He shone his torch down. The mountainside fell away sharply from the pathway. It was almost a sheer drop to the rocky valley far below.

On a ledge about five metres down lay a man. With one hand he held on to a black and white colllie and with the other he clutched the stump of a small bush growing out of the mountainside.

Charlie could see the danger of the situation at once. The ledge sloped downward. If the man loosened his grip on the bush he and his dog would probably slip forward and fall to their deaths below.

"Thank God you're here. I don't think I can hold on much longer." The man spoke with a posh accent. He's not a local farmer, thought Charlie.

"Are you OK? Are you hurt?" Charlie blurted out.

"This fool of a dog of mine made her way down here, after a rabbit or something. She couldn't get back up so I climbed down to get her. I twisted my ankle when I was climbing down and now I can't make my way back up. Can you get help? I can't hold on much longer."

"I'll get help. Can you hold out for half an hour or so?"

"An hour at the most," gasped the man.

"Hang on then. I'll be back".

As Charlie trotted back down the hillside path in the gathering dusk he tried to form a plan in his mind. Where was the nearest house? Where was the nearest phone? He didn't know. His best bet, he decided, was to head back to the hostel. He needed help and the only help that was available were the students of 3G.

He arrived back breathless to find the entire class sitting in the common room. Some sat together on chairs. Others were sprawled on the floor and seemed half-asleep. Their silence surprised him.

"I thought some of you would be in bed," he said.

"Some of us were, but we heard odd noises coming from the attic . . . " one replied.

"Is this place haunted, Sir?" another asked.

Charlie realised that they were scared. Probably a few mice or bats in the attic had them scared. He almost smiled.

"It could be," he said, "but a ghost in the attic is not our problem just now."

He then told them about the injured man and the dog trapped on the ledge. He was surprised when they listened attentively.

"I want five or six volunteers and no messing. This is for real. If we don't do something — and do it quick — that man will fall to his death."

All sixteen of them put up their hands.

"Sixteen is too many. I can't take all of you. It's too dangerous." Charlie told them.

"I'm not staying here on my own."

"I'm not either. I'm sure this place is haunted."

Charlie realised that he had no choice but to bring the lot! He must be mad, he thought to himself.

"OK. We all go. But no messing and do what I say. Is that OK by everyone?"

They sensed a new firmness in his voice. They nodded.

"Right. Boil a kettle and make a flask of tea. This guy will need something to warm him when we get him up. I'm going to search for rope. There's bound to be some around. And roll up a few sleeping bags. We'll need them."

Five minutes later Charlie, surrounded by 3G, left the hostel and headed back out into the night. Outside the gate that led from the hostel garden into the field stood the cattle.

"We can't go out. We can't go through this field. The bulls . . . " someone muttered fearfully.

"Right. Get into a tight group. We'll walk slowly across the field towards the gate. I'll stay between you and the cattle. You'll be alright."

"Are you sure, Sir?"

"I promise. Trust me."

A strange parade made its way across the moonlit field. It was led by 3G, huddled together. Next came Charlie walking backwards and flashing his torch at the dozen or so curious cattle who followed from behind.

When they reached the safety of the road sixteen timid voices muttered "Thanks, Sir".

Charlie couldn't help smiling.

## Questions & Assignments — PART 2

1. What happened on the way to Wicklow?
2. Why were the pupils afraid of the cattle? Was Charlie pleased about this? Explain your answer.
3. As Charlie set off from the hostel on his walk the writer says that — *'3G had watched his progress, their mouths hanging open in admiration.'* Why does he use the word *'admiration'*?
4. What happened during the walk?
5. Were you surprised by the way the class reacted when Charlie told them about the injured man?
6. Why did the writer use the phrase *'a strange parade'* when describing how Charlie and the class left the hostel to rescue the man on the ledge?

## PART 3

As a rescue team, 3G were perfect. They followed every instruction without question. A rope was tied around Charlie's waist and he was slowly and carefully lowered on to the ledge. Each order was carried out carefully. A second rope was used to lower down a sleeping bag. The dog was bundled into the sleeping bag and hauled swiftly to safety. One of the pupils took charge of the dog and the rope was lowered again. Charlie tied it under the injured man's arms and around his waist. Slowly and carefully they hauled him up the steep mountainside. Then they hauled Charlie back up. The hot tea quickly revived the injured man. His ankle was swollen badly and he couldn't walk.

Two stout branches were found and pushed through the sleeping bag to make a crude stretcher. Soon the rescue party was making its way back down the mountain in the moonlight, the pupils taking it in turns to carry the stretcher with the injured man on board.

Dawn was breaking when they reached the road that ran along the valley. A passing van driver was hailed down. He had a mobile phone and a short time later an ambulance arrived. Darren Hosford said he'd mind the dog, who trotted along wagging her tail.

"Before I go I better introduce myself," said the injured man, as he was lifted into the ambulance. "I'm James Andrews."

"I'm Charlie Murray . . . "

" . . . and we're 3G from Kilmoone Community School in Dublin," chimed in Darren Hosford.

"I'll be in touch" said James Andrews.

A few moments later the ambulance was on its way to Wicklow Hospital with the injured man inside.

"The best thing that we can do now is to go back to the hostel and get a few hours sleep," said Charlie.

When they reached the field the cattle were at the gate to greet them — until the little collie caught sight of the cattle. She leapt forward straining at her lead, barking and growling. The cattle raised their tails in the air, turned and galloped back across the field. 3G cheered.

A half hour later 3G and their teacher were sleeping soundly — utterly exhausted but satisfied after a good night's work.

\* \* \* \* \*

Mrs. Chawke, the Minister for Education, was just finishing breakfast when the news came on. It was the usual mixture of good and bad. Middle East talks breaking down, interest rates to remain steady, farmers planning a protest in Dublin and — "A dramatic rescue operation took place near Glencree early this morning when a group of Dublin schoolchildren and their teacher, Mr. Charlie Murray, hauled the millionaire businessman James Andrews and his dog from a ledge on to which he had fallen, while walking his dog. Shaken and bruised, but comfortable, Mr. Andrews is recovering in Wicklow Hospital. The children and their teacher, who are from Kilmoone Community School in

Dublin, are understood to have been hostelling in the area. More on this story later."

Kilmoone Community School — that rang a bell in the minister's head. Yes, that was the school that she was due to visit that afternoon. The very school!

Perfect, she thought. Just perfect. Now I'll have my picture in the papers and I'll be on TV as well. There was nothing the minister liked more than having her picture in the paper or being on TV. She picked up the phone and rang her secretary.

"Sean? Minister Chawke here. You heard the news about the kids from Kilmoone Community School . . . ? Good. I want them there when we arrive this afternoon. I want to be photographed with them . . . How do you mean? How might it be difficult . . . I know they are in Wicklow. Get on to the school and get them back there . . . I don't care how you do it . . . just do it... and, by the way, make sure that there's a newspaper photographer and a TV camera person with us on the helicopter . . . no excuses, Sean . . . I want to be seen on national TV and in the papers congratulating those brave children and their teacher . . . "

"Yes, Minister," sighed Sean.

\* \* \* \* \*

Charlie was woken by loud banging on the hostel door. He looked at his watch. It was midday. When he opened the door he was surprised to see Mr. Bacon standing outside and the minibus parked on the road outside. What was that man up to, he wondered to himself.

Mr. Bacon stepped in and shook Charlie by the hand. He seemed excited to the point of agitation. His little eyes twinkled and he hopped from one foot to the other, rubbing his hands together gleefully.

"Great show last night, Charlie. Great show. Splendid! Splendid! Great for the school's reputation."

One by one the students of 3G arrived from upstairs, yawning and rubbing their eyes.

"What's up?" they muttered.

"As you know, boys and girls," announced Mr. Bacon, "the Minister for Education is visiting the school today and has specially asked that she meet you all in person to congratulate you on your brave and wonderful deed, rescuing the millionaire businessman, Mr. James Andrews. I'm sure that he will want to reward the school in some way... so pack up your things and get everyone on the bus. We must hurry. Can't keep the Minister waiting. Ha-ha-ha."

There were a few surprised mutters of "What millionaire?" but most were too exhausted to do anything other than what they were being told.

3G had barely taken their seats on the bus when they fell sound asleep. Charlie did likewise. Mr. Bacon drove behind the bus in his Toyota.

3G awoke just as the bus was pulling into the school yard. The students of the school were lined up in the yard, class by class, and all wearing neat uniforms. In the distance could be heard the whirring of an approaching helicopter. Mr. Bacon scurried to the bus and led 3G over to the steps near the main entrance where the teachers and the board of management stood. 3G looked out of place with their runners and scruffy tracksuits.

Overhead the whirring grew louder and a bright green helicopter swooped down and circled over the school.

Kilmoone Community School was a single storey building. It had flat roof, covered in black felt. Class 3A had spent most of Tuesday afternoon on that roof, painting *Welcome Minister Chawke'* in white big letters. On Tuesday night a number of changes were made to the message by a group of students from 3G. They painted over the first and last letter of the minister's surname with black paint. They then added the word *'face'* in white letters. Underneath they painted the words — *'Signed Mister Piggy Bacon – The Boss'*. And underneath that again was a drawing of a pig's head. It was this message that caught the minister's eye as the helicopter descended towards the school. It also caught the eyes of the cameramen on board. Inside the helicopter cameras clicked and whirred.

"Don't photograph that!" cried the Minister for Education, but she couldn't be heard above the roar of the engine. When the helicopter touched down in the school football pitch the minister's face was white with fury.

Mr. Bacon, followed by his wife, trotted towards the helicopter to greet the minister. He was beside himself with excitement. He shook her hand and smiled his best smile. He couldn't help noticing that she did not smile back. He led her back to the steps and made a short speech of welcome. He finished up by saying that he hoped that she liked the message of welcome on the school roof.

"I'm sorry to disappoint you, Mr. Bacon but I did not like the message at all," began the minister, giving Mr. Bacon an icy stare. She then went on to speak about the need to respect public property, the evils of vandalism and the responsibility of teachers — and especially principal teachers — to train their pupils to be model citizens. After each sentence of her speech she glared at Mr. Bacon. She ended by saying that the principal, pupils and staff had a lot to learn from the example shown by those brave and noble boys and girls of class 3G and their teacher, Mr. Murray.

"I would now like to meet them, Mr. Bacon," she said ending her speech. Mr. Bacon was in a panic. He made a brief announcement that the students gathered in the yard could have the remainder of the day off and that they were to leave quietly. He couldn't understand why the minister seemed very cross about the welcome message on the roof. And she had said nothing yet about the computers.

He lead her towards 3G and introduced her to Charlie Murray. They spoke for a while and he seemed to cheer her up. Then she began speaking to the pupils of 3G. She spent a long time talking to them and their teacher. She actually seems to be enjoying their company, thought Mr. Bacon bitterly. God knows what they are telling her!

The other teachers and the members of the board stood around. They wanted to go inside and grab a bite to eat and something to drink, but felt that it would be impolite to go in until the minister was ready to do so. Would she ever stop chatting with that bunch, they thought to themselves. Finally the minister beckoned Mr. Bacon.

"Mr. Bacon. I'm told that these brave boys and girls have not eaten all day. Is there something for them to eat here?"

"Well, not really. There are some sandwiches and sausage rolls and wine and soft drinks, but they are for yourself — and the staff and the board of management, of course."

"Nonsense, Mr. Bacon. I'm not in the least bit hungry, and I'm sure that the teachers and the board of management aren't either. I'd love if these brave boys and girls would join us while we eat. I'm sure that there will be plenty there for all."

"Yes, Minister," he muttered

The minister turned to 3G. "Now boys and girls you go ahead in and get something to eat. Mr. Bacon is going to introduce me to the teachers and the board. We'll be in after you."

3G didn't need to be told twice. They disappeared towards the canteen in a flash.

" By the way, Mr. Murray tells me that he teaches them Irish and English and Religion. They seem strange subjects for a teacher who is qualified in Maths and Computers. Do they not, Mr. Bacon?"

"Er . . . Um . . . " Mr. Bacon was lost for words.

"I have decided to let the school have the computers . . . "

"Oh, thank you so much, Minister . . . "

" . . . on condition that Mr. Murray is in charge of them. I want somebody responsible in that position. And, by the way, Mr. Murray tells me that he is on probation this year. I have assured him that he has no worries in that regard. There will be a job for him in this school for as long as he wants it."

"Yes, of course, Minister," muttered the principal.

"Now please introduce me to these people and then we'll join the brave boys and girls and have something to eat . . . "

3G arrived into the canteen to find a feast laid out before them. There were sausage rolls, cocktail sausages, sandwiches and cakes of every colour, all waiting to be eaten.

When the minister and her followers arrived in, a short time later, there were four sausage rolls, three cakes and a half dozen sandwiches (tomato and lettuce) left. All the cocktail sausages were gone. In the corner Darren Hosford sipped a glass of red wine.

"This is awful!" screamed Miss Donovan, who had prepared the food. "They've eaten everything!"

"Indeed it is!" snapped Mr. Bacon.

"Nonsense!" said the minister. "They deserve it. The little dears must have been starving."

"But, Mrs. Chawke, we have nothing left to offer you to eat."

"Don't worry about me, Mr. Bacon. I'm on a diet. Perhaps it's something you should consider yourself."

Before Mr. Bacon could think of a suitable reply the minister's secretary approached her with a note. She scanned it quickly and then cleared her throat.

"Attention everybody. I have just got a message from Mr. James Andrews. Perhaps Mr. Bacon would like to read it out?"

Mr. Bacon took the paper and began to read. "I am recovering well from my fall. I want to express my great gratitude to you brave boys and girls, and your teacher of course, for saving my life. And, as a token of my appreciation . . . "

The room was silent.

" . . . I want to give you all a holiday,

including your teacher, Mr. Murray, in Disneyworld in Florida. And in order that you all enjoy yourselves fully there I will include two hundred pounds spending money for each of you. Once again many thanks. Yours sincerely, James Andrews."

For a moment 3G were speechless. Then they began to cheer.

Later that evening in Darren Hosford's house a number of 3G gathered to watch a video clip from the six o'clock news. It was a shot of the roof of their school. They watched it over and over, admiring their art work.

In his house, Mr. Bacon only watched it once.

## Questions & Assignments — PART 3

1. Does the reader find out that the injured man was a millionaire before Charlie and the class find out? Explain your answer.
2. What do we learn about the Minister for Education from the story?
3. Why was Mr. Bacon in a happy mood when he arrived at the hostel? At this point in the story what did you hope would happen (a) to Mr. Bacon and (b) to Charlie at the end of the story?
4. Why was the Minister angry when she arrived at the school? Who was responsible for making her angry?
5. Did you enjoy the ending of this story? Give reasons for your answer.

## word power!

Find the words in the story which have similar meanings to each of the words and phrases below. The number in brackets after each one indicates the number of letters in the answer. The words appear in the story in the same order as the meanings given below.

CLUES

1. head-teacher (9)
2. a difficult task (9)
3. stuttered (9)
4. short (5)
5. similarity (10)
6. unrelaxed (6)
7. very happy (9)
8. trial period in a job (9)
9. unhappily (9)
10. holding (9)
11. spoke very quietly (9)
12. very tired (5)
13. ate grass (6)
14. ran quickly (8)
15. walked slowly (6)
16. just before nightfall (8)
17. vanished (11)
18. barely noticeable (5)
19. out of breath (10)
20. order (11)
21. transports injured people (9)
22. good name (10)

## ASSIGNMENT

Write a short story entitled 'A School Tour'. Divide your work in to paragraphs as follows:

### Paragraph 1 (4 – 5 sentences)
When did your teacher tell the class about the tour?
*On the first day back after Christmas . . .*
When your teacher announced the tour what words did he/she use? Use quotation marks.
*"I was thinking that this year we would . . ."*
How did the class respond?

### Paragraph 2 (3 – 4 sentences)
What time did you leave?
Describe the weather as you left your town on the morning of the tour.
*As we drove up the hill and away from Kilowen, the sky . . . and the . . .*
What did you do to pass the journey?
How long did the journey take?

### Paragraphs 3, 4 and 5
The next three paragraphs will describe how the day was spent.

# SPOT THE ERRORS

The following **Spot the Errors** exercise is aimed at sharpening your basic writing skills. Spot the 20 errors in the Passage below and rewrite the passage correctly. (Note: Refer to the Guidelines on pages 1—15.)

## 6   In Search of Hamish — A Black and White Sheepdog

Fergus walked home in good spirits, kicking a pebble in front of him and huming under his breath. There was a breath of spring in the air and snowdrop's were blooming in sheltered spots and one could believe that the trees would bud and sprout leafs again.

"Hamish got out," his mother said the moment he opened the door. "The gas man called to read the meter and…"

Fergus waited to here no more. He lifted Hamishs lead from the hook in the hall. He ran across the meadows, calling and whisling as he went. Two dogs played together on an open stretch, prancing and barking. Neither of them was a black and white sheepdog.

From their Fergus went to Queen's park. It was a large place, covering many acres. His steps slowed he could not check out the hole area, and besides, dusk was already closing in. He tried their favorite paths, without success. He must go home since that was what Hamish was lightly to do after he had had his jaunt.

Cars and buses now had their sidelights on; room's were lit up but as yet uncurtained. He walked briskly, scanning every side street, stopping on every corner to look in each direction.

And then he saw hamish. He was on the other side of the road, trotting along with his tale up and his tongue out as if he had slowed from a long run.

Hamish! cries Fergus in relief, and regretted it instantly.

Hamish turned and saw Fergus and, like an arrow, came towards him. A dark red and white double decker bus was coming down the hill. The paths of the dog and the bus coincided. As Fergus saw Hamish meet the offside wheel of the bus he felt as if a firework had exploded inside his head.

# THE GREATEST GIFT
### Philip Van Doren Stern

## PART 1

The little town straggling up the hill was bright with coloured Christmas lights. But George Pratt did not see them. He was leaning over the railing of the iron bridge, staring down moodily at the black water. The current eddied and swirled like liquid glass, and occasionally a bit of ice, detached from the shore, would go gliding downstream to be swallowed up in the shadows under the bridge.

The water looked paralysingly cold. George wondered how long a man could stay alive in it. The glassy blackness had a strange, hypnotic effect on him. He leaned still farther over the railing . . .

"I wouldn't do that if I were you," a quiet voice beside him said. George turned resentfully to a little man he had never seen before. He was stout, well past middle-age, and his round cheeks were pink in the winter air as though they had just been shaved.

"Wouldn't do what?" George asked sullenly.

"What you were thinking of doing."

"How do you know what I was thinking?"

"Oh, we make it our business to know a lot of things," the stranger said easily.

George wondered what the man's business was. He was a most unremarkable little person, the sort you would pass in a crowd and never notice. Unless you saw his bright blue eyes, that is. You couldn't forget them, for they were the kindest, sharpest eyes you ever saw. Nothing else about him was noteworthy. He wore a moth-eaten old fur cap and a shabby overcoat that was stretched tightly across his paunchy belly. He was carrying a small black satchel. It wasn't a doctor's bag — it was too large for that and not the right shape. It was a salesman's sample kit, George decided distastefully. The fellow was probably some sort of pedlar, the kind who would go around poking his sharp little nose into other people's affairs.

"Looks like snow, doesn't it?" the stranger said, glancing up appraisingly at the overcast sky. "It'll be nice to have a white Christmas. They're getting scarce these days – but so are a lot of things." He turned to face George squarely. "You all right now?"

"Of course I'm all right. What made you think I wasn't? I— "

George fell silent before the stranger's quiet gaze.

The little man shook his head. "You know you shouldn't think of such things – and on Christmas Eve of all times! You've got to consider Mary – and your mother, too."

George opened his mouth to ask how this stranger could know his wife's name, but the fellow anticipated him. "Don't ask me how I know such things. It's my business to know 'em. That's why I came along this way tonight. Lucky I did too." He glanced down at the dark water and shuddered.

"Well, if you know so much about me," George said, "give me just one good reason why I should be alive."

The little man made a chuckling sound. "Come, come, it can't be that bad. You've got your job at the bank. And Mary and the kids. You're healthy, young, and— "

"And sick of everything!" George cried. "I'm stuck here in this mudhole for life, doing the same dull work day after day. Other men are leading exciting lives, but I – well, I'm just a small-town bank clerk that even the Army didn't want. I never did anything really useful or interesting, and it looks as if I never will. I might just as well be dead. I might better be dead. Sometimes I wish I were. In fact, I wish I'd never been born!"

The little man stood looking at him in the growing darkness. "What was that you said?" he asked softly.

"I said I wish I'd never been born," George repeated firmly. "And I mean it too."

## Questions & Assignments — PART 1

1. What details in the first paragraph tell us that (a) it was Christmas time and (b) it was very cold?
2. What do you think George Pratt was considering as the story opens? What sentence in the story supports your answer?
3. What did he notice particularly about the stranger?
4. What was the stranger carrying?
5. How did the stranger surprise George?
6. What was George's attitude to life?
7. What do you expect to happen in the next part of the story?

## Word Power!

Find the words in the story which have similar meanings to each of the words and phrases below. The number in brackets after each one indicates the number of letters in the answer. The words appear in the story in the same order as the meanings given below.

### CLUES

1. now and then (12)
2. in a bad-tempered manner (8)
3. notable (10)
4. cloudy (8)
5. not plentiful (6)
6. think about; take into account (8)
7. expected (11)
8. looked quickly (7)
9. shook; shivered (9)
10. said something more than once (8)

# PART 2

The stranger's pink cheeks glowed with excitement. "Why that's wonderful! You've solved everything. I was afraid you were going to give me some trouble. But now you've got the solution yourself. You wish you'd never been born. All right! Okay! You haven't!"

"What do you mean?" George growled.

"You haven't been born. Just that. You haven't been born. No one here knows you. You have no responsibilities – no job – no wife – no children. Why, you haven't even a mother. You couldn't have, of course. All your troubles are over. Your wish, I am happy to say, has been granted – officially."

"Nuts!" George snorted and turned away.

The stranger ran after him and caught him by the arm.

"You'd better take this with you," he said, holding out his satchel. "It'll open a lot of doors that might otherwise be slammed in your face."

"What doors in whose face?" George scoffed. "I know everybody in this town. And besides, I'd like to see anybody slam a door in my face."

"Yes, I know," the little man said patiently. "But take this anyway. It can't do any harm and it may help." He opened the satchel and displayed a number of brushes. "You'd be surprised how useful these brushes can be as an introduction – especially the free ones. These, I mean." He hauled out a plain little handbrush. "I'll show you how to use it." He thrust the satchel into George's reluctant hands and began. "When the lady of the house comes to the door you give her this and then talk fast. You say: 'Good evening, madam. I'm from the World Cleaning Company, and I want to present you with this handsome and useful brush absolutely free – no obligation to purchase anything at all.' After that, of course, it's a cinch. Now you try it." He forced the brush into George's hand.

George promptly dropped the brush into the satchel and fumbled with the catch, finally closing it with an angry snap. "Here," he said, and then stopped abruptly, for there was no one in sight.

The little stranger must have slipped away into the bushes growing along the river bank, George thought. He certainly wasn't going to play hide and seek with him. It was nearly dark and getting colder every minute. He shivered and turned up his coat collar.

The street lights had been turned on, and Christmas candles in the windows glowed softly. The little town looked remarkably cheerful. After all, the place you grew up in was the one spot on earth where you could really feel at home. George felt a sudden burst of affection even for crotchety old Hank Biddle whose house he was passing. He remembered the quarrel he had had when his car had scraped a piece of bark out of Hank's big maple tree. George looked up at the vast spread of leafless branches towering over him in the darkness. The tree must have been growing there since Indian times. He felt a sudden twinge of guilt for the damage he had done. He had never stopped to inspect the wound, for he was ordinarily afraid to have Hank catch him even looking at the tree. Now he stepped out boldly into the road to examine the huge trunk.

Hank must have repaired the scar or painted it over, for there was no sign of it. George struck a match and bent down to look more closely. He straightened up with an odd, sinking feeling in his stomach. There wasn't any scar. The bark was smooth and undamaged. He remembered what the little man at the bridge had said. It was all nonsense, of course, but the non-existent scar bothered him.

When he reached the bank, he saw that something was wrong. The building was dark, and he knew he had turned the vault light on. He noticed, too, that someone had left the window shades up. He ran around to the front. There was a battered old sign fastened on the door. George could just make out the words:

**FOR RENT OR SALE**
Apply JAMES SILVA, Real Estate.

Perhaps it was some boy's trick, he thought wildly. Then he saw a pile of ancient leaves and tattered newspapers in the bank's ordinarily immaculate doorway. And the windows looked as though they hadn't been washed in years. A light was still burning across the street in Jim Silva's office. George dashed over and tore the door open.

Jim looked up from his ledger-book in surprise. "What can I do for you, young man?" he said in the polite voice he reserved for potential customers.

"The bank," George said breathlessly. "What's the matter with it?"

"The old bank building?" Jim Silva turned around and looked out of the window. "Nothing that I can see. Wouldn't like to rent or buy it, would you?"

"You mean – it's out of business?"

"For a good ten years. Went bust during the depression. Stranger 'round these parts, ain't you?"

George leaned weakly against the wall. "I was here some time ago," he said weakly. "The bank was all right then – I even knew some of the people who worked there."

"Didn't know a feller named Marty Jenkins, did you?"

"Marty Jenkins! Why, he—" George was about to say that Marty had never worked at the bank – couldn't have, in fact, for when they had both left school they had applied for a job there and George had gotten it. But now, of course, things were different. He would have to be careful. "No, I didn't know him," he said slowly. "Not really, that is. I'd heard of him."

"Then maybe you heard how he skipped out with fifty thousand dollars. That's why the bank went broke. Pretty near ruined everybody around here." Silva was looking at him sharply. "I was hoping for a minute maybe you'd know where he is. I lost plenty in that crash myself. We'd like to get our hands on Marty Jenkins."

"Didn't he have a brother? Seems to me he had a brother named Arthur."

"Art? Oh, sure. But he's all right. He don't know where his brother went. It's had a terrible effect on him, too. Took to drink, he did. It's too bad – and hard on his wife. He married a nice girl."

George felt the sinking feeling in his stomach again. "Who did he marry?" he demanded hoarsely. Both he and Art had courted Mary.

"Girl named Mary Thatcher," Silva said cheerfully. "She lives up on the hill just this side of the church – Hey! Where are you going?"

But George had bolted out of the office. He ran past the empty bank building and turned up the hill. For a moment he thought of going straight to Mary. The house next to the church had been given to them by her father as a wedding present. Naturally Art Jenkins would have gotten it if he had married Mary. George wondered whether they had any children. Then he knew he couldn't face Mary – not yet anyway. He decided to visit his parents and find out more about her.

## Questions & Assignments — PART 2

1. At the end of the first part of the story George wishes that he had never been born. What is surprising about the stranger's response to this wish?
2. Why did the stranger give the satchel to George?
3. What unexpected thing happened when George was about to give the satchel back?
4. Would you agree that George's mood changed after the stranger left? Give a reason for your answer.
5. Why did George quarrel with Hank Biddle?
6. Why do you think George felt uneasy when he examined the bark of the maple tree?
7. Why did George realise something was wrong when he reached the bank?
8. *'George leaned weakly against the wall.'* Explain clearly why George leaned weakly against the wall.
9. What do we learn about (a) Marty Jenkins and (b) Art Jenkins?
10. (a) What does George hope will happen when he visits his parents?
    (b) What do you expect will happen?

## Word Power!

Find the words in the story which have similar meanings to each of the words and phrases below. The number in brackets after each one indicates the number of letters in the answer. The words appear in the story in the same order as the meanings given below.

CLUES

1. answer to a problem (8)
2. obligations; duties (16)
3. closed noisily (7)
4. not eager (9)
5. buy (8)
6. bad-tempered (9)
7. examine; look at (7)
8. very old (7)
9. torn in shreds (8)
10. very clean; spotless (10)
11. ran very quickly (6)

# PART 3

There were candles burning in the windows of the little weather-beaten house on the side street, and a Christmas wreath was hanging on the glass panel of the front door. George raised the gate latch with a loud click. A dark shape on the porch jumped up and began to growl. Then it hurled itself down the steps, barking ferociously.

"Brownie!" George shouted, "Brownie, you old fool, stop that! Don't you know me?" But the dog advanced menacingly and drove him back behind the gate. The porch light snapped on, and George's father stepped outside to call the dog off. The barking subsided to a low, angry growl. His father held the dog by the collar while George cautiously walked past. He could see that his father did not know him. "Is the lady of the house in?" he asked.

His father waved towards the door. "Go on in," he said cordially. "I'll chain this dog up. She can be mean with strangers."

His mother, who was waiting in the hallway, obviously did not recognise him. George opened his sample kit and grabbed the first brush that came to hand. "Good evening, ma'am," he said politely. "I'm from the World Cleaning Company. We're giving out a free sample brush. I thought you might like to have one. No obligation. No obligation at all . . ." His voice faltered.

His mother smiled at his awkwardness. "I suppose you'll want to sell me something. I'm not really sure I need any brushes."

"No'm. I'm not selling anything." He assured her. "The regular salesman will be around in a few days. This is just – well, just a Christmas present from the company."

"How nice," she said. "You people never gave such good brushes away before."

"This is a special offer," he said. His father entered the hall and closed the door.

"Won't you come in for a while and sit down?" his mother said. "You must be tired walking so much."

"Thank you, ma'am. I don't mind if I do." He entered the little parlour and put his bag down on the floor. The room looked different somehow, although he could not figure out why.

"I used to know this town pretty well," he said to make conversation. "Knew some of the townspeople. I remember a girl named Mary Thatcher. She married Art Jenkins, I heard. You must know them."

"Of course," his mother said. "We know Mary well."

"Any children?" he asked casually.

"Two – a boy and a girl."

George sighed audibly. "My, you must be tired," his mother said. "Perhaps I can get you a cup of tea."

"No, don't bother," he said. "I'll be having supper soon." He looked around the little parlour, trying to find out why it looked different. Over the mantelpiece hung a framed photograph which had been taken on his kid brother Harry's sixteenth birthday. He remembered how they had gone to Potter's studio to be photographed together. There was something odd about the picture. It took him a full minute to realise what it was. It showed only one figure – Harry's.

"That your son?" he asked.

His mother's face clouded. She nodded but said nothing.

"I think I met him, too," George said hesitantly. "His name's Harry, isn't it?"

His mother turned away, making a strange choking noise in her throat. Her husband put his arm clumsily around her shoulder. His voice, which was always mild and gentle, suddenly became harsh. "You couldn't have met him," he said. "He's been dead a long while. He was drowned the day that picture was taken."

George's mind flew back to the long-ago August afternoon when he and Harry had visited Potter's studio. On their way home they had gone swimming. Harry had been seized with a cramp, he remembered. He had pulled him out of the water and had thought nothing of it. But suppose he hadn't been there!

"I'm sorry," he said miserably. "I guess I'd better go. I hope you like the brush. And I wish you both a very Merry Christmas." There, he had put his foot in it again, wishing them a Merry Christmas when they were thinking about their dead son.

Brownie tugged fiercely at her chain as George went down the porch steps and accompanied his departure with a hostile, rolling growl.

He wanted desperately now to see Mary. He wasn't sure he could stand not being recognised by her, but he had to see her.

## Questions & Assignments — PART 3

1. As this part of the story opens it becomes more and more clear to George that his wish was granted. What evidence is there of this?
2. Why did Harry die?

### word power!

Find the words in the story which have similar meanings to each of the words and phrases below. The number in brackets after each one indicates the number of letters in the answer. The words appear in the story in the same order as the meanings given below.

CLUES

1. came forward (8)
2. in a threatening manner (10)
3. settled down (8)
4. very carefully (10)
5. in a friendly manner (9)
6. awkwardly (8)
7. not friendly (7)

# PART 4

The lights were on in the church, and the choir was making last-minute preparations for Christmas vespers. The organ had been practising *Holy Night* evening after evening until George had become thoroughly sick of it. But now the music almost tore his heart out.

He stumbled blindly up the path to his own house. The lawn was untidy, and the flower bushes he had kept carefully trimmed were neglected and badly sprouted. Art Jenkins could hardly be expected to care for such things.

When he knocked at the door there was a long silence, followed by the shout of a child. Then Mary came to the door.

At the sight of her, George's voice almost failed him. "Merry Christmas, ma'am," he managed to say at last. His hand shook as he tried to open the satchel.

"Come in," Mary said indifferently. "It's cold out."

When George entered the living room, unhappy as he was, he could not help noticing with a secret grin that the too-high priced blue sofa they often had quarrelled over was there. Evidently Mary had gone through the same thing with Art Jenkins and had won the argument with him, too.

George got his satchel open. One of the brushes had a bright blue handle and vari-coloured bristles. It was obviously a brush not intended to be given away, but George didn't care. He handed it over to Mary. "This would be fine for your sofa," he said.

"My, that's a pretty brush," she exclaimed. "You're giving it away free?"

He nodded solemnly. "Special introductory offer. It's one way for the company to keep excess profits down – share them with its friends."

She stroked the sofa gently with the brush, smoothing out the velvety nap. "It's a nice brush. Thank you. I – "

There was a sudden scream from the kitchen, and two small children rushed in. A little, homely-faced girl flung herself into her mother's arms, sobbing loudly as a boy of seven came running after her, snapping a toy pistol at her head. "Mommy she won't die," he yelled. "I shot her a hunert times, but she won't die."

He looks just like Art Jenkins, George thought. Acts like him too. The boy suddenly turned his attention to him. "Who're you?" he demanded belligerently. He pointed his pistol at George and pulled the trigger. "You're dead. Why don't you fall down and die?"

There was a heavy step on the porch. The boy looked frightened and backed away. George saw Mary glance apprehensively at the door.

Art Jenkins came in. He stood for a moment in the doorway, clinging to the knob for support. His eyes were glazed, and his face was very red. "Who's this?" he demanded thickly.

"He's a brush salesman," Mary tried to explain. "He gave me this brush."

"Brush salesman!" Art sneered. "Well, tell him to get outa here. We don't want no brushes." Art hiccoughed violently and lurched across the room to the sofa where he sat down suddenly. "An' we don't want no brush salesmen neither."

"You'd better go," Mary whispered to George. "I'm sorry."

The boy edged toward George. "G'wan, go 'way. We don't want no brushes. An' we don't want no ole brush salesman neither."

George looked despairingly at Mary. Her eyes were begging him to go. Art had lifted his feet up on the sofa and was sprawling out on it, muttering unkind things about brush salesmen. George went to the door, followed by Art's son who kept snapping his pistol at him and saying: "You're dead – dead – dead!"

Perhaps the boy was right, George thought when he reached the porch. Maybe he was dead, or maybe this was all a bad dream from which he might eventually awake. He wanted to find the little man on the bridge again and try to persuade him to cancel the whole deal.

## Questions & Assignments — PART 4

1. What sentence tells us that the garden was not cared for? Why do you think that the writer included this detail?
2. List all the details that the author gives which suggest that Art Jenkins was drunk.
3. Do you think that the Jenkins' home was a happy one? Give reasons for your answer.

## Word power!

Find the words in the story which have similar meanings to each of the words and phrases below. The number in brackets after each one indicates the number of letters in the answer. The words appear in the story in the same order as the meanings given below.

### CLUES

1. evening church service (7)
2. walked unsteadily (8)
3. not cared for (9)
4. threw (5)
5. weeping loudly (7)
6. in a rude manner (13)
7. in a nervous and anxious manner (14)
8. walked very unsteadily (7)
9. finally (10)

## PART 5

He hurried down the hill and broke into a run when he neared the river. George was relieved to see the little stranger standing on the bridge. "I've had enough," he gasped. "Get me out of this – you got me into it."

The stranger raised his eyebrows. "I got you into it! I like that! You were granted your wish. You got everything you asked for. You're the freest man on earth now. You have no ties. You can go anywhere – do anything. What more can you possibly want?"

"Change me back," George pleaded. "Change me back – please. Not just for my sake but for others too. You don't understand. I've got to get back. They need me here."

"I understand right enough," the stranger said slowly. "I just wanted to make sure you did. You had the greatest gift of all conferred upon you – the gift of life, of being a part of this world and taking a part in it. Yet you denied that gift." As the stranger spoke, the church bell high up on the hill sounded, calling the townspeople to Christmas vespers. Then the downtown church bell started ringing.

"I've got to get back," George said desperately. "You can't cut me off like this. Why, it's murder!"

"Suicide rather, wouldn't you say?" the stranger murmured. "You brought it on yourself. However, since it's Christmas Eve — well, anyway, close your eyes and keep listening to the bells." His voice sank lower. "Keep listening to the bells."

George did as he was told. He felt a cold, wet snowdrop touch his cheek – and then another and another. When he opened his eyes, the snow was falling fast, so fast that it obscured everything around him. The little stranger could not be seen, but then neither could anything else. The snow was so thick that George had to grope for the bridge railing.

As he started toward the village, he

thought he heard someone saying: "Merry Christmas," but the bells were drowning out all rival sounds, so he could not be sure.

When he reached Hank Biddle's house he stopped and walked out into the roadway, peering down anxiously at the base of the big maple tree. The scar was there, thank Heaven! He touched the tree affectionately. He'd have to do something about the wound – get a tree surgeon or something. Anyway, he'd evidently been changed back. He was himself again. Maybe it was all a dream, or perhaps he had been hypnotised by the smooth-flowing black water. He had heard of such things.

At the corner of Main and Bridge Streets he almost collided with a hurrying figure. It was Jim Silva, the real estate agent. "Hello, George," Jim said cheerfully. "Late tonight, ain't you? I should think you'd want to be home early on Christmas Eve."

George drew a long breath. "I just wanted to see if the bank is all right. I've got to make sure the vault light is on."

"Sure it's on. I saw it as I went past."

"Let's look, huh?" George said, pulling at Silva's sleeve. He wanted the assurance of a witness.

He dragged the surprised real estate dealer around to the front of the bank where the light was gleaming through the falling snow. "I told you it was on," Silva said with some irritation.

"I had to make sure," George mumbled. "Thanks — and Merry Christmas!" Then he was off like a streak, running up the hill.

He was in a hurry to get home, but not in such a hurry that he couldn't stop for a moment at his parents' house, where he wrestled with Brownie until the friendly old dog waggled all over with delight. He grasped his startled brother's hand and wrung it frantically, wishing him an almost hysterical Merry Christmas. Then he dashed across the parlour to examine a certain photograph. He kissed his mother, joked with his father, and was out of the house a few seconds later, stumbling and slipping on the newly fallen snow as he ran on up the hill.

The church was bright with light, and the choir and the organ were going full tilt. George flung the door to his home open and called out at the top of his voice: "Mary! Where are you? Mary! Kids!"

His wife came toward him, dressed for going to church, and making gestures to silence him. "I've just put the children to bed," she protested. "Now they'll—" But not another word could she get out of her mouth, for he dragged her up to the children's room, where he madly embraced his son and his daughter and woke them up thoroughly.

It was not until Mary got him downstairs that he began to be coherent. "I thought I'd lost you. Oh, Mary, I thought I'd lost you!"

"What's the matter, darling?" she asked in bewilderment.

He pulled her down on the sofa and kissed her again. And then, just as he was about to tell her about his odd dream, his fingers came in contact with something lying on the seat of the sofa. His voice froze.

He did not even have to pick the thing up, for he knew what it was. And he knew that it would have a blue handle and vari-coloured bristles.

## Questions & Assignments — PART 5

1. Why did George return to the stranger?
2. What did the stranger want George to understand?
3. What were the first, second and third signs that George was *'changed back'*?
4. Why did he examine the photograph in his parents' home?
5. Would you agree that George was very affectionate towards his family? Refer to the text to support your answer. Suggest why he was.
6. What, in your view, is the author trying to suggest in the final paragraph?

**General Questions**

1. In what ways did George realise that his life was worthwhile?
2. What lesson or message do you get from this story?
3. Explain the title *The Greatest Gift*.
4. There is a saying — 'There are two kinds of people in the world; those who cause problems and those who solve problems.' Does the story illustrate this? Explain your answer.

---

**Word Power!**

Find the words in the story which have similar meanings to each of the words and phrases below. The number in brackets after each one indicates the number of letters in the answer. The words appear in the story in the same order as the meanings given below.

### CLUES

1. spoke in a breathless manner (6)
2. begged (7)
3. spoke in a quiet voice (8)
4. hid; made less clear (8)
5. crashed against; bumped against (8)
6. held tightly (7)
7. puzzlement (12)

# ASSIGNMENTS

1. Write a Short Story entitled 'A Wish That Came True'.

2. The best things in life are free. What's your opinion?

[Answer Guidelines]

1. Opt for an essay modelled on this story but set it in your own life – get the wish granted in the first few lines.
   **For example:**
   It had been a lousy day. It started with a big row with my mother and father over smoking. I walked out and slammed the door. In school it got worse. I gave a very rude answer to the principal when he asked me for my journal. Now I have a suspension note in my bag to bring home. I'm standing at . . . dreading what I have to face at home. There is nobody around except an old man . . .
   "I wish … " sighed the old man.
   "And I wish…" I snapped back.
   "No problem," he replied. "Your wish is granted."

   Now continue…

2. You can agree or disagree — or opt for the middle ground. You will need to identify what you regard as the 'best things in life' and show how they are or are not 'free'. Remember that the word 'free' can have a broad meaning, i.e. some things are often bought with something other than money, such as persistence, practice, patience, hard work etc.

### Remember
Poor handwriting – where every word presents a difficulty for the reader – takes a great deal from a piece of writing. Good handwriting is your responsibility. Make it neat and legible by slowing down.

## Points to Note

### POINT OF VIEW

Omniscient means 'all seeing'. Stories in which the author is directly addressing the readers are narrated from the omniscient point of view. **Omniscient narrators** are like **invisible observers** with the power to **see everything.** They can observe separate events as they occur simultaneously and know the **inner thoughts and feelings of all the characters** in the story. However, the narrator **must be careful** to reveal just enough information to hold the interest of the reader.

It is important to note that the omniscient point of view is not always impartial. Authors often describe a character or a situation in such a way as to get the reader to adopt a certain attitude.

### SCIENCE FICTION

Science fiction stories and films are very popular nowadays. (Can you explain the term 'science fiction'?) Many science fiction stories are set in distant planets, populated by strange looking beings armed with gadgets that can carry out amazing and incredible tasks.

Science fiction stories are also set in the real world where the writer sets out to explore 'what would happen if . . . ?'
- What would happen if wishes could be granted?
- What would happen if a person could become invisible?
- What would happen if a person could travel back in time?
- What would happen if a person read the minds of others?
- What would happen if a person could control the moods of others?

Very often the writer shows that such impossible inventions can lead to more harm than good.

# Strangers
## Karel Capek

"Well, I'm surprised at you!" cried Mistress Dinah. "If they'd been decent folk they'd have gone to the mayor instead of begging their way like this! Why didn't you send them to Simon's house? Why on earth must we be the ones to take them in? Aren't we as good as Simon? I know his wife would never let riff-raff like that into her house! I'm surprised at you, I really am, for lowering yourself to have anything to do with such people!"

"Don't shout so," grunted old Isachar, "they'll hear what you say."

"Let them hear!" shouted Mistress Dinah, raising her voice still more. "What next! It's a nice look-out if I'm not even to whisper in my own house because of tramps like that! Do you know them? He says she's his wife. His wife, is she? I know the sort of thing that goes on among those tramps. Aren't you ashamed to let such people into the house?"

Isachar wanted to point out that he had only let them into the cow-house, but he kept it to himself; he liked a quiet life.

"And that woman," Mistress Dinah went on indignantly, "it's obvious what her condition is. My God, as if things weren't bad enough without that! Just think of all the gossip there will be! What can you have been thinking of?" Mistress Dinah paused for breath. "Of course, you can't say no to a young thing like that. She's only to look sweet at you and you can't do enough for her. You wouldn't have done as much for me, Isachar! Just make yourselves comfortable, good people, there's lots of straw in the cow-house . . . As though we were the only people in all the town who have a cow-house! Why didn't Simon give them a truss of straw? Because his wife wouldn't put up with such behaviour from her husband, do you understand? It's only I who am such a poor, downtrodden wife that I put up with it all without a murmur."

Old Isachar turned to the wall. Will she ever stop? he thought. She's partly right, but to make such a fuss about a poor —

"Bringing strangers into the house!" went on Mistress Dinah in righteous anger. "Who knows what sort of people they are? Now I shan't close an eye all night long for fright! But a lot you care whether I do or not! Everything for strangers, nothing for me! You might just once have a little consideration for your overworked and ailing wife! And in the morning I shall have to clear up after them! If the fellow really is a carpenter, why hasn't he got a job? And why must I be the one to have all this trouble? Are you listening, Isachar?"

But Isachar, with his face to the wall, pretended to be asleep.

"Heavens," sighed Dinah, "what a life I have of it! I shall be awake all night now worrying . . . And there he sleeps like a log! They might carry off the whole house while he's snoring away . . . My God, the worries I have!"

And there was silence except for old Isachar's regular snoring.

Towards midnight he was waked out of a doze by a woman's stifled moans. "Damn it," he thought in alarm, "that was in the cow-house next door! I only hope it won't wake Dinah . . . She'll start fussing again!"

And he lay without moving, as if he were asleep.

A moment later there was another moan. "God, be merciful! Oh God, grant that Dinah doesn't wake up," prayed old Isachar in anguish, but just then he felt Dinah stir beside him, raise herself and listen in strained attention. It'll be awful, thought Isachar, but he lay low and said nothing.

Mistress Dinah got up without a word, flung a rug round her and went out into the yard. Maybe she'll throw them out, thought Isachar helplessly. I'm not going to be mixed up in it. She can do what she likes . . .

After a strangely long and whispering moment, Dinah came back. Drowsily, Isachar thought he heard the snap and crackle of wood, but he decided not to move. Perhaps Dinah felt cold he thought, and was lighting a fire.

Then Dinah slipped away again quietly. Isachar half-opened his eyes and saw a kettle of water over the blazing fire. Whatever's that for? he thought in astonishment, and fell asleep again at once. He did not wake till Dinah went hurrying out into the yard with queer, eager, important little steps, carrying the steaming kettle.

Isachar was very puzzled. He got up and put on a few clothes. I must see what's going on, he said to himself, but in the doorway he ran into Dinah.

Gracious, what a hurry you're in! he wanted to snap at her, but he had no time.

"What are you standing there gaping for?" she burst out at him, and hurried into the yard again with her arms full of scraps of stuff and strips of linen. She turned on the threshold. "Go back to bed" she cried harshly, "and . . . . don't come bothering us and getting in the way, d'you hear?"

Old Isachar didn't go back to bed though. Instead he wandered out into the yard. At the door of the cow-house he saw a man standing at the door and went towards him. "Well, well" he muttered in a friendly whisper, "Dinah has turned you out and has taken charge, I suppose. She's a very bossy woman is Dinah . . ." The man nodded in response but said nothing. He looked dazed; probably exhausted, thought Isachar. Then Isachar became aware that there was something different about the night. There seemed to be a strange brightness about. He looked towards the sky and gasped in wonder. "Look, the star!" he said, "Did you ever see such a star?"

*Karel Capek (Adapted)*

1. At the start of the story Mistress Dinah was
   (a) weeping
   (b) crying
   (c) screaming
   (d) shouting.
   What sentence in the story supports your choice?
2. *'Riff-raff'* is a term used to describe
   (a) religious people
   (b) people who are looked down on
   (c) people who travel
   (d) saints.
3. Isachar was awakened by
   (a) Dinah's snores
   (b) the cries of a child
   (c) an alarm clock
   (d) a noise from the stable.
   What sentence in the story supports your choice?
4. *'Stifled'* means
   (a) loud
   (b) muffled
   (c) painful
   (d) clear.
5. Why was Mistress Dinah angry with her husband?
6. Why, according to Mistress Dinah, did Isachar let the couple stay in the cow-house?
7. Mistress Dinah describes herself as a *'downtrodden'* wife. Would you agree? Give reasons for your answer.
8. Using all the information given to you in the story, write a description of Isachar.
9. Why was Isachar worried that his wife would wake up?
10. What sentence in the story tells us that Mistress Dinah woke up?
11. What do you think happened when Mistress Dinah went out into the yard?
12. Explain how Mistress Dinah's attitude to the strangers changes over the course of the story.
13. Does Mistress Dinah's attitude to Isachar change over the course of the story? Refer to the story to support your answer.
14. Would you agree that this story deals with a special event in the history of mankind? Refer to the information in the story to explain your answer.

# Spectrum 2

[Answer Guidelines]

13. Fill in the blank spaces with words from the box below. The letters in each missing word have been mixed up.

Mistress Dinah's attitude to Isachar (1) _____ (2) _____ change over the course of the story. She (3) _____ at him, complains (4) _____ him and shows no (5) _____ for him. Later, when she is (6) _____ the woman in the cow-house, she is still unpleasant (7) _____ Isachar and (8) _____ harshly to him.

| | | | |
|---|---|---|---|
| twarods | sode | hlpineg | aobtu |
| skspea | perctes | nto | outhss |

## ASSIGNMENTS

**PERSONAL WRITING**

1. Write a letter that Isachar might have written to his brother, telling him about the events of that night and the days that followed.

2. (a) The story *Strangers* looks at the birth of Christ from an unusual point of view. Pick another event from the life of Christ and write about it from the point of view of a person who was there.
   (b) Pick an event from history and describe it from the point of view of an onlooker.

3. Write an essay or a short story entitled 'A Christmas Surprise'.

[Answer Guidelines]

2. (a) You could be a guest at the wedding feast at Cana; an onlooker at the Crucifixion or one of the soldiers guarding the tomb.
   (b) Two young people, walking on a beach, notice an unusual and frightening sight. They, of course, do not realise that they are witnessing (i) the arrival of the first Vikings to Ireland or (ii) the arrival of Christopher Columbus in the West Indies.

**Remember**
If you want to use an interesting word but you're not sure of its spelling — attempt it or look it up in a dictionary.

Strangers

## word power!

Find the words in the story which have similar meanings to each of the words and phrases below. The number in brackets after each one indicates the number of letters in the answer. The words appear in the story in the same order as the meanings given below.

CLUES
1. respectable (6)
2. people (4)
3. amazed (9)
4. speak under your breath (7)
5. angrily; feeling unjustly treated (11)
6. clear (7)
7. talk about other people's personal affairs (6)
8. at ease; warm (11)
9. actions (9)
10. someone kept in a low or inferior position (11)
11. unnecessary activity or unnecessary excitement (4)
12. someone who works too hard (10)
13. light sleep (4)
14. distress (7)
15. threw (5)
16. amazement (12)
17. confused (7)
18. doorway (9)
19. very tired (9)
20. unusual (7)

151

## 7 Flat-hunting

Betsy Brian and Mary went with they're parents to view the flat at Tollcross. It was a top floor flat, three flights up.

"Itll keep us fit," said Tom cheerfully, as they moved up the damp stone staircase towards the light.

The flat had prevously been occupied by an elderly woman who had just died. Dark stains blotched the wallpaper, obliterating roses and violets; the woodwork was the colour of treacle; water dripped from aincent taps into discoloured sinks.

"A lick of paint and it'll look quiet different?" said Tom.

"Yes, don't be put off by the decoration," said Willa. And a good scrub will soon get rid of the smell.

They walked around silently, gazing at the walls, the windows, the view across the street.

"It's a very good property," said the agent. "All the windows are intact, you'll notice. And the chimneys work. Coal fires are making a big comeback."

Two rooms were up a small narrow stair these were the rooms which Tom and Willa taught would be suitable for Mary and Brian. The rooms had sloping ceiling's and dormer windows that gave a view of the roof-tops across the street and the sky.

"Quite spacious aren't they?" said tom.

"Not bad," admitted Mary.

"I want this room," said Betsy, standing on her toes to luck out of the window.

"You are going to sleep downstairs beside us," said Willa.

"Are we going to buy it then" asked Mary.

"No, no, we haven't decided yet, but if we do—" A bell tolled somewhere below.

"Excuse me," said the Estate agent. "That'll be the next viewers. Im just about run off my feat. There are so many people after the place." He went clattering down the stairs whistling.

"They always say that," says Tom, "to make you feel keen."

# THE ANNIVERSARY
### Anon

## PART 1

At 8.00 a.m. Bill Jordan pulled into the lorry park. He switched off and pulled on the handbrake. Then he reminded himself that it was twenty-five years to the minute since he had come out of prison. He recalled looking back at the prison gates on this same day twenty-five years before and vowing that he would never go 'inside' again. Five years, for robbery and violence, had been the sentence and he had served the full term. Once he had struck a warder who had taunted him and his remission was automatically lost. That incident was Bill's salvation. He learned at last that violence did no good. From that day on, whenever people tried to provoke or upset him, he forced himself to react in the mildest possible way. As the years went by, his mates came to marvel at the calmness of the former convict. These were his thoughts as he strode towards the transport café. One more thought struck him. Apart from his lorry and four motor bikes parked side by side, the lorry park was empty.

As Bill made his way to the counter, he saw that the only customers were four Hell's Angels. They obviously owned the bikes outside. They were at the other end of the room and they had drawn chairs up to the juke box, which they had going full blast. One had his feet up on the machine itself. The noise was so deafening that they did not even notice Bill's entrance. The proprietor came out from the kitchen as Bill got to the counter. They had known each other for years, years when the café had been alive with customers at all hours of the day and night, before the new motorway was opened and the café had died.

"Usual?" asked the proprietor, and Bill nodded. The café owner went into the kitchen and returned soon afterwards with Bill's breakfast — sausage, bacon and egg, toast, marmalade and a huge mug of tea. Bill paid and took his tray. At that moment the juke box switched itself off and Bill's footsteps sounded unnaturally loud in the sudden silence as he took his tray to a table near the window.

*Spectrum 2*

## Questions & Assignments — PART 1

1. What was Bill Jordan's job?
2. What time of day did he leave prison? Give a reason for your answer by referring to the story.
3. *'Once he had struck a warder who had taunted him and his remission was automatically lost.'* Explain this sentence in more simple language.
4. Explain how the incident with the warder changed Bill's life.
5. What do you think was Bill's first impression of the other customers in the café?
6. What information is the reader given about the café?
7. What do you think is going to happen in the next episode? Give reasons for your answer.

### [Answer Guidelines]

5. Fill in the blank spaces with words from the box below. The letters in each missing word have been mixed up.

   As (1) _____ as Bill saw the gang in the café he (2) _____ expected trouble. He would know from (3) _____ that Hell's Angels (4) _____ cause trouble. The juke box was playing (5) _____ . This showed that they had no (6) _____ for anybody else in the café. Also, one of them had his feet on the jukebox. This showed an (7) _____ attitude.

   | | | |
   |---|---|---|
   | onfte | onso | aganrrot |
   | ulodly | caontisideron | eerienxpce |
   | obaprbly | | |

## PART 2

**B**ill's progress to the window table seemed to fascinate the four Hell's Angels at the far end of the room. They lost all interest in the juke box. The one with his feet up swung them down. He said to his mates, "Come on. Let's go and say good morning to the gentleman."

As Bill started to sip his tea, the four Hell's Angels came to the next table and each took a chair. The chairs were placed side by side facing Bill and the gang sat on them like spectators in the ringside seats at a wrestling match. They sat and watched Bill sip his tea. As Bill put down his mug and took up his knife and fork, one of the gang said, "Good morning". Bill did not answer. He had been through all this years before in prison. The fact that now there were four louts looking for a bit of fun made little difference. Bill had had years of practice in controlling his emotions and he had learned to behave in situations of this kind as though his tormentors were not there. He cut his sausage into pieces, stuck one on his fork, dipped it in his egg yolk and put it into his mouth as though eating in front of eight insolently staring eyes were the commonest thing in the world.

"You got cloth ears?" asked the one who was apparently the leader of the pack. "I said good morning."

Bill did not even look up. He stabbed a piece of bacon and carried on eating.

"Well now," went on the leader, "either you're a very bad talker or you just have bad manners. Come to think of it, you *are* bad-mannered. Here's the four of us all mad hungry and you stuffing away like a pig and you haven't offered one of us a bite to eat. Now Johnny here is famished, aren't you mate? Just fancy a piece of sausage, don't you Johnny? Well mate, have a piece on me." So saying, he took a piece of sausage from Bill's plate and gave it to Johnny. Johnny leaned over, dipped the sausage in Bill's egg, winked to his pals, and chewed at the morsel noisily.

"Mm. Good that," murmured Johnny. "You try some, Dave." At this a third Hell's Angel grabbed a piece of sausage, dusted it with salt and pepper, coated it with tomato sauce and popped it into his mouth.

Bill Jordan took a mouthful of toast and started to chew it, apparently unaware of the vultures around him.

The leader spoke up again. "Now, young Nosher here," he said, pointing to the fourth member of the group. "You don't like sausage much, do you, Nosher? You'd rather have bacon, wouldn't you, Nosher? Now there's a lovely rasher right on that plate there. Be my guest, Nosher, old mate." Thereupon the leader picked up a piece of Bill's bacon and gave it to Nosher. As he handed it over he said to Bill, "Oo! Sorry mate, I'm afraid I've spilt your tea."

## Questions & Assignments — PART 2

1. *'Come on. Let's go and say good morning to the gentleman.'* Describe the tone of voice in which you think these words were spoken. Give a reason for your answer.
2. What simile or comparison does the writer use to describe the gang?
3. (a) Describe, briefly, the behaviour of the gang as they sat opposite Bill.
   (b) How did he respond?
   (c) How did you think he would respond?
4. (a) What do you expect to happen in the final episode?
   (b) What would you like to see happening in the final episode?

## PART 3

Bill did not need telling. The hot liquid had gone through his jacket and soaked his shirt. Though it dripped off the table into a steady trickle down his trousers, he did not change his position. All he did was to feel in his pocket for a 10p piece which he placed on the table.

"What's that for?" asked Nosher. "More tea?"

"No. More music," said Bill, glancing at the juke box.

"Well you might be a bad talker," said the leader, "but you're not a bad sport. I'll put the Stones on for you myself."

"And I'll go and put some dry clothes on," said Bill.

As Bill went out through the door the Stones filled the room with deafening sound. A few minutes later the proprietor came out and started wiping the counter. The Hell's Angels, sensing the chance of more fun, came over to the counter.

"Very bad talker, that chap," the leader said.

"Which chap's that?"

"The feller that's just gone out."

"I don't know him," said the owner. "He's never been in here before."

"Well, he's certainly a bad talker."

"Oh?" said the owner. "He's a bad driver too."

"How do you know that if he hasn't been in here before?" asked the leader.

"Well," said the owner, "he's just driven a twenty-ton lorry straight over four motor bikes and he's gone straight out on to the road as if he never even saw them. You couldn't hear the noise because you had the juke box on so loud."

By then Bill Jordan was a kilometre away and smiling happily. It had been an unusual way of celebrating a twenty-fifth anniversary.

## Questions & Assignments — PART 3

1. Describe, briefly, what happens in the final episode.
2. Outline, in not more than five sentences, the plot of the story.
3. Discuss the difficulties that a film producer would have in making this story into a film.

# The Anniversary

**Word Power!**

Find the words in the story which have similar meanings to each of the words and phrases below. The number in brackets after each one indicates the number of letters in the answer. The words appear in the story in the same order as the meanings given below.

## CLUES

1. remembered (8)
2. promising to himself (6)
3. a punishment by a judge (8)
4. hit (6)
5. prison guard (6)
6. mocked; jeered (7)
7. time taken off a prison term for good conduct (9)
8. event; occurrence (8)
9. saving from ruin or trouble (9)
10. to make somebody angry (7)
11. respond (5)
12. admire (6)
13. criminal (7)
14. walked quickly (6)
15. observe (6)
16. owner of a business (10)
17. interest greatly (9)
18. observers of a sporting event (10)
19. thugs (5)
20. feelings (8)
21. people who make trouble for others (10)
22. feeling very hungry (8)
23. a piece of food (6)
24. looking quickly (8)

## PERSONAL WRITING

## ASSIGNMENTS

1. Describe an occasion when somebody's patience or kindness or wickedness made a particular impression on you.

2. Gangs. Write about how they form; the types of people who lead gangs; the people who are victims of gangs; the advantages and disadvamtages of being in a gang.

3. Write a short story entitled 'Revenge'.

**Remember**
A piece of dialogue is often a good way to start an essay or story.

## Points to Note

### PLOT

All stories have three basic ingredients: plot, characters and setting. The plot of a story – sometimes called the **'bones'** of a story – refers to the important events in the story and how they are **linked.** When writing about the plot of a story you should be able to pick out the main events and explain how they happened. In most plots, events take an **unexpected** turn at some point. This element of **surprise** is one reason why people enjoy reading stories.

#### Assignment — Plot

Below is a description of the plot of the story *The Anniversary* in seven sentences. Rewrite it filling in the blank sections.

> The story takes place (where?) and (what time?).
> Bill Jordan was a truck driver.
> He spent time in prison for striking someone.
> While there he vowed that he would never do so again.
> In the café a group of motorbike thugs taunt Bill as he . . .
> Despite . . . , he does not . . .
> Later . . .

### CONFLICT

All plots have conflict in them. The word conflict means a **struggle** or a **contest.** Conflict usually **arises** at an early point in the story when a character has a **goal** and is faced with an **obstacle** that **prevents** him from **achieving** that goal. The obstacle is usually another character (or characters) but sometimes it can be a natural obstacle such as a storm at sea.

Often the obstacle a character faces is his or her own **beliefs** and **principles.** When a character struggles with his or her beliefs and principles or is facing a **difficult decision** we can say that the character is experiencing **internal conflict** as the conflict is taking place within the character.

In all situations of conflict, one side eventually wins out. When this occurs we say that the conflict is **resolved.** Discovering the outcome of conflict – who wins and who loses – is one of the pleasures of reading.

# Night Train
## Nuala Lavin

"God knows, Jim, is there ever going to be an end to this weather?" remarked Dermot Duffy, the fireman, to his companion, Jimmy Gleeson.

"It's a dirty night to be heading for Cork right enough," agreed Jimmy as the pair of them strolled along the platform towards the locomotive that hissed quietly at the head of the Cork train.

It was a dirty night. The dim lamps of the station yard beyond the platform were shrouded in steam but the falling rain was still visible in these patches of light. The rain belt that had been over the country for the past three days still showed no sign of lifting. The station was quiet, even for a Friday night, and those few passengers heading south would have no trouble finding seats on the train.

"We'll break no speed records tonight, Jimmy!" joked Dermot as he climbed on to the footplate of the big locomotive. "You can say that again!"

The glowing heat from the firebox was welcome as the two men set about preparing for the journey. Dermot began stoking the fire while Jimmy cast his eye over the gauges in the smoky cab, checking steam pressure, brake pressures and water temperatures. Gazing across the bleak rain-soaked station yard with its network of tracks glistening through the darkness, Jimmy wished he was home in Inchicore, his feet up before the fire, listening to the wireless or doing the crossword in the evening paper. He was not looking forward to the journey, thundering through one hundred and sixty miles of darkness and driving rain while watching for each green signal indicating a clear track ahead. Yet the run to Cork on a summer's day was so different. From the cab, he enjoyed the view of the countryside with its constant changes brought by the ebb and flow of the seasons.

Still, he wasn't complaining. He had a job. Security. A steady wage. Even though the company was closing down many of the branch lines, it would be a long time before they decided to close the Dublin – Cork line and give him his walking papers! At least, he reflected, he was never forced to emigrate in search of work. Somehow, England never took his fancy. In his years on the railway he had seen many partings on station platforms and heartbreaking affairs they were. Young men and women bidding farewell to ageing parents and older men with battered suitcases leaving wives and children to head for the mail boat of Dunlaoghaire and on to the factories and building sites of England.

Jimmy's thoughts were interrupted by the shrill sound of the guard's whistle from the other end of the platform.

"We're off, Dermot," he remarked. He pushed a lever forward. The wheels spun for a brief moment on the wet track before gripping and the train, puffing loudly, slipped away from the platform, rumbled over the points in the station yard and on into the wet windy night.

The lights of the city gave way to the dimmer lights on the streets of the new suburb of Ballyfermot, as the train continued to gather speed. Then a brief glimpse of the brightly-lit Clondalkin

Paper Mills marked, for Jimmy, the outer limits of his native city before the train plunged into the darkness, heading for the open plains of Kildare.

"It's one awful night!" shouted Dermot as he offered Jimmy a cigarette from a crumpled packet of Woodbines, "I wouldn't be surprised if there was flooding on the line."

"Doubtful," replied Jimmy, "I've been on this run now for nearly twenty years and I have rarely seen floods. The line is banked well above ground level for most of the way. Still it's a night to keep a careful eye on the signals."

They lapsed into silence then as the roar of the wind rushing past the sides of the open cab, the hiss of steam and the rattle of the wheels on the rails combined to make conversation almost impossible.

Twenty minutes after pulling out of Kingsbridge station, the six-fifteen Dublin–Cork express thundered through the little station of Hazelhatch on the border of counties Dublin and Kildare. Jimmy noted the friendly wave from the figure in the signal box and the green glow of the signal light which promised a clear line ahead to Sallins.

As the train travelled on southwestward – over the swollen rivers and streams, past the rain-drenched fields, through the dimly-lit towns and stations – Jimmy's thoughts turned to home.

He missed Danny around the house, but then he knew that all fathers must face the day when their children will leave to set up homes of their own. It only seemed like a year or two since Danny took his first faltering steps. How he loved the walks along the canal banks watching and waving at the barges with their cargoes of stout. "Hey Da, won't I be a bargeman when I'm big?" and Jimmy would tell him that he would. Then came the engine driver phase when young Danny would proclaim that when he was big he'd be an engine driver "just like me Da!" But Jimmy Gleeson had different plans for his only child. If he had his way, Danny would never work on a steam loco – not for his son the long hours, the nights away from home, the constant deafening rattle, the taste of steam, smoke and coal dust always in his throat. No, times were changing. The changes were slow and almost imperceptible, but Jimmy could see them. There were now more opportunities for young lads starting out, especially those with brains. There were scholarships to be won, scholarships that would take care of school and college fees and would eventually lead to well-paid, secure and comfortable jobs.

Jimmy smiled to himself at how things turned out. Occasionally, he himself had to put a little pressure on Danny, but the boy's alert mind and love of reading made his school career as successful as Jimmy had hoped it would be. The scholarships came, first to the Brothers in Synge Street and then to study engineering at university. This led to what Jimmy regarded as a fine job in the E.S.B. Then came Anne, a cheerful and easygoing girl. Their wedding last June he would always remember . . .

Despite the weather, they were only five minutes late arriving at Limerick Junction. Only a few passengers boarded and soon the train was thundering onwards through the darkness and driving rain at seventy miles an hour.

His thoughts drifted again, this time to his own boyhood. His own father was only a series of blurred episodes in his memory, like the trailer of a film. He

remembered the halfpenny every Friday when his father arrived home from work. It could be exchanged for a bag of sweets at a pokey little corner shop. He had hazy memories of a trip to the sea at Bray one sunny day and paddling in the shallow wavelets, holding his father's hand; later, lines of men in uniforms, his father among them, marching to the strains of *It's a Long Way to Tipperary*. His most vivid memory was of his mother crying while he felt a mixture of pride and confusion as he gazed at his father framed in the front door with his smart uniform and kit-bag, setting off to fight the war to end all wars. He'd be back before the summer was over and they'd go to Bray again and they'd have great fun in the sea.

He didn't come back. All that came was a telegram and, later on, a Victoria Cross, awarded posthumously for 'bravery beyond the call of duty'. He still had them at home in a drawer. The telegram he must have read a thousand times. "James 'Stoker' Gleeson. Killed in action. Somme, July 3rd, 1916". Strange, he thought, how they included the nickname – 'Stoker' – on an official document. He never discovered how his father got the nickname ... but as a boy he was known as 'Stoker' Gleeson's son.

The glimpse of a bearded man frantically waving a red lamp, on a dimly lit platform brought Jimmy's thoughts sharply back to the present. Instinctively, he applied full brakes. He could feel the whole train shudder as the brakes gripped the spinning wheels, but the engine, thirty-two tons of steel, racing along wet rails was putting up a fight. Bracing himself for impact, Jimmy closed the throttle and shut off steam and the train slowly began to lose speed.

It was a little over a minute before the train finally came to rest and Jimmy breathed a silent prayer of thanks.

"What's wrong, Jimmy?" enquired

Dermot. "Why did you stop?"

"Didn't you see?"

"See what?"

"Back the line there at Castleduff station . . . someone on the platform waving a red lamp. I just caught a quick glimpse of him but I wasn't taking any chances."

"I noticed nothing, but we'd better climb down and see what's the problem," said Dermot.

The two men lowered themselves from the footplate and carefully made their way through the driving rain up along the side of the hissing engine to see what problem lay ahead. The weak beam from their lamp was no match for the pitch darkness and Jimmy wondered for a moment had he imagined the man with the beard and the red lamp. Then he knew it wasn't his imagination when, out of the blackness, came a lamp, heading shakily towards them, and the sound of a soft southern accent as the light drew closer.

In the lamplight stood an elderly man with wellington boots and a coat covered in mud.

"Dirty ol' night, men! I was worried that Barry wouldn't make it in time. But you got the warning. You're lucky that you're not dead!"

"Yes, we got the warning," replied Jimmy. "What's the problem?"

"A landslide. Five or six hundred yards further on. I was crossing a field near the line less than half an hour ago, meself and Barry, the son, checking on cattle, when we heard a loud rumbling noise. When we went to look we saw a pile of rocks, some very big, had come loose from the side of the cutting and rolled down on to the tracks. This rain must have loosened them. So I walked on up the line, and I sent Barry, my son, to run to the station at Castleduff and tell them the lines were blocked. I knew the Cork train was due to pass."

"We owe you a great deal of thanks, Mister," said Dermot, "that was quick thinking on your part."

"It sure was," echoed Jimmy, "thank God your son Barry made it to Castleduff station in time. Otherwise I'd hate to think what might have happened."

"What do we do now?" enquired the farmer.

"Nothing", replied Jimmy. "The lads in Castleduff will have telephoned ahead to Mallow and back to Limerick Junction. You can bet the line is closed now. There's no fear of any other train ploughing into the pile of rocks. So we just reverse the train back to Castleduff and tell the passengers what happened. The company will lay on buses to bring them to Cork. As for Dermot here and myself – we'll most likely head back to Dublin with an empty train."

"And yourself?" replied Dermot. "Do you live far from here?"

"Not too far. A half mile across the fields there," replied the man, nodding towards the embankment above them.

"You must be soaked to the skin. You need to get home and get dried off."

"Men, would you mind very much if I went back with you to Castleduff. You see, Barry will be there and we can head on home together . . ."

"Course not," replied Jimmy. "Come back here and climb on board!"

The three men climbed back on the locomotive and Jimmy slowly reversed the train back into Castleduff station. On their arrival, the station master ran down the platform and warmly greeted the three men on the locomotive.

"Am I glad to shake your hand!" he declared. "For a minute or two I thought . . . ," his voice trembled slightly, " . . .

I thought the worst was going to happen. Good man, Jerry. Your action saved a lot of lives."

Jimmy Gleeson and Dermot Duffy nodded in vigorous agreement. "We have things in control here," the station master continued, "I got a message through to Limerick Junction and to Mallow. The line is closed both ways and there are buses already on the way from Mallow to take the passengers on to Cork. I'll get the porter to explain what has happened and then we'll get you men a cup of tea – or maybe something stronger – in my parlour. I'm sure you could all do with one!"

"You can say that again!" replied Jerry. "And men, I'd like you to meet my son, Barry," he added as a young man, in his early twenties, emerged from the shadows and shyly shook hands with the driver and the fireman. "That was a great bit of running you did tonight, you deserve a gold medal for it," joked Dermot.

"And more!" added Jimmy.

A big fire blazed in the parlour of the station master's house, giving the room a comfortable glow.

The station master raised his glass.

"Good luck!" he declared. The others around the fire echoed the words of the station master.

"We certainly had our share of luck tonight!" remarked Jimmy.

"I would have thought Jerry that you had the biggest share," said the station master.

"Me?" said Jerry surprised. "Why me?"

"You were taking your life in your hands when you walked up the tracks with only a dim lamp to stop the express. You were lucky that the driver spotted your lamp and stopped. If there had been a crash you could have been caught in it too."

Puzzled looks flickered across the faces of Jerry and the crew of the engine.

"But I didn't stop the train. It was already stopped when I reached it. I thought you signalled it to stop after Barry warned you about the landslide," said Jerry to the station master.

"Barry warned me alright!" replied the station master. "But the trouble was that the train beat him to it. He ran in here with the news just as the train passed through. It was too late for me to take any action. So the question is," continued the station master turning to Jimmy Gleeson, the driver, "if Barry didn't warn you and nobody here warned you, why did you stop?" Jimmy shook his head in a half bemused, half-puzzled way. He seemed lost for words.

"Surely you saw him? At the end of the platform? Waving a red lamp?"

"Saw who?"

"I don't know *who*. I only caught a glimpse of him standing at the end of the platform waving a lamp. He had a beard, a very long one, a bit old fashioned looking like you'd see in the old photographs. The signalman with the long beard – he's the one who warned me."

"A signalman with a long beard, waving a lamp at the end of the platform. That's strange!" declared the station master.

"Why?" asked Dermot Duffy.

"Because, for a start, there's no signalman here with a beard and also because there wasn't a sinner at the end of that platform when you passed through," came the reply.

"That's true," added Barry. "We ran out and watched the last carriage go by. There was nobody at all on the platform."

A brief silence descended on the gathering, as they pondered on the mystery. Then Jerry spoke.

"A beard you said?"

The driver nodded, though slowly and a little uncertainly.

"There's not many fellows around here with beards but when I was a young lad they were all the go," continued Jerry. "In fact, I remember a signalman who worked here and who had a beard."

"I don't remember him," said the station master.

"He was around before your time," replied Jerry. "We had a nickname on him but it has slipped my mind. He was in the Great War, the Somme. He came back badly shell-shocked. For a year or two he couldn't talk about anything except the war, the poor devil. Made little or no sense. He eventually got over it and got a job here in the station. He's dead and gone now this last ten years, God rest him."

"Maybe it was his ghost you saw," the station master said with an uneasy laugh.

"I have it!" said Jerry, snapping his fingers, "'Stoker!' That's what they called him. He'd go around the village declaring *'Stoker Somebody-or-other saved my life'*. That's all he'd say. Nothing more. So that's how he got his nickname!"

"You don't remember who that somebody-or-other was?" asked Jimmy, almost in a whisper. "It wasn't Gleeson was it? Stoker Gleeson?"

"Now, come to think of it, it was!" said Jerry. "How did you know that?"

## Questions & Assignments

1. (a) Where does the opening episode of the story take place?
   (b) What details help us to picture the scene?
2. Why was Jimmy not looking forward to the journey?
3. Did Jimmy like his job? Refer to the story to support your answer.
4. What insights into emigration do we get from the story?
5. What do we learn about Jimmy's (a) son and (b) father?
6. Why did Jimmy apply the brakes?
7. (a) Who first noticed the landslide?
   (b) What did they do?
8. *"I'd hate to think what might have happened,"* said Jimmy. What do you think might have happened?
9. The station master praises Jerry for stopping the train. Why were Jerry and the engine crew puzzled by the station master's words?
10. Did Barry warn the station master in time about the landslide? Give a reason for your answer.
11. As the story closes the men *'pondered on the mystery'*. What was the mystery?
12. Explain what Jerry and his son Barry did in the story.
13. What do we learn about the man with the beard?
14. Would you describe this story as a ghost story? Explain your answer.
15. (a) The story ends with a question. Do you think the ending was effective? Give a reason.
    (b) Extend the ending by a paragraph or two, to include Jimmy's reply to Jerry's question and the reaction of the others in the room.

Night Train

## word power!

Find the words in the story which have similar meanings to each of the words and phrases below. The number in brackets after each one indicates the number of letters in the answer. The words appear in the story in the same order as the meanings given below.

CLUES
1. friend (9)
2. walked slowly (8)
3. engine for pulling trains (10)
4. able to be seen (7)
5. instruments for measuring (6)
6. shining (10)
7. go to live in a foreign country (8)
8. high-pitched (6)
9. came together (8)
10. canal boats (6)
11. always there; continuous (8)
12. clear (5)
13. shake violently (7)
14. a way of speaking in a particular region (6)
15. considered (8)

## Personal Writing

### Assignment

There are a number of old traditions surrounding ghosts. The most common ones are that they are (a) spirits of the dead, denied rest, until some wrong done to them or by them has been put right, (b) apparitions sent with a message or a warning to a living person and (c) hallucinations as a result of a guilty conscience.

Make up a Ghost Story set in your local area.

#### Remember
Always include a few sentences to help your reader 'see' where the events in your writing are taking place. One or two details will be enough to set the scene.

## Points to Note — GHOST STORIES

Gruesome events such as corpses coming back to life or coffins bursting open are the main elements of some ghost stories. Incidents that are less dramatic and yet still defy any normal explanation form the basis of others. The story *Night Train* is an example of the latter. A high speed train stops in the night; there is a suggestion that a ghost was involved. The writer doesn't claim any ghostly involvement. He merely tells us what those involved saw (or thought they saw) and lets us decide for ourselves.

The following **Spot the Errors** exercise is aimed at sharpening your basic writing skills. Spot the 20 errors in the Passage below and rewrite the passage correctly. (Note: Refer to the Guidelines on pages 1—15.)

## 8  Searching for Kate

Two Policemen came and writ down the details: Kates age, description and when she was last seen. Peter felt sick as he described her dark red, curly hair, snub nose and green duffel coat. Why didn't they go out and start searching, Peter wanted to shout at them, instead of all this writing in notebooks?

At last the policemen took they're flashlights and went to look. Peter acommpanied them but aunt Ethel would not allow maria to leave the house. She seemed to think that if she let her out of her site she might never see her again either.

They went into every passage, going through to the back green where they flashed their lights and Peter called out "Kate" as instructed. His voice sounded thin and week, drifting up into the night air. It was bitterly cold. Frost was silvering over the grass and the clothes-lions glitered.

The door leading into the sixth back green was stuck. One of the policemen put his shoulder to it and it jerked open.

"Kate!" called Peter, but no one answered.

Then they saw her lying in a huddle on the ground beside the wall. Peter reached her first her face felt as cold as marbell.

"Is she dead" he cried.

"Asleep more likely." the policeman lifted her gently up into his arms. But she's frozen, poor girl. Just as well she didn't lie here all night. We'll need a doctor quickly.

Kate's eyelids flickered and settled again. They carried her upstairs and laid her, rapped in a quilt, in front of the fire. The doctor came soon and said he thought they'd better have her taken to hospital.

# The Goalkeeper's Revenge
## *Bill Naughton*

Sim Dalt had two long, loose arms, spindly legs, a bony face with gleaming brown eyes, and, from the age of twelve, was reckoned to be a bit touched in the head.

Goalkeeping was the main interest in Sim's life. In his nursery days the one indoor pastime that satisfied him was when his mother kicked a rubber ball from the living-room into the kitchen, while Sim stood goal at the middle door. It was rare even then that he let one pass.

He later attended Scuttle Street elementary school, where he was always gnawed with the ferocious wish for four o'clock, when he could dash to the cinder park to play goalie for some team or other. Even in the hot summer days, Sim would cajole a few non-players into a game of football. "Shoot 'em in, chaps," he would yell, after lovingly arranging the heaps of jackets for the goalposts, "the harder the better."

At twelve he was picked as goalkeeper for his school team. "If you let any easy 'uns through," the captain, Bob Thropper, threatened him, "I'll bust your shins in!"

But he had no need to warn Sim, for it was rare indeed that anyone could get a ball past him.

It was near the end of the season, and Scuttle Street were at the top of the league and in the final for the Mayor's Shield, when a new and very thorough inspector visited the school. He found Sim's scholastic ability to be of such a low order that he directed him at once to Clinic Street special school.

"I suppose you could continue to play for us until the end of the season," said Mr. Speckle, at a meeting of the team, "and then, at least, you'll be sure of a medal."

"What, sir!" interposed Bob Thropper. "*A cracky school* lad play for us? Ee, sir, that *would* be out of order!"

"But what shall we do about a goalkeeper?" asked the teacher.

"Goalkeepers!" snorted Bob. "I could buy 'em and sell 'em."

"What," asked Sim, staring at Bob, "what do you mean, buy 'em an' sell 'em?"

"I mean that they're ten a penny," grunted Bob, "especially daft 'uns." And having made his point he snapped: "Off with them togs, mate — we want 'em for our next man." And Sim sadly removed his boots, stockings, and shorts, but when it came to the jersey, he hesitated, but Bob grabbed at it: "Buy 'em an' sell 'em," he growled, "that's me."

There was a tear close to Sim's eye. "I'll never buy you," he hissed, "but I might *sell* you one day."

In adapting himself to his new life he was quick enough to grasp any advantage it might offer. He organised games in the schoolyard, and for two years enjoyed some hectic, if not polished, goalkeeping. And at the age of fifteen, when his mother took him round to different factories for work, he simulated idiocy so as not to be taken on.

"Now stop this shinanikin," his mother scolded him, "you're no more barmy than I am. And you know it."

"You shoulda told the school-inspector that," remarked Sim.

Every morning, with the 'normal intelligence' boys gaping enviously at him through the factory windows, Sim would set out for the cinder park, bouncing and heading a football along the street.

At the age of nineteen he accepted his first job, since it did not interfere with his way of life; also, it had possibilities. It was at Brunt's Amusement Arcade, where the chief attraction was a 'Beat the Goalie' game. There were goalposts that appeared to be full size, and a real football, and all comers were invited to try to score. It cost threepence for a try, and anyone who scored received sixpence in return. Sim, of course, got the job of goalkeeper.

Maggie Brunt, the owner, was a wizened, red-eyed woman. "How's it goin', lad?" she would say, giving sly slaps of apparent goodwill on various parts of the goalkeeper's person. By this cunning form of greeting she had caught out a stream of employees who had been fiddling — having one pocket for Maggie and one for themselves.

She tried it out on Sim, time after time, and never once was there the faintest jingle of metal, until finally she decided that the lad must be simple, if not honest. The fact was that Sim — who did things with singular efficiency when he had to — had constructed a special pocket, copiously insulated with cottonwool, and provided with various sections for different coins. Had Maggie turned him upside-down and shaken him like a pepper-pot she would not have heard the faintest jingle, so expertly was it contrived.

There came a day, after some six thrifty years, when Maggie decided to sell the Arcade — and Sim was able to buy it from her. "Bless you, lad," sighed Maggie, "they say you're gone in the head, but I wish there were more like you."

"It wouldn't do," remarked Sim, and not without a touch of regret he removed the cottonwool from his pocket.

Bob Thropper's visit to the Arcade was the start of a remarkably prosperous boom for Sim. Bob was a thickset, dark-jowled footballer by this time, and the idol of the Hummerton crowd. His tremendous kicking power had broken many goal-nets, winded or knocked senseless a number of goalkeepers, and on one occasion, it was said, had actually smashed a crossbar.

One night, just after a cup-tie victory, Bob and his team-mates, merry though not drunk, were passing the Arcade, when one suggested having some sport with Sim.

"Skipper," whispered Stan Mead, "you smash one in!"

Stan Mead dived into his pocket for threepence, when Sim called out: "Like to make it pounds instead of pence?"

The challenge was taken up at once, and in a moment eleven pound notes were flung down, and Sim covered these with as many out of his pocket. Then Bob Thropper drew back, took his short, confident run, and let go one of his famous drives. Sim was up like a flash, and brought it down with a stylish assurance.

Then with a casual air he threw the ball back. "Are you covering the twenty-two quid?" he asked.

The money was covered in two minutes. "What about waiting till somebody nips off for your football boots?" asked Stan Mead.

Bob shook his head. "I could lick this loon," he snorted, "in my bare feet" — and with that he took a second shot. It was good — but not good enough. Sim leapt and caught it on his chest. Bob's face went darker than ever. "Fetch my boots," he hissed at Stan Mead, "an' I'll smash him to bits."

A huge crowd swayed the Arcade when Bob Thropper prepared to make the third attempt. The forty-four pounds had been covered, so that there was a pile of pound notes on an orange box, with a brick on top of them. After having his boots tied up, Bob Thropper removed his jacket, took off his collar and tie, and nodded to Stan Mead to place the ball. The crowd went silent as he took the short run, and then kicked.

The ball flashed forward — it went like lightning, a knee-high shot. "*Goal!*" yelled a voice from behind. But a long thin figure whizzed through the air. There was a thud, the figure dropped to the ground. Nobody could be sure what had happened — until Sim stood up. His face was white. But he had the ball clutched against his heart. Slowly he went towards the orange box and picked up the money. "Closing time!" he whispered in a low, clear voice. The crowd set up a sudden cheer — volley after volley.

From that night on Sim Dalt became famous as "The goalie Bob Thropper could never beat!" The Arcade flourished. Sim got offers from many teams, including one from Hummerton club itself.

"When I join your club," he told them, "it'll not be as a goalie."

And it was not many years before Sim's words came true, for there came a chance for him to buy a considerable portion of club shares, and he was voted a director.

One September morning early in the season he was taken round and introduced to all the players.

"Meet Bob Thropper," said the co-director, "our most famous centre-forward."

Sim looked at the man before him. "Centre-forwards," he remarked significantly, "I can buy 'em an' sell 'em — or," he added, "I can at least sell 'em."

Some vague and long-forgotten moment of memory was evoked in Bob Thropper at these words.

He stood there frowning. Then, as Stan Mead nudged him and spoke, it all came back to him clearly.

"Bob, you'd better be looking for a nice pub to retire to," Stan whispered feelingly, "because this chap means it."

## Questions & Assignments

1. What is your first impression of
   (a) Sim Dalt?
   (b) Bob Thropper?
2. Explain fully why Sim was dropped from the Scuttle Street school team.
3. Why was Sim not offered a factory job?
4. Describe his first *'job'*.
5. How did Maggie Brunt check if her employees were *'fiddling'*?
6. How did Sim manage to buy the arcade?
7. Would you agree that Sim Dalt got double revenge on Bob Thropper? Explain your answer.
8. Did you consider the ending satisfying? Why?
9. Imagine that you are a judge in a short story competition. Mark the story out of ten and explain briefly why you marked it as you did.

## Word Power!

Find the words in the story which have similar meanings to each of the words and phrases below. The number in brackets after each one indicates the number of letters in the answer. The words appear in the story in the same order as the meanings given below.

### CLUES

1. very thin (7)
2. hobby (7)
3. persuade (6)
4. warned of punishment (10)
5. unusual (4)
6. interrupted (10)
7. snapped (7)
8. paused for a moment (9)
9. making a change to suit new conditions (8)
10. exciting and energetic (6)
11. pretended (9)
12. jealously (9)
13. took up an offer (8)
14. shrivelled (7)
15. protected (9)
16. thought out (9)
17. sorrow (6)
18. an offer of a contest (9)
19. appearing relaxed and unconcerned (6)
20. dull sound (4)
21. held tightly (8)
22. grew successful (10)
23. part (7)
24. hazy; unclear (5)
25. called to mind (6)

## About Bill Naughton

Bill Naughton was born in Co. Roscommon but left as a child to live in the north of England when his parents emigrated. He was a successful writer of short stories, plays and screenplays. He died in 1992 when he was in his seventies.

# The Goalkeeper's Revenge

## Points to Note — INTEREST

It is likely that, at an early stage in the story *The Goalkeeper's Revenge* you wanted Sim Dalt to get the better of Bob Thropper. Good authors create characters that **interest** the readers. We **admire** or **pity** certain characters in a story and want them to succeed; we **dislike** other characters and **hope** that they will meet their downfall. Either way the author will have succeeded in creating interest when a reader feels strongly about a character. If we had no interest in a character we would not be interested in reading on to find out what happens to that character.

When writing about how a story grabbed your interest you should identify the character(s) or situation that has aroused your interest and outline your feelings on the character(s).

## WORD PUZZLE

Solve each of the word puzzles below. Some clues are provided to help you. The clues are not in the same order as the anagrams. For example, the first clue 'To give the wrong information' refers to puzzle 14 — 'MSIINORFM'. Can you spot a **similarity** in the spelling patterns of each word?

1. SSUEMI
2. MTSEAIK
3. OMNITCUSCD
4. ILSAMY
5. SFMTII
6. ISFTNRUOME
7. MELSPLIS
8. ALMSIED
9. RNIMTPSI
10. HAMSIP
11. DMSUDNRENATSI
12. RIEMS
13. EISBEARLM
14. MSIINORFM
15. SITM

- To give the wrong information
- Spell wrongly
- One who hoards money
- To lead astray
- Not the right size
- Unfortunate accident
- Bad behaviour
- Bad luck
- In bad spirits
- To lose
- Not understand fully
- Fog
- Error in a book
- Treat wrongly
- Incorrect idea or action

**The following Spot the Errors exercise is aimed at sharpening your basic writing skills. Spot the 20 errors in the Passage below and rewrite the passage correctly. (Note: Refer to the Guidelines on pages 1—15.)**

## 9     Gilly Plays Basketball

Just then a ball bounced lose from the basketball game nearby and rushed towards her. She grabbed it, She hugged it and ran over to the basket and through it up, but she had been in to much of a hurry. The ball touched the rim but refused to go in for her. Angrily she jumped and caught it before it bounced. She was dimly aware of a protest from the players. She aimed again, this time with care. The ball arched and sank cleanly into the net. She pushed someone out of the way and grabed it just below the net.

Hey! Who do you think you are shouted one of the boys.

Another of the boy's, as tall as she, tried to pull the ball from her hands. She spinned round, nocking him to the concrete, and shot again, bouncing the ball off the back-board and neatly into the net. She grabbed it once more.

Now all the boys where after her. She began to run across the playground, laughing and clutching the ball she could here the boys screaming behind her, but she was more faster than them. She ran all the way back to the basketball post and threw the ball again, missing wildly in her glee. The boys tried to grab the ball from her. She fought back, scratching and kicking for all she was worth.

"Hey! Hey! Whats going on here?" Miss harris towered above them. The fighting evaporated under her glare. She marched all seven of them to the principle's office. Gilly noted with satisfaction a long red line down the tall boys cheek. She'd actually drawn blood in the fracas. The boys looked a lot worse than she felt. Six to one — pretty good odds, even for Gilly.

# Spit Nolan
## Bill Naughton

Spit Nolan was a pal of mine. He was a thin lad with a bony face that was always pale, except for two rosy spots on his cheekbones. He had quick brown eyes, short, wiry hair, rather stooped shoulders, and we all knew that he had only one lung. He had had a disease which in those days couldn't be cured, unless you went away to Switzerland, which Spit certainly couldn't afford. He wasn't sorry for himself in any way, and in fact we envied him, because he never had to go to school.

Spit was the champion trolley-rider of Cotton Pocket; that was the district in which we lived. He had a very good balance, and sharp wits, and he was very brave, so that these qualities, when added to his skill as a rider, meant that no other boy could ever beat Spit on a trolley – and every lad had one.

Our trolleys were simple vehicles for getting a good ride downhill at a fast speed. To make one you had to get a stout piece of wood about five feet in length and eighteen inches wide. Then you needed four wheels, preferably two pairs, large ones for the back and smaller ones for the front. However, since we bought our wheels from the scrapyard, most trolleys had four odd wheels. Now you had to get a poker and put it in the fire until it was red hot, and then burn a hole through the wood at the front. Usually it would take three or four attempts to get the hole bored through. Through this hole you fitted the giant nut-and-bolt, which acted as a swivel for the steering. Fastened to the nut was a strip of wood, on to which the front axle was secured by bent nails. A piece of rope tied to each end of the axle served for steering. Then a knob of margarine had to be slanced out of the kitchen to grease the wheels and bearings. Next you had to paint a name on it: *Invincible* or *Dreadnought*, though it might be a motto: *Death before Dishonour* or *Labour and Wait*. That done, you then stuck your chest out, opened the back gate, and wheeled your trolley out to face the critical eyes of the world.

Spit spent most mornings trying out new speed gadgets on his trolley, or searching Enty's scrapyard for good wheels. Afterwards he would go off and have a spin down Cemetery Brew. This was a very steep road that led to the cemetery, and it was very popular with trolley-drivers as it was the only macadamised hill for miles around, all the others being cobblestones for horse traffic. Spit used to lie in wait for a coal-cart or other horse-drawn vehicle, then he would hitch *Egdam* to the back to take it up the brew. *Egdam* was a name in memory of a girl called Madge, whom he had once met at Southport Sanatorium, where he had spent three happy weeks. Only I knew the meaning of it, for he had reversed the letters of her name to keep his love a secret.

It was the custom for lads to gather at the street corner on summer evenings and, trolleys parked at hand, discuss trolleying, road surfaces, and also show off any new gadgets. Then, when Spit gave the sign, we used to set off for Cemetery Brew. There was scarcely any evening traffic on the roads in those days, so that we could have a good practice before our evening race. Spit, the unbeaten champion, would inspect every trolley and rider, and allow a start which was reckoned on the size of the wheels and the weight of the rider. He was always the last in the line of starters, though no matter how long a start he gave it seemed impossible to beat him. He knew that road like the palm of his hand, every tiny lump or pothole, and he never came a cropper.

Among us he took things easy, but when occasion asked for it he would go all out. Once he had to meet a challenge from Ducker Smith, the champion of the Engine Row gang. On that occasion Spit borrowed a wheel from the baby's pram, removing one nearest the wall, so it wouldn't be missed, and confident he could replace it before his mother took baby out. And after fixing it to his trolley he made that ride on what was called the 'belly-down' style – that is, he lay full stretch on his stomach, so as to avoid wind resistance. Although Ducker got away with a flying start he had not that sensitive touch of Spit, and his frequent bumps and swerves lost him valuable inches, so that he lost the race with a good three lengths. Spit arrived home just in time to catch his mother as she was wheeling young Georgie off the doorstep, and if he had not made a dash for it the child would have fallen out as the pram overturned.

It happened that we were gathered at the street corner with our trolleys one evening when Ernie Haddock let out a hiccup of wonder: "Hey, chaps, wot's Leslie got?"

We all turned our eyes on Leslie Duckett, the plump son of the local publican. He approached us on a brand-new trolley, propelled by flicks of his foot on the pavement. From a distance the thing had looked impressive, but now, when it came up among us, we were too dumbfounded to speak. Such a magnificent trolley had never been seen! The riding board was of solid oak, almost two inches thick; four new wheels with pneumatic tyres; a brake, a bell, a lamp, and a spotless steering-cord. In front was a plate on which was the name in bold lettering: *The British Queen*.

"It's called after the pub," remarked Leslie. He tried to edge it away from Spit's trolley, for it made *Egdam* appear horribly insignificant. Voices had been stilled for a minute, but now they broke out:

"Where'd it come from?"

"How much was it?"

"Who made it?"

Leslie tried to look modest. "My dad had it specially made to measure," he said, "by the gaffer of the Holt Engineering Works."

He was a nice lad, and now he wasn't sure whether to feel proud or ashamed. The fact was, nobody had ever had a trolley made by somebody else. Trolleys were swopped and so on, but no lad had ever owned one that had been made by other hands. We went quiet now, for Spit had calmly turned his attention to it, and was examining *The British Queen* with his expert eye. First he tilted it, so that one of the rear wheels was off the ground, and after giving it a flick of the finger he listened intently with his ear close to the hub.

"A beautiful ball-bearing race," he remarked, "it runs like silk." Next he turned his attention to the body. "Grand piece of timber, Leslie – though a trifle on the heavy side. It'll take plenty of pulling up a brew."

"I can pull it," said Leslie, stiffening.

"You might find it a shade *front-heavy*," went on Spit, "which means it'll be hard on the steering unless you keep it well oiled."

"It's well made," said Leslie. "Eh, Spit?"

Spit nodded. "Aye, all the bolts are counter-sunk," he said, "everything chamfered and fluted off to perfection. But—"

"But what?" asked Leslie.

"Do you want me to tell you?" asked Spit.

"Yes, I do," answered Leslie.

"Well, it's got none of *you* in it," said Spit.

"How do you mean?" says Leslie.

"Well, you haven't so much as given it a single tap with a hammer," said Spit. "That trolley will be a stranger to you to your dying day."

"How come," said Leslie, "since I *own* it?"

Spit shook his head. "You don't own it," he said, in a quiet, solemn tone. "You own nothing in this world except those things you have taken a hand in the making of, or else you've earned the money to buy them."

Leslie sat down on *The British Queen* to think this one out. We all sat round, scratching our heads.

"You've forgotten to mention one thing," said Ernie Haddock to Spit, "what about the *speed*?"

"Going down a steep hill," said Spit, "she should hold the road well – an' with wheels like that she should certainly be able to shift some."

"Think she could beat *Egdam*?" ventured Ernie.

"That," said Spit, "remains to be seen."

Ernie gave a shout: "A challenge race! *The British Queen* versus *Egdam*!"

"Not tonight," said Leslie. "I haven't got the proper feel of her yet."

"What about Sunday morning?" I said.

Spit nodded. "As good a time as any."

Leslie agreed. "By then," he said in a challenging tone, "I'll be able to handle her."

Chattering like monkeys, eating bread, carrots, fruit, and bits of toffee, the entire gang of us made our way along the silent Sunday-morning streets for the big race at Cemetery Brew. We were split into two fairly equal sides.

Leslie, in his serge Sunday suit, walked ahead, with Ernie Haddock pulling *The British Queen*, and a bunch of supporters around. They were optimistic, for Leslie had easily outpaced every other trolley during the week, though as yet he had not run against Spit.

Spit was in the middle of the group behind, and I was pulling *Egdam* and keeping the pace easy, for I wanted Spit to keep fresh. He walked in and out among us with an air of imperturbability that, considering the occasion, seemed almost godlike. It inspired a fanatical confidence in us. It was such that Chick Dale, a curly-headed kid with a soft skin like a girl's, and a nervous lisp, climbed up on to the spiked railings of the cemetery, and, reaching out with his thin fingers, snatched a yellow rose. He ran in front of Spit and thrust it into a small hole in his jersey.

"I pwesent you with the wose of the winner!" he exclaimed.

"And I've a good mind to present you with a clout on the lug," replied Spit, "for pinching a flower from a cemetery. An' what's more, it's bad luck." Seeing Chick's face, he relented. "On second thoughts, Chick, I'll wear it. Ee, wot a 'eavenly smell!"

Happily we went along, and Spit turned to a couple of lads at the back. "Hey, stop that whistling. Don't forget what day it is – folk want their sleep out."

A faint sweated glow had come over Spit's face when we reached the top of the hill, but he was as majestically calm as ever. Taking the bottle of cold water from his trolley seat, he put it to his lips and rinsed out his mouth in the manner of a boxer.

The two contestants were called together by Ernie.

"No bumpin' or borin'," he said.

They nodded.

"The winner," he said, "is the first who puts the nose of his trolley past the cemetery gates."

They nodded.

"Now, who," he asked, "is to be judge?"

Leslie looked at me. "I've no objection to Bill," he said. "I know he's straight."

I hadn't realized I was, I thought, but by heck I will be!

"Ernie here," said Spit, "can be starter."

With that Leslie and Spit shook hands.

"Fly down to them gates," said Ernie to me. He had his father's pigeon-timing watch in his hand. "I'll be setting 'em off dead on the stroke of ten o'clock."

I hurried down to the gates. I looked back and saw the supporters lining themselves on either side of the road. Leslie was sitting upright on *The British Queen*. Spit was settling himself to ride belly-down. Ernie Haddock, handkerchief raised in the right hand, eye gazing down on the watch in the left, was counting them off – just like when he tossed one of his father's pigeons.

"Five – four – three – two – one – *Off!*"

Spit was away like a shot. That vigorous toe push sent him clean ahead of Leslie. A volley of shouts went up from his supporters, and groans from Leslie's. I saw Spit move straight to the middle of the road camber. Then I ran ahead to take up my position at the winning-post.

When I turned again I was surprised to see that Spit had not increased the lead. In fact, it seemed that Leslie had begun to gain on him. He had settled himself into a crouched position, and those perfect wheels combined with his extra weight were bringing him up with Spit. Not that it seemed possible he could ever catch him. For Spit, lying flat on his trolley, moving with a fine balance, gliding, as it were, over the rough patches, looked to me as though he were a bird that might suddenly open out its wings and fly clean into the air.

The runners along the side could no longer keep up with the trolleys. And now, as they skimmed past the half-way mark, and came to the very steepest part, there was no doubt that Leslie was gaining. Spit had never ridden better; he coaxed *Egdam* over the tricky parts, swayed with her, gave her her head, and guided her. Yet Leslie, clinging grimly to the steering-rope of *The British Queen*, and riding the rougher part of the road, was actually drawing level. Those beautiful ball-bearing wheels, engineer-made, encased in oil, were holding the road, and bringing Leslie along faster than spirit and skill could carry Spit.

Dead level they sped into the final stretch. Spit's slight figure was poised fearlessly on his trolley, drawing the extremes of speed from her. Thundering beside him, anxious but determined, came Leslie. He was actually drawing ahead – and forcing his way to the top of the camber. On they came like two charioteers – Spit delicately edging to the side, to gain inches by the extra downward momentum. I kept my eyes fastened clean across the road as they came belting past the winning-post.

First past was the plate *The British Queen*. I saw that first. Then I saw the heavy rear wheel jog over a pothole and strike Spit's front wheel – sending him in a swerve across the road. Suddenly then, from nowhere, a charabanc came speeding round the wide bend.

Spit was straight in its path. Nothing could avoid the collision. I gave a cry of fear as I saw the heavy solid tyre of the front wheel hit the trolley. Spit was flung up and his back hit the radiator. Then the driver stopped dead.

I got there first. Spit was lying on the macadam road on his side. His face was white and dusty, and coming out between his lips and trickling down his chin was a rivulet of fresh red blood. Scattered all about him were yellow rose petals.

"Not my fault," I heard the driver shouting. "I didn't have a chance. He came straight at me."

The next thing we were surrounded by women who had got out of the charabanc. And then Leslie and all the lads came up.

"Somebody send for an ambulance!" called a woman.

"I'll run an' tell the gatekeeper to telephone," said Ernie Haddock.

"I hadn't a chance," the driver explained to the women.

"A piece of his jersey on the starting-handle there . . ." said someone.

"Don't move him," said the driver to a stout woman who had bent over Spit. "Wait for the ambulance."

"Hush up," she said. She knelt and put a silk scarf under Spit's head. Then she wiped his mouth with her little handkerchief.

He opened his eyes. Glazed they were, as though he couldn't see. A short cough came out of him, then he looked at me and his lips moved.

*"Who won?"*

"Thee!" blurted out Leslie. "Tha just licked me. Eh Bill?"

"Aye," I said, "old *Egdam* just pipped *The British Queen*."

Spit's eyes closed again. The women looked at each other. They nearly all had tears in their eyes. Then Spit looked up again, and his wise, knowing look came over his face. After a minute he spoke in a sharp whisper:

"Liars. I can remember seeing Leslie's back wheel hit my front 'un. I didn't win – I lost." He stared upward for a few seconds, then his eyes twitched and shut.

The driver kept repeating how it wasn't his fault, and next thing the ambulance came. Nearly all the women were crying now, and I saw the look that went between the two men who put Spit on a stretcher – but I couldn't believe he was dead. I had to go into the ambulance with the attendant to give him particulars. I went up the step and sat down inside and looked out the little window as the driver slammed the doors. I saw the driver holding Leslie as a witness. Chick Dale was lifting the smashed-up *Egdam* on to the body of *The British Queen*. People with bunches of flowers in their hands stared after us as we drove off. Then I heard the ambulance man asking me Spit's name. Then he touched me on the elbow with his pencil and said:

"Where *did* he live?"

I knew then. That word 'did' struck right into me. But for a minute I couldn't answer. I had to think hard, for the way he said it made it suddenly seem as though Spit Nolan had been dead and gone for ages.

*Spectrum 2*

### Questions & Assignments

1. What evidence in the first paragraph suggests that Spit Nolan did not belong to a rich family?
2. According to the narrator what were the qualities of a good trolley rider?
3. List the items needed to make a trolley.
4. Why was Cemetery Brew different from other roads in the district?
5. How do we know that Spit Nolan and the narrator were very close friends?
6. On two occasions the narrator tells us that Spit Nolan was impossible to beat in a trolley race. Find the sentences in the story where we are told this and write them out.
7. Describe the Ducker Smith episode from Spit's point of view.
8. Why do you think that Leslie *'wasn't sure whether to feel proud or ashamed'*?
9. During your first reading of this story
    (a) Who did you want to win the race? Why?
    (b) Who did you think would win? Why?
10. (a) Explain why Spit had a good start in the race?
    (b) What helped Leslie catch up with him?
    (c) What detail in the story gives us a good idea of the speed at which the riders travelled?
11. Explain how the accident happened.
12. Close to the ending of the story our fears grow that Spit will not survive. What details does the narrator include to cause us to fear that Spit will die? At what stage do we know for certain?
13. Do you regard this story as sad or happy? Give reasons for your answer. (Think for a few moments before you make your choice!)
14. Imagine that you are a judge in a short story competition. Mark the story out of ten and explain briefly why you marked it as you did.
15. Both *Spit Nolan* and *The Goalkeeper's Revenge* were written by Bill Naughton. In what ways are the two stories similar? Consider not only the plots but also the settings and the way the stories are told.

### [Answer Guidelines]

7. Remember in your answer that it is Spit who is speaking. You might begin as follows:

*One day Ducker Smith challenged me to a race. Ducker Smith was the champion trolley rider of the Engine Row gang.*

Your answer should be at least six sentences in length.

## PERSONAL WRITING

# ASSIGNMENTS

1. Describe an occasion when you or friends of yours were involved in an accident. Write at least three paragraphs:

   **Paragraph 1:** The events that led up to the accident
   **Paragraph 2:** The accident itself
   **Paragraph 3:** What happened after the accident.

   Begin each new paragraph a little in from the margin on a new line.

**Remember**
Names of people always begin with a capital letter.

2. The opening paragraph of *Spit Nolan* consists of a short pen portrait of Spit Nolan.
   Write pen portraits of two people you know and two imaginary (fictitious) people, <u>closely</u> modelled on this opening paragraph. Each portrait should consist of at least <u>five</u> sentences.

   **Sentence 1:** General introduction.
   　　　'Tom Thumb was a . . . pal/neighbour/ teacher . . .'
   **Sentences 2 and 3:** Appearance.
   　　　'He was . . . , with a . . . and a . . .'
   **Sentence 4:** An unusual or interesting fact about the person.
   **Sentence 5:** The person's attitude to life or a striking characteristic.
   (You could include an additional sentence — **Sentence 6:** What other people thought of the person.)

## Points to Note — EXPECTATION

When Ernie Haddock appears on the street with his new trolley in the story *Spit Nolan,* we expect something interesting to develop.

In good stories the readers' **expectations** are **built up** when an author leads them to think that something interesting is **likely to happen.** We may meet a character who quickly finds himself in a situation where a particular thing is likely to happen. We keep turning the pages to find out if our **expectations** will be **fulfilled.** This sense of expectation is exciting and is one of the elements that makes a plot gripping and enjoyable.

When writing about how a story aroused your expectations you should state your expectations clearly and how the author creates these expectations. It may be through conflict, details of events or setting, dialogue, inner thoughts of a character . . . etc.

### Word Power!

Find the words in the story which have similar meanings to each of the words and phrases below. The number in brackets after each one indicates the number of letters in the answer. The words appear in the story in the same order as the meanings given below.

#### CLUES

1. were jealous of (6)
2. attached; tied (8)
3. fault-finding (8)
4. put back to front (8)
5. talk about (7)
6. examine closely (7)
7. very sure (9)
8. came towards (10)
9. silent from a surprise or a shock (11)
10. filled with air (9)
11. unimportant; not standing out (13)
12. skillful (6)
13. carefully (8)
14. expecting things to go well (10)
15. grabbed suddenly or quickly (8)
16. barely noticeable (5)
17. people involved in a contest (11)
18. strong; energetic (8)
19. a slight bulge along the middle of a road (6)
20. without warning (8)
21. holding tightly (8)
22. force created by a moving body (8)
23. a crash between two objects (9)
24. spoke quickly and with little thought (7)
25. saying (something) over and over again (9)

# THE BOY JUDGE
## *John Turvey*

In the time of the Caliph Haroun, a man called Ali Cogia lived in Baghdad. Ali was not rich: he was a seller of sweets and cakes. But he had no wife and family to look after, and had enough for his own needs.

Under the floor of the room at the back of his shop he kept a jar; and every week he put a small gold piece into it. The money was for him to use when he was old or ill. For, as he often said, "I have no sons to look after me when I am old and cannot work."

One day, when Ali was about fifty years old, he took out the jar and counted the money. There were more than a thousand gold pieces inside. "More than enough for the time when I am old," he said to himself, and he began to think.

Now, Ali was a good man. He went to the mosque every Friday; he gave money to the poor. But there was one thing which he had not done. He had not made the journey to Mecca.

From that day Ali thought more and more about the journey. He had the money. Poorer men than him had gone. Yet, life in Baghdad was easy, and the road to Mecca was hard. Not everyone who went there came back. But the thought had come into his head and would not go out. The time for the journey was near, and at last he said to his friends: "This year I will go."

So he sold his shop and got ready for the journey. But one difficulty remained — the jar with the gold. "Who will look after it while I am away?" he thought.

At last he thought of something. He went into a shop and bought some olives. Then he filled the jar with them so that they covered the gold. Lastly he

closed the top of the jar and took it to his friend Hussein, who kept the shop next to his.

"Brother Hussein," he said, "you know that I am going, if God wishes, to Mecca. I have sold everything, and have only this jar of olives. I do not like to waste good food. Can I leave it with you till I come back?"

"That is a small thing to ask a friend," said Hussein. "Put it here in this corner of my shop. Nobody will touch it there. And may God bring you safely back to Baghdad."

After many weeks Ali reached Mecca. There he did all the things that people have to do there. Then the time came for him to leave. This was the first journey that Ali had ever made. Before, he had been afraid to travel. Now, he found that he rather liked it. So he did not go straight back home.

In Mecca he had met some Egyptian merchants. "Come back with us to Cairo," they said. "There is always work there for a maker of sweets."

So Ali went with them and stayed two years. After that he moved on to Damascus. Time passed. It was nearly seven years since he had left Baghdad.

"It is long enough," he said one day. "I shall sell my shop here and go back to my own city of Baghdad to die among my friends."

On the very day that Ali Cogia left Damascus, Hussein's wife needed some olives. There were none in the house, and the shop in their street was shut. "What shall I do?" she asked.

"There are some olives in my shop," said Hussein. "Do you remember? Seven years ago old Ali Cogia left a jar of them with me. He never came back from Mecca. Some people say he went to Cairo, but he is surely dead by now."

"So let us eat his olives," said his wife. "They are doing no good to a dead man."

Hussein went into his shop, and there, still in its corner, stood the jar. Nobody had touched it in all those seven years. But when he opened it and looked inside, he saw that the olives at the top were quite dry. He put his hand deeper into the jar, but even those lower down were dry. So he put his whole arm in. When he pulled it out, black, oily and salty, he was holding a gold piece.

He put his hand into the jar again and found more gold. Many thoughts flew round his head. At last he put the gold into the jar again and went back to his wife. To her he only said: "Those olives were too old and dry."

The next day he took the olives out of the jar and threw them away. Then he took the gold out and buried it in his yard. Next, he went and bought new olives. He filled the jar with these, and closed it as it had been before.

"Seven years is a long time," he said to himself, "but I cannot be sure that Ali Cogia is dead. If he does come back, I shall have a jar of olives to give him. And that is what he asked me to look after — a jar of olives."

A few weeks later Ali Cogia came back to Baghdad. The first thing he did was to go round to Hussein's house. After they had talked for some time, Ali asked him about the jar of olives.

"Olives?" said Hussein. "What olives?"

"You remember. Before I left, I gave you a jar of olives to keep for me," said Ali. "You put it in a corner of your shop."

"Ah, perhaps you did give me a jar," said Hussein. "I had forgotten. Seven years is a long time. Let us go into my shop and see if it is still there."

Hussein's words had made Ali feel afraid. But when he saw the jar, just where he had left it, he felt much better. "My friend," he said, "you have looked after this jar for seven years. Now I want to give you something. You will see what is in the jar which you have kept so well."

With these words Ali put his arm into the jar and pulled out — not the gold pieces which he wanted to give to Hussein — but olives. He tried again and again, but the same thing happened every time.

"Where is my gold?" he asked at last.

"Gold? What gold?"

"The gold I put in this jar."

"You said nothing about a jar of gold. You only gave me this jar of olives."

"My friend, if you needed the money, do not be afraid to say. You may pay it back, a little every week, but . . . ."

"I have not touched your jar, and know nothing of any gold . . . ."

At last, after this had gone on for some time, Ali said: "Enough. I shall go to the judge. He will know which of us is telling the truth, and the law will punish the other."

"I don't mind," said Hussein. "Let us see if the judge is foolish enough to believe the story you have just told me."

The next day Ali and Hussein took the matter to the judge.

"Did anyone see you put the gold in

# The Boy Judge

the jar?" the judge asked Ali.

"No, I was alone. I have no wife or family."

"Did you tell anybody about putting the gold in the jar?"

"No, I did not want anybody to know."

"What did you tell Hussein was in the jar?"

"Olives."

Then the judge turned to Hussein. "Did anyone tell you there was gold in the jar?"

"No."

"Did you at any time open the jar?"

"No."

"Ali Cogia," said the judge, "how can you waste our time in this way? There is nothing to show that there was ever any gold in your jar. You are an old man. You do not remember what you did seven years ago."

Ali was angry at the judge's words. But there was one more thing he could do. He wrote a letter to the Caliph about the whole matter and gave it to one of the Caliph's servants.

By this time the story of the jar of olives had passed through all the markets of Baghdad. Everybody was talking about it, some believing Ali, and others believing Hussein. So when the Caliph got Ali's letter, he read it with care. He liked to know everything that went on in the city.

That night he called for his vizir and said: "Let us put on plain clothes tonight and walk about the streets. I want to hear what people are saying about this Ali Cogia. Is he a fool, or a man of truth, or a thief?"

As they were walking through that part of the city where Ali lived, they heard children speak the names of Ali and Hussein.

"You can be Ali."

"Let me be Hussein."

"All right, and I shall be the judge."

The two men stopped and looked into the yard where the voices were coming from. The children were sitting under a tree playing a game. One boy was playing the judge, and two more were playing Ali and Hussein. There were others, too. As the game went on, the Caliph listened more and more carefully. The boy judge was asking good questions.

At last, the Caliph said to the vizir: "Go in and speak to this boy. Tell him to come to the palace tomorrow morning. I also want to see the judge, Ali Cogia, Hussein, two olive merchants and the jar of olives."

The next day all these people came before the Caliph. Every one of them felt afraid: the judge was afraid because he thought he might have made a mistake; Ali was afraid because the Caliph might think *he* was a thief; Hussein was afraid because he *was* a thief; the merchants were afraid because they did not know what the Caliph might know about them, and the boy was afraid because he had never seen such a wonderful palace before.

"Come, boy," said the Caliph. "Sit down beside me. I heard you judge these two men in play last night. Today you shall really do it. — And you," he said to the judge, "listen to this child and learn how to tell truth from untruth, right from wrong, and good men from thieves."

Although still afraid, the boy spoke clearly. "Bring me the jar," he said. And the jar was put before him. "Is this the jar you gave to your friend?"

"Yes," said Ali.

"Is this the jar that Ali gave you?"

"Yes," said Hussein.

The boy put his hand in the jar and took out some olives. He gave some to the Caliph and to Ali and Hussein. Then he slowly ate one himself. "They are very good olives," he said.

Then to Hussein he said: "Did you eat any of them before today?"

"Not one," he answered. "I did not touch that jar from the time it came into my shop to the day Ali Cogia came back to Baghdad."

The boy then turned to the olive merchants. "You try them," he said. "They are good olives, although seven years old."

"Seven years old?" cried one of the merchants. "I can see by looking at them that they are not so old. They are this year's olives. No olive is any good after three years."

"Even after two years they lose their colour," said the second merchant.

"And yet Hussein says that these olives have been in the jar for seven years," said the boy.

"I have bought and sold olives for twenty years," said the first merchant, "and I know that olives do not last for seven years."

Hussein's face had gone white. His eyes were turned to the ground. "I took the gold," he said. "It is in a hole in my yard."

The Caliph then spoke: "You know how the law punishes thieves."

But before Hussein could answer, Ali said: "O great Caliph, do not cut off his hand. He was once a good friend to me. I did wrong to leave the gold with him. Let him go with a beating."

The Caliph looked at the boy judge. "A beating would be enough," the boy said.

"Then let it be so," said the Caliph.

So Hussein kept his hand, but lost his good name; Ali lost a friend, but got back his gold; and the boy judge was sent by the Caliph to study law. For as the great Haroun said: "Twenty jars of gold cannot buy a good judge."

*The Boy Judge*

In the case of questions 1–4 write out the sentence (or sentences) from the story that support your choice of answer.

1. Ali Cogia saved
   (a) fifty gold pieces
   (b) a thousand gold pieces
   (c) about a thousand gold pieces
   (d) at least one thousand and one gold pieces.
2. The story tells us that Ali had a shop in
   (a) Baghdad only
   (b) Damascus only
   (c) in both Baghdad and Damascus.
3. The day after he discovered Ali's gold, Hussein
   (a) changed it to a new hiding place
   (b) threw the jar away
   (c) buried the dried olives
   (d) bought a new jar.
4. Hussein's wife
   (a) heard that Ali was dead
   (b) hoped that Ali was dead
   (c) assumed that Ali was dead
   (d) knew that Ali lived in Damascus.
5. Why did Ali Cogia put away a gold piece every week?
6. Why do you think the writer says of Mecca: *'Not everyone who went there got back'*?
7. Why did Ali buy olives?
8. Why did Ali decide to go on to Cairo from Mecca?
9. What sentence tells us that Ali wanted to reward Hussein for minding his jar of gold?
10. Why was Ali unable to prove to the judge that there had been gold in the olive jar?
11. (a) Who was the Caliph?
    (b) Why did the Caliph put on plain clothes?
12. List all the people who were ordered to appear before the Caliph.
13. Explain how the boy judge showed that Hussein was not telling the truth?
14. Should Ali have told Hussein about the gold in the jar before he left for Mecca? Give a reason for your answer.
15. Do you think that Hussein was right to decide to use his friend's jar of olives? Give a reason for your answer.
16. Why do you think Hussein decided not to tell his wife about the gold in the jar?
17. *"Olives?"* said Hussein. *"What olives?"* Why did Ali feel afraid when he heard these words?
18. Describe the game the children were playing.
19. What details in the story suggest that Ali was a good man?

[Answer Guidelines]

14. Many questions on stories, poems, plays and media have no 'right' or 'wrong' answers. These are usually questions which require you to give your view on something in the story. These type of questions are usually put in one of the following ways:
    – Do you think that . . .
    – Give your views on . . .
    – In your opinion . . .
    – Would you agree that . . .

Your view is an important part of the answer but more important is the information in the story on which your view is based. The following Sample Answer to Question 14 shows how two different views can each form an acceptable answer.

> I think Ali should have told Hussein about the gold. If Hussein realised that it was Ali's life savings I don't think he would steal it. After all the two men were friends and neighbours.
>
> **or**
>
> I think Ali was right not to tell Hussein about the gold. If Hussein knew about it he might be tempted to steal it. Ali's plan was a good one and it would have worked if he had come straight back from Mecca. The longer he stayed away, the greater the chance was of the gold being found.

## Points to Note — SETTING

The setting of a story refers to the **place** and **time** that the events in the story happened. It is important to be aware of the setting because things that happen in one particular setting might not happen in another. For example many of the incidents in *The Boy Judge* could not happen in a modern setting.

Authors establish the setting of a story by describing the places where the events happened. If the author can help us 'see', in our imaginations, the places where the events of the story happen then the story comes more to life.

## PERSONAL WRITING

# ASSIGNMENTS

**Writing for Young Children**

Writing stories for young children is not as simple as it may seem. The story must be told in a clear and straightforward way and the language must be easily understood by the child.

Write a fairy story suitable for reading to the 5 – 7 age group. You can make up one yourself or retell an old favourite such as *Cinderella* or *Jack and the Beanstalk*.

How will you begin? 'Once upon a time . . .' of course!

**Remember**

Start all your sentences with a capital letter and end with a full stop.

**Functional Writing**

Write a newspaper report on one of the two court scenes in the story. Include headlines.

## Word power!

Find the words in the story which have similar meanings to each of the words and phrases below. The number in brackets after each one indicates the number of letters in the answer. The words appear in the story in the same order as the meanings given below.

### CLUES

1. problem (10)
2. a distance to travel; a trip (7)
3. closed (4)
4. ideas (8)
5. put underground (6)
6. purchased; paid for (6)
7. think back; recall (8)
8. someone who hears court cases (5)
9. penalise (6)
10. stupid; silly (7)
11. very cross (5)
12. ordinary; simple (5)
13. robber (5)
14. where kings live (6)
15. people who buy and sell (9)
16. error (7)
17. learn about something (5)

## About the Story

This story is from a collection of stories called <u>The Arabian Nights</u>, also known as <u>The Thousand and One Nights</u>. They are old folk tales of Arabic and Indian origin and were collected by an Egyptian story-teller around five hundred years ago. The collection of these stories was translated into English around one hundred and fifty years ago and became a bestseller in its day. One of the best known of the Arabian Nights tales is that of <u>Ali Baba and the Forty Thieves</u>.

The following **Spot the Errors** exercise is aimed at sharpening your basic writing skills. Spot the 20 errors in the Passage below and rewrite the passage correctly. (Note: Refer to the Guidelines on pages 1—15.)

## 10 Fashion

The first cloths were probaly maid just to protect people from the cold. But men and women soon wanted there clothes to be more than practical – they wanted them to be beuatiful too. The more advanced a society became, the more attention was paid to the manner of dress. by the time the egyptians had built the great piramyds, fashion was as important as it is today.

Until recently, beautiful clothes were made by hand they were usually elaborate and allways expensive. Fashion was for the royal, the rich and the famous now mass production has made stylish clothes available to almost everyone. The modern fashion buisness, from the design room to the store window, is one of the most busy, most imaginative and most glamorous activities in the world.

In designing a dress the fashion designer works with three things: shape fabric, and color. The fashion designer works in a design room. Here the fabric's are brought together, the shape of the garment developed and the colours decided upon. First, a sketch is made of the garment. From the sketches sample garments are made of muslin, a cheep cotton. if the muslin sample is satisfactory then the item is made in the desired fabric.

# On My Mother's Life
### *Eamonn Burke*

The wet shiny streets glistened in the orange lights of a grey November evening.

Outside the shopping centre, huddled in a dark corner, were four boys. All wore jeans and dark anoraks with furry hoods pulled over their heads. One could see the red glow of a cigarette as it passed from one hand to another.

The boys were bored. They were waiting for something to happen, for it to get darker, for the car park to become quieter, for working men to drive in and go for a few drinks in the pub across the road. They were the best. The boys wanted to drive. They would just borrow a car. It would be a Toyota or a Nissan, but if they were really lucky, a BMW. As Skinner, the leader of the group, said "Nothing can catch a BMW."

Soon the car park was deserted. The younger boys looked at Skinner and waited. He was the leader, the boss. He was cool. He was never caught robbing or messing and could talk his way out of anything. He was staring at the dark green Nissan that had been parked twenty yards away. He walked slowly to the car. In his hand, deep in his pocket, he was holding the 'blackhead' with which he would open the car.

He glanced inside. No car lock, no alarm. He was about to open the door when he sensed that he was not alone. The tall imposing figure of Garda Delaney loomed across the car park towards him.

"Damn! Babyface. I am snared rapid," he thought. He almost panicked but then remembered he had done nothing wrong. His hands were still in his pockets, the 'blackhead' feeling like a hammer in his hand.

"You there, what are you doing?"

"Me," said Skinner. "Nothing, just walking home from the chemist with some tablets for my mother. She is sick."

"You were not looking into that car were you?"

"On my mother's life, I was not. I never robbed a car in my life. Ask anyone."

The three boys in the corner all smiled when they heard Skinner's voice. They had heard the same excuse so often in the past and it always worked. In school, whenever he was suspected of some kind of indiscipline, Skinner would always say — "On my mother's life I did not do that."

The Garda looked long and hard at Skinner and said in a low voice, "You better be going home to your sick mother with the tablets."

Skinner walked quickly away in the direction of the nearest houses. When he was out of sight of the Garda he quickly returned to his pals.

"That was a close call. What did you say Skinner?"

"I told them that my mother was sick and I was getting tablets for her," he replied. They all laughed at this.

"She is not too sick to be going playing Bingo," said one of the smaller boys.

Skinner thought of his mother and the gold bracelet and the rings she wore every time she went out. He smiled to himself. Why does she bother to dress up just to play Bingo? His attention returned to the Nissan in the car park.

He slowly walked over to the car, looking around him. Then he quickly pulled the blackhead from his pocket and opened the car. To the boys watching, it seemed that Skinner just vanished into the car.

"Will he be able to get it going? Is there a car lock?" they whispered, feeling a mixture of fear and hope.

As the boys all stared, the lights went on and the sound of a powerful engine broke the stillness of the car park. The big car drove straight at the boys, screeched to a halt and all the boys climbed in quickly. The car surged forward and accelerated down the main road, spray flying from its wheels.

The boys in the car were all shouting now, except for Skinner who was concentrating on driving.

"Let's go to town," said Anto.

"No, let's go to the airport," said Gazzer.

"What about Kerry?" suggested Darren, a little uncertainly.

"No. We'll just cruise around here. It's as good as anywhere and if we're spotted we know where to hide", said Skinner.

Skinner felt really good. He was always happy in a car. As the boys continued to shout, he just kept smiling.

"Do you want a bit of skid?" he said. Before anyone could answer, he suddenly shoved his foot down hard on the accelerator.

"Hold tight," said Skinner as he slammed on the brakes and pulled hard on the steering wheel.

The car skidded around the corner and spun once, but Skinner did not lose control.

"Take it easy, Skinner," screamed one of the boys.

Skinner just laughed and accelerated again. He again slammed on the brakes, pulled on the steering wheel and slipped around another corner.

He did not see the woman crossing the road. Nobody in the car felt the thud when the rear of the car swung and struck her.

A man on his way home from work found her lying on the road. He noticed that a gold bracelet lay on the ground. Searching through the woman's handbag for identification, all he found was a purse and a book of used bingo tickets.

\* \* \* \* \*

The car screeched to a halt and the boys tumbled out at the end of a dark cul-de-sac. They all ran in different directions. At his front door Skinner looked at his watch. He was late.

His father shouted at him, "Where have you been till this time?"

"Just out with my friends . . . talking."

His father stared at him long and hard — "I hope you were not in trouble." Skinner blushed and said, "On my mother's life I was not."

On My Mother's Life

### Questions & Assignments

1. What are your feelings towards (a) Skinner and (b) the other boys.
2. Briefly describe the setting of the story.
3. What is the feature of the story that the author leaves to the reader to decide?
4. Is there an important lesson to be learned from this story?
5. Do you think the title is suitable? Give a reason for your answer.
6. Give a short outline of the story in your own words.

### [Answer Guidelines]

6. You might begin as follows:
   *One November night a group of boys huddled together in a car-park. They were planning to steal a car. Skinner was their leader.*

   Use the following 'sentence starters' to continue.
   When the car park was deserted, Skinner approached . . .
   As he was about to . . .
   He told the Garda that . . .
   The boys laughed when he . . .
   He thought of his . . .
   When the Garda had gone . . .

### Word Power!

Find the words in the story which have similar meanings to each of the words and phrases below. The number in brackets after each one indicates the number of letters in the answer. The words appear in the story in the same order as the meanings given below.

#### CLUES

1. sparkled (9)
2. crowded closely together (7)
3. a light (without a flame) (4)
4. empty of people (8)
5. looking with a fixed gaze (7)
6. got a feeling (6)
7. impressive; overpowering (8)
8. jewellery worn on the wrist (8)
9. interest (9)
10. disappeared (8)
11. silence (9)
12. moved very quickly (6)
13. directing all his attention (13)
14. increased speed (11)
15. a dead-end street (8)
16. went red in the face (7)

The following **Spot the Errors** exercise is aimed at sharpening your basic writing skills. Spot the 20 errors in the Passage below and rewrite the passage correctly. (Note: Refer to the Guidelines on pages 1—15.)

## 11  A Night in the Takeaway

The door opened and a man came in he was dressed in a very old, brown coat with the pocket hanging off. His face was covered with dirt And his filthy, grey hair hanged in greasy lumps over his collar. He appeared to have grate dificulty in keeping still for he was weaving about all over the place and had to hold on to the counter to stop himself falling over backwards.

Sandwich, guv! he shouted in an odd, aggressive way. "Chicken, make it a chicken, OK?"

The man behind the counter begun making up the sandwich. He had very curly, black hair and a white overall, underneath which he was wearing a string vest. He didn't look at all pleased with the new customer.

"Eat hear or take away" He asked.

The new customer jerked his head towards the street to indicate that he wants to take the food away. In doing so, he overbalanced and fell against the plate glass window. I realised that he must be drunk.

"You got the money this time, Duke?" asked the sandwich man. "This isnt a charity shop you know."

"I got money!" shouted the customer. "I'm rich. Rolling in the stuff."

He fumbeld in his trouser pocket and brought out a handful of silver. The counter man took some of the coins and rang them up on the till. He pressed the rest of the money into one of Dukes hands and the sandwich into the other.

"On your way now, duke, OK?" he said.

Duke seemed pacified and made for the door. He didn't see the glass and walked smack into it then he jerked the door open and disapeared with a strange, bouncing step into the night crowds.

# Spoil the Child
## Howard Fast

### PART 1

The first morning Pa was gone, I tried to ride one of the mules. I didn't think that would hurt, because the mules were unharnessed anyway. But Maude told Ma, and Ma slapped me. Ma was in the wagon, and she wouldn't have seen. I told Maude I'd remember.

Pa left about six in the morning while Ma still slept. "Goin' after meat?" I asked him. He had his rifle.

He nodded.

"Can I go?"

"Stay with Ma, sonny," he said. "She ain't well."

"You said I could hunt—"

"You stay with Ma, sonny."

Maude got up a few minutes after that. I could see Pa like a black dot out on the prairie. I pointed to him.

I said: "That's Pa out there huntin'."

Maude was combing her hair, not paying a lot of attention to me. Then I tried to ride the mule. Pa would never let me ride his horse. It was only half-broken, cost four hundred dollars. Ma was always saying we could have lived a year on what that horse cost.

Maude woke Ma. My mother was a tall, thin woman, tired looking. She wasn't well. I could see that she wasn't well.

"Dave, get off that mule," she said. "Where's Pa?"

"Went out to hunt."

"Come here. Can't ever get it into your head to behave." I went over, and she slapped my face. "Don't bother them mules. When'll he be back? We can't stay here."

"He didn't say."

"Get some chips for a fire," Ma told me. "My land, I never seen such a lazy, shiftless boy." But she didn't say it the way she always did, as if she would want to bite my head off. She seemed too tired to really care.

I guess Ma walloped me every day. She said I was bad – a lot worse than you'd expect from a boy of twelve. You didn't expect them to be bad that young.

"You learn to leave the mules alone," Maude called.

"You shut up," I told her. Maude was fifteen and pretty. She had light hair and a thin, delicate face. Ma said that someday Maude would be a lady. She didn't expect much from me. She said I would be like Pa.

I walked away from the wagon, looking for chips. By now, Pa was out of sight, and where he had gone the prairie was just a roll of yellow and brown, a thread of cloud above it. It frightened me to be alone on the prairie. Pa laughed at it, and called it a big meadow. But it frightened me.

We had been on the prairie for a week now. Pa said in another few weeks we'd reach Fort Lee, due west. He said that if he had cattle stock, he'd settle down right on the prairie. This way, he'd cross the mountains, grow fruit, maybe, in California. Ma never believed much he said.

I went back to the wagon and started a fire. Ma had gone inside, and Maude sat on the driver's seat.

"You might gimme a hand," I told Maude.

"I don't see you overworking," Maude said.

"You'd better learn to shut up."

From inside the wagon, Ma yelled: "You hold your tongue, Dave, or I'll wallop you!"

"You're a little beast," Maude said.

"You wait," I told her.

I went to the keg, drew some water, and set it up to boil. I could tell by the sound that there wasn't a lot of water left in the keg. Pa had said we'd reach water soon.

When I came back to the fire, I glanced up at the sky. It was an immense bowl of hot blue, bare except for a single buzzard that turned slowly, like a fish swimming. I guess I forgot. I kept looking up at the buzzard.

Ma climbed down from the wagon slowly. "You're the same as your Pa," she said. "Lazy an' bad." Her face was tight-drawn. For the past few weeks she had hardly smiled, and now it seemed that she wouldn't smile again.

"And fresh," Maude said.

I put the water on the fire, not saying anything.

"Spare the rod and spoil the child," Ma said.

Then her face twisted in pain, and she leaned against the wagon. "Well, don't stand there," she told me. "Water the mules."

I went to the keg. I knew there wasn't enough water for the mules. I hoped Pa would come back soon; I had a funny, awful fear of what would happen if he didn't come back soon. I kept glancing out at the prairie.

Pa had an itch in his feet. Ma said I would grow up the same way – having an itch in my feet. She was always sorry that she had married a man with an itch in his feet. Sometimes she said that the war had done it, that after the war between the North and the South, men were either broken or had to keep moving, like Pa. Always west.

We lived in Columbus. Then we moved to St Louis; then Topeka. Pa couldn't stop, and Ma got more and more worn out. She said that a wild land was no place to raise children. It was hard on Ma, all right. Pa didn't do much, except when we were moving west, and then he would be like a different person. Ma never complained to him. She walloped me instead.

I gave the mules enough water to cover the bottoms of their pails.

Ma came over, said: "That's not enough water."

"There ain't a damn sight more."

"Don't swear!" Ma exclaimed. She clapped a hand across my head.

"He's always swearing," Maude said. "Thinks he's grown up."

Ma stared at me a moment, dully; then she went over and prepared breakfast. It was gruel and hardtack.

"Fresh meat would be good," Ma said. She looked over the prairie, maybe looking for Pa. I knew how much she cared for Pa. She would talk a lot about itching feet, but that didn't matter.

After breakfast, I gave the mules some oats, and Maude cleaned up the dishes. I kept glancing at Maude, and she knew what I meant. She didn't care, until Ma went back into the wagon. It hurt me to look at Ma.

"He'll be back soon, I guess," Ma said. Then she climbed into the wagon. It was a big sixteen-foot wagon, the kind they called freighters, with a hooped top, covered over with dirty brown canvas.

Maude said: "You leave me alone."

"I'll leave you alone now," I told Maude. "I gotta leave you alone now. Maybe you know what's the matter with Ma?"

"That's none of your business," Maude said.

"It's my business, all right."

"You're just a kid."

I went to the back of the wagon and pulled out Pa's carbine. It was the one he had used during the war, a short cavalry gun.

Ma saw me; she lay inside, and I could hear her breathing hard.

She said: "What're you up to now; Pa back?"

"Not yet."

"Well, you tell me soon as he gets back. And don't get into any mischief."

"All right."

In front of the wagon, I sat down on a feed box, and cleaned the gun with an old rag. Maude watched me. Finally, she said – "I'm gonna tell Ma you're fooling with Pa's gun.'

"You keep your mouth shut."

Ma groaned softly then, and we both turned around and looked at the wagon. I felt little shivers crawl up and down my spine. Where was Pa? He should have been back already. I put down the gun and walked around the wagon. In a circle, the prairie rose and fell, like a sea of whispering yellow grass. There was nothing there, no living thing.

Maude was crying. "Why don't Pa come back?" she said.

I didn't answer her. I guess it occurred to me for the first time that Pa might not come back. I felt like crying. I felt like getting into a corner and crying. I hadn't felt so small for a long time. It would be a comfort to have Ma slap me now. You get slapped, and you know you're a kid, and you don't have to worry about anything else.

I said to Maude: "Go inside the wagon and stay with Ma."

"Don't you order me around."

"All right," I said. I turned my back on her. I didn't hold much with girls when they're that age.

Then Maude went inside the wagon. I heard her crying, and I heard Ma say: "You stop that crying right now."

I loaded the carbine. I untethered one of the mules, climbed onto it, and set out across the prairie in the direction Pa had taken. I didn't know just what I'd do, but I knew it was time Pa came back.

## Questions & Assignments

### PART 1

1. Why did Pa get up early and go out on the prairie?
2. Why did Dave (the boy who is telling the story) say that Pa was *'like a black dot out on the prairie'*?
3. Why were the family travelling out west?
4. Dave asks Maude if she knows what's the matter with Ma. Why does she not tell him?
5. To what does Dave compare the prairie? Do you think it is a good comparison? Give a reason for your answer.
6. Why did Dave set off on the mule at the end of this section of the story?
7. (a) What details help us to discover where and when the story takes place?
   (b) What kind of difficulties are the travellers likely to come across in such a setting?
8. How does Ma feel about (a) Pa, (b) Maude and (c) Dave?
9. (a) What did Ma mean when she said that Pa had *'an itch in his feet'*?
   (b) What reason did she give for it?
   (c) What evidence is there in the story to show that she was right?
10. What does Dave want to happen and what is he afraid may happen at this point in the story?

### word power!

Find the words in the story which have similar meanings to each of the words and phrases below. The number in brackets after each one indicates the number of letters in the answer. The words appear in the story in the same order as the meanings given below.

CLUES

1. a type of gun (5)
2. flat land covered in grass, with no trees (6)
3. annoy (6)
4. slapped (8)
5. looked quickly (7)
6. very big (7)
7. empty (4)
8. a bird of prey (7)

## PART 2

It wasn't easy, riding the mule just with harness straps. Mules have a funny gait. And we didn't go very fast. I was glad Ma and Maude were in the wagon, otherwise Ma would probably hit me.

In about a half hour, the wagon was just a tiny black dot. It might have been anything. I kept glancing at the sun to remember the direction I had taken. Then a swell hid the wagon. I kept on going. I knew that if I stopped, even for a little while, I'd cry my head off.

I saw a coyote. He stood like a dog and watched me. An antelope hopped close, and I might have shot at them. But I couldn't bring myself to fire a rifle there. It would have done something to me.

I found Pa. I guess I had been riding for about an hour when I saw him, over to one side. A buzzard flapped up, and I felt my throat tighten until I thought it would choke me. I didn't want to go over to him. I got down from the mule, and I walked over slowly. But I didn't want to; something made me.

He was dead, all right. Maybe it was Indians and maybe it wasn't; I didn't know. He was shot four times, and his gun was gone.

The buzzard wouldn't go away; I shot the buzzard. I didn't cry. The carbine kicked back and made my shoulder ache. I was thinking about how Pa always called me an undersized, freckled little runt. He said I wouldn't grow up. Maybe that's why I didn't cry.

I went away a little distance and sat down. I didn't look at Pa. I tried to remember where we were, what Pa had told me about going west. When I thought of Ma, I had a sense of awful fear. Suppose it happened now.

The mule walked over and nuzzled my shoulder. I was glad the mule was there then. If he wasn't, I don't know what I would have done.

Pa had to be buried. I knew that men had to be buried, but I couldn't do it. The prairie was hard, baked mud. I went back to Pa and stood over him; I guess that was the hardest thing I had ever done in my life. I straightened his clothes. I pulled off his boots. Men in the West were always talking about dying with their boots on. I didn't know how it meant anything, one way or another, but I thought Pa would be pleased if he didn't have his boots on.

Then I climbed up on the mule and started back for the wagon. I tried not to think that I was twelve years old. If you get to thinking about that, then you're no good at all. When I got back, Ma would lick me plenty.

The mule must have found its way back, because I didn't pay much attention to that. I let the reins loose, holding onto the harness straps, and I kept swallowing. Then I saw the wagon.

I thought: "I can't tell Ma now – maybe later." Nobody had ever told me about a thing like that, but I knew it wouldn't do to tell Ma now. I guess I only felt it instinctively, but I knew that the importance wasn't in Pa any more. All that was important was life, and life was just a fleck of dust in the prairie. It was like a nightmare to think of the distance of the prairie, and how we were alone.

I rode up to the wagon, and Maude and Ma were both standing next to it. I could tell from Ma's face how worried she had been about me.

"There he is!" Maude screamed.

Ma said: "I guess there ain't nothing a body can do with you. Dave. Get off that mule."

I slipped off, tethered the mule. My whole body was twisted up with the strain of keeping what I had seen off my face. I came over to Ma.

"Where have you been?" she demanded.

"Hunting."

"I reckon there's nothing else for a little loafer like you. Spare the rod and spoil the child. Come here."

I went over and bent down, and she walloped me a bit, not too hard. She wasn't very strong then, I guess. I cried, but I wasn't crying because of the licking. I had had worse lickings than that and never opened my mouth. But it seemed to break the tension inside of me, and I had to cry. I went over and sat down with my back against one of the wagon wheels.

Maude walked past me and said: "I guess that learned you."

I just looked at her, without answering. I took out my jack-knife and began to pare at one of the wagon boards. Then my eyes travelled to the water keg.

I got up and went around to Ma. She was still standing there, staring off across the prairie in the direction Pa had gone.

Without turning, she said to me: "Seen anything of your Pa?"

"No."

The sun was westward now, a splotch of red that blazed the whole prairie into a fire. I could get a little of how Ma felt; I could see the loneliness.

"Get a fire going," she said. "He ought to have enough sense to come back early. Stop that whimpering. God help a woman when a man has itching feet."

I gathered chips and started the fire. When I took water from the keg for mush, the keg was just about empty. I didn't mention that to Ma. She went about preparing supper slowly, awkwardly, and Maude watched her, frightened.

Ma kept glancing at the west.

"Be dark soon," I said.

"Guess Pa'll be here any minute," Ma said dully. I could tell that she didn't believe that.

"I guess so," I nodded.

We ate without speaking much. Ma didn't eat a great deal. As soon as we had finished, she went into the wagon.

Maude was saying: "I don't see how I can clean dishes without water. You fetch some water, Dave."

"There ain't no water," I said.

Maude stared at me, her eyes wide and frightened. She had heard stories, just the same as I had, about pilgrims who ran out of water. She opened her mouth to say something.

"What about Ma?" I asked her quietly, nodding at the wagon.

"Why don't Pa come back?"

"Ain't no sense thinking about Pa if he ain't here. What about Ma? I guess it won't be long."

She shook her head.

"You don't need to be scared," I muttered. "It won't do no good to be scared. I reckon the worst part of this trip is over."

"Where's Pa?" she whispered. "What happened?"

"How do I know what happened? You girls make me sick. I never seen anything to beat you girls."

I got up and went over to the water keg. I shook it, hoping, without having any reason to hope. I knew it was just about empty. We had plenty of food – dried meat and meal and dried beans – enough to last a month, I guess. But Ma would need water.

Maude was crying.

"Why don't you go to bed?" I told her.

"Don't order me around."

"Well, you go to bed," I said. "Go in

and sleep with Ma. I'll stay out here."

"You're not big enough to stay out here alone," Maude said, but I knew she was afraid to stay inside the wagon with Ma. I knew how she felt, and I didn't blame her for the way she felt, she was such a kid, with Ma petting her all the time. We couldn't talk it over between ourselves, and that would have made it a lot better. But we couldn't.

"I'm plenty big enough," I said.

Inside the wagon Ma groaned, and out on the prairie a coyote was barking. There's nothing like a coyote barking to make your insides crawl. I was all shivers, and I could see that Maude wanted to stay close to me. But that wouldn't have made it any better.

"Get in the wagon, damn you!" I cried. I was glad Ma couldn't hear me swear. Ma would lick me good and plenty when I swore like that.

Surprised, Maude stared at me. Then, without a word, she went into the wagon.

## Questions & Assignments — PART 2

1. *'A buzzard flapped up'* Do you think the word 'flapped' is a good choice to describe the movement of the buzzard?
2. Why did Dave not bury Pa?
3. *'I tried not to think I was twelve years old.'* Explain why Dave tried not to think about that.
4. Read the paragraph beginning *'I thought: I can't tell Ma . . .'* and answer the following questions:
    (a) *'. . . and life was just a fleck of dust on the prairie.'* What do you think Dave meant by this statement?
    (b) Why was it like a nightmare?
5. (a) What decision does Dave have to make before he returns to the wagon?
    (b) Do you think that he made the right decision? Explain why.
6. Maude, like Dave, had heard stories about pilgrims who ran out of water? What kind of stories do you think they might have heard?
7. Describe the mood of Maude and Dave as nightfall approaches.

## Word Power!

Find the words in the story which have similar meanings to each of the words and phrases below. The number in brackets after each one indicates the number of letters in the answer. The words appear in the story in the same order as the meanings given below.

### CLUES

1. a way of walking (4)
2. a type of deer (8)
3. pain (4)
4. rubbed with his nose (7)
5. straps for steering a horse (5)
6. a small particle (5)
7. tied up (an animal) (8)
8. getting ready (9)
9. use vulgar language (5)

## PART 3

I stood there, outside, for a while. It had grown quite dark. In the sky there was a faint, reflected light of the sun, but it was quite dark. I walked over to the wagon and picked up one of the mule blankets that hung on the shafts. It was a warm night, summertime; I decided to put the blanket under the wagon and lie down on it.

I heard Maude saying her prayers in the wagon, but no sound from Ma. I couldn't say my prayers. Usually, Ma saw to it that I did, but tonight I couldn't say a word aloud. I tried, opening my mouth, but no words came out. I thought them, as much as I could. I tried not to think about Pa. Spreading the blanket, I lay down on it, holding the carbine close to me. It seemed a part of Pa and all that was left; I hugged it.

I couldn't sleep. I tried for a long time, but I couldn't sleep. It was quite dark now, with no moon in the sky. The mules were moving restlessly; probably because they wanted water.

I think I dozed a little. When I opened my eyes again, the moon was just coming up, yellow and bloated. I felt chilled thoroughly. Bit by bit, what had happened during the day came back, and now it was all more real than it had been in the daytime. While I lay there, thinking about it, I heard horses' hooves; at first not noticing them, and only becoming aware of them when the horses bulked out of the night, two men riding slowly.

They were in the moonlight, and I was hidden in the shadow of the wagon. They didn't see me. They stopped just about a dozen yards from the wagon, sitting on their horses and eyeing the mules. The mules moved restlessly.

When I realised they were Indians I couldn't move, just lay there and watched them. They were naked to the waist, with their hair in two stiff braids to their shoulders. They both carried rifles.

I thought of Pa. I thought of screaming to wake Maude and Ma. I thought: "If they shot Pa—" They were cutting loose the mules.

I felt for the carbine, twisted around, so I lay on my belly. One of the men had dismounted and was coming towards the wagon. He held his gun in one hand and had drawn a knife with the other. I sighted the centre of his breast and fired.

I remember how the sound blasted out the silence of the prairie. In the wagon, someone screamed. The Indian stopped, seemed to stare at me, swayed a bit, and crumpled to the ground. I remember the sharp pain in my shoulder from the blow of the recoil.

The mounted man's horse had wheeled about. He pulled it back, and fired at me. The shot threw sand in my face. I had a few cartridges and caps in my pocket, and I tried frantically to reload. The cartridges slipped through my fingers.

Then the Indian was gone. He had taken the other horse with him, and I heard their hooves thundering across the prairie. I dropped the carbine. My shoulder ached terribly. Inside the wagon, Maude was whimpering, my mother groaning.

I climbed from under the wagon. The Indian lay on his back, his face hard and twisted. I stood there, looking at him.

Maude climbed down out of the wagon. "What is it?" she cried. Then she saw the Indian and screamed.

"All right – I shot him."

She stood there, holding her hand to

her mouth.

"You get back in the wagon. I guess he killed Pa, all right. Don't tell that to Ma."

She shook her head. Ma was groaning. "I can't go back," Maude said.

"Why?"

And then I knew. I should have known from the way Ma was groaning. I went up to Maude and slapped her face. She didn't seem to feel it. I slapped her again.

"Get in there with Ma."

"I can't — it's dark."

"Get in there!" I yelled.

We had lanterns on the outside of the wagon. I took one and lit it. I wasn't trembling so much now. I gave the lantern to Maude, who was still standing the way she had been before.

"Go inside," I said.

Maude climbed into the wagon, taking the lantern with her. Then I cried. I crouched under the wagon, clutching the carbine and crying.

Finally, I went over to the Indian. I forced myself to do that. He lay half across the rifle he had carried. I pulled it out, and it was my father's rifle, all right.

I don't know how long I stood there holding the rifle. Then I put it under the seat, along with the carbine. I didn't want to look at the wagon.

I walked over to the mules, led them over to the shafts. It was hard to harness them. I had to balance myself on the shafts to get at their backs. When it was done, I ached all over, and my shoulder was swollen where the carbine had rested.

I climbed to the driver's seat. The curtains were down, and I couldn't see into the wagon, but the light still burned. Taking down Pa's whip, I let it go onto the mules' backs. I had seen Pa do that, and sometimes he let me try. The whip was fourteen feet long and I couldn't do much with it, but I got the mules moving. They had to keep moving. We had to find water.

At night, under the moon, the prairie was black and silver at the same time. Somehow, it didn't frighten me, the way it had during the day. I sat there thinking, I guess, of nothing at all, only awfully aware of the change inside me.

We drove on like that. I kept the mules at a slow pace, so the freighter wouldn't roll much. I was very tired, and after a while I didn't use the whip at all.

Then Maude came out of the wagon, sat down next to me. She looked at me and I looked at her, but she didn't say anything. She pressed close to me.

I whistled at the mules.

Inside the wagon something was whimpering. It made me tremble to hear that.

"Reckon we'll find water soon," I told Maude.

She nodded mechanically. Her head kept nodding and I dozed, myself. I guess I kept dozing through the night, fell asleep towards morning.

Maude woke me. The wagon had stopped, and the sun was an hour up. The mules had stopped on the bank of a slow, brown stream, lined with cottonwoods as far as I could see.

Maude was pointing at the water.

"Don't you start crying now," I said, rubbing my eyes.

"I won't," Maude nodded.

Ma called me, not very loud: "Dave come here."

I climbed inside the wagon. Ma was lying on the bed, her arm curled around something. I peered at it.

"Do you know?" she said.

"I reckon I do. I reckon it's a boy. Girls ain't much use."

Ma was crying – not much; her eyes were just wetting themselves slowly.

"Where are we?" Ma asked me.

"We been travelling through the night. There's a river out there. I guess we don't need to worry about water."

"All night — Pa back?"

I said, slowly: "I killed an Indian last night, Ma. He had Pa's gun."

Then she just stared at me, and I stood there, shifting from one foot to another, wanting to run away. But I stood there. It must have been about five minutes, and she didn't say anything at all. The baby was whimpering.

Then she said: "You harnessed the mules?"

"Uh-huh. Maude didn't help me— "

Ma said: "You don't tease Maude. You don't tease Maude, or I'll take a stick to you. I never seen a boy like you for teasing."

"Uh-huh," I nodded.

"Just like your Pa," Ma whispered. "It don't pay to have a man whose heels are always itching – it don't pay."

"No use cryin'," I said.

Ma said: "What are we going to do?"

"Go on west. Ain't hard now to go a few hundred miles more. Reckon it won't be hard. Pa said— "

Ma was staring at me, her mouth trembling. I hadn't ever seen her look just like that before. I wanted to put my head on her shoulder, hide it there.

I couldn't do that. I said: "Pa told me. We'll go west.'

Then I went outside. I sat down on the wagon seat, looking at the river. I heard the baby making noises.

I said to Maude: "A man feels funny — with a kid."

## Questions & Assignments

### PART 3

1. In the night two men approach the wagon. Describe in around six sentences what happened to them.
2. Do you think that Dave should have told his mother about Pa? Do you think that he picked a good time to tell her? Explain.
3. At what point in the story do we learn that Ma has given birth to a child?
4. 'A suspense-filled story.' Would you regard this as an accurate description of the story? Give reasons for your answer.
5. As the boy drives the wagon across the dark prairie he thinks of the *'change inside me'*. Outline the way in which Dave changed over the course of the story. Pay particular attention to the final line of the story.
6. Is this story a sad one? Give reasons for your answer.
7. How does this story give us a sense of the hardships that people had to endure in the past?

### [Answer Guidelines]

4. Remember that suspense (or tension) is present in a story when we fear something unpleasant may be about to happen and we are hoping that it will not – or vice versa. After the event the tension is broken. Suspense is created in this story in at least three separate events. Outline these and show how the suspense was created by saying what you feared might happen and what you hoped would happen.

Spoil the Child

## word power!

Find the words in the story which have similar meanings to each of the words and phrases below. The number in brackets after each one indicates the number of letters in the answer. The words appear in the story in the same order as the meanings given below.

### CLUES
1. slept lightly (5)
2. became aware (8)
3. ammunition (10)
4. crying softly (10)
5. lamp (7)
6. holding tightly (9)
7. hitch mules to the wagon (7)

## Points to Note

### Author and Narrator

Do not confuse the terms **author** and **narrator.** An author is the person in the real world who sits down and writes the story. A narrator is a character in the story who tells the story in the way it happened to him (or her). In this story Dave, a twelve-year-old boy, is the narrator.

### Suspense and Tension

There are many moments of suspense and tension in the story *Spoil the Child*. Suspense and tension are two important terms you will need to remember when writing about stories. They both refer to the same thing – the **excitement (fear and hopes)** experienced by a reader when **something important** is **about to happen** in the story.

When writing about suspense and tension you should identify why the reader is feeling apprehensive. Explain what it is that the reader **fears** might happen and what it is that the reader **hopes** will happen. Experiencing suspense (in the safety of an armchair) adds to the enjoyment of reading.

### Relief

**Relief** is the relaxing of tension that we feel when we discover the **outcome** of a story. Throughout a story the reader will have hoped or feared that something was going to happen. Whether the reader feels disappointed or happy about the outcome there will still be an experience of relief.

### Surprise

Frequently things do not turn out **quite as expected** in stories. Most stories have surprises in them when events may take a **novel twist** (hence the term 'novel'). These surprises may result in us changing our attitude towards a character or our expectations on the direction of the story.

**The following Spot the Errors exercise is aimed at sharpening your basic writing skills. Spot the 20 errors in the Passage below and rewrite the passage correctly. (Note: Refer to the Guidelines on pages 1—15.)**

## 12 The Beano

The *Beano* comic, which gave life to Dennis the menace, celebrated its 60th birthday in july 1998.

A special double issue of the comic, which also brought readers the Bash Street Kids and minnie the minx, appeared this week on newsagent's shelves.

At it's peak, the comic sold more than two million copys a week, although it now sells only 250,000. A recent British survey put it ahead even of football magazines as the favorite reading matter of boys aged nine to fourteen.

Dennis the Menace, who has terrorised the comics pages with his faithful dog gnasher since 1951, even boasts a fan club with more than a million members.

Since the *Beano* was first published in July 1938, only tree characters have ever appeared on the comic's cover. These were Biffo the Bear Dennis the Menace and the original cover star, Big Eggo, an ostrich with an appetite for unexploded bombs.

The first issue costed two old pence. Surviving copies are now worth thousands of pounds. The *Beano* was the first british comic to use the american technique of putting speech bubbles to characters' mouths, rather than use captions below the pictures.

The *Beano*'s Editor, Mr Euan Kerr, said: "Wer'e very careful to make changes only gradually. It is our reader's who decide which charachters stay and which go."

But the future for the comic is becoming more international, with Dennis the Menace already speaking German, French and Irish in an animated television series.

"He's on his way to becoming an international terrorist, he said.

# THE WITCH'S FIRE
*Anon*

## PART 1

When King Henry VIII quarrelled with the Pope, life was very difficult for the Catholics in England. Laws were passed making them swear the oath of supremacy. This meant that they had to say in public that the king was the head of the church in England. If they refused to take the oath they were punished by fines, prison and sometimes death. Many took the oath in public but kept up their faith in private. One such person was Anne Musgrave, a young woman of twenty whose parents had died and left her quite well off. She was engaged to a young man named Richard Holgrove. His family was Catholic too. Privately they kept up their old religion. They used their home as a secret meeting place for Catholics of the district. At one such meeting a spy was present. He later betrayed the family to Judge Harding, one of the King's officers. The judge hated the Catholics. He had closed down many abbeys in his time. He soon brought the Holgrove family to trial for hiding priests. Spies were paid to say that they had seen priests saying mass in the Holgroves' house. Judge Harding ordered Richard Holgrove and his father to be executed for this crime.

Anne begged the judge to spare the life of her fiancé. When Judge Harding saw the lovely young woman he fell in love with her at once. He would not change his verdict. He hinted, though, that if Anne forgot Richard and married him, he would protect her. But when Anne saw that nothing she could do would save Richard, she turned her back on the judge. She walked out vowing that if Richard Holgrove was not to be her husband, no other man would be. The next day Richard and his father were beheaded. Their heads were fixed to the gateposts of their home as a warning to other Catholics in the district.

From that day Anne never spoke to a man. She stayed in her house and was never seen outside its doors.

### Questions & Assignments — PART 1

1. How, according to the story, did life become very difficult for Catholics in England after Henry VIII quarrelled with the Pope?
2. Explain how some Catholics got around these difficulties.
3. What evidence is there in this episode that Anne Musgrave was a rich lady?
4. Explain why Richard Holgrove and his father were executed.
5. Why was Anne not punished?
6. What action did Anne take after her fiancé was executed?
7. What do you expect to happen in the next episode? Why?
8. Why is the reader tempted to continue reading the story after the first episode?

## PART 2

After some years Judge Harding had become a rich man. The monasteries had a lot of money, and when the judge closed them down he kept a good deal of it for himself. He got a reputation as an enemy of the Catholics. To reward him for his efforts the king granted him the Holgroves' house and all their lands. Judge Harding moved into his new home and so became a neighbour of Anne Musgrave. The judge had not forgotten the young woman's beauty and made up his mind to marry her. He called at Anne's house but the servants would not let him in. He sent expensive presents but they were returned without a word. He wrote long letters telling Anne that he loved her and she would be rich and powerful if she agreed to marry him. The letters were returned unopened. Harding was furious at this treatment. He swore that if he could not marry Anne, no one else would. He would see to that.

People were very superstitious in those days. The judge planned to make use of this to bring Anne under his power. He paid the same false witnesses who had brought down the Holgrove family to spread rumours in the district of strange goings-on at Anne's house. Because she never went out, people already thought she was rather strange. Harding's men spread gossip at inns, fairs and markets that Anne Musgrave was a witch. People were paid to whisper that Anne had put their cattle under a spell and made them die. There was much sickness in those days because people were poor and their houses were dirty. However, when people fell ill or died, hints were dropped that the victims had been bewitched by Anne. She had put the evil eye on them, they said.

As time went on Anne Musgrave was accused of many things. She was arrested on charges of witchcraft. The night before her trial Anne was secretly brought from her cell for a private meeting with Harding. He promised that she would go free if she agreed to marry him. She refused.

"Then you have chosen death," muttered Harding. "Before the end of this week you will burn at the stake in the market place." He rang for the guards, who took Anne back to her cell.

### Questions & Assignments — PART 2

1. How did Judge Harding become a rich man?
2. Explain how the judge became a neighbour of Anne's.
3. How did he try to win Anne's favour?
4. When he failed to do so what did he decide to do?
5. What evidence is there in this episode that the people were superstitious?
6. (a) What do you *expect* to happen in the final episode?
   (b) What do you *hope* will happen in the final episode?

### [Answer Guidelines]

5. The writer suggests that many people believed that the deaths of farm animals and humans were caused by spells worked by witches. The real reasons for the deaths of people were illness, poverty and squalor but some believed otherwise.

## PART 3

The next day the trial began. The charges were read out and the evidence was heard. Anne was brilliant. She had answers to all the accusations that were made and, though he tried as hard as he could, Harding knew that she could not be proved guilty. So he announced that the next day the case would be decided by the drawing of lots. There would be two folded papers, on one of which would be written the word 'guilty'. The other paper would read 'not guilty'. Whichever paper Anne chose would decide her fate.

That night Anne was again brought secretly from her cell for a final meeting with the judge.

"This is your last chance," Harding warned her. "You cannot escape the drawing of lots and I have arranged it so that, whichever paper you choose, you will die. Look!" He drew a curtain. "Your funeral fire is already being made. Tomorrow it will be lit and you will be burned alive."

For the last time Anne refused to marry the judge and she was taken back to her cell.

The judge then took the two pieces of paper which would be used as lots on the following day. He wrote 'guilty' on both of them. As he folded both papers he smiled grimly at the thought that whichever paper she chose, Anne Musgrave would die.

The next morning, in front of all the people, the judge held out the folded papers, one in each hand. The funeral fire was ready, and soldiers with burning torches were waiting to light it. Anne asked for one thing before she drew the lot. She asked for the fire to be lit first, so that if she did have to die, she would die quickly. This was done and the fire crackled into flame.

Anne then took one of the papers, unfolded it and immediately threw it into the blazing fire. She then asked one of the soldiers to read out the words on the paper left in the judge's hand.

"Guilty," he read out in a loud voice.

Anne then said, "The other paper must have said 'not guilty' then, mustn't it?"

The onlookers agreed and a great shout went up. Everyone was relieved that she was innocent.

Judge Harding realised that Anne had cleverly guessed what he would do with the papers and that she had finally tricked him. He was so angry at this that he had a heart attack and a few days later he was dead.

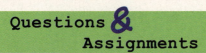

### Questions & Assignments — PART 3

1. Was the judge able to prove that Anne was a witch? Write out the sentence which supports your answer.
2. Was drawing lots a fair and just way to try Anne? Give a reason for your answer.
3. Explain why the judge wrote 'guilty' on both pieces of paper.
4. Give a clear explanation of how Anne tricked the judge.
5. Briefly describe the setting of the story.

## PERSONAL WRITING

# Assignments

### Writing for Young Children

1. Write about a lucky escape you had **or** one that you know about.

2. Describe an occasion when you were treated unfairly **or** an occasion when you witnessed someone being treated unfairly.

3. Write about a place where you would not like to live **or** a time in the past when you would not like to have lived. Explain why.

**Remember**

If you run out of ideas, imagine someone interviewing you about the subject. They will ask questions beginning with Who? What? When? Where? Why? and How? The answers you would give will be your material.

# Novels

### Danny the Champion of the World — by Roald Dahl

Danny thinks the world of his father, who has looked after him since his mother died when Danny was just four months old. But as he grows up, Danny discovers that his father's secret spells adventure and trouble for both of them!

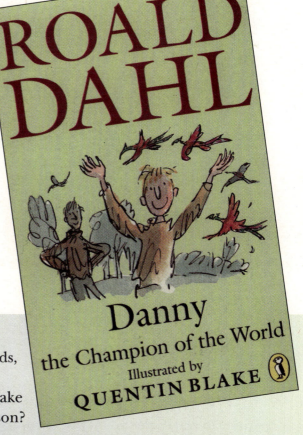

### Questions & Assignments

1. Describe, in your own words, Danny's home. (Chapter 1)
2. How did Danny's father make life interesting for his son? (Chapter 3)
3. Outline some of the poaching methods that Danny's father knew about.
4. Why did Danny's father enjoy poaching Mr. Hazell's pheasants?
5. (a) Describe the character, Captain Lancaster.
   (b) Why did he accuse Danny of cheating?
6. (a) Write about the way Danny and his father set about poaching two hundred pheasants in Mr. Hazell's wood.
   (b) What part of this episode did you find (i) exciting and (ii) amusing?
7. Write a review of *Danny the Champion of the World*.

## Buddy — by Nigel Hinton

Buddy would give anything to have a more ordinary dad on the night of the meeting with his class teacher at school. In the past, his mum would go to these meetings on her own, but she left home six months ago and hasn't been heard from since. That's something else that worries Buddy, because he thinks he's responsible for her leaving. It's a bewildering time for him as he struggles to understand the adult world and come to terms with the embarrassment and the love that he feels for both his parents.

### Questions & Assignments

1. (a) Explain why Buddy stole from his mother's purse. (Chapter 1)
   (b) Do you blame him? Give reasons for your answer.
2. Describe Buddy's appearance and explain why he was sensitive about it. (Chapter 2)
3. What does the 'fruit shop' joke reveal about (a) Mr. Normington and (b) Class 3E? (Chapter 2)
4. Disappointment, anger, guilt — does Buddy experience these feelings in Chapter 3? Illustrate your answer by referring to Chapter 3.
5. What sentence in Chapter 4 suggests that Buddy's father's job was not an ordinary one?

6. What events in Chapter 5 give Buddy a sense of achievement?
7. What insights can be found in Chapter 5 into the ways in which young people can be kind or cruel towards each other?
8. How does the plot develop in Chapter 6?
9. (a) Describe the atmosphere in the Rybeero household.
   (b) What details help to establish this atmosphere?
   (c) How does it differ from the atmosphere in Buddy's home? (Chapter 7)
10. Explain how Buddy suffers in Chapter 9.
11. Would you agree that Chapter 10 ends with a mood of suspense? Explain your answer by referring to the story.
12. What features of the author's description of the Beast makes him appear fearful? (Chapter 11)
13. (a) Trace the build up of tension in Chapter 11.
    (b) At what point is the tension relieved?
14. Was Buddy justified in being ashamed of his father? (Chapter 13) Give reasons for your answer.
15. Would you agree that Buddy's mother's reasons for leaving were good ones? (Chapter 14) Explain your answer.
16. (a) Explain the problem Buddy faces at the close of Chapter 16.
    (b) What would you do if you were in that situation?
17. Was Mrs. Rybeero right to let Buddy leave? (Chapter 20) Give reasons for your answer.
18. What features of the author's description of the countryside did you find particularly vivid and impressive?
19. Give your views on the ending of the story.
20. Would you agree that the characters of both Buddy's father and mother were a little unreal? Support your answer by referring to the story.
21. Write a review of the novel and say why you think it would or would not make an enjoyable read for someone of your age.

# [Answer Guidelines]

8. Rewrite this answer, filling in the spaces from the words below.

This chapter introduces a new _____ to the story. As Buddy _____ from the disco with his friends, Julius and Charmian Rybeero, he tells them about 56 Croxley Street and even _____ a few more gory details. They _____ to go and look at the house. Our curiosity is aroused. What will they find there? What will _____ to them?

The house turns out to be a _____ and forbidding sight with its _____ gardens and boarded windows. Out of _____ they approach the house, cautiously at first. Julius shows off his courage by knocking at the front door and then _____ through the letter box. What he sees makes him take to his _____ . Buddy and Charmian then take a look and see a sight that _____ them with fear – a pale skull-like face lit by candlelight and staring back at them. In _____ , they run away as fast as they can. What began as _____ fun ended with a terrifying experience.

The occupant of 56 Croxley Street gives the plot a new element. Is it a ghost? What kind of _____ can it be? How will it tie in with Buddy's plight? We want to read on to find the answers to these questions.

| | |
|---|---|
| bravado | returns |
| peering | happen |
| invents | creature |
| harmless | gloomy |
| decide | heels |
| mystery | chills |
| overgrown | panic |

# [Answer Guidelines]

**13.** (a) Buddy, Julius and Charmian have _____ the 'Beast' leaving number 56 and they decide to go in and _____ while he is _____ . We see that they are taking a risk and _____ begins to build up. We wonder will they get back out _____ before the 'Beast' returns or will there be someone else in the house. We _____ that there is danger ahead for them.

Buddy is looking for a link _____ the house and his father's work. We wonder will he discover such a link.
They explore the house without making any dramatic _____ and eventually reach the attic. The _____ grows when they spot the 'Beast' returning.

In an _____ to escape, they creep down the stairs and attempt to leave through the front door. It is locked and from the other end of the hallway the 'Beast' is _____ towards them, holding a knife. The author gives us a picture of his skull-like face and his red-rimmed sunken eyes as he slowly asks 'What you doing?' At this point the tension is at its highest.

(b) The tension is _____ when Charmian asks him about the cat he is supposed to have strangled. He _____ like a child who has been accused in the wrong and denies killing the cat. It is then clear that the 'Beast' presents no _____ to Buddy, Charmian and Julius.

| | |
|---|---|
| behaves | sense |
| discoveries | tension |
| absent | effort |
| suspense | explore |
| safely | relieved |
| advancing | threat |
| between | observed |

### The Runaways — by Victor Canning

On a night of wild storms, two lonely creatures escape from captivity. One is a boy, Smiler, wrongly convicted of stealing; the other, a cheetah, Yarra, leaving the Longleat Wildlife Park to have her cubs in privacy.

Both are in danger from the outside world and each other, but somehow their lives become inextricably bound up as they fight for survival on the edge of Salisbury Plain.

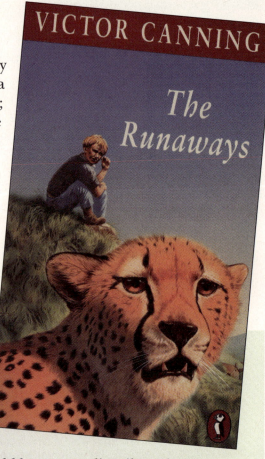

### Questions & Assignments

1. Describe (a) Smiler's and (b) Yarra's first day of freedom up to the point where they both settle down to rest for the night.
2. Smiler, according to his father, could be extraordinarily patient and industrious. Say how he shows patience and industry during his first days at Ford Cottage.
3. Yarra presents Smiler with a couple of difficulties in Chapter 4. Explain how Smiler deals with these.
4. Smiler gives his situation serious thought and decides on a plan. Outline this plan and the progress he makes in Chapter 5.
5. Why didn't Yarra return to the barn?
6. Describe Smiler's job at Danebury House.
7. What kind of character is Joe Ringer?
8. How does Yarra die?
9. Describe how Smiler trained the cubs.
10. Why did Smiler run away a day earlier than planned?
11. Write a note on each of the following characters:
    (a) Major Collingwood
    (b) Mrs. Lakey
    (c) Miss Milly
    (d) Pat Bagnall
    (e) Ethel.

## Roll of Thunder, Hear My Cry — by Mildred D. Taylor

Cassie was content with life on her family's Mississippi farm — especially in the school holidays, when she could run through the cool forest and wade barefoot in the pond. Besides, there were lots of things that bothered her about going to school, apart from having to wear a dress instead of trousers and sit all day in a classroom, things she took for granted yet didn't understand. Why was the Great Faith School so shabby and badly equipped, while Jefferson Davis County, the school for white children, was smart and well-cared for? Why did the Jefferson Davis pupils travel by bus, while she and her brothers had to walk to school in all weathers? Cassie didn't think about these differences much, but they were there in the back of her mind.

Behind her everyday life of homework and helping on the farm, with its rare treats like a trip into town or the great jamboree of the annual 'revival', Cassie sensed deep fears and tensions in her family. The Thirties were hard times for poor people, and her father had to take a second job on the railroad to try to make ends meet. But worse dangers than poverty threatened them. Cassie overheard talk about the sinister night riders, and she knew how their neighbour Mr. Berry and his nephews had been set on fire by a group of white men. Slowly, she began to realise that many white Southerners hated and despised her own people just for being black. It was painful knowledge, and the hardest lesson to learn was that she couldn't always fight back after an insult — for as her father told her, she had to weigh her own hurt against what a vicious gang might do to the whole community. Some things were too important, though, you had to take a stand, and it was up to her to decide what those things were.

This powerful and moving book is based on the experience of Mildred Taylor's own family, and its clear-eyed account of their struggle to hold on to their integrity through the hardships of the Thirties rings true in every word. *Roll of Thunder, Hear My Cry* was awarded the Newbery Medal for 1977.

### Chapter 1
1. From whose point of view is the story told?
2. At what point in time does the story begin?
3. What do we learn about Cassie and her family?
4. (a) Describe the school book episode.
   (b) Briefly outline what insights into Mississippi society of the 1930s are provided in the episode.
   (c) What do we learn about the character of Mama from the episode?

### Chapter 2
1. What do we learn about Mr. Logan's circumstances in this chapter?
2. (a) What features of Mr. Morrison made a big impression on the children?
   (b) A phrase in this chapter hints that Mr. Morrison will play a significant part in the story. Can you find the phrase? Explain your choice.
3. What event in this chapter underlines how difficult and precarious life was for the black people?

### Chapter 3
1. (a) Describe how the driver of the Jefferson Davis school bus humiliated Little Man.
   (b) Describe the children's revenge.
2. Comment on the character of Jeremy Simms.
3. Explain how the visit of Mr. Avery increased tension at this point of the story.

### Chapter 4
1. What is your impression of T. J. Avery. Refer to Chapter 4 to support your answer.
2. What does Harlan Granger want from Big Ma?
3. Do you think Mama acted wisely by bringing the children to see Mr. Berry?
4. (a) Explain briefly why the people were forced to shop at the Wallace Store.
   (b) What was Mama's plan to change this situation?

### Chapter 5
1. What examples of racism are to be found in the events of this chapter?

### Chapter 6
1. What are your first impressions of Uncle Hammer?
2. Would you agree that this chapter contains both moments of tension and humour? Refer to the chapter to support your answer.
3. What episode in this chapter shows Mama's wisdom and tolerance?

### Chapter 7
1. Describe Christmas at the Logan household.
2. What was the purpose of Mr. Jamison's visit?
3. Would you agree that the chapter closes on a note of tension? Explain your answer.

### Chapter 8
1. Describe Cassie's revenge on Lillian Jean Simms.
2. Why is Mama sacked?
3. Do you feel pity or contempt for T. J. Avery at the end of this chapter? Give reasons for your answer.

### Chapter 9
1. This chapter opens with a description of spring. What two features of the description impressed you?
2. What do we learn of T. J. Avery's '*friendship*' with the Simms brothers?
3. Do you blame Mr. Avery and Mr. Lanier for leading the boycott of Wallace's store? Give reasons for your answer.
4. What episode in this chapter created suspense?
5. Outline clearly and briefly what happened during the ambush.

### Chapter 10
1. Describe the problems which the Logan family faced at this point of the story.
2. What do we learn about the character of (a) Mr. Morrison and (b) Kaleb Wallace from the trunk episode?
3. What characteristics are displayed by Stacey during the conversation with Jeremy?
4. Was Papa pleased when he heard that Uncle Hammer sold the Packard? Explain your answer.
5. What details in the final part of the chapter suggest that T. J. Avery is about to get into trouble?

### Chapter 11
1. Write a brief and clear summary of the events of this chapter.
2. Would you agree that Chapter 11 ends on a note of tension? Explain briefly.

### Chapter 12
1. In your opinion was the fire accidental or deliberate? Give reasons for your answer.
2. Is there a lesson to be learnt from the way that both the blacks and the whites responded to the fire?

*Spectrum 2*

**General Questions**

1. (a) What features of the novel appealed to you?
   (b) Did the novel help you to achieve a deeper understanding of the issues in the story? Explain your answer.
2. Discuss how the different families in the story are portrayed.
3. Do you think that narrating the story from the point of view of Cassie was effective?

## [Answer Guidelines]

2. The Logans are a close-knit family; the parents and grandmother are warm, caring, hard-working, honest, with high personal integrity. They foster a sense of community. They treat the children fairly but firmly. They give sound advice to the children whenever it is sought and help them see the importance of making decisions and considering the consequences instead of acting irrationally. (Give one or two examples.) Hammer's love for his family is reflected in his selling of the car. (Give a few other examples.)

   Mr. Morrison, whose entire family was savagely killed, valued highly the warmth and love of the Logan household. This is shown by the manner in which he guards the house night after night. (Give other examples.) Comment briefly on some of the other families: the Averys, the Wallaces, the Simms. How do they differ from the Logan family?

3. Rewrite this answer, filling in the spaces with words from the box below.

   Cassie is nine; her _____ on events and people are _____ and straightforward; while she may not _____ at once the significance of many of the things that she sees and hears, it is always _____ to the reader. Because she is nine she cannot be _____ at all events. The adults often keep important _____ to themselves in order not to frighten the children.

   The author allows Cassie to _____ on a number of adult _____ in order to convey to the reader the course of events as seen from the adult point of view. The author does this on _____ to get the reader to work on the story. By not giving the full facts, but revealing important details, the author allows the readers the pleasure of working things out for themselves. (Give a few examples.)

   | eavesdrop | observations | information |
   | conversations | honest | purpose |
   | clear | present | understand |

# Our Day Out

## by Willy Russell

Willy Russell was born in 1947 in Whiston near Liverpool where his father owned a chip shop. As a schoolboy his performance was well below average. After leaving school at sixteen with unimpressive O level results — passing English only — Willy began work as a trainee ladies' hairdresser. He soon grew tired of life in the salon and became a labourer in a warehouse. His next career move took him to Ford Motors as a night-shift cleaner. It was during this time that he began studying by day for A levels. After success in these examinations he began training to become a teacher. During his time in teacher training college, he wrote and produced his first play.

He worked as a teacher for a year or two but the success of his musical *John, Paul, George, Ringo and Bert* in London in the mid 1970s enabled him to turn to writing as a full-time occupation. Since then he has enjoyed great success as a writer for both stage and screen. His best known works include the musical *Blood Brothers* and the screen plays *Educating Rita* and *Shirley Valentine*.

*Our Day Out* is a play about an outing of the Progress class (a class for children who have difficulty with reading and general school work) in a school from a poor part of Liverpool. The class are being taken on a day trip by coach to a sea-side resort in Wales. Mrs. Kay, the Progress class teacher, has organised the outing but the headmaster asks Mr. Briggs, another teacher, to go along 'to keep an eye on things'. The play chronicles the behaviour of the children on the coach, at a café, at the zoo, at an old castle and at the beach and the varied responses of the teachers and others with whom they come into contact.

The play has some very funny moments but it also explores a number of serious issues in a realistic and unsentimental manner. It may even develop our understanding, sympathy and affection for those who are sometimes regarded as life's losers.

## Presenting the Play

*Our Day Out* was originally written as a television play. Furthermore, it was not written as a play to be recorded in a television studio but as a film to be made on location — i.e. in a natural outdoor setting. Nevertheless, it has been successfully presented as a stage play by a number of Irish schools over the past ten years.

Stage plays cannot compete with film (including television) and radio in terms of sets and scenery. Film and radio can make speedy changes from one scene to another; and can also include scenes involving travel which would be difficult to depict accurately on stage. However, by using your imagination you should be able to adapt *Our Day Out* for stage. You may find the following suggestions useful.

- Recorded sound effects. Describe each sound effect and where it is to be located.
- Slides projected on to a backdrop. Slides need to be specially photographed. Say what type of photographs (slides) will be needed.
- Convert directions into stage directions. These may need to be changed or added to.
- Should stage furniture and props be kept to a minimum to preserve the fast pace of the play? What props are not needed? What props are essential?
- Should an extra part be written for another member of the Progress class (or staff)? Who would act as a commentator or story-teller? Care should be taken that such an additional character does not hold up the action.

# Our Day Out

## Characters

***THE TEACHERS:***
**Mrs Kay** *(in her early forties)*
**Susan** *(early twenties)*
**Colin** *(early twenties)*
**Briggs** *(early thirties)*
**Headmaster**

***THE KIDS:***
**Carol** *(13)*
**Reilly** *(15)*
**Digga** *(15)*
**Linda** *(15)*
**Karen** *(15)*
**Andrew** *(13)*
**Ronson** *(13)*
**Kevin** *(12)*
**Jimmy** *(12)*
**Maurice** *(12)*
**Other kids** *(all around 12 or 13)*

***OTHER ADULTS:***
**Les,** the 'lollipop man'
**The Driver**
**Mrs Roberts**
**Waitress**
**John**
**Mac**
**Animal Keeper**
**Two other Animal Keepers**

# Our Day Out

## Scene 1: In the street

[*The street is in the inner city of Liverpool.* **Kids** *are streaming in one direction. It is approaching 9 a.m. The* **Kids** *are pushing, shoving, rushing, ambling, leering and jeering. A group of older kids cross the road, ignoring the lollipop man's assistance. He points them out to a passing woman, obviously disgusted.* **Carol** *rushes along the street wearing a school uniform which doubles as a street outfit and her Sunday best. She is eating half a sandwich and clutching a supermarket carrier bag. She arrives at the roadside and, as there isn't a vehicle in sight, goes to cross without bothering to enlist the aid of the lollipop man,* **Les**. *He stops her from stepping off the pavement*]

**Les:** 'Ey you!
**Carol:** [*Stopping*] What?
**Les:** Come here. Come on!
**Carol:** [*Approaching him*] Agh ey, Les. Come on. I wanna get t' school.
**Les:** That makes a bloody change.
**Carol:** We're goin' out. On a trip.
**Les:** Now listen. Are you listenin'? Y' don't cross the road without the assistance of the lollipop man. And that's me!
**Carol:** There's nott'n comin', though.
**Les:** Now just you listen; I know it might look as though there's nothin' comin' but how do you know that a truck or car isn't gonna come speedin' out of that side road? Eh?
**Carol:** [*Looking*] Oh yeh. I never thought of that.
**Les:** No. I know y' didn't. Y' never do. None of y'. That's why the government hired me to look after y' all.
**Carol:** Ta Les.
**Les:** Ey. Where y' goin' today then?
**Carol:** It's somewhere far away. I forget.
**Les:** They all goin'?

**Carol:** Only the kids who go to the Progress Class.
**Les:** What's that?
**Carol:** What? Y'don't know what the Progress Class is? It's Mrs Kay's class. Y' go down there in the week if y' can't do sums or writing. If y' backward like.
**Les:** By Christ, I'll bet she's kept busy. They're all bloody backward round here.
**Carol:** I know. Come on Les. I wanna get there.

[**Les** *looks up and down the road. Not a vehicle in sight*]

**Les:** Just hold it there.
**Carol:** There's nott'n comin'.

[**Les** *looks down the road In the distance a car is just appearing*]

**Carol:** Oh come on, Les.

[**Les** *holds out his arm to prevent her from crossing. Only when the car is within striking distance does he walk out with his 'Stop' sign. The car pulls to a halt.* **Les** *waves* **Carol** *across*]

**Les:** [*Quietly to* **Carol** *as she passes*] I got him that time. Arrogant get that one is.

[**Carol** *continues on her way. The driver of the car glares as* **Les** *waves him on*]

## Scene 2: The school gates

[*A coach. Various groups of* **Kids** *are scattered near by. One group surrounds a teacher,* **Mrs Kay**, *all of them after her attention. Cries of, 'Miss, miss, miss, me mum said I could go, miss,' and 'Miss, can I come if I haven't got enough money?' and, 'Miss, can I come, miss?'*]

**Mrs Kay:** All right, all right. Will you just let me have a minute's peace and I'll get you all sorted out. Right. Now those who've got permission to come on the trip but haven't yet paid, I want you to come over here.

[*She moves a short distance away and all the kids follow her.* **Briggs** *surveys this scene*]

**Mrs Kay:** [*Bright*] Good morning, Mr Briggs.
**Briggs:** [*Begrudged*] Morning.

[*He turns and enters the school*]

**Briggs:** [*To a couple of boys*] Come on, move!

### SCENE 3: The Headmaster's office

[*The Headmaster is talking to* **Briggs**, *who was the driver of the car*]

**Headmaster:** Well I'd like you to go with her, John. We can get Frank Collins to take over your examination classes for the day. I'd just like you to be there and keep an eye on things. I don't want to be unprofessional and talk about a member of staff but I get the impression she sees education as one long game.
**Briggs:** Well . . . if the antics in her department are anything to go by . . . ! She always reminds me of a mother hen rather than a teacher . . .
**Headmaster:** Well, anyway, just try and keep things in some sort of order.

### SCENE 4: The school gates

[**Mrs Kay** *is talking to two young teachers,* **Colin** *and* **Susan**. *Around them are excited, lively kids – not lined up but in random groups*]

**Mrs Kay:** [*Shouting to a Kid*] Maurice! Come away from that road will you?

[*The* **Kid** *does so. Two older* **Kids** *come rushing out of school and up to the* **Teachers**]

**Reilly:** Miss . . . miss, can we come wit' y'? Can we?
**Mrs Kay:** Oh, Brian! You know it's a trip for the Progress Class.
**Reilly:** Agh, ay, miss, we used t' be in the Progress Class though.
**Susan:** But you're not now, Brian. Now you can read and write you're back in normal classes.
**Mrs Kay:** Look Brian. You know I'd take you. But it's not up to me. Who's your form teacher?
**Reilly:** Briggsy.
**Mrs Kay:** Well, you'll have to go and get his permission.
**Reilly:** [*As he and* **Digga** *rush off*] You're ace, miss.
**Mrs Kay:** Brian!

[*He stops*]

Bring a note.
**Reilly:** [*Worried*] Ah . . . what for, miss?
**Mrs Kay:** [*Smiling*] Because I wasn't born yesterday, Brian Reilly, and if I don't ask you for a note you'll just hide behind the corner for ten minutes and say he said you could go.
**Reilly:** [*Knowing she's got him sussed*] As if we'd do a thing like that, miss!
**Carol:** [*Still tugging*] Where are we goin', miss?
**Mrs Kay:** Carol . . . Miss Duncan's just told you, Conway. We're going to Conway.
**Carol:** Miss, is that in England, eh?
**Colin:** It's in Wales, Carol.
**Carol:** Will we have t' get a boat?
**Mrs Kay:** Carol . . . we're going on a coach. Look, it's there. You can get on now.

[*She shouts out to the rest of the* **Kids**]

Go on . . . you can all get on now.

[*There is a wild rush of* **Kids** *to the coach doors. The* **Driver** *appears and blocks the way*]

**Driver:** Right. Just stop there. Don't move.
**Kid:** Miss said we could get on.
**Driver:** Oh, did she now?
**Kids:** Yeh.
**Driver:** Well, let me tell youse lot something now. Miss isn't the driver of this coach. I am. An' if I say y' don't get on, y' don't get on.
**Mrs Kay:** Is anything wrong, Driver?
**Driver:** Are these children in your charge, madam?
**Mrs Kay:** Yes.
**Driver:** Well y' haven't checked them, have y'?
**Mrs Kay:** Checked them? Checked them for what?
**Driver:** Chocolate an' lemonade! We don't allow it. I've seen it on other coaches madam; fifty-two vomittin' kids . . . it's no joke. No, I'm sorry, we don't allow that.
**Mrs Kay:** [*To* **Susan**] Here comes Mr Happiness. All right, Driver . . . I'll check for you.

[*To* **Kids**]

. . . Now listen, everyone. If anybody's got any chocolate or lemonade I want you to put your hands up.

[*A sea of dumb faces and unraised hands.* **Mrs Kay** *smiles at the* **Driver**]

There you are, Driver. All right?
**Driver:** No, it's not all right. Y' can't just take their word for it. They have to be searched. Y' can't just believe kids.

[*Pause.* **Mrs Kay** *stares at him. She could blow up but she doesn't*]

**Mrs Kay:** Can I have a word with you, Driver, in private?

[*Reluctantly the* **Driver** *gets off the coach and goes across to her. She manoeuvres it so that he has his back to the coach and the* **Kids**]

What's your name, Driver?
**Driver:** Me name? I don't usually have to give me name.
**Mrs Kay:** Oh, come on . . . what's your name?
**Driver:** Suttcliffe, Ronny Suttcliffe.
**Mrs Kay:** Well, Ronny, [*Pointing*] take a look up these streets. [*He does and she motions the other teachers to be getting the* **Kids** *on the coach*] Ronny, would you say they were the sort of streets that housed prosperous parents?
**Driver:** We usually only do the better schools.
**Mrs Kay:** All right, you don't like these kids. I can tell that. But do you have to cause them so much pain?
**Driver:** [*Shocked*] What have I done? I only told 'em to wait . . . .
**Mrs Kay:** Ronny, the kids with me today don't know what it is to *look* at a bar of chocolate. Lemonade never touches their lips. [*We almost hear the violins*] These are the children, Ronny, who stand outside shop windows in the pouring rain, looking and longing and never getting. Even at Christmas, at Christmas-time when your kids from the better schools are opening presents and singing carols, these kids are left to wander the cold cruel streets.

[*Pause as she sees the effect she is having. The* **Driver** *is griefstricken*]

### SCENE 5: Inside the coach

[*The kids are stuffing themselves with sweets and lemonade. The* **Driver** *comes on board and by the time he turns to face the* **Kids** *there is not a bottle of lemonade or chocolate bar in sight. The* **Driver** *puts his hand into his pocket and pulls out a pound note*]

**Driver:** Here you are, son, [*To* **Kid** *in front seat*] run over to the shops an' get what sweets y' can with that.

[*The* **Kid** *takes the money and gets off the*

coach. **Susan**, *the young teacher, leans across to* **Mrs Kay**]

**Susan:** What did you do?
**Mrs Kay:** Lied like hell, of course!

[*She gets up and faces the kids*]

Now, will you listen everyone. We'll be setting off for Conway in a couple of minutes.

[*Cheers*]

Now listen! We want everyone to enjoy themselves, so let's have no silly squabbling or doing anything that might be dangerous to yourselves or to others. That's the only rule we have today: think of yourselves, but think of others as well.

[**Reilly** *and* **Digga** *rush into the bus*]

**Reilly:** Miss, miss, we're comin' wit' y', miss. He said it's all right.
**Mrs Kay:** Brian, where's the note?
**Reilly:** He didn't give us one, miss. He's comin' himself. He said to wait.

[**Digga** *and* **Reilly** *go to the back of the coach.* **Mrs Kay** *looks at* **Colin** *and* **Susan**]

**Colin:** He's coming to keep an eye on us.
**Susan:** Make sure we don't enjoy ourselves.
**Mrs Kay:** Ah well. We'll just have to deal with him the best way we can.

[*She sits down next to* **Carol**. *On the back seat of the coach* **Reilly** *and* **Digga** *are facing some small kids*]

**Reilly:** Right, punks. Move!
**Little Kid:** Why?
**Reilly:** Cos we claimed the back seat, that's why.
**Little Kid:** You're not even in the Progress though.
**Digga:** We used to be though, so move.
**Reilly:** Yeh. Respect y' elders!

[*At the front of the coach,* **Briggs** *is climbing aboard. He stands at the front and stares and glares. The* **Kids** *sigh - he is a cloud on the blue horizon*]

**Briggs:** [*Suddenly barks*] Reilly. Dickson. Sit down!
**Reilly:** Sir, we was only . . . .
**Briggs:** [*Staccato*] Sit down, now, come on, move!

[**Reilly** *and* **Digga** *sit on the two small kids who move to make room for them*]

**Briggs:** Go on, sort yourselves out!

[*He leans across to* **Mrs Kay** *and speaks quietly*]

You've got some real bright sparks here, Mrs Kay. A right bunch.
**Mrs Kay:** Well, I think we'll be safe now that you've come to look after us.
**Briggs:** [*Looking at the* **Kids**] There's a few of 'em I could sling off right now.
**Mrs Kay:** Oh, you are coming with us then?
**Briggs:** The Boss thought it might be a good idea if you had an extra member of staff.

[*Stands to address the* **Kids**]

Right, listen.

[*Pause*]

We don't want you to think that we don't want you to enjoy yourselves today, because we do! But a lot of you haven't been on a school visit before so you won't know *how* to enjoy yourselves. So I'll tell you. To enjoy a coach trip we sit in our seats. We don't wander up and down the aisle. We talk quietly to our neighbour, not shout at our mates four seats down.

[*Staccato*] Are you listening, girl! We look nicely out of the windows at the scenery. And we don't do anything else.

[*Throughout the speech the* **Kids** *look disappointed*]

Don't worry, I've driven in my car behind school coaches and seen it. A mass of little hands raised in two-fingered gestures to the passing cars. Yes. But we won't do that will we? Will we?

[*Chorus of: 'No, sir.'*]

**Briggs:** No, sir. We won't.

[*The* **Kid** *returning from the shop, armed with sweets, climbs onto the bus*]

**Kid:** I've got them . . . I've got loads . . .
**Briggs:** Where've you been?
**Kid:** Gettin' sweets, sir.
**Briggs:** Sweets?
**Mrs Kay:** [*Reaching for sweets*] Thank you, Maurice.
**Briggs:** Sweets?

[*The* **Driver** *taps* **Briggs** *on the shoulder*]

**Driver:** Excuse me, can I have a word with you, please?
**Briggs:** [*Puzzled*] Yes.

[*The* **Driver** *gets off the coach and* **Briggs** *follows.* **Mrs Kay** *gives the sweets to* **Susan** *who starts to dish them out. We hear a snatch of the* **Driver's** *speech to* **Briggs**]

**Driver:** The thing is, about these kids, they're like little souls lost an' wanderin' the cruel heartless streets . . .

[*Inside the coach,* **Colin** *has joined* **Susan** *in giving out the sweets.* **Colin** *is at the back seat*]

**Reilly:** How y' gettin' on with miss, eh sir?
**Digga:** We saw y', sir, goin' into that pub with her, sir.

[**Susan** *is watching in the background*]

**Colin:** [*Covering his embarrassment*] Did you?
**Reilly:** Are you in love with her, sir? Are y'?
**Colin:** [*Making his escape*] All right . . . you've all got sweets have you?
**Reilly:** Sir's in love, sir's in love!

[**Reilly** *laughs and jeers as* **Colin** *makes his way down the aisle*]

**Susan:** Watch it, Brian!
**Reilly:** [*Feigned innocence*] What?
**Susan:** You know what.
**Reilly:** Agh ey, he is in love with y' though, isn't he, miss.
**Digga:** Miss, I'll bet he wants t' marry y'.
**Reilly:** You'd be better off with me, miss. I'm better lookin'.
**Susan:** [*Giving up playing it straight. She goes up to him, leans across and whispers*] Brian . . . little boys shouldn't try to act like men. The day might come when their words are put to the test!

[*She walks away*]

**Reilly:** [*Jeering*] Any day, miss . . . . any day . . . . [*Laughs*]
**Digga:** What did she say? What did she say?
**Reilly:** Said she fancied me.

[*At the front of the coach,* **Briggs** *and the* **Driver** *are climbing back on board. Briggs sits opposite* **Mrs Kay.** *He leans across to her*]

**Briggs:** [*Quietly*] We've got a right head case of a driver.

[*The engine roars into life. The* **Kids** *cheer.* **Briggs** *turns round with a warning look as the coach pulls away from the school. Thousands of little fingers raise in a V-sign out of the windows*]

Spectrum 2

## Questions & Assignments

1. What information do we get from Carol in Scene 1 on the setting and the direction of the action of the play?
2. What are your impressions of Carol from these scenes?
3. What insights do we get into the nature and the causes of the children's poverty from the first 5 scenes?
4. Would you say that Mrs. Kay was (a) silly, (b) easily fooled, (c) clever, (d) soft-hearted? Support your answer by referring to the text.
5. Do you think Mrs. Kay was right to allow Reilly and Digga to go? Give reasons for your answer.
6. (a) What are your impressions of Mr. Briggs at this point of the play?
   (b) Do you think that his presence on the outing will add to *or* take from our enjoyment of the play? Give reasons for your answer.

## [Answer Guidelines]

6. (a) We first meet **Briggs** in Scene 1 as the driver of the car. He *'glares'* at the lollipop man who, in turn, describes him as *'an arrogant get'*. In Scene 2, **Briggs** responds to **Mrs. Kay's** greeting in a *'begrudged'* way. When he is talking to the headmaster he is eager to criticise **Mrs. Kay** and the way she deals with her class. It is clear that he agrees to go in order to keep on the right side of the headmaster. When he boards the bus, the children sigh and he, in turn, glares at them. He talks to **Mrs. Kay** about the children in an unkind and sarcastic way *'You've got some real bright sparks here . . . '*
   **Mr. Briggs** tells the children how to enjoy themselves but it is clear from their reaction that their idea of enjoyment and his idea of enjoyment differ a great deal. His remark about the driver, *'We've got a right head case of a driver'* could suggest that Briggs has no sympathy or understanding of the poverty and deprivation of the children and that he regards those who show any pity for them as 'head cases'.
   **Briggs** is clearly a figure of feared authority, a teacher who gets his way by bullying and frightening the children, rather than by winning their affection and respect.

   (b) I think that **Briggs** will add a great deal to the enjoyment of the play. An important element in the plot of any play is conflict and Briggs' presence on the trip is sure to result in conflict both between him and the other teachers and, of course, between him and the children. The form the conflict will take and whether Briggs will or will not come off worse, adds to our interest in the play. Therefore, while Briggs' presence on the tour is not likely to provide added enjoyment for the children, it will provide added interest and enjoyment for the audience or readers.

## Points to Note — CHARACTERS IN PLAYS

Here are some points to remember when writing about a character in a play. You should base your assessment of the character on:

- what he or she says.
- actions and gestures of the character. Pay particular attention here to stage directions.
- what other characters say of him or her.
- how others respond to the character in question.

Conclude with your overall impressions of the character and see how he or she contributes to the interest of the play.

Finally, take care not to confuse 'bad characters' and 'bad people'. While certain characters, such as Briggs, would obviously be unpleasant to have around in real life, they can be great dramatic creations who add much excitement and enjoyment to plays. In fact, 'nasty' characters often add more **interest** to plays than 'good' characters.

## PERSONAL WRITING

### ASSIGNMENT

#### Writing Drama

Create an unpleasant character by writing a short scene based on one of the following situations. Remember the kind of behaviour we dislike in others — boasting, mocking, being greedy, bullying, boring etc.

- You and your family are awaiting the arrival of an unpopular relative. He or She arrives . . .
- A new teacher arrives in your class . . .
- A new boy or girl arrives in your neighbourhood and attempts to join your 'crowd' . . .

### SCENE 6: Leaving the city

[*As the coach goes along the city streets the* **Kids** *are talking and laughing and pointing. On the back seat,* **Reilly** *secretly takes out a packet of Number Six cigarettes. The* **Little Kid** *sees them*]

**Digga:** Reilly, light up.
**Reilly:** Where's Briggsy?
**Digga:** He's at the front, I'll keep dixie. Come on, we're all right, light up.
**Little Kid:** Agh 'ey. You've got ciggies. I'm gonna tell miss.
**Reilly:** Shut up you an' open that friggin' window.
**Little Kid:** No . . . I'm gonna tell miss.
**Digga:** Go'n tell her. She won't do nott'n anyway.
**Kid:** I'll tell sir.
**Reilly:** You do an' I'll gob y'.
**Digga:** Come on . . . open that window, you.
**Kid:** Why?
**Reilly:** Why d' y' think? So we get a bit of fresh air.
**Kid:** Well there's no fresh air round here. You just wanna smoke. An' smokin' stunts y' growth.
**Reilly:** I'll stunt your friggin' growth if y' don't get it open.

[**Andrews** *gets up and reaches for the window*]

**Andrews:** I'll open it for y' Reilly.

[**Reilly** *ducks behind the seat and lights up*]

**Andrews:** Gis a ciggy.
**Reilly:** Get y' own ciggies.
**Andrews:** Ah go on. I opened the window for y'.
**Digga:** Y' can buy one off us.
**Andrews:** I can't. I haven't got any money.
**Reilly:** Course y've got money.
**Andrews:** Me ma wouldn't give me any. She didn't have any.
**Digga:** Go 'way . . . your ma's loaded.
**Andrews:** Well *I've* got no money . . . honest.
**Digga:** Well, y've got no ciggies either.
**Andrews:** I'll give y' half me sarnies for one ciggie.
**Reilly:** What's on 'em?
**Andrews:** Jam.
**Reilly:** I hate jam.

[*They have become lax about keeping an eye out and do not notice* **Briggs** *getting up from his seat and approaching the back of the coach.* **Digga** *suddenly looks up and sees him*]

**Digga:** Briggs!

[**Reilly** *passes the cigarette to* **Andrews**]

**Reilly:** Here!
**Andrews:** Ta.

[**Andrews** *takes it and, making sure that his head is out of sight, he takes a huge drag. When he looks up,* **Briggs** *is peering down at him*]

**Briggs:** Put it out!
**Andrews:** Sir, sir, I wasn't . . .
**Briggs:** Put it out. Now get to the front of the coach.
**Andrews:** Sir, I was just . . .
**Briggs:** I said get to the front!

[**Andrews** *sighs, gets up and goes to the front of the coach.* **Briggs** *sits in Andrews' seat*]

**Briggs:** Was it your ciggie, Reilly?
**Reilly:** Sir, I swear on me mother.
**Digga:** Don't believe him, sir. How can he swear on his mother? She's been dead for ten years.
**Briggs:** All right, all right. We don't want any argument. There'll be no more smoking if I stay up here, will there?

[**Carol**, *who is sitting next to* **Mrs Kay**, *is staring out of the window*]

**Carol:** Isn't it horrible, eh, miss.
**Mrs Kay:** Mm?
**Carol:** Y' know . . . all the thingy like. The dirt an' that.

[*Pause*]

I like them nice places.
**Mrs Kay:** Which places?
**Carol:** Y' know them places on the telly. Where they have gardens an' trees outside an' that.
**Mrs Kay:** You've got trees in Pilot Street, haven't you?
**Carol:** We did have till last bommy night - the kids chopped 'em all down an' burnt them all. [*Pause*] Miss, y' know when I grow up, miss. Y' know if I started to work hard now an' learned how to read, eh? Well, d' y' think I'd be able to live in one of them nice places?

[*Pause*]

**Mrs Kay:** Well you could try, couldn't you, love. Eh?
**Carol:** Yeh.

[**Mrs Kay** *smiles at her and links her arm. At the back, the kids are all stifled and bored by* **Briggs'** *presence*]

**Briggs:** [*Pointing out of the window at the South Docks*] Now just look at that over there.

[**Digga** *looks but sees nothing*]

**Digga:** What?
**Briggs:** What? Can't y' see? Look, those buildings. Don't you ever bother looking at what's around you?
**Reilly:** It's only the docks, sir.
**Briggs:** You don't get buildings like that anymore. Just look at the work that must have gone into that.
**Reilly:** D' you like it down here, sir?
**Briggs:** I'm often down here at weekends, taking notes, photographs. [*Sharply*] Are you listening, Reilly? There's a wealth of history that won't be here much longer.
**Reilly:** Me old man works down here, sir.
**Briggs:** What does he think about it?
**Reilly:** He hates it.
**Briggs:** His job or the place.
**Reilly:** The whole lot.
**Briggs:** Well, you tell him to stop and have a look at what's around him. Yes, he might see things a bit differently then.

[**Briggs** *looks up and sees* **Linda** *kneeling up on her seat and talking to the girl behind her*]

**Karen:** Wales is cracker.
**Briggs:** Linda Croxley!
**Linda:** [*Not even looking up*] What?

[**Briggs** *gets up and goes across to her. She waits until the last possible moment before sitting 'properly' in her seat*]

**Briggs:** What sort of outfit's that for a school visit?

[*She is dressed in the prevailing pop outfit of the day*]

**Linda:** [*Chewing. Contemptuous. Looking out of window*] What!
**Briggs:** Don't you 'what' me young lady. [*She shrugs*] You know very well that on school visits you wear school uniform.
**Linda:** Well. Mrs Kay never said nott'n about it.
**Briggs:** You're not talking to Mrs Kay.
**Linda:** Yeh. I know.

[*Pause*]

**Briggs:** [*Leaning in close. Threatening*] Now listen here young lady - I don't like your attitude one bit!
**Linda:** What have I said? I haven't said nott'n yet, have I?
**Briggs:** I'm talking about your attitude. [*Pause*] I'm telling you now. Carry on like this and you'll be spending your time in Conway inside this coach.
**Linda:** I don't care. I don't wanna see no crappy castle anyway.

**Briggs:** [*Pointing*] Count yourself lucky you're not a lad. [*Pause*] Now I'm warning you, Miss Croxley, cause any more unpleasantness on this trip and I'll see to it that it's the last you ever go on. [*Pause*] Is that understood? Is it?
**Linda:** [*Still looking out of window*] Yes. [*Sighs*]
**Briggs:** It better had be.

[*He makes his way down to the front of the coach and takes his seat next to **Andrews**. Across the aisle **Briggs** sees that **Mrs Kay** has taken off her shoes and has her stockinged feet curled up under her. **Carol** has her arm linked through **Mrs Kay's** and is snuggled up to her – they look more like mother and daughter than teacher and pupil. Behind **Briggs**, **Linda** is kneeling up again, **Reilly** and company have started smoking and there are lots of kids eating sweets, drinking lemonade and larking about. He addresses the kid next to **Andrews**]*

**Briggs:** Right, what's your name?

[*Pause*]

**Briggs:** Wake up!
**Maurice:** Sir, me!
**Briggs:** What's your name?
**Maurice:** McNally, sir.
**Briggs:** Right, McNally, go and sit at the back.
**Maurice:** Sir, what for?
**Briggs:** Never mind what for, just do what you're told, lad.

[**Maurice** *goes to the back of the coach*]

**Briggs:** [*To **Andrews***] Right, move up! How long have you been smoking, Andrews?
**Andrews:** Sir, I don't smoke.

[*Pause as **Briggs** looks at him*]

Sir, since I was eight, sir.
**Briggs:** And how old are you now?
**Andrews:** Sir, thirteen, sir.
**Briggs:** What do your parents say about it?
**Andrews:** Sir, sir, me mum says nott'n about it but when me dad comes home, sir, sir, he belts me.
**Briggs:** Because you smoke?
**Andrews:** Sir, no sir, because I won't give him one.

[*Pause*]

**Briggs:** Your father goes to sea does he?
**Andrews:** What? No, sir.
**Briggs:** You said 'when he comes home,' I thought you meant he was away a lot.
**Andrews:** He is, sir, but he doesn't go to sea.
**Briggs:** What does he do?
**Andrews:** I dunno, sir, sir, he just comes round every now an' then an' has a barney with me mam. Then he goes off again. I think he tries to get money off her but she won't give him it though. She hates him. We all hate him.

[*Pause*]

**Briggs:** Listen. Why don't you promise yourself that you'll give up smoking. You must realise it's bad for your health.
**Andrews:** Sir, I do, sir. I've got a terrible cough.
**Briggs:** Well, why don't you pack it in?
**Andrews:** Sir, sir, I can't.
**Briggs:** Thirteen and you can't stop smoking!
**Andrews:** No, sir.
**Briggs:** [*Sighing, shaking his head*] Well you'd better not let me catch you again.
**Andrews:** No, sir, I won't.

[*Pause as they each go into their respective thoughts. **Briggs** turns and looks at **Mrs Kay**. She looks at him and smiles warmly. He tries to respond but doesn't quite make it. **Colin** walks along the aisle generally checking that everything is all right. As he gets near **Linda's** seat her friend, **Karen**, taps her and points him out. **Linda** immediately turns round and smiles at **Colin**. It's obvious that she fancies him*]

**Linda:** Sir, y' comin' to sit by me are y'?

**Karen:** [*On the seat behind Linda*] Don't sit by her sir . . . come an' sit by me.
**Colin:** I've got a seat at the front, thanks.
**Linda:** 'Ey, sir.
**Colin:** What, Linda?
**Linda:** Come here, I wanna tell y' somethin'.
**Colin:** Well, go on.
**Linda:** Ah ey sir, I don't want everyone to hear. Come on, just sit down here while I tell y'.
**Karen:** Go on, sir . . . she won't harm y'.
**Linda:** Come on, sir.

[*Reluctantly* **Colin** *sits by her.* **Karen's** *head is poking through the space between the seats and both girls laugh*]

**Colin:** What is it?

[*They laugh*]

You're not goin' to tell me a joke, are you?

[*The girls laugh even more*]

Well, I'll have to go.

[**Linda** *quickly links her arm through his and holds him there*]

**Linda:** No, sir . . . Listen. Listen, she said, I wouldn't tell y' . . . but I will. [*Pause*] Sir, I think you're lovely.
**Colin:** [*Quickly getting up. Embarrassed*] Linda!

[*He walks away from the girls to the back of the coach*]

**Linda:** I told him. I said I would. Ooh . . . he's ace isn't he?
**Karen:** You've got no chance. He's goin' with miss.
**Linda:** I know. [*Pause*] He might chuck her though an' start goin' with me. He might marry me.
**Karen:** [*Shrieking*] Ooer! Don't be stupid, you. You won't get a husband like sir. You'll end up marryin' someone like your old feller.

**Linda:** You're just jealous you, girl.
**Karen:** Aaght.

[**Colin** *talks to the lads on the back seat.* **Reilly** *hides a cigarette in his cupped hand*]

**Colin:** All right lads . . . it shouldn't be too long before we're getting into Wales.
**Little Kid:** That's in the country, Wales, isn't it, sir?
**Colin:** A lot of it is countryside, yes.
**Reilly:** Lots of woods, eh sir?
**Colin:** Woods and mountains, lakes . . . .
**Reilly:** You gonna take miss into the woods, are y', sir?
**Colin:** [*Pause*] Now just watch it, Brian, all right?
**Reilly:** Sir, I just meant was y' gonna show her the trees an' the plants . . . .
**Colin:** I know quite well what you meant.

[*Turns to go*]

And if I was you I'd put that fag out before you burn your hand. If Mr Briggs sees that you'll be spending the rest of the day alongside him. Now come on, put it out.

[**Reilly** *takes a last mammoth drag and then stubs out the cigarette.* **Colin** *walks back along the aisle*]

**Reilly:** [*Shouting after him*] I'll show her the woods for y', sir.

[**Colin** *pretends not to hear.* **Reilly** *leans across to the* **Little Kid** *in the seat in front and knocks him*]

**Reilly:** Give us a sweet you, greedy guts.
**Kid:** I've only got a few left.
**Digga:** You've got loads.
**Kid:** I haven't.
**Reilly:** Let's have a look then.

[*The* **Kid** *falls for it and shows him the bag.* **Reilly** *snatches it*]

Ta!

> ### Questions & Assignments
>
> 1. (a) Give some examples of slang used in this scene.
>    (b) Do you think the use of slang adds to or takes from the play? Explain your answer.
> 2. What did you find humorous in this scene?
> 3. (a) What 'attitude' does Linda display towards Briggs?
>    (b) How does she succeed in displaying this attitude?
> 4. What are your feelings towards (a) Carol, (b) Andrews and (c) Mrs. Kay, at this point in the play?
> 5. What insights do we get into the home backgrounds of some of the children?

### Scene 7: In the country

[*The coach is on a country road.* **Mrs Kay** *is talking to the* **Driver**]

**Mrs Kay:** Ronny, I was just wondering, is there somewhere round here we could stop and let the kids stretch their legs a bit?

**Driver:** Well I'll tell y' what, Mrs Kay, there's a few cafés a bit further on. D' y' want me to pull into one of them?

**Mrs Kay:** Smashing.

### Scene 8: A roadside café

[*Outside the café there are signs saying 'Open' and 'Coaches Welcome'. Inside the café, a* **Waitress** *is working on the tables. There is also a woman,* **Mrs Roberts**, *working behind the counter*]

**Waitress:** [*Looking up and seeing coach in distance*] Better be getting some cups ready, Mrs Roberts. There's a coach comin'.

**Mrs Roberts:** [*Moving over to window*] Where is it?

**Waitress:** Probably pensioners so early in the season.

**Mrs Roberts:** [*Worried*] No. I don't . . . I don't think so.

[*She moves behind the counter and produces a pair of binoculars*]

Let me see.

[*She lifts the binoculars and looks at the coach. She can see the kids and the destination indicator which reads: 'Liverpool to Conway'. She lowers the binoculars and frowns a worried frown*]

Right! Come on, action!

### Scene 9: Inside the coach

[**Mr Briggs** *is addressing the* **Kids**]

**Briggs:** Now the folk who run these places provide a good and valuable service to travellers like us . . . so remember what I've said.

### Scene 10: Back at the café

[*The café is alive with activity: the shutters are coming down, the 'Coaches Welcome' sign is replaced by 'Absolutely no Coaches' and the 'Open' sign by one saying 'Closed'. The doors are locked and bolted;* **Mrs Roberts** *and the* **Waitress** *lean against the door*]

### SCENE 11: In the coach

[*The coach has pulled up. The* **Driver** *and* **Mrs Kay** *are looking at the café*]

**Mrs Kay:** Perhaps it's because it's so early in the season. Maybe if they knew there was the chance of some business they'd open for us. I'll go and give them a knock.

### SCENE 12: In the café

[*Inside, the two women are silent, terrified. They hear footsteps coming up the drive. The door is knocked upon.* **Mrs Kay** *is on the other side of the door watched by the* **Kids** *from the coach windows. She knocks again*]

**Mrs Roberts:** [*From within*] We are closed!
**Mrs Kay:** You couldn't possibly . . . .
**Mrs Roberts:** [*Firm*] We are closed.

[**Mrs Kay** *moves away. As the two women hear the receding footsteps, they sigh*]

**Mrs Roberts:** I only ever did it once, take a Liverpool coachload. I tell you not one word of a lie Miss Powell, they'd rob your eyes if you wasn't lookin'.

[*The coach pulls away. The* **Kids** *give V-signs to the café and cross their legs to stop themselves from wetting*]

### SCENE 13: A café and shop

[*On the window a sign reads: 'Under New Management'. Inside, two men,* **John** *and* **Mac***, are behind the counter generally preparing their place for the season*]

**John:** Look, how many times, listen, it's only the start of the season innit? Eh? Course it is. We can't make a bloody fortune before the season's begun, can we?
**Mac:** See, it's no' that what's worryin' me. What I think, see, is we bought the wrong place. If you was askin' me, I'd say the coaches'll stop at the first café they come to. An' that's up the road.
**John:** Some of them will, yeh. But there'll be enough for us as well. Give it a month, that's all; y' won't be able t' see this road for coaches. Thousands of school kids with money t' burn. We'll clean up, mate.

[*They hear the sound of brakes and of tyres pulling up.* **John** *looks out of the window*]

Now what did I say, eh?
**Mac:** [*Looking out of window. Brightening*] Look at that. Christ, there's hundreds of them.
**John:** Right. Let's go. Come on.

[*Moves to the counter and points out the items quickly*]

**John:** Jelly Babies: 15p a quarter.
**Mac:** I thought they was only 12.
**John:** Ice creams 9p.
**Mac:** They was only 7p yesterday.
**John:** Listen, mate, can I help inflation?
**Mac:** [*Getting the picture*] Oh right. I get the picture.
**John:** Passin' trade mate. Always soak the passin' trade. Y' never see them again so it don't matter. Bubble Gum 2p — no make that 3. Ice lollies 10p. Come on . . . get those doors open. We'll milk this little lot.

### SCENE 14: In the car park

[*The* **Kids** *are tumbling off the coach.* **Mrs Kay** *takes out a flask and sits on a bench in the café garden.* **Briggs** *is frantic*]

**Briggs:** Stop! Slater, walk . . . walk! You, boy . . . come here. Now stop. All of you . . . stop!
**Mrs Kay:** [*Pouring out coffee*] Mr Briggs, they'll . . .

**Briggs:** [*To a boy,* **Ronson**, *who is rushing for the door of the shop*] Ronson! Come here!

[**Ronson** *stops and walks back to* **Briggs**, *shrugging*]

**Mrs Kay:** Mr Briggs . . . as long as they don't go near the road I don't think there's any . . .
**Briggs:** All right, Mrs Kay.

[**Ronson** *stands in front of him*]

Now just where do you think you are?

[**Ronson** *is puzzled*]

Well?

[**Ronson** *looks round for help in answering. There is none*]

**Ronson:** [*Sincerely*] Sir, Wales?

### Scene 15: Inside the shop

[*The counter cannot be seen for pushing, impatient* **Kids.** *The two men are working frantically as orders are fired at them from all quarters. As the orders are shouted, the* **Kids** *are robbing stuff left, right and centre - it's the usual trick but the two men are falling for it - the* **Kids** *point to jars high up, as the men turn their backs, racks of chocolate bars disappear into eager pockets*]

### Scene 16: Outside the shop

**Briggs:** And don't let me catch you at it again. Now go on. Walk.

[*He watches as* **Ronson** *walks into the shop. Satisfied, he turns to* **Mrs Kay**]

Now, Mrs Kay, what was it you wanted?
**Mrs Kay:** Well, I just thought you might like to have a sit down away from them for a few minutes.
**Briggs:** To be quite honest, Mrs Kay, I think we should all be inside, looking after them. Do you think it was wise just letting them all pour in there at once?
**Mrs Kay:** Ooh . . . leave them. They've been cooped up for over an hour. They'll want to stretch their legs and let off a bit of steam.
**Briggs:** I don't mind them stretching their legs. It's not the children I'm concerned about.
**Mrs Kay:** Well, just who are you concerned about?
**Briggs:** There's not only our school to think about, you know. There's others who come after us and they're dependent upon the goodwill of the people who run these places.
**Mrs Kay:** [*Pouring out another cup of coffee*] Considering the profit they make out of the kids I don't think they've got much to complain about.
**Briggs:** [*Taking cup*] Thanks. [*Pause*] You know, I'll have to say this to you, Mrs Kay, there are times when I really think you're on their side.

[*Pause*]

**Mrs Kay:** And I'll have to say this to you, Mr Briggs, I didn't ask you to come on this trip.
**Briggs:** No, but the Headmaster did.

### Scene 17: Outside the coach

[*The last few stragglers climb on board*]

**Mrs Kay:** [*To the* **Kids**] Are you the last? Anyone left in the toilet?
**Susan:** [*As she finishes counting heads*] That's the lot. We've got them all.
**Mrs Kay:** All right Ron.
**Driver:** Right love. [*Starts engine*]

### SCENE 18: In the shop

[*The* **Kids** *have gone and the shelves are almost bare. The two men sit back, exhausted but satisfied*]

**Mac:** If I hadn't seen it with m' own eyes.
**John:** I told y'.
**Mac:** We'll have to re-order.
**John:** An' that's just one coachload.
**Mac:** We must've took a bloody fortune.
**John:** There was sixty quid's worth of stock on those shelves an' most of it's gone.
**Mac:** Come . . . let's count up.

[*He gets up, goes to the till and opens it. It contains a lot of change but hardly any notes. He is puzzled*]

Was you lookin' after the notes?

**John:** Which notes? I thought you was takin' care of them.
**Mac:** Well, we must of taken a load of notes.

[*He looks at the bare shelves*]

### SCENE 19: Inside the coach

[*The* **Kids** *are weighed down with sweets*]

### SCENE 20: The shop

**Mac:** The thievin' little bastards!

[*He rushes for the door.* **John** *follows. As he flings back the door he sees the coach just pulling away down the road. They run after the disappearing coach. The back window is a mass of two-fingered gestures. The two men are finally left standing in the road*]

### SCENE 21: In the coach

[**Mrs Kay** *leaves her seat and goes over to* **Susan's** *seat.* **Susan** *is playing 'I Spy' with a couple of girls who are sitting with her*]

[**Briggs** *moves across to talk to* **Colin**. *He is conspiratorial*]

**Briggs:** You know what her problem is, don't you?
**Colin:** [*Trying to keep out of it. Looking out of window*] Mm?
**Briggs:** Well, she thinks I can't see through all this woolly-headed liberalism, you know what I mean? I mean, all right, she has her methods, I have mine but I can't see why she has to set herself up as the great champion of the non-academics. Can you? It might look like love and kindness but if you ask me I don't think it does the kids a scrap of good.
**Colin:** Erm . . .
**Briggs:** I mean, I think you have to risk being disliked if you're going to do any good for these type of kids. They've got enough freedom at home, haven't they, with their two quid pocket money and television till all hours, haven't they? [*Pause*]
I don't know what you think but I think her philosophy is totally confused. What do you think?

[**Briggs** *waits for an answer*]

**Colin:** Actually, I don't think it's got anything to do with a philosophy.
**Briggs:** What? You mean you haven't noticed all this, sort of, anti-establishment, let the kids roam wild, don't check them attitude?
**Colin:** Of course I've noticed it. But she's like that all the time. This trip isn't organised according to any startling theory.
**Briggs:** Well what is the method she works to then? I mean, you tell me, you know her better than I do.

**Colin:** The only principle behind today is that the kids should have a good day out.
**Briggs:** Well that's all I'm saying, but if they're going to have a good and stimulating day then it's got to be planned and executed better than this.

[*While* **Briggs** *is talking,* **Mrs Kay** *has moved to have a word with the* **Driver**. *Suddenly the coach swings into a driveway.* **Briggs** *is startled and puzzled*]

What's this . . . where are we . . .
**Mrs Kay:** It's all right, Mr Briggs . . . . I've checked it with the Driver. I thought it would be a good idea if we called into the zoo for an hour. We've got plenty of time.
**Briggs:** But I thought this trip was organised so that the kids could see Conway Castle.
**Mrs Kay:** We'll be going to the castle after. [*To the* **Kids**] Now listen, everybody. As a sort of extra bonus, we've decided to call in here and let you have an hour at the zoo.

[*Cheers*]

**Briggs:** Look, we can't . . . .
**Mrs Kay:** Now the rest of the staff and myself will be around if you want to know anything about the animals – mind you, there's not much point in asking me, because I don't know one monkey from the next.
**Reilly:** [*Shouting from back*] Apart from Andrews, miss, he's a gorilla.

[**Andrews** *gives him a V-sign*]

**Mrs Kay:** And yourself, Brian, the Orang Utang.

[*The* **Kids** *laugh.* **Reilly** *waves his fist*]

**Digga:** Don't worry, miss, he's a big baboon.
**Mrs Kay:** Now let's not have any silly name-calling.
**Briggs:** [*Whispering in* **Mrs Kay's** *ear*] Mrs Kay . . .
**Mrs Kay:** [*Ignoring him*] Now as I was saying, I don't know a great deal about the animals but we're very lucky to have Mr Briggs with us because he's something of an expert in natural history. So, if any of you want to know more about the animals you see, Mr Briggs will tell you all about them. Come on, leave your things on the coach.
**Kid:** Agh, great.

[*The* **Kids** *begin to get up*]

## Questions & Assignments

1. Why do you think the ladies in the first café behaved as they did?
2. Do you think Mac and John deserved to be robbed? Give reasons for your answer.
3. This part of the play consists of a series of very short scenes. While these would present little difficulty to produce on film, they would present quite a challenge in a stage version. Suggest in some detail how they might be best presented on stage.

## Points to Note — IRONY

**IRONY** is present when the result of a sequence of events turns out to be the opposite to what was expected or intended. Irony is a device used frequently by authors and playwrights to give plots their unexpected twists and turns that add interest and enjoyment to stories and plays.

In relation to the café scenes we can say – *The events in the café are rich in **irony*** or ***it is ironic*** that, although the men set out to 'rob' the children by overcharging them, they end up being robbed by the children.

### Scene 22: The zoo

[*The **Kids** wander around in groups – pulling faces at the animals, pointing and running, girls walking arm in arm. They point and shriek with delight at the monkeys. **Mr Briggs** is with a group of **Kids** looking at a large bear in a pit*]

**Briggs:** . . . and so you can see with those claws it could give you a very nasty mark.

**Andrews:** An' could it kill y', sir?

**Briggs:** Well, why do you think it's kept in a pit?

**Ronson:** I think that's cruel. Don't you?

**Briggs:** No. Not if it's treated well. And don't forget it was born in captivity so it won't know any other sort of life.

**Ronson:** I'll bet it does, sir.

**Girl 1:** How do you know? Sir's just told y' hasn't he? If it was born in a cage an' it's lived all its life in a pit, well, it won't know nothin' else so it won't want nothin' else, will it?

**Ronson:** Well, why does it kill people then?

**Andrews:** What's that got to do with it?

**Ronson:** It kills them cos they're cruel to it. They keep it in a pit so when it gets out it's bound to be mad an' wanna kill people. Don't you see?

**Andrews:** Sir, he's thick. Tell him to shurrup, sir.

**Ronson:** I'm not thick. If it lived there all its life it must know, mustn't it, sir?

**Briggs:** Know what?

**Andrews:** Sir, he's nuts.

**Ronson:** It must know about other ways of living, sir. Y' know, free, like the way people have stopped it livin'. It only kills people cos it's trapped an' people are always stood lookin' at it. If it was free it wouldn't bother people at all.

**Briggs:** Well, I wouldn't be so sure about that, Ronson.

**Andrews:** Sir's right. Bears kill y' cos it's in them t' kill y'.

**Girl 2:** Agh come on, sir . . . let's go to the Children's Zoo.

**Andrews:** Let's go to the big ones.

**Briggs:** It's all right . . . we'll get round them all eventually.

**Girl 1:** Sir, we goin' the Children's Zoo then.

**Briggs:** If you want to.

**Girl 1:** Come on.

[**Briggs** *starts to walk away. The two girls link his arms, one on either side. He stops*]

**Briggs:** Oh! [*Taking their arms away*] Walk properly.

**Girl 2:** Agh ey, sir, the other teachers let y' link them.

[**Mrs Kay** *is with another group. She sees* **Briggs**]

**Mrs Kay:** Oh hello. How are you getting on? They plying you with questions?
**Briggs:** Yes, they've been very good.
**Mrs Kay:** I'm just going for a cup of coffee. Do you want to join me?
**Briggs:** Well I was just on my way to the Children's Zoo with these.
**Andrews:** It's all right, sir. We'll go on our own.
**Mrs Kay:** Oh come on. They'll be all right.
**Briggs:** Well, I don't know if these people can be trusted on their own, Mrs Kay.
**Mrs Kay:** It's all right, Susan and Colin are walking round and the place is walled in. They'll be all right.
**Andrews:** Go on, sir. You go an' get a cuppa. Y' can trust us.
**Briggs:** Ah! Can I though? If I go off for a cup of coffee with Mrs Kay can you people be trusted to act responsibly?

[*Chorus of 'Yes, sir'*]

**Briggs:** All right Mrs Kay. We'll trust them to act responsibly.
**Mrs Kay:** Come on.

[*They walk off to the zoo café*]

## Questions & Assignments

1. What do we learn of the approach to teaching of (a) Mrs. Kay and (b) Mr. Briggs from his conversation with Colin?
2. What impression do you get of Colin from the conversation?
3. (a) What is Mr. Briggs' attitude to the zoo visit?
   (b) Is his attitude understandable? Explain.

### SCENE 23: The bird house

[*Two boys are slowly repeating, 'Everton, Everton' to two blue and yellow macaws*]

**Boy:** Go on, just tweek it out, you dislocated sparrow . . . speak!

### SCENE 24: The children's zoo

[*The* **Kids** *watch a collection of small animals – rabbits, gerbils, guinea pigs, bantam hens – all contained in an open pit.* **Ronson** *looks fondly at a rabbit*]

**Ronson:** They're great, aren't they?
**Carol:** They're lovely.
**Ronson:** [*Bending over and stroking a rabbit*] Come on . . . come on . . .
**Carol:** Ey' you. Y' not supposed t' touch them.

[**Ronson** *answers by picking up the rabbit and gently stroking it.* **Carol** *reaches over to join him stroking the rabbit but he pulls it close to him protectively*]

**Carol:** Well. I'll get one of me own.

[*She bends down and picks up a guinea pig which she strokes affectionately*]

These are better anyway!

### Drama — Our Day Out

#### SCENE 25: The zoo café

[**Mr Briggs** and **Mrs Kay** *are waiting for coffee at the service rail*]

**Briggs:** How many sugars, Mrs Kay?
**Mrs Kay:** Call me Helen. I hate being called Mrs Kay all the time. Makes me feel old. I tried to get the kids to call me Helen once. I had the full class chanting it. Two minutes later they were calling me Mrs Kay again. No, no sugar, thank you.

#### SCENE 26: The children's zoo

[*More* **Kids** *have followed* **Ronson's** *example. Quite a few of them are now clutching furry friends*]

**Carol:** I'm gonna call mine Freddy. Hiya, Freddy. Hello, Freddy. Freddy.

#### SCENE 27: The zoo café

[**Mrs Kay** *and* **Briggs** *are sitting at a table; she lights a cigarette*]

**Briggs:** They're really interested, you know, really interested in the animals.
**Mrs Kay:** I thought they'd enjoy it here.
**Briggs:** Perhaps when we're back in school we could arrange something; maybe I could come along and give them a small talk with some slides that I've got.
**Mrs Kay:** [*Enthusiastic*] Oh, would you?
**Briggs:** You should have asked me to do something a long time ago.
**Mrs Kay:** Well, don't forget you've never offered before.
**Briggs:** To tell you the truth I didn't think the kids who came to you would be too interested in animals.

### Questions & Assignments

1. Describe the attitudes of the children towards the animals.
2. (a) Would you agree that at this point in the play the relationship between Mrs. Kay and Mr. Briggs is improving? Give reasons for your answer by referring to the text.
   (b) Do you think this improved relationship will last? On what does it depend?

### [Answer Guidelines]

2. (a) At this point in the play both Mrs. Kay and Mr. Briggs make an effort to be more friendly towards one another. Mrs. Kay asks Mr. Briggs to call her 'Helen'. Mr. Briggs, in turn, is impressed by the interest that the children showed in the animals and this makes him see Mrs. Kay in a new light. He offers to give her class a talk with slides and she is delighted. Pleased with her reaction, Mr. Briggs tells her that she should have asked before.

   (b) The new friendship is being built on very shaky grounds. Mr. Briggs is having coffee because the children have promised to act responsibly in his absence. There is a chance – but only a slight chance – that they will live up to their promise but if they don't then the new friendship between Mrs. Kay and Mr. Briggs may not last.

## SCENE 28: The children's zoo

[*The animal pit is empty. The children have gone*]

## SCENE 29: The coach

[**Briggs** *and* **Mrs Kay** *approach*]

**Briggs:** Don't worry, we'll get that arranged as soon as we get back to school.

[**Susan** *and* **Colin** *stand by the coach with the* **Driver**]

**Colin:** [*To* **Driver**] You should have come round with us, it's a grand zoo.
**Driver:** A couple of hours kip — seen it all before.
**Colin:** You'd have had a good time.
**Mrs Kay:** All on board?
**Susan:** Yes. We wandered back and most of them were already here.
**Mrs Kay:** Oh! That makes a change.
**Briggs:** All checked and present. Right. Off we go.

[*The* **Driver** *and the teachers climb on board. In the distance the* **Animal Keeper**, *polonecked and wellied, runs towards the coach. Inside the coach the* **Kids** *sit like angels. The coach pulls away but the* **Animal Keeper** *waves it down. It stops. The* **Keeper** *strides on board*]

**Mrs Kay:** Have we forgotten something?
**Keeper:** Are you supposed to be in charge of this lot?
**Mrs Kay:** Why? What's the matter?
**Keeper:** Children. They're not bloody children. They're animals. That's not a zoo out there. This is the bloody zoo, in here!
**Briggs:** Would you mind controlling your language and telling me what's going on.
**Keeper:** [*Ignoring him and pushing past him to the* **Kids**] Right. Come on. Where are they?

[*The* **Kids** *look back innocently*]

Call yourselves teachers. You can't even control them.
**Briggs:** Now look. This has just gone far enough. Would you tell me exactly what you want please?

[*A clucking hen is heard. The* **Keeper** *turns and looks. A* **Kid** *is fidgeting with his coat. The* **Keeper** *strides up to him and pulls back his coat, revealing a bantam hen. Two more* **Keepers** *come on board. The first* **Keeper** *grabs the hen and addresses the* **Kids**]

**Keeper:** Right! And now I want the rest!

[*There is a moment's hesitation before the flood-gates are opened. Animals appear from every conceivable hiding place. The coach becomes a menagerie.* **Mrs Kay** *raises her eyebrows to heaven. The* **Keepers** *collect the animals.* **Briggs** *stares icily*]

## SCENE 30: The coach, moments later

[**Briggs** *is outside talking to the* **Keepers**, *who have collected all the animals in small cages. They walk away and* **Briggs** *climbs onto the coach. His face is like thunder. The* **Kids** *try to look anywhere but at him – trying to avoid the unavoidable.* **Briggs** *pauses for a long, staring, angry and contemptuous moment*]

**Briggs:** I trusted you lot. [*Pause*] I trusted you. And this, is the way you repay me. [*Pause*] I trusted all of you, but it's obvious that trust is something you know nothing about.
**Ronson:** Sir, we only borrowed them.
**Briggs:** [*Shouting*] Shut up, lad! [*Pause*] Is it any wonder that people won't do anything for you? The minute we start to treat you as real people, what happens? That man was right, you act like animals, animals! [*Pause*] Well I've learned a lesson today. Oh, yes, I have. I've learned that trust is

something you people don't understand. Now, I'm warning you, all of you, don't expect any more trust from me!

[*The* **Kids** *are resigned. They have heard it all before.* **Briggs** *turns to* **Mrs Kay**]

Mrs Kay when we get to the castle we'll split up into four groups. Each member of staff will be responsible for one group.

[**Mrs Kay** *looks at him*]

## Questions & Assignments

1. Did you find this scene sad or amusing or a mixture of both? Give reasons for your answer.
2. (a) Explain the significance of Scene 30.
   (b) Do you think that the next scene would be more effective if Scene 30 were omitted? Explain your answer.

### SCENE 31: Conway Castle

[**Briggs**, *with a group of ordered children standing behind him, points to a spot high up on the castle. The* **Kids** *all look up, bored*]

**Briggs:** Now you see these larger square holes, just below the battlements there – well, they were used for . . . long planks of wood which supported a sort of platform, and that's where the archers used to stand and fire down on the attackers of the castle. Now what's interesting is, if you look at the side of that tower it's not quite perpendicular.

[*In another part of the castle,* **Kids** *are rushing about playing medieval cowboys and Indians.* **Mrs Kay** *sits on a bench overlooking the estuary.* **Carol** *and* **Andrews** *are with her. In a secluded passage of the castle,* **Reilly** *and* **Digga** *are smoking. They are concealed in an alcove.* **Colin's** *voice can be heard. He approaches,* **Karen** *and* **Linda** *follow close behind him*]

**Colin:** So, although these walls are nearly fifteen feet thick in places, you still have the wind blasting in through the arrow slits and with no proper heat, you can imagine just how cold it must have been.

**Linda:** Sir, I wonder what they did to keep warm in the olden days?

**Colin:** [*Stopping and turning*] Well, obviously they . . . Where's everybody else gone? Where are the others?

**Karen:** Sir, they kept dropping out as you were talkin'.

**Colin:** Oh God.

**Linda:** It's all right, sir. Y' can keep showin' us round. We're dead interested.

**Colin:** [*Sighing*] All right Linda . . . what was I saying?

**Linda:** Sir, y' was tellin' us how they kept warm in the olden days.

**Colin:** [*Continuing down the passage*] They wore much thicker clothing . . . All right, Linda?

**Linda:** Sir, it's dead spooky. It's haunted isn't it?

**Colin:** Don't be silly.

**Linda:** Sir, I'm frightened [*Linking his arm for protection*]

**Colin:** Now, don't do that, Linda!

**Linda:** [*Holding on*] But I'm frightened, sir.
**Karen:** [*Grabbing his other arm*] Sir, so am I.
**Colin:** [*Firmly, freeing himself*] Now, girls, stop being silly. Stop it. There's nothing to be frightened of! Now, come on.

[*He leads them along the passage. As they pass the alcove where* **Reilly** *and* **Digga** *are concealed,* **Reilly** *leans out and just gently touches* **Linda's** *shoulder. She screams and flings herself at* **Colin**, **Karen** *reacts and does the same. Even* **Colin** *is slightly startled*]

**Linda:** Sir, it touched me.
**Colin:** What did?
**Linda:** Oh, it did.

[**Colin** *looks worried. They hear laughter. Just at the point when the three of them are about to run,* **Reilly** *and* **Digga** *fall laughing out of the alcove. In the distance* **Briggs** *shouts,* 'Reilly!' **Reilly** *and* **Digga** *hear him and leg away past* **Colin** *and the terrified girls. Outside,* **Mrs Kay**, **Carol** *and* **Andrews** *still sit looking out over the estuary*]

**Mrs Kay:** Why don't you go and have a look around the castle grounds. You haven't seen it yet.
**Carol:** Miss, I don't like it. It's horrible. I just like sittin' here with you, lookin' at the lake.
**Mrs Kay:** That's not a lake, love. It's the sea.
**Carol:** That's what I meant, miss.
**Andrews:** Miss, wouldn't it be great if we had something like this round ours. Then the kids wouldn't get into trouble if they had somewhere like this to play, would they?
**Carol:** Miss. Couldn't have nothin' like this round our way could they?
**Mrs Kay:** Why not?
**Carol:** Cos we'd only wreck it, wouldn't we?
**Andrews:** No, we wouldn't.
**Carol:** We would, y' know. That's why we never have nothin' nice round our way – cos we'd just smash it up. The Corpy knows that so why should they waste their money, eh? They'd give us things if we looked after them, but we don't look after them, do we?
**Andrews:** Miss, miss, y' know what I think about it, eh, miss.
**Mrs Kay:** Go on, John. What do you think?
**Andrews:** Miss, if all this belonged to us, miss, and it was ours, not the Corpy's but, ours, well, we wouldn't let no one wreck it would we? We'd defend it.

[**Briggs** *approaches, obviously angry*]

**Briggs:** You two . . . off! Go on. Move.
**Carol:** Sir, where?
**Briggs:** Anywhere, girl. Just move. I want to speak to Mrs Kay. Well, come on then.

[*The two kids,* **Carol** *and* **Andrews**, *wander off.* **Briggs** *waits until they are out of hearing range*]

**Mrs Kay:** I was talking to those children.
**Briggs:** Yes, and I'm talking to you, Mrs Kay. It's got to stop, this has.
**Mrs Kay:** What has?
**Briggs:** What has? Can't y' see what's goin' on? It's a shambles, the whole ill-organised affair. Look at what they did at the zoo. Just look at them here.

[*All around the castle they can see, from where they sit,* **Kids** *running, pulling, laughing and shouting*]

They're just left to race and chase and play havoc. God knows what the castle authorities must think. Look, when you bring children like ours into this sort of environment you can't afford to just let them go free. They're just like town dogs let off the lead in the country. My God, for some of them it's the first time they've been further than Birkenhead.
**Mrs Kay:** [*Quietly*] I know. And I was just thinking; it's a shame really, isn't it, eh? You know, we bring them to a crumbling pile of bricks and mortar and they think they're in the fields of heaven.

[*Pause. He glares at her*]

**Briggs:** [*Accusing*] You *are* on their side, aren't you?

**Mrs Kay:** [*Looking at him*] Absolutely, Mr Briggs. Absolutely!

**Briggs:** Look! All I want to know from you is what you're going to do about this chaos.

**Mrs Kay:** Well, I'd suggest that if you want the chaos to stop, then you should stop seeing it as chaos. All right, the Headmaster asked you to come along — but can't you relax? There's no point in pretending that a day out to Wales is going to furnish them with the education they should have had long ago. It's too late for them. Most of them were rejects on the day they were born, Mr Briggs. We're not going to solve anything today. Can't we just try and give them a good day out? At least we could try and do that.

**Briggs:** [*The castle looming behind him*] Well, that's a fine attitude, isn't it? That's a fine attitude for a member of the teaching profession to have.

**Mrs Kay:** [*Beginning to lose her temper ever so slightly*] Well, what's your alternative? Eh? Do you really think there's any point pretending? Even if you cared, do you think you could educate these kids, my remedial kids? Because you're a fool if you do. You won't educate them because nobody wants them educating . . .

**Briggs:** Listen Mrs Kay . . .

**Mrs Kay:** No! You listen, Mr Briggs . . . If these kids, and all the others like them, had real learning the factories of England would empty overnight. And don't you try and tell me that there's kids who, given the choice, would still empty bins and stand on production lines, but don't give me that because that's the biggest myth of all. Give them education – choice – and they'd want what we've got, what the best-off have got. And that's why you won't educate them, Mr Briggs. You're in a job that's designed to fail, because no matter what the rest of us want, the factories of England must have their fodder.

**Briggs:** And I suppose that's the sort of stuff you've been pumping into their minds, is it?

**Mrs Kay:** [*Laughing*] And you really think they'd understand?

**Briggs:** Listen, I'm not going to spend any more time arguing with you. You may have organised this visit, but I'm the one who's been sent by the Headmaster to supervise. Now, either you take control of the children in your charge or I'll be forced to abandon this visit and order everyone home.

[*Pause. She looks at him*]

**Mrs Kay:** Well . . . that's your decision. But I'm not going to let you prevent the kids from having some fun. If you want to abandon this visit then you'd better start walking because we're not going home. We're going to the beach.

**Briggs:** The beach!!

**Mrs Kay:** We can't come all the way to the seaside and not go down to the beach!

[*She turns and walks away*]

## Questions & Assignments

1. In this scene both Carol and Andrew comment on their neighbourhood and environment. From their comments explain how they see themselves.
2. Conflict develops between Mrs. Kay and Mr. Briggs in this scene. Trace the cause of the conflict to its final outcome. Who comes off best?
3. Would you agree that a new side to Mrs. Kay's character is revealed in this scene? Give reasons for your answer.
4. *You are on their side, aren't you?* Briefly state what you think this remark reveals about Mr. Briggs' character.

## Points to Note — CONFLICT

The word **'conflict'** means a contest or a struggle and is present in the plots of most stories and plays. Conflict occurs when somebody is against somebody or something else. It is usually between two individuals but can also occur between an individual and nature (e.g. a character facing a dangerous mountain climb); between an individual and an organisation or between an individual and his or her conscience.

When one side in a conflict wins, or a struggle is settled amicably, we say that the conflict has been **resolved**.

In order to give a story a degree of excitement the outcome of any conflict cannot be too obvious and is often unexpected. The plots of short stories and short one-act plays are usually based on one single conflict.

However, in longer plays and novels there can be a network of conflicts linked together. One is no sooner resolved than another begins to develop.

### Scene 32: The beach

[**Briggs** *sits on a rock apart from the main group.* **Mrs Kay** *is paddling, dress held above her knees looking old-fashioned, with a group of kids. Girls are screaming in delight and boys are laughing and running. Two boys,* **Kevin** *and* **Jimmy**, *are near* **Mrs Kay**]

**Jimmy:** 'Ey, miss, we could have brought our costumes an' gone swimmin'.
**Kevin:** We could go swimmin' anyway, couldn't we, miss?
**Carol:** [*Trailing behind* **Mrs Kay**] Miss, when do we have to go home?
**Jimmy:** What? In your undies?
**Kevin:** Yeh. Why not?
**Mrs Kay:** No. Not today.
**Kevin:** Agh . . . why not, miss.
**Mrs Kay:** Because . . .
**Jimmy:** If y' went swimmin in just y' undies, the police would pick y' up, wouldn't they, miss?
**Mrs Kay:** Look, the reason I don't want you to go swimming is because there aren't enough staff here to guarantee that it would be safe. I want to go home with a full coachload, thank you.
**Carol:** Miss, when d' we have t' go . . . .
**Kevin:** Agh, miss, I'd be all right, miss . . . I wouldn't get drowned, miss.
**Mrs Kay:** [*Warning*] Kevin!

**Kevin:** Oh, miss.
**Mrs Kay:** Kevin, I've already explained why I don't want you to go swimming . . .
**Kevin:** Oh . . . Miss . . .
**Mrs Kay:** Carry on like that and I'll have to sort you out.
**Kevin:** Agh . . .

[*She stops him with a warning look. He tuts. Satisfied that he won't take it any further, she turns to* **Carol**]

**Mrs Kay:** Right . . .
**Kevin:** Just for five minutes, miss.
**Mrs Kay:** [*Turning and walking towards him*] Kevin Bryant . . . come here.
**Kevin:** [*Backing away. Laughing*] Ah, miss, I didn't mean it . . . honest miss. I never meant it.

[**Mrs Kay**, *glaring in mock seriousness, comes after him. He is laughing. He breaks and runs. She chases him, skirts trailing in the water, with the other kids shouting and jeering and urging her to catch him.* **Kevin** *is hardly able to run because of laughing so much.* **Mrs Kay** *charges on through the water, looking incongruous.* **Kevin** *suddenly stops, turns, bends down in the water and prepares to send up a spray*]

**Kevin:** Don't, miss . . . don't or I'll spray y'.
**Mrs Kay:** Kevin Bryant . . . you'll do what? . . . You wait till I get hold of you.

[*They face each other. The* **Kids** *at the water's edge chant and shout: 'Get him, Miss', 'Duck him, Miss', 'Throw him in', 'Y've had it now, Bryant'.* **Kevin** *makes the mistake of turning to the group of* **Kids** *to answer them. In a flash she is on him and turns him upside down. She ducks him and he comes up spluttering and laughing. The other* **Kids** *cheer and laugh*]

**Kevin:** Oh no, miss.
**Mrs Kay:** Now who wanted to go swimming, Kevin?

**Kevin:** Oh miss, miss. Me 'air's all wet.

[*She quickly lifts him so that she is carrying him, cradle fashion, out of the water.* **Briggs** *looks on. He turns away.* **Mrs Kay** *and* **Kevin** *walk away from the water. He shakes water from his hair*]

**Kevin:** Miss . . . I might get a cold though. I hate that.
**Mrs Kay:** Oh, you're like an old woman. Come on then.

[*She reaches in her bag and produces a towel. She wraps the towel round his head and rubs vigorously. Beneath the towel* **Kevin** *is beaming and happy*]

**Kevin:** Ta miss.
**Carol:** [*At side of* **Mrs Kay**] Miss, when do we have t' go home?
**Mrs Kay:** What's the matter, love? Aren't you enjoying it?
**Carol:** Yeh, but I don't wanna go home. I wanna stay here.
**Mrs Kay:** Oh, Carol, love . . . we're here for at least another hour. Why don't you start enjoying yourself instead of worrying about going home.
**Carol:** Cos I don't wanna go home, miss.
**Mrs Kay:** Carol, love . . . We have to go home. It can't be like this all the time.
**Carol:** Why not?
**Mrs Kay:** [*Looks at her. Sighs*] I don't know, love.

Spectrum 2

> **Questions & Assignments**
>
> 1. The kind of relationship Mrs. Kay has with the children is brought into sharp focus in this scene. Describe this relationship by referring to the events in the scene.

### Scene 33: The beach

[*A game of football is in progress.* **Mrs Kay** *is in goal. She makes a clumsy save and the* **Kids** *cheer.* **Briggs** *watches from a distance.* **Mrs Kay** *leaves the game and goes to meet* **Colin** *and* **Susan** *who are approaching*]

**Mrs Kay:** Wooh . . . I'm pooped.
**Andrews:** [*Shouting from game*] Agh, miss, we've not got a goalie now.
**Mrs Kay:** [*Shouting back*] It's all right, Carol can go in goal for you now.

[*She looks amongst the group.* **Colin** *and* **Susan** *look on*]

Where is she?
**Susan:** Who?
**Mrs Kay:** Carol. She went to look for you.
**Colin:** We haven't seen her.
**Mrs Kay:** Well, where is she?

[**Mrs Kay** *scans the beach.* **Carol** *cannot be seen.* **Mrs Kay** *looks at* **Susan**]

You haven't seen her at all?

[**Susan** *shakes her head*]

**Mrs Kay:** [*Looks over beach again*] Oh she couldn't. Could she?
**Susan:** Lost?
**Mrs Kay:** Don't say it. Perhaps he's seen her.

[*She shouts across*]

Mr Briggs . . . Mr Briggs.

[**Briggs** *looks up, rises and then comes over to her*]

**Susan:** I hope he has seen her.
**Mrs Kay:** Yeh. The only trouble is she didn't go that way.
**Briggs:** [*Approaching*] Is that it? Are we going home now?
**Mrs Kay:** Have you seen Carol Chandler in the last half hour?
**Briggs:** Look! I thought I'd made it quite plain that I was having nothing more to do with your outing.
**Mrs Kay:** Have you seen Carol Chandler?
**Briggs:** No. I haven't.
**Mrs Kay:** I think she might have wandered off somewhere.
**Briggs:** You mean you've lost her.
**Mrs Kay:** No. I mean she might have wandered off.
**Briggs:** Well, what's that if it's not losing her? All I can say is it's a wonder you haven't lost half a dozen of them.
**Colin:** Listen, Briggs, it's about time someone told you what a burke you are.
**Briggs:** And you listen, sonny. Don't you try telling me a word because you haven't even earned the right. Don't worry, when we get back to school, your number's up. As well as hers. [*He motions to* **Mrs Kay**] When we get back, I'll have the lot of you!
**Mrs Kay:** Would you mind postponing your threats until we've found Carol. At the moment I'd say the most important thing is to find the girl.
**Briggs:** Don't you mean try and find her?
**Mrs Kay:** Susan . . . you keep these lads playing football. We'll split up and look for her.

[**Mrs Kay**, **Colin** and **Briggs** *walk off in separate directions*]

## Scene 34: The cliff

[*Below the cliff-top, the sea is breaking on rocks in a cave mouth. In the distance,* **Mrs Kay** *is shouting 'Carol, Carol' and* **Colin** *is searching the far end of the beach.* **Carol** *is standing on top of the cliff watching the waves below. She looks out over the sea. Alone on the cliff-top, she is at peace with the warm sun and small breeze upon her – a fleeting moment of tranquillity*]

**Briggs:** Carol Chandler!

[**Briggs** *approaches. On seeing her he stops and stands a few yards off*]

Just come here.

[*She turns and stares at him*]

Who gave you permission to come up here?
**Carol:** No one.

[*Turning, she dismisses him*]

**Briggs:** I'm talking to you, Carol Chandler.

[*She continues to ignore his presence*]

Now just listen here, young lady . . .

[*As he goes to move towards her, she turns on him*]

**Carol:** Don't you come near me!
**Briggs:** [*Taken aback. Stopping*] Pardon!
**Carol:** I don't want you to come near me.
**Briggs:** Well, in that case just get yourself moving and let's get down to the beach.

[*Pause*]

**Carol:** You go. I'm not comin'.
**Briggs:** You what?
**Carol:** Tell Mrs Kay that she can go home without me. I'm stoppin' here . . . in Wales.

[*Pause*]

**Briggs:** Now just you listen to me — I've had just about enough today, just about enough, and I'm not putting up with a pile of silliness from the likes of you. Now come on . . . .

[*He starts to move towards her. She takes a step towards the edge of the cliff*]

**Carol:** Try an' get me an' I'll jump over.

[**Briggs** *stops, astounded. There is an angry pause. She continues to ignore him*]

**Briggs:** Now come on! I'll not tell you again.

[*He moves forward. Again, she moves nearer to the edge. He stops and they look at each other*]

I'll give you five seconds. Just five seconds. One . . . two . . . three . . . four . . . I'm warning you, five!

[*She stares at him blankly.* **Briggs** *stares back in impotent rage*]

**Carol:** I've told y' . . . I'm not comin' down with y'.

[*Pause*]

I'll jump y' know . . . I will.
**Briggs:** Just what are you trying to do to me?
**Carol:** I've told you. Leave me alone and I won't jump.

[*Pause*]

I wanna stay here. Where it's nice.
**Briggs:** Stay here? How could you stay here? What would you do? Where would you live?

**Carol:** I'd be all right.
**Briggs:** Now I've told you . . . stop being so silly.
**Carol:** [*Turning on him*] What do you worry for, eh? Eh? You don't care, do y'? Do y'?
**Briggs:** What? About you? Listen . . . if I didn't care, why am I here, now, trying to stop you doing something stupid.
**Carol:** Because if I jump over, you'll get into trouble when you get back to school. That's why, Briggsy! So stop goin' on. You hate me.
**Briggs:** Don't be ridiculous — just because I'm a school teacher it doesn't mean to say that . . .
**Carol:** Don't lie, you! I know you hate me. I've seen you goin' home in your car, passin' us on the street. And the way y' look at us. You hate all the kids.

[*She turns again to the sea, dismissing him*]

**Briggs:** What . . . makes you think that? Eh?
**Carol:** Why can't I just stay out here, eh? Why can't I live in one of them nice white houses an' do the garden an' that?
**Briggs:** Look . . . Carol . . . you're talking as though you've given up on life already. You sound as though life for you is just ending, instead of beginning. Now why can't, I mean, if it's what you want, what's to stop you working hard at school from now on, getting a good job and then moving out here when you're old enough? Eh?
**Carol:** [*Turns slowly to look at him. Contempt*] Don't be friggin' stupid.

[*She turns and looks down at the sea below*]

It's been a great day today. I loved it. I don't wanna leave here an' go home.

[*She moves to the edge of the cliff.* **Briggs** *is alarmed but unable to move*]

If I stayed though, it wouldn't be no good. You'd send the coppers to get me.
**Briggs:** We'd have to. How would you survive out here?
**Carol:** I know.

[*Pause*]

I'm not goin' back though.
**Briggs:** Please . . . .
**Carol:** Sir, sir, y' know if you'd been my old feller, I woulda been all right, wouldn't I?

[**Briggs** *slowly holds out his hand. She moves to the very edge of the cliff.* **Briggs** *is aware of how close she is*]

**Briggs:** Carol. Carol, please come away from there. [*Stretching out his hand to her*] Please.

[**Carol** *looks at him and a smile breaks across her face*]

**Carol:** Sir . . . sir, you don't half look funny, y' know.
**Briggs:** [*Smiling back at her*] Why?
**Carol:** Sir, you should smile more often, y' look great when y' smile.
**Briggs:** Come on, Carol. [*He gingerly approaches her*]
**Carol:** What'll happen to me for doin' this, sir?
**Briggs:** Nothing. I promise you.
**Carol:** Sir, y' promisin' now, but what about when we get back t' school?
**Briggs:** [*Almost next to her now*] It won't be even mentioned.

[*She turns and looks down at the drop then back at* **Briggs'** *outstretched arm.* **Carol** *lifts her hand to his. She slips.* **Briggs** *grabs out quickly and manages to pull her to him.* **Briggs** *wraps his arms around her*]

> ### Questions & Assignments
>
> 1. (a) Trace how suspense is built up in these scenes.
>    (b) At what point does it reach a climax?
> 2. What effect do you think Carol's remarks will have on Mr. Briggs?
> 3. What is your response to Carol's comments about her own life and the prospects which life holds for her?
> 4. In the case of both Carol and Mr. Briggs, describe how you think each of them views the situation that has developed in this scene.

## Points to Note — SUSPENSE AND TENSION

As we have seen, **conflict** is an important ingredient in all plots. Conflict holds the attention of the reader and audience. They are anxious to find out what happens next; what the outcome of a particular conflict will be. This feeling of anxiety, impatience and uncertainty on the part of the audience is known as **suspense** or **tension**.

To achieve this, the outcome of a conflict should never be completely predictable. The outcome may often be unexpected and unlikely but it should be still within the bounds of possibility.

### CLIMAX

The climax of any plot is when the suspense and tension is at its highest.

### SCENE 35: The beach

[**Susan** *still waits anxiously on the beach whilst the* **Kids** *play football. Other* **Kids** *watch the game, including* **Linda** *and* **Karen**. **Reilly** *challenges* **Digga** *for the ball and gets it from him*]

**Karen:** [*Shouting*] Go on, Digga . . . get him, get him.
**Linda:** Come on, Brian.

[**Reilly** *gets the ball past* **Digga**, *then around two more defenders, and scores.* **Linda** *cheers;* **Reilly** *sees her and winks.* **Mrs Kay** *and* **Colin** *approach.* **Susan** *looks up in inquiry;* **Mrs Kay** *shakes her head.* **Susan** *sighs*]

**Mrs Kay:** [*As she approaches*] I think we'd better let the police know.
**Susan:** Shall I keep them playing . . .

[*Behind* **Mrs Kay**, **Susan** *can see* **Briggs** *and* **Carol** *in the distance*]

Oh, look . . . he's found her.
**Mrs Kay:** Oh, thank God. [*She turns and starts hurrying towards them*]
**Colin:** I'll bet he makes a bloody meal of this.
**Susan:** I don't care as long as she's safe.
**Colin:** Yeh, well, we'd better round them up. It'll be straight off now.

[**Mrs Kay** approaches **Carol** and **Briggs**]

**Mrs Kay:** Is she all right? Carol, the worry you've caused us!
**Briggs:** It's all right, Mrs Kay. I've dealt with all that.
**Mrs Kay:** Where were you?
**Carol:** On the cliff, miss.
**Mrs Kay:** On the . . . .
**Briggs:** Mrs Kay, I've found her. Now will you just let me deal with this.
**Mrs Kay:** [*Shaking her head as they walk up the beach towards the others*] Carol Chandler.
**Briggs:** Right.

[*The main group are preparing to leave as* **Mrs Kay**, **Carol** *and* **Briggs** *reach them*]

**Briggs:** Right . . . come on. Everyone on the coach.

[*General 'tuts'and moans of: 'Why can't we stay' etc.*]

Come on . . . all of you, on.

## SCENE 36: The coach

[*The staff stand by the coach doors as the* **Kids** *file by onto the coach*]

**Driver:** Right. [*To* **Briggs**] Back to the school then?
**Briggs:** School . . . back to school?

[**Mrs Kay** *looks up*]

It's only early, isn't it?

[*To* **Mrs Kay**] Anyway, you can't come all the way to the seaside and not pay a visit to the fair.

[**Carol** *overhears them as she climbs onto the coach. She rushes inside*]
**Carol:** [*Loud whisper*] We're goin' the fair, we're goin' the fair. . . Sir's takin' us t' the fair.

[*The word is spread like fire inside the coach. Outside,* **Mrs Kay** *is intrigued — half-smiling*]

**Briggs:** Play your cards right, I might take even you for a ride on the waltzer.

## SCENE 37: A fairground

[*Rock and roll music. On the waltzer the* **Kids**, *including* **Briggs** *and* **Carol** *together in a car, are spinning round.* **Mrs Kay** *takes a photograph of* **Briggs** *and* **Carol** *climbing out of the waltzer car.* **Mrs Kay**, **Colin** *and* **Susan**, **Reilly** *and* **Linda**, **Digga** *and* **Karen**, **Andrews**, **Ronson**, **Carol** *and some of the other kids are all photographed in a group.* **Briggs** *is snapped eating candy-floss, then again on the highest point of the bigwheel with mock fear on his face and* **Carol** *next to him her eyes closed in happy terror. Then he is photographed playing darts, then with a cowboy hat on, handing a goldfish in a plastic bag to* **Carol**]

## SCENE 38: Back at the coach

[*As the* **Kids** *pile onto the coach,* **Briggs**, *still wearing his cowboy hat, stands by the coach door*]

**Kids:** [*As they get onto coach*]
  Sir, thanks, sir.
  Sir, that was Ace.
  We had a great laugh, didn't we, sir?
  Sir, we gonna come here again?
**Ronson:** Can we come tomorrow, sir?
**Briggs:** Oh, get on the bus, Ronson.

[*Everyone is singing as the coach moves along. One of the kids is collecting for the* **Driver**; **Reilly** *has his arm around* **Linda**; **Digga** *is with* **Karen**; **Carol**, *with her goldfish, sits next to* **Mrs Kay**; **Ronson** *has a white mouse; the back seat is now occupied by Andrews and other kids.* **Briggs** *is also on the back seat - cowboy hat on, tie pulled down and singing with them.* **Mrs Kay** *takes a photograph of them*]

**Mrs Kay:** Say 'Cheese'.

### SCENE 39: Back in the city

[*The city can be seen out of the coach windows. Inside the coach the kids are tired and worn out now. Some are sleeping, some are singing softly to themselves, some stare blankly out of the window*]

**Linda:** Y' glad y' came?
**Reilly:** Yeh.
**Linda:** It was great, wasn't it, eh?
**Reilly:** It'll be the last one I go on.
**Linda:** Why?
**Reilly:** Well I'm leaving in the summer aren't I?
**Linda:** What y' gonna do?
**Reilly:** [*Looking out of window*] Dunno. [*Looks out of the window at the City*] It's friggin' horrible when y' come back to it, isn't it?
**Linda:** What is?
**Reilly:** That. [*Nods at window*]
**Linda:** Oh, yeh. [*Resigned*]

[**Briggs**, *with* **Andrews** *asleep next to him, sees the familiar surroundings and the kids hanging about in the streets. He sits up, puts his tie back to normal, goes to straighten his hair and feels the cowboy hat. He takes it off and puts it on* **Andrews**. *He then takes out a comb and combs his hair; puts on his jacket and walks down the aisle to* **Mrs Kay**]

**Briggs:** Well, nearly home.
**Mrs Kay:** [*She is taking the completed film from her camera*] I've got some gems of you here. We'll have one of these up in the staff room when they're developed.
**Briggs:** Eh? One of me?
**Mrs Kay:** Don't worry . . . I'm not going to let you forget the day you enjoyed yourself.
**Briggs:** [*Half laughs. Watches her put the film into its box*] Look . . . why don't you give it to me to develop?
**Mrs Kay:** Would you?
**Briggs:** Well, it would save you having to pay for it. I could do it in the lab.
**Mrs Kay:** [*Handing it over*] I don't know, using school facilities for personal use.

[*He smiles at her and takes the film. He puts it in his pocket*]

## Questions & Assignments

1. (a) Describe how Mr. Briggs has changed.
   (b) Do you think it will last? Give reasons for your answer.

### Scene 40: Outside school

[*It is evening as the coach turns into the street outside the school and pulls up.* **Briggs** *gets out, then the* **Kids** *pour out shouting 'Tarars' and running up the street.* **Reilly** *and* **Linda** *get off the coach together*]

**Briggs:** Right! Come on, everyone out!
**Reilly:** 'Night, sir. Enjoyed yourself today, didn't y', sir?
**Briggs:** Pardon?
**Reilly:** I didn't know you was like that, sir. Y' know, all right for a laugh an' that. See y' tommorer, sir.
**Briggs:** Eh — Linda.

[*She stops.* **Briggs** *turns*]

We'll, erm, we'll let the uniform go this time.

[*Pause*]

But Linda, don't let me catch you dressing like that in the future, though.

[*She shrugs and walks off with* **Reilly**. *The other kids make their way home.* **Mrs Kay** *gets off the coach*]

**Mrs Kay:** Nothing left behind. 'Night Ronny.
**Susan:** Good night.

[*The coach pulls away. The* **Driver** *toots good-bye and they wave*]

Ooh! . . . That's that. I don't know about anyone else but I'm off for a drink.
**Colin:** Oh, I'll second that.
**Susan:** Good idea.
**Mrs Kay:** [*To* **Briggs**] You coming with us?
**Briggs:** [*The school looming behind him*] Well, actually I've . . . .
**Susan:** Oh, come on . . . .
**Briggs:** No . . . I'd better not. Thanks anyway. I've, um, lots of marking to do at home. Thanks all the same though.
**Mrs Kay:** Oh well, if we can't twist your arm.

[*Pause*]

Thanks for today.

[*She turns and goes to her car accompanied by* **Susan** *and* **Colin**. *She pulls away and toots good-bye.* **Briggs** *moves to his own car, puts his hand in his pocket and produces car keys and the roll of film. He looks at the film and then up at the school. He pulls open the film and exposes it to the light, crumples it up and puts it into his pocket. He then gets into his car, pulls away and at the junction turns right.* **Carol**, *walking along the street with the goldfish in her grasp, looks up at the disappearing car*]

**The End**

### Questions & Assignments

1. (a) Outline your response to the final scene.
   (b) Say why you think he destroyed the film.
2. Write an alternative ending to the play.

## Assignments

1. Write a scene based on each of the following situations:
   (a) It is a week later. Mrs. Kay approaches Mr. Briggs about the film.
   (b) The Headmaster invites Mr. Briggs to his office next day to give an account of the trip.
   (c) Mrs. Kay sees Mr. Briggs destroying the film. She confronts him on the matter on the following day.
   (d) Imagine that Carol had jumped or fallen from the cliff and seriously injured herself as Mr. Briggs approached her. Write a scene set in the Headmaster's office later in the day. Present are the Headmaster, Mr. Briggs, Mrs. Kay and Carol's parents.
   (e) Carol and Andrews walk home together discussing the events of the day.
2. (a) Describe, briefly, the three scenes from the play which you found
   (i) most amusing, (ii) most sad and (iii) most exciting.
3. (a) Describe the scene from the play that would be most difficult to stage. Give reasons for your choices.
   (b) Explain how you would approach the task of staging a particular scene of your choice.
4. (a) In your view, what serious issues were explored in the play?
   (b) Did your study of the play change your view on any of these issues *or* did it provide you with a new insight into any of them? Explain your answer fully.

## SPOT THE ERRORS

The following Spot the Errors exercise is aimed at sharpening your basic writing skills. Spot the 20 errors in the Passage below and rewrite the passage correctly. (Note: Refer to the Guidelines on pages 1—15.)

### 13  Listening to a Storm

Lying in bed, john could hear the wind rising. Already the bows in the trees were stirring and a loose shuter in the outbuilding was banging. It was that, he supposed, which had woken him. He lay with the blanket's clutched around him to shut out the invading wind, but sleep would not come.

He heard his Father and Mother come upstairs to bed, their low conversation the noises as each went to the bathroom and then silence fell inside the house. He still could not sleep. He blamed the wind, for it was getting wilder, But he wondered why it should disterb him tonight, for no storm before had kept him awake for more than a few miuntes.

He slips out of bed and went two the window. The wind was as fierce as he had ever known the branches of the elms opposite were creaking and swaying and he heard a loud crack as one gave under the force of the gust. Leafs swept across the garden in a mad flurry and he imagined his mothers rose bushes bending and the discarded petals scattering over the border. The moon was full and high, riding among swift, sweeping clouds. It's light cast sharp moving shadows across the countryside. John wished he was good at art; there was a beauty about the seen that he would have liked to paint.

He was suddenly struck with the strangeness that their was in the world about him, that anything as rough as this night and its Storm could hold such magic.

# Film Studies

## THE AUTHOR AND THE NOVEL

The author, Nelle Harper Lee had a childhood that in many ways was similar to that of her narrator, Scout Finch. She was born in 1926 and grew up in Monroeville, Alabama, USA, where her father, Amasa Lee, was a lawyer. He also served in the state legislature in Alabama. Her playmates were her older brother and a young neighbour, Truman Capote, who himself was to become a famous novelist. She was an avid reader as a child.

When she was seven years old, the Scottsboro trial, one of the most famous court cases in American history, was being held and was covered in great detail by the newspapers. The Scottsboro trial was similar in many ways to the trial of Tom Robinson.

Like the fictional trial of Tom Robinson, the Scottsboro trial took place in the 1930s in Alabama; the defendants were black men and the accusers were white women.

After leaving school Harper Lee studied law in the State University of Alabama, but left before completing her final exams and moved to New York.

*To Kill A Mockingbird* was written during the beginning of the Civil Rights era (from about 1955 to 1958). Alabama was very much in the news at this time with the Montgomery bus boycott, Martin Luther King's rise to leadership, and Autherine Lucy's attempt to enter the all-white University of Alabama graduate school.

The novel was published in 1960, a time of intense racial strife in America, as the struggle in the Civil Rights movement grew violent and spread into the American consciousness on TV screens and the nightly news. The novel was an astonishing success, shooting to the top of the Best Seller list and making a remarkable impact on a divided nation.

*To Kill A Mockingbird* was Harper Lee's only novel. It won numerous literary awards, including the Pulitzer Prize in 1961. Since then it has sold around 30 million copies and has been translated into many languages. In 1962 a film, based on the book, was made.

## BACKGROUND AND SETTING

The events of the story take place in the 1930s, some years after the economic crash of 1929 which resulted in massive unemployment and poverty throughout the United States. Throughout the nation millions of people had lost their jobs, their homes, their businesses, or their land, and everything that made up their way of life. In every American city of any size, long 'bread lines' of unemployed people formed to receive basic food supplies, their only means of subsistence. Many people lived in shanty towns, their shelters made of sheet-metal and scrap.

It was the time of 'The New Deal', a name given to the policies of President Roosevelt which were aimed at relieving the effects of the Great Depression.

Although slavery came to an end with the defeat of the Confederate States of the South by the Union States of the North in the American civil war of the 1860s, many whites regarded black people as inferior and resented their new-found freedom.

*To Kill A Mockingbird* is set in the sleepy old town of Maycomb, a fictitious town in the southern state of Alabama, a town inspired by the author's own hometown.

Throughout the novel we are given many detailed pictures of the town, its inhabitants and their place in the social order, their customs and beliefs, their attitudes and their everyday concerns. These are essential in helping us to understand fully the events of the story by providing us with an insight into the background.

## PLOT

The events of the story take place between the beginning of the summer of 1933 and end at Hallowe'en of 1935. They centre on the encounters and problems faced by the central characters of the novel, Atticus Finch, a lawyer and a widower, and his children Jean Louise (Scout) and her older brother Jem.

The story is divided into two parts. In the first part the action centres on the children's immediate neighbourhood and the conflict between the children and the imagined terror of the Radley Place. In the closing chapters of the first part of the novel, events in the larger community of

Maycomb begin to cast a shadow over the safe world of their neighbourhood.

In the second part of the story unfolding events bring the children beyond the safe confines of their own neighbourhood to encounter real dangers, as their father, Atticus, undertakes a task that will bring him and his children into conflict with various sections of Maycomb's community.

In the final chapters of the story the two strands of the plot combine to bring about a dramatic and surprising ending.

## NOVEL TO FILM

It has been said that a film adaptation of a novel is seldom as satisfying as the book. What we often mean is that incidents in books may be more detailed and there may be many sub-plots which would simply make a film seem too confusing. An average screenplay is 125 to 150 pages long, while the average length of a novel is twice that. On the other hand a film is capable of transmitting a great deal of information about setting, atmosphere and dramatic action through one striking image, something which might take many pages to describe in a book.

Film directors are limited in a number of ways which do not restrict the writer. For instance they have a shooting schedule which must be drawn up to accommodate actors, locations, climate, sound and lighting crews. They also have the all-important film budget.

Many factors influence the cost of making a film and films can often run way over budget. Actors can command very large fees. Night scenes are very expensive. Special effects, aerial shots, certain settings and locations, good cinematographers, post-production and pre-launch publicity all add to the cost of the film.

Writers on the other hand, can sit at their desks, whenever they please, for as long as they choose. Their locations, characters and props are all in their minds and they are not dependent on anyone else to create their work, however long they decide it will be.

Consequently film directors may make significant changes to the original story in order to reduce the filming time, and so restrict expenditure. They will also present the story as they want the viewers to see it, highlighting certain aspects and playing down others. All of these factors influence how a novel will be adapted to the screen.

## FILM TECHNIQUES

When studying a film or writing about it, you should be able to comment on how the camera is used to create certain effects. You should understand and be able to recognise a number of terms and techniques.

**Shot:** A continuous section of unedited film. Just as the sentence is a basic building block in writing, the shot is the basic building block in film. Shots vary in length from a few seconds to several minutes, however the average length is around 20 seconds. Shots are described in terms of distance, angles and movement.

**Distance:** Extreme close-up; close-up; medium shot; long shot; extreme long shot – each of these types of shot can highlight or emphasise whatever aspects of the scene a director considers important. For example an extreme close-up could be used to show the audience an inscription on a ring, or to show an expression on a character's face. Medium and long shots are used to show the whole body, the person's immediate situation or the location of the character in relation to a wider scene.

**Establishing shot:** This is generally a long shot showing the audience the general location of the scene which follows.

**Camera angle:** The angle from which a character or scene is photographed can convey certain traits of character or situation. It can also influence the audience's attitude to that character or situation. There are three angles: high angle, eye level and low angle.

A low-angle shot is one where the camera is positioned lower than the character. On screen this produces the effect of the character looking down on the viewers and can convey the impression of power, importance and authority. Conversely a high-angle shot is one where the camera is positioned higher than the character and can make the character appear weak, insignificant or inferior.

**Movement:** A tracking shot is one where the camera moves from one point to another, either sideways or in and out to follow a moving subject. The camera can roll on tracks or be hand held.

**Pan:** Moving the camera from left to right or right to left to take in a large scene is known as panning.

**Tilt:** This is when the camera is tilted up or down.

**Roll:** This is when the camera swivels vertically.

**Boom shot:** This involves putting the camera on some sort of crane to give the viewers an aerial view.

**Scene:** A series of linked shots taking place in the same location.

**Sequence or Episode:** A number of linked scenes that combine to form an event in the story.

### TO KILL A MOCKINGBIRD – SCREENPLAY BY HORTON FOOTE

For the purposes of detailed study we have divided the film into 14 episodes. We recommend that the following questions and assignments are attempted after viewing each episode.

Nelle Harper Lee, the author of the novel, wrote in her introduction to Horton Foote's published screenplay of the novel, 'If the integrity of a film adaptation is measured by the degree to which the novelist's intent is preserved, Mr. Foote's screenplay should be studied as a classic.'

When the film appeared in 1962, To Kill a Mockingbird was honoured by five Oscar nominations and Academy Awards for Best Actor (Gregory Peck), Best Adapted Screenplay, and Best Black-and-White Art Direction. It also won special humanitarian awards for its treatment of racial injustice.

#### EPISODE 1 OPENING SEQUENCE (CREDITS)

1. List the objects in the box shown in the opening sequence. When you have seen the entire film consider if any of these objects is a symbol of an important issue in the film. Note the drawing of the bird. Does this sequence in any way echo the story of the film? Explain.

#### EPISODE 2 MR. CUNNINGHAM'S VISIT

1. What does the voice-over and the opening shot of the town reveal about the time in which the film is set?
2. Why does Mr. Cunningham visit the Finch household?
3. (a) What questions does Scout ask Atticus?
   (b) How does Atticus deal with Scout's questions?
4. Explain why Jem refuses to come down from the tree?
5. What does Miss Maudie say about Atticus?
6. What kind of camera angle is used to introduce the arrival of John Baker Harris (Dill)? Suggest why this particular camera angle is used.
7. What does Jem do when Scout persists in questioning Dill about his father?
8. (a) What does Jem tell Dill about Boo Radley?
   (b) Do you think he is making it up? Why?
9. (a) What has Dill's aunt to say about the Radleys?
   (b) What effect will these revelations have on the audience?
10. What are your impressions of the following characters at this point in the film: (a) Atticus, (b) Jem, (c) Scout, (d) Dill, (e) Cal, and (f) Mr. Cunningham?
11. Identify one issue or question that has arisen at this point which you expect to be resolved over the course of the film.

### EPISODE 3 ATTICUS AND SCOUT READING

1. What was Atticus's attitude towards the Radleys?
2. Explain briefly how the music contributes to the atmosphere of this scene.
3. As Scout talks to Jem about their mother, Atticus overhears. How does he react? Why would the audience find this scene moving?
4. Outline the purpose of Judge Taylor's visit?
5. '*I'll take the case.*' In what way do Atticus's words arouse the interests and expectations of the audience?
6. As this sequence closes, a noise is heard in the distance. What is the noise? Can you suggest why it was put in?

### EPISODE 4 MORNING AND A TRIP IN A TYRE

1. How do the opening shots of this episode contrast with the closing shots of the previous episode? Refer to the music and scenery.
2. Describe the tyre episode.
3. What does Jem's action, following the 'rescue' of Scout, reveal about him?

### EPISODE 5 A VISIT TO THE COURTHOUSE

1. Describe the scene outside the courthouse.
2. What does Dill say about the events in the court?
3. (a) Describe Bob Ewell's appearance.
   (b) What is your response to this character?
   (c) What are your expectations of the role Bob Ewell is likely to play in the story?

### EPISODE 6 A VISIT TO THE RADLEY HOUSE

1. What techniques are used in this episode to establish gripping suspense?
2. Describe the camera angles used as the children make their way to the Radley house. Can you suggest the reason for these particular camera angles?
3. What do we learn from Jem about Atticus when he decides to go back for his pants?
4. At what points in this episode is tension high? At what points does it ease?

### EPISODE 7 SCOUT GOES TO SCHOOL

1. Why was Scout unhappy about going to school?
2. Jem invites Walter to lunch. What does this reveal about Jem's character?
3. What do we learn about Walter's life from the conversation at lunch?
4. What does this scene reveal about the standard of behaviour expected of Jem and Scout by Atticus and Cal?
5. In her conversation later with Atticus what does Scout reveal about (a) the teacher and (b) the Cunningham family?
6. What '*compromise*' do Atticus and Scout agree on at the end of this episode?
7. The significance of the title of the film is revealed in this episode. Explain how.
8. Explain how the voice-over heard at the end of this episode leads us to the next scene.

### EPISODE 8 THE DOG ON THE STREET

1. Describe the shot showing the dog.
2. How is it suggested that the dog is dangerous?
3. Show how the tension builds up in this episode. Comment on the close-ups and the sound effects.
4. Comment on Jem's expression before and after the shooting.

### EPISODE 9 A VISIT TO THE ROBINSONS

1. How does the set suggest that the Robinsons are poor?
2. Comment on the significance of Jem's actions towards the boy.
3. How is Bob Ewell presented in this scene? Are there any similarities between this episode and the previous episode? Consider the figure of Bob Ewell on the roadway.
4. Atticus declares that Ewell is '*all bluff*'. Do you agree? Is this episode foreshadowing something? Explain your answer.
5. What happens to Jem while Calpurnia is being brought home? Does Jem succeed in overcoming a long-held fear at this point? Explain.

### EPISODE 10 SCOUT FIGHTS – AGAIN

1. Comment on the voice-over heard at the opening of this episode. What expectations does it build up?
2. (a) Why does Scout fight with Cecil Jacobs?
   (b) Describe the reaction of Atticus when he learns of the fight.
3. (a) Why has Atticus agreed to defend Tom Robinson?
   (b) What does this tell us about the character of Atticus?
4. Describe the scene at the tree.
5. Jem reveals the contents of the box – and some surprising information – to Scout. Explain the importance of these revelations to the plot of the film.
6. How does the voice-over, which bridges this episode with the next one, sustain the interest of the audience?

### EPISODE 11 SUMMER AGAIN

1. (a) '*Thought he'd be safer there . . .*' Explain the significance of these words.
   (b) How does Jem respond to the remark?
2. How does the tension in this episode begin to build?
3. What do we fear will happen during the episode at the courthouse?
4. Explain how the conflict is resolved. In your opinion, do Scout's words have greater significance than she realises? Explain.
5. What evidence of discrimination and racial prejudice is there in the film up to this point?

## Episode 12 The Trial

**Note:** Be clear on the meanings of each of the following terms before watching this episode: **defence; prosecution; witness; evidence; summation; jury.**

1. Show how the the director emphasises the importance of the trial for the people of Maycomb.
2. Do you think that the actors playing the parts of Bob and Mayella Ewell played their parts well during the trial scene? In your answer refer to gestures, expressions, tones of voice etc.
3. What evidence suggests that Tom Robinson is innocent?
4. We get a number of close-ups of Jem during the trial. What do these close-ups convey?
5. Describe the manner of the prosecution towards Tom Robinson. What is your response to it?
6. Outline the main points of Atticus's summation.
7. How is the tension maintained during this episode? Note the use of pauses as the jury returns.
8. Describe the reactions of (a) Jem and (b) the Judge to the verdict.
9. 'The trial scene closes on a highly charged emotional note.' Discuss.
10. What direction do you expect the plot to take at the ending of the trial scene?

## Episode 13 A Visit from the Sheriff

1. Describe the reaction of Atticus to the sheriff's news.
2. Outline the main events of the visit to the Robinson place.
3. At what point was the suspense at its height? How was it resolved?
4. Were you disappointed at the action of Atticus? Explain your answer.

## Episode 14 Halloween

1. Explain how the 'voice-over' signals that the most important part of the story is now about to commence.
2. Describe the sequence of events from the opening of this episode to the end of the film.
3. 'The final episode of the film contains some memorably frightening moments and some very tender moments.' Discuss this statement and show how camera angles, sound-effects and music contribute.
4. Comment on the reference to the title of the film in this scene.

# Reading & Media

## DICK KING-SMITH

Almost twenty five years ago, a primary-school teacher who lived in south-west England walked into a bookshop and saw, for the first time, his name on the cover of a book. "My God," he remembers thinking, "I'm a children's author. Fantastic!"

He was 56 years old at the time, a former soldier, farmer, travelling salesman and shoe factory worker. Today, Dick King-Smith is probably the most popular living children's author, with about six million books sold in Britain alone. He was beaten only by the late Roald Dahl and the American author R. L. Stine in a recent BBC poll of young readers' favourites.

At 76, he continues to publish a new book every three or four months. And *Babe*, the film of his book *The Sheep-Pig*, made him famous round the world.

He and Myrle, his wife of 55 years, live in a seventeenth-century cottage in a village between Bristol and Bath, in the south of England. King-Smith still writes in the same small room where he wrote that first book, *The Fox-Busters*, 22 years ago. More than 90 books have emerged from that room, although some are very short. For a couple of hours most mornings, King-Smith sits here and writes his stories in long hand with a pencil. In the afternoon he types them up, one-fingered, on an old portable typewriter.

The King-Smiths are an amusingly combative couple. He is tall and gangly, with a shock of white hair and ancient clothes, like the farmers in some of his books. She is neat, slight and rather frail. Between them flows constant good-humoured banter. He reads his stories to her and if they don't come up to scratch he starts again.

Their life together has been a long and bumpy journey. "He's had a lot of knocks in life," says Joanna Goldsworthy, the editor who nursed into print his first six books, including *The Sheep-Pig*. "He was just so amazed when he succeeded as a writer."

It was a case, he says, of "at last finding something I'm good at". He wrote *The Fox-Busters* in 1976, when he had been teaching for just a year. It owed its existence to an incident in his farming days, when many of his chickens were massacred by a fox. Wouldn't it be fun, he thought at the time, to write a story in which the chickens fought back? But he didn't find the time for more than a decade, when he was first faced with the six-week school summer holiday. "Because I'd had the story in my head so long. I wrote it in three weeks."

He made a list of 20 children's publishers from the *Writers' and Artists' Yearbook* and sent the story to each of them in turn. Number three was Victor

> "In an ideal world I'd have stayed a farmer, but I was a bad businessman and went bust. I'm very happy that things have turned out the way they have."

Gollancz, where it was read by Joanna Goldsworthy. She told him she liked the story — in which chickens learn to dive-bomb their tormentors — but that he hadn't a clue how to write for children. "Because it was a war story, I wrote it like a war correspondent's report. There was no characterisation and practically no dialogue. She more or less said, 'Look, are you prepared to do a lot of work on this?' And I said, 'Yes,' and I did, and eventually she published it."

"It was very sophisticated and rather wordy for a children's book," recalls Goldsworthy. "But the basic idea was terrific and there was a real knowledge of how animals behave." King-Smith's plots often involve what film-makers call a 'high concept' premise: a pig that learns to be a sheepdog, a hedgehog who wants to find a safe way of crossing the road, a chicken that is taught to speak, parrot-fashion.

But his lifelong involvement with animals sets him apart from those authors who write about them without any real understanding. It was with his second published book, *Daggle Dogfoot*, about a pig with deformed feet, that King Smith "really found the voice that he has made his trademark," says Goldsworthy. Or rather, the voices. Although the animals in his books never wear clothes, they all talk.

Goldsworthy continued to ask him to simplify his stories and his language. He grumbled, but he learned. His pre-war private education and his grandfatherly age (he now has 11 grandchildren and a great granddaughter) gives his writing a timeless quality and a formality that children seem to like. He never tries to be their best friend. Nor does he shield them from the grisly fate of animals. "It's a deceit to your readers to do that," he says. "They're terribly tough. They can take things." Annie Eaton, his current editor at Transworld, agrees. "He doesn't pull his punches. If a pig is in danger of being butchered he will say so, although he will usually save him."

Dick King-Smith was born in Bitton, a village only three miles from where he lives now. His younger brother followed father and grandfather into the family paper mill business, but Dick was more interested in animals. "We always had masses of pets at home, not just the usual dogs." On Christmas Day 1935, when he was 13, he was introduced to a girl called Myrle England. "I didn't think much of girls, but she was interested in budgerigars. And she liked dogs . . ." They wrote to each other during Dick's schooldays at Marlborough, and continued to keep in touch when he left to take up a farming apprenticeship in Wiltshire.

They married in 1943 and that September, as a 21-year-old platoon commander in the Grenadier Guards, King-Smith landed in Salerno, Italy. In July 1944, south of Florence, a German paratrooper picked up a discarded British grenade and threw it at him. Luckily, it hit a tree first. "It nearly knocked me off," he says. "I had about 120 bits of metal in me. I still feel 'em occasionally." After a year's recuperation, he briefly returned to his regiment, but his military career was over. He was sent on an ex-servicemen's farming course and then, in 1947, he plunged into 20 years of farming.

His family bought a 50-acre dairy farm, ostensibly to provide milk and eggs for the paper mill's canteen but really to support the wounded soldier and his children: his first daughter was born in 1945, with a second daughter and a son following shortly after. "We kept as many different sorts of animals as we could. We treated them all like pets. We gave them all names." This was not a recipe for serious farming. When the paper mill closed at the beginning of the 1960s, the farm had to be sold too. King-Smith then began renting a bigger farm. "Although I'm quite a good stockman, I'm hopeless with business," he admits. Six years later, the bank manager told the King-Smiths to call it a day.

After a succession of jobs, Dick took a four-year teacher-training course, then started work at a village primary school, only five miles from home. He taught for seven years, but there was trouble over his efforts to teach mathematics to eight-year-olds. "Their maths skills have not improved," commented the head mistress. "They have deteriorated."

King-Smith was now 60. His parents had recently died leaving some money, and he calculated that if he stopped work he and Myrle would be able to scrape together an income of about £5,000 a year. "I'll manage on it," Myrle assured Dick. He had by this time written his first four books, though he did not expect to earn much from them. But the books started "popping up like mushrooms". He even had a spell on television, introducing children to animals and telling them stories.

King-Smith's output was prolific. He produced a book every six weeks, concentrating on the seven to elevens at first, then adding picture books for younger readers. He kept the children's departments of two and sometimes three publishers busy.

Recently, he has become more ambitious, with adolescents and young adults in mind. The first of these books, *Godhanger*, appeared in 1997. "It's very dark, very stark," he says. "I've allowed myself to use interesting language for once, instead of having to keep to the plot, do a few little jokes and get on with it." The result is an impressive but rather unusual book. King-Smith vowed that if it was badly received, he'd go back to "pigsty comedy".

That has not been necessary. A second novel in a similar vein, The *Crow-Starver*, appeared in July last year. Success has proved an uncomplicated joy. There was no new house, no swimming pool. Selling the film rights to *The Sheep-Pig* did not transform King Smith's fortunes. He won't say what he was paid, but some people put it as low as £15,000. The film made almost 250 million dollars.

It is likely that he was paid more for the sequel *Babe: Pig in the City*, released last month, in which the talented sheep-pig goes on tour to raise money to save his injured owner's farm. Babe is King-Smith's character so Universal Studios has to pay him to use him, but it is not his story and he has had nothing to do with the film.

Universal Studios has licensed seven new Babe books, created without Dick King-Smith's involvement, not to mention all the soft toys, clothes and kitchenware.

Whatever doubts he has about *Babe II*, he does appreciate the technical possibilities opened up by *Babe*: for the first time, real animals appeared to be actually speaking in a film. For an author whose books are crammed with talking animals, this is a promising development.

This year, he hopes that *The Water Horse*, the story of some children who find a sea monster, will be made into a British film. And although he generally scorns cartoons, he seems pleased that *The Fox-Busters* is set to appear as an animated television version.

He will not be retiring, he maintains, not while the ideas continue to flow. "I enjoy writing stories," he says, with deep satisfaction. "And somebody pays me for it."

## Questions & Assignments

1. In what year was Dick King-Smith born? Explain how you arrived at your answer.
2. List all the occupations Dick King-Smith has had in his life.
3. What evidence is there to show that Dick King-Smith is a very popular author?
4. (a) Describe Dick King-Smith's method of writing?
   (b) Do you think that he should change it? Explain your answer.
5. (a) When and how did Dick King-Smith get the idea for his first book?
   (b) When did he write it?
6. Were the publishers happy with the version of the story that he sent to them? Explain your answer.
7. What do you think is meant by the film-makers' term *'a high-concept premise'*? Consider the full sentence in which the phrase occurs.
8. (a) What kind of work does an editor who works in a book publishers do?
   (b) In your view was Joanna Goldsworthy a good editor?
9. What are Dick King-Smith's attitudes towards his readers?
10. (a) Did his family need to buy the farm to supply the paper mill's canteen? Explain your answer.
    (b) *'This was not a recipe for serious farming.'* What do you think is meant by this statement?
11. Why do you think that the bank manager told Dick King-Smith to *'call it a day'*?
12. Do you think that Dick King-Smith was a good teacher? Explain your answer.
13. *'King-Smith's output was prolific.'* What do you think this statement means?
14. In recent years he has changed his writing style. Explain how.
15. What involvement has Dick King-Smith in the film *Babe: Pig in the City*?
16. Why did the film *Babe* mark a technical breakthrough in film-making? Explain why this is a *'promising development'* for Dick King-Smith.
17. Write a short biography of Dick King-Smith based on this passage. You may use words and phrases but not any complete sentences from the passage.
18. From reading the passage say why you would or would not like to make your living as a writer.

The following **Spot the Errors** exercise is aimed at sharpening your basic writing skills. Spot the 20 errors in the Passage below and rewrite the passage correctly. (Note: Refer to the Guidelines on pages 1—15.)

## 14 A Little Help from her Friends

Some people might think that Wendy has a brass neck. she has no close relatives. She was busy and active until, earlier this year, she suddenly needed a big operation followed by a long coarse of treatment. She new she wouldn't be able to drive for quiet some time and that she'd have very little strengh. She worried about how she would cope.

So wendy made a list of all the thing she was worried about. She would need somebody to walk her dog regularly and help tidy the garden. Also, getting the shopping home from the supermarket would be to difficult on her own, and transport to the bridge club and to Hospital for her follow-up treatment was another problem. She'd have to solve.

She says, I'd often heard people complaining that no-one offered them help, yet I no that most people are only too glad to be of use, if only they knew what to do. Perhaps I was cheeky, but I decided that I'd simply ask for the help I needed. I got the idea from brides who give people lists of the wedding present's they'd like, and let them choose what to give."

She showed the list to everyone who visited her, and no one minded a bit indeed, over the past months theyve all lent a cheerful hand, which she's sure has helped her recovery. Its a good thing to offer help — but perhaps it takes more trust in friendship for an independant sole to ask for it.

# Holiday in Clare

**Carlo Gébler recalls the holiday in Clare when he and his brother magically received forbidden fruit — toy guns**

We lived in Morden, a grim suburb in south London. Each summer we were sent to east Clare, my younger brother and I, to my mother's people. Our London house smelt of coal dust and the sulphur we sprayed on the grapes that grew under the verandah. The Irish house smelt of marmalade, soda-bread and grandfather's Gold Flake cigarettes. That summer, the magic summer, we were nine and seven.

In London, toy guns were forbidden. As were toy bazookas which fired ping-pong balls, Airfix models of the *Bismarck* and the *HMS Hood*, Roman centurion sword, scabbard and shield outfits, and Colt .45 cap-guns. No military toys of any sort were permitted. Even playing with a stick that happened, by chance, to have the handle/barrel shape of a gun was forbidden.

The rule against war toys came from my father. He didn't like them, he said, because they were shoddy and dangerous. Now I am a father myself, I think he just hated the noise and high jinks that went with these toys. So, in London, we lived in a largely war toy free zone.

In Ireland, on the contrary, it was Liberty Hall. We were free. We made spears and swords out of ash sticks. We made Webley revolvers and Winchester repeating rifles out of broom handles. We made pea shooters from copper pipe. We made catapults with 'Y's of beech and strips of inner tube. But no matter how hard we tried, no matter how inventive we were, everything we made looked handmade, which it was. And nothing had the finish or the gloss of a proper war toy from a shop. It was a terrible situation. We were free to play war but owned no weapons that looked like the real thing.

In the circumstances the only alternative was magic. There was a fairy ring at the bottom of the avenue. It was a perfect circle of beech and oak trees with wild irises growing between them. Furthermore, which had not escaped our attention, no matter how bad the storm, the cattle never went in here.

So, off we set. Tramping down the avenue, we were in the normal everyday world of grass, bird song and cattle dung. But once we slipped inside the ring we were in a different world. It was incredibly dark for a start; it took ages for our eyes to adjust to the gloom. It was also very quiet, while at the same time familiar sounds like the rasping bray of our donkey appeared to be far further away than in fact we knew was the case. We had noticed the same effect in churches. The ring also had a unique smell. It was a chalky, musty odour, like the incense we sniffed at Sunday Mass.

But its most important feature, undoubtedly, was the lichen-covered stones in the middle. This was the altar. Here we placed our offerings. These were a penny, a headless toy soldier, a broken set of Rosary beads, a Lady Finger biscuit and an old light bulb from the milking parlour. Then we knelt on the brown carpet of beech nuts and, until our bare knees could stand it no longer, we begged the powers to grant us one wish: a double-barrelled shot gun with a spring mechanism that fired cork plugs for each of us.

We went back to the ring the next day. Our offerings were gone. Miracle of miracles. We knelt and prayed. We went back again the day after. On the night following our third visit, my brother woke me in the middle of the night. He had something to show me. I stared out into the velvety darkness. I blinked in disbelief. It couldn't be. It was. Three gold figures hovered outside: a blind fox (quite how I knew it was blind eludes me now), a bat and a fairy in a pointed hat. It was an encouraging sign. I knew at once we needn't go back to the ring.

Some days later the post van pulled up and the postman fetched two long parcels out of the back. There were sealing wax blobs along the brown paper seams. One was addressed to Master Carlo, the other to Master Sasha Gébler. We carried the parcels into the kitchen and opened them. Inside were the double-barrelled shotguns we coveted. There was also a note from my mother. My grandmother read it out.

My mother said she had bought the guns on impulse. She hoped we liked them. We were advised not to bring them home. Yes, I said and shrugged. I knew what this letter meant. Grandmother had written off to her. But the guns would have come even if she hadn't. The powers would have seen to it. I knew that.

I unpicked the string which attached the corks to the gun-barrel ends and hurried outside to shoot a few Tommies.

## Questions & Assignments

1. Do you think that the writer preferred to be in London or Clare? Give a reason for your answer.
2. According to the passage was it illegal for people to have toy guns in London? Explain your answer.
3. Was the writer's father a strict parent? Refer to the passage to show how you arrived at your opinion.
4. What did the writer enjoy doing in Ireland?
5. How does the writer show that the fairy ring was a magical place?
6. What was their purpose in going to the fairy ring?
7. Do you think that the author actually saw three gold figures in the darkness? Give a reason for your answer.
8. *'My mother said she had bought the guns on impulse.'* What is the meaning of this sentence? Did he believe his mother? Explain your answer.
9. Suggest an alternative title or heading to print on top of the story.

## PERSONAL WRITING

### ASSIGNMENT

Write about a magical moment from your childhood.

# GARDA COP CRIME ON

**Geraldine Comiskey reports**

IS IT a bird? Is it a plane? No – it's the Cop 'Copter.

The Garda helicopter has whirled into action, shining giant searchlights into gardens and windows to catch criminals on the run.

Armed with a plane and helicopter, each equipped with the latest hightech gadgets, the GASU (Garda Air Support Unit) are a force to be reckoned with.

### GARDENS

This week, I reckoned it was time to meet the Helicops – and join them on a patrol in the supercool Squirrel helicopter.

It looked like the sort of machine you would expect to find Robocop flying – but I was surrounded by real action men on my day with GASU.

With two Garda Observers – Sergeants Greg McGovern and Paul Kinsella – and Air Corps pilot Captain John Finn taking the controls, we took off from Casement military aerodrome in Baldonnel, Dublin, where the special unit is based.

### SPECIAL

The Air Corps supply the pilots and technicians for both the chopper and the plane, but the Garda Observers decide where to go.

The unit is linked by radio to the control in Harcourt Square, where all the 999 calls are taken.

The helicopter also picks up calls from various bases throughout the county, on a multi-channel radio inside the craft.

At the base, members of the unit on 'ground duty' man the telephones and keep in touch with their colleagues in the air by radio.

With the whole country to patrol, both chopper and plane are kept busy, landing only to refuel.

Just seconds after leaving the airfield, we were on our first mission – to catch a burglar in Dalkey, Dublin, about 20 miles away as the crow flies.

In less than three minutes, we had reached the east coast and were hovering above exclusive Sorrento Point – or Millionaire's Row, as it's known to showbiz fans, auctioneers, and of course burglars.

### SHOWBIZ

We could see a patrol car on the narrow road below as we spiralled down towards the rooftops.

Sitting beside the pilot, Paul used a complicated-looking set of controls to manoeuvre the camera, which dangles from under the chopper's nose.

## It's no flight of fancy at all

SKY patrol is the most coveted beat in the Gardai – and there was no shortage of applicants for the special airborne unit.

Over 100 applied, but after stringent physical tests, only 16 were chosen (four sergeants and 12 Gardai).

Only the super-fit can fly eight hours a day, every day, without the luxury of a pressurised cabin, and a surgeon specialising in aviation disorders has been assigned to the unit.

The stress on the body is similar to that experienced by divers.

Ears, sinuses, veins and various other body tissues are all under tremendous strain because of the constant change in air pressure.

The changes in G-force caused by the sudden rising, swooping and gyrating can also make you quite queasy, and every crew member carries a sickbag.

### AEROBATICS

Luckily, we didn't need them on our mission, but even Greg admitted his stomach was doing aerobatics when the copter suddenly banked.

Sergeant Noel Mostyn describes the special training at Templemore as "a few weeks of hell".

Experts monitored them for over-all fitness and the ability to stay alert after very little sleep – so they could be ready for any situation.

"We were tested to our limits," says Noel, who was based on Harcourt Terrace before joining the Air Support Unit.

But Noel and the others in the team says it was worth any discomfort. "I get a great buzz out of it," says Sergeant Greg McGovern.

Pilot John Finn, who is an Air Corps Captain assigned to the Garda Unit, gets his kicks in another way when he lands – on the Kildare football team.

The unit also includes a woman, Garda Lorraine Boyle.

# THE BLADE RUNNER

He panned the camera along the row of houses, occasionally zooming in and focusing on a garden.

**HOUSES**

Beside Greg in the back seat, I got a birds-eye view of everything – a screen mounted on a stand behind the pilot's seat showed me what the camera saw, and the windows all round give a wide view of Dublin Bay.

Only the blades of the chopper could be heard as we stayed silent, listening watching and waiting for more instructions – and scaring the wits out of a burglar who might be lurking below.

After a few minutes, we were told that the burglar had been caught.

**RADIO**

"Mission Over," said Paul over the radio as we banked sideways and shot up into the air.

Seconds later, we were thundering over Stephen's Green like a giant bug, low enough to observe the surprised expression on a number of sunbathers' faces.

We could even see what sort of sandwiches they were eating.

No one seemed to be committing any crime, so we moved on.

**NOISE**

As we dropped out of the sky, a high-pitched bleeping noise warned us we had passed the 50-feet mark – the pilot can adjust this device to suit mountainous areas.

Back at the base, the crew logged the flight's details, while I watched video footage of other missions.

Car chases on the M50, speeding, swerving motorbikes in suburban housing estates as well as prisoners on the run from Mountjoy – they were all caught on candid cameras.

## EASY TARGETS

THEY take no prisoners, but the Garda Air Support Unit (GASU) have made over 200 arrests since they took to the skies last September.

Hovering above the criminals, they keep their giant searchlights on their targets until the patrol cars arrive.

They have also recovered over 100 stolen cars – and millions of pounds of property, including illegal drugs.

Both the Squirrel helicopter and Defender plane have more than earned their keep since they were commissioned.

Together, they keep a 24-hour watch over every street, garden and hedgerow in Ireland.

Co-operation with the Air Corps has added to the efficiency of GASU.

If an extra craft is needed, or if one of the craft is being serviced, the Gardai can request an Air Corps helicopter complete with pilot.

**REQUEST**

The Air Corps also provide mechanics and technicians like Sergeant Nick McNulty, who checked the Squirrel before we departed.

A typical eight-hour patrol is hectic, as the choppers only land to refuel – giving the crew a few minutes to log details of the last mission.

The chopper can stay up for two-and-a-half hours max before refuelling, while the plane can fly five hours non-stop.

The Squirrel is valued at about £1·2m on its own – but £4·5m with the equipment.

The equipment, which is common to both aircraft, includes a camera which can zoom in close enough to read car registration numbers.

The camera's special 'thermal heat imaging' device can detect the body heat of people hiding in bushes.

Some criminals are very cunning – like the three trespassers on a factory rooftop recently, who lay one on top of the other to fool the cops into thinking there was only one.

But it didn't work and all the criminals were caught.

## Questions & Assignments

1. Is the reporter impressed by the Garda helicopter? Give reasons for your answer.
2. What is the name of the Garda unit that operates the helicopter?
3. Where are the unit's headquarters located?
4. How many members are in the unit? Is the Garda helicopter piloted by Gardai? Refer to the passage to support your answer.
5. Name the people who were on board the Garda helicopter on the day that the reporter flew in the helicopter.
6. Explain the phrase *'as the crow flies'* or give an example of when you might use that phrase.
7. Describe the equipment that the Garda helicopter carries.
8. Describe the mission to Dalkey to catch the burglar.
9. What task does the crew carry out when they return to base?
10. In what ways has the Garda helicopter *'earned its keep'* since it was commissioned?
11. Would you agree that working as a crew member in the Air Support Unit is demanding work? Explain your answer.
12. (a) The report is divided into three sections. In the case of the headline of each section explain why you do or do not think it is suitable.
    (b) Comment on the main title of this feature.

## PERSONAL WRITING

## ASSIGNMENTS

1. Imagine that you are a member of the Garda Air Support Unit. Write an account of a day you spent on duty in the Garda helicopter.
2. Write a detailed description of the photograph accompanying this report.

Reading & Media

# SPOT THE ERRORS

The following Spot the Errors exercise is aimed at sharpening your basic writing skills. Spot the 20 errors in the Passage below and rewrite the passage correctly. (Note: Refer to the Guidelines on pages 1—15.)

## 15 Flying Saucers

The first report of flying saucers was recieved in 1947. That year a aeroplane pilot claimed to have scene nine saucers flying around Mount rainier since then the United States air force has received thousands of similar reports. It set up a system for the investigation of Unidentified Flying Objects (UFO's for short). Many people believed that the saucers were spaceships that had flown to the earth from other planets. Aboard them we're believed to be strange beings who had come to study us.

Nearly everyone who reports a flying saucer has seen something. But what have they actually seen In some cases the 'something' has been a weather balloon, a satellite a cloud, a meteor, a star, or a bird. In other cases it has been a comet, a Planet, or fireworks.

Hear is a case of a saucer report, togeter with an explanation of what really happened. An american pilot, flying night patrol over the U.S. naval base at Guantanamo bay in Cuba, spotted a saucer and gave chase. The saucer took the form of an orange light that out-turned, out-climbed and out-dived the plane. Finally the light made a turn to the left and slowed down. It hovered above the water for a moment and then disapeared. The pilot was surprised to learn that he had been chasing a weather balloon. Air currants had carryed the balloon up, down and around. And so the pilot had taught it was an aircraft of some kind.

**TOP 2FM** disc jockey Ian Dempsey dramatically switched sides and yesterday moved his breakfast show to RTE's arch rival, independent radio station, Today FM.

The presenter who attracted 250,000 listeners in his key morning radio slot is believed to have crossed sides for a 'substantial' six figure sum.

Dempsey, who has been with the national station for nineteen years is a major broadcasting coup for 100–102 Today FM which has as many listeners daily as Dempsey had for his RTE Monday–Friday slot.

It is understood that the independent station is jubilant at Dempsey's decision to sign up for a three year contract and regards the presenter as a key tool in the scramble to haul in more listeners.

At the Today FM base in Dublin city centre yesterday, the DJ refused to comment on the six figure sum, more than £100,000, to be paid when he begins his breakfast show in September.

"It is a new challenge and a new chapter in my career. I am happy with the offer. The negotiations were going on for the best part of a year and I was asked how much it would take," he commented.

And added: "I am very excited about the new challenge. I was a long time at RTE and I made some great friends but it's time for a change in my career. The show is going to be the same format and hopefully some of my listeners will follow me."

Dempsey yesterday hung up his headphones at RTE to take holidays before starting his new show which will be broadcast from 7am to 10am from September 21. Meanwhile, Gareth O'Callaghan is to replace Ian Dempsey in RTE's morning slot from Monday.

## Questions & Assignments

1. Why is Today FM delighted that Ian Dempsey has joined them?
2. Is there any firm evidence in the article on the amount that he is being paid? Explain your answer.
3. How long did Ian Dempsey work for RTE?
4. Will his new show on Today FM be different to his breakfast show on RTE? Give a reason for you answer.
5. Write a suitable headline for the story.
6. Did Ian Dempsey leave RTE immediately after announcing his plans? Give a reason for your answer.
7. Why do you think that he refused to comment on the amount that he is being paid?
8. Rewrite the important points of this story. Your report should be between 75 and 100 words in length. While you can use words and phrases from the article you should not copy any complete sentence from the article.

## Assignments

**Personal Writing**

1. Write a brief review of your favourite radio programme.
2. Imagine that you are a radio DJ. Name three records that you would like to play on your show and write out what you would say about each record before playing it.
3. If you were the producer of a morning 'breakfast' show on radio describe some of the ways you would make it attractive to listeners.
4. Imagine you were the photographer sent to cover this story. Describe the photograph that accompanies the report and say why you think it works well.
5. (a) If you were a newspaper reporter sent to cover this story write out five questions that you would put to Ian Dempsey.
   (b) Name someone else that you would like to interview in connection with the story. What questions would you ask?

# TAKE A DIVE

When an island-hopping holiday is mentioned, Inis Bofin, Inis Turk and Clare Island are probably the last places most people would think of — but an underwater 'weekend safari' is the break with a difference currently being offered by a diving company in Connemara. Diving has become an increasingly popular sport in Ireland over the past few years, with many tourists travelling here specifically to dive and Bord Fáilte promoting our underwater attractions.

Asa Eldisaksson, from Sweden, came for the diving – and has stayed for the past three months. She is now working as an instructor for the Connemara diving company Scubadive West, and has done the 'dive safari' twice.

"The safari is terrific," she says. "The weather was really windy when I did it, but it didn't make any difference. The trip out to the islands is easy, the accommodation is great and the people are lovely. From the islands it is only 10 or 15 minutes to the dive sites. When I went diving in other countries it took up a lot of the day just getting to the sites. I worked in Egypt for a year and when I came here it was the first time I had dived in really cold water, but it was brilliant. The visibility is great and there is a lot of variety in the sea life you get to see. You can do cave diving, wall diving or drift diving."

For those who have no experience of diving, Scubadive West offers a Try-a-Dive course which takes about three hours and the cost is very reasonable. For anyone who thinks they may enjoy it, this reporter highly recommends it; you get professional tuition and are then taken out on a 30-minute supervised dive. It is all surprisingly easy.

It takes only a short time to get used to the equipment; it feels quite heavy at first, but once you go underwater you almost forget about it. Breathing with the equipment is simple, and the sense of freedom you get swimming underwater looking at the sea life is like none other. If you are looking for a fast-moving sport, however, this is not for you. It is all very slow-moving and peaceful and really is a chance to see another world.

Scubadive West is run by Shane and Olli Gray and their four sons Cillian, Tiernan, Breffni and Ronan. The Grays owned and ran a scuba-dive centre in Dalkey, Co. Dublin, before they moved to Renvyle in Co. Galway. Shane learned to dive in the Army. "I decided the set-up in the existing scuba-diving clubs wasn't adequate to cater for the interests of beginners," he says, "so I started a school, offered the courses on a fee-paying basis, and provided the equipment."

"We had a lovely set-up in Dalkey at Colliemore Harbour. However, from the mid–to–early 1980s the water quality visibly deteriorated from year to year. By the late 1980s it was just pea soup and we decided we didn't have a product to sell any more. There was no joy in diving there," Shane explains.

"Ireland is an ideal destination for anyone interested in diving. We have the most westerly coastline in Europe and are sitting right in the path of the Gulf Stream. We get the full benefit of this, which means that the waters are milder and this provides for better marine life and colour. We have a magical natural ingredient here. The broken nature of the coastline on the west means there is lots of shelter and variety. The islands provide even more variety."

"What were missing for many years were facilities. Bord Fáilte set up a marketing group with those involved in diving around the country and part-funded a five-year marketing plan. The group is called Discover Underwater Ireland and we have seven or eight dive centres along the west coast."

Ronnie Fitzgibbon, the chairman of Discover Underwater Ireland, says substantial numbers of visitors have been attracted by the seven Bord Fáilte-approved dive centres. "I would estimate that most of them bring in an excess of 1,000 each year," he says. "These are tourists who come specifically for diving activities. In relative terms the centres spend a lot on marketing each year, and our growth is fairly substantial."

Fitzgibbon, who runs Waterworld in Tralee, says the good thing about the dive centres is that they all offer different kinds of diving holiday.

So where did the inspiration for Scubadive West's dive safari come from? "The safari was my idea," says Shane Gray. "You have to be innovative as you are competing with other dive centres in Ireland as well as internationally. You are competing with warm-water destinations and therefore you have to make your product as interesting as possible. There has been so much interest that we have had to put on extra safaris. The novelty of visiting three very beautiful islands attracts people, apart altogether from the very high quality of the diving available off these islands. Warm-water destinations offer 'live-aboard diving holidays' where you stay on the boat. So the dive safari offers the next best thing."

The dive safari lasts four days, The price of about £180 covers 3 nights B&B, dinners, travel to the three islands, six dives and all the equipment. Contact Scubadive West on (095) 43922 or e-mail Scuba@anu.ie.

*Spectrum 2*

## Questions & Assignments

1. What sentence tells us that more and more people are taking up the sport of diving?
2. What nationality is Asa Eldisaksson?
3. What impressed Asa Eldisaksson about Ireland?
4. On the Try-a-Dive course what length of time does the diving tuition take?
5. How does the writer show that using the diving equipment is not difficult?
6. Why do you think the reporter says that diving *'is a chance to see another world'*?
7. When did Shane Gray begin diving?
8. How many members of the Gray family are involved in the running of Scubadive West?
9. Why do you think the company is called Scubadive West?
10. Explain why the Grays moved to Connemara.
11. How does Shane Gray show that the west coast is a good place for anyone interested in diving?
12. What do we learn about Ronnie Fitzgibbon from the article?
13. Approximately how many tourists come to Ireland each year to take part in diving?

## Assignments

**Personal Writing**

1. You have been asked to devise a small advertisement for Scubadive West to be placed in a British newspaper. Write out the text of the advertisement.
2. Imagine that you were a reporter sent to interview Shane Grey. List eight questions that you would put to him.

Reading & Media

The following **Spot the Errors** exercise is aimed at sharpening your basic writing skills. Spot the 20 errors in the Passage below and rewrite the passage correctly. (Note: Refer to the Guidelines on pages 1—15.)

## 16  The Titanic

The sinking of the *Titanic* was one of the worst maritime disasters in history. The Luxury Liner *Titanic*, on its maiden voyage from Southampton to new York City, struck an Iceberg about 170 km south of the Grand Banks of Newfoundland just before midnight on April 14, 1912. Of the more than 2,220 persons aboard, 1,513 died. Including the American millionaires John Jacob Astor, Benjamin Guggenheim and Isidor Straus.

The ship had been proclaimed insinkable because of its sixteen watertight compartments. However the iceberg punchured five of them, one more than had been considered possible in any accident, and the *Titanic* sank in less than three hours. Investigations into the accident found that the ship had been steaming too fast in dangerous waters, that lifeboat space had been provided for only about half of the passengers and crew and that the *californian*, a ship that was passing close to the seen at the time, had not come to the rescue because it's radio operator was off juty and asleep. These findings led to many reforms, such as lifeboat space for every person on a ship, lifeboat drills, the maintenance of a full-time radio watch while at sea and an International ice patrol.

The sinking of the *Titanic* has been the subject of several books and films, but not until september 1985 was the actual reck found and the area photograped, by a joint French–US Expedition, through the use of robot submarines equipped with television cameras. In July 1986 the US researchers explored the *Titanic* in a small three-person submarine. They took pictures of the interior, but recovered no artifacts. The following year a controversial french salvage effort retrieved dishes, jewels, currency and other artifacts. Which were exhibited in Paris in September 1987.

# The Phantom of the Point

**They may need an exorcist soon at the Point Theatre in Dublin if a jinx which seems to have haunted its production of *The Phantom of the Opera* fails to go away.**

The 'Phantom of the Point' struck twice during a matinée performance on Saturday, causing the sound system to fail and the machinery used to change the scenery to jam, bringing the show to a premature end.

The cancellation followed an incident last month when an actress in the lead role fell ill on stage at a time when the understudy was also unwell.

Management at the Point have been eager to dispel any rumours that a supernatural force is at play. But many staff members are worried that there is 'something out there'.

"Since the show started there have been all sorts of weird things happening," said one employee. "The cleaning staff are convinced their Hoovers are starting all by themselves."

In a strange case of life imitating art, the show was interrupted on Saturday by a faceless voice announcing tales of woe. It wasn't the Phantom himself but an unfortunate Point employee who had to explain to the 2,500 capacity crowd that the show had to be at first delayed and finally cancelled.

The first interruption, lasting about 15 minutes, occurred shortly after the show began. Someone apparently unplugged the computer system which operated the orchestra keyboards. Who? The mystery remains.

The second incident occurred during the interval when the computers used to operate the scenery for the show 'crashed', leaving the audience, some of whom had travelled from as far away as Tyrone and Cork, trailing home early.

"Whatever caused it, it's ruined our day completely," said Ms. Sheila Malone from Mallow, Co. Cork, who had gone to the show with her mother and grandmother to celebrate the latter's 70th birthday.

A Point spokesman said that all ticket-holders would be refunded but he could not guarantee that travel expenses would be paid.

Future performances of the show should not be affected by the system failure, the cause of which, although not human, was not supernatural either, he said. "The fact is that when you have a show that lasts three months people are going to go sick and you are going to have incidents like this. There is nothing suspicious about it."

Others might disagree, however, as Saturday's performance was the second in almost as many weeks to be disrupted. And as we all know, these things tend to come in threes.

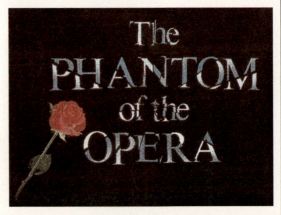

Reading & Media

## Questions & Assignments

1. Who is the 'Phantom of the Point'?
2. Explain the opening sentence clearly.
3. What is the name of a person who is called to take over if an actor is unable to perform?
4. Are the workers in the Point concerned that some strange happenings are occurring? Explain your answer.
5. Why was the worker who made the announcements to the audience described as *'a faceless voice'*?
6. At what stage was the show cancelled — close to the beginning, middle or end? Give a reason for your answer.
7. For how long had the show been running in the Point?
8. What evidence is there in the article that the show was very popular?
9. What do you understand by the last sentence in the report?
10. The show was disrupted on a previous occasion. Explain why the disruption occurred.

## Personal Writing

### Assignments

1. Imagine that you are the Ms. Malone referred to in the report. Write a letter to the management of the Point outlining your views on the question of refunds and travel expenses.

2. Imagine that you are the worker who had to make the two announcements to the audience. In each case write out the exact words you would use.

# SUPERMARKET TECHNIQUES

So you think you're too clever to be tricked into buying unwanted goods by cunning retailers? Well sadly it seems that none of us is. Experts recently monitored shoppers and found that French accordion tunes made French wine walk off the shelves. Yet, when questioned, most shoppers hotly denied that the music directed their choice – which goes to show how much we can be manipulated.

Music is only one tool that the retail trade uses to lighten your wallet. A survey of Californian supermarkets found that high-priced goods were placed invitingly at eye level, with goods aimed at children cunningly placed on lower shelves. You've probably noticed how chocolate bars are stacked at child height next to the checkout, where mums and dads wait with bored kids.

Scientific studies show that any particular brand of product on supermarket shelves have about one second to grab your eye as you browse the shelves. Packaging hype is a great way to catch your eye, and it should all be taken with a hefty pinch of salt. '10% Extra Free' sounds good until you discover a competitor's product already offers this 'extra' anyway.

Beware, too, of the 'colour con'. Supermarkets can use lush greens and fake grass in their greengrocery sections and cool blues near frozen foods to suggest fresh products. At the deli counter, special lighting effects make meat look more appetising.

Watch aisles as well. End-of-aisle displays are often stocked with goods near their expiry dates. And a narrow, messy aisle packed with disorderly goods is an attempt to give an impression of a bargain basement 'pile-it-high, sell-it-cheap' store. The 'bargains' are nearly always bang on their 'best before' date.

The oldest trick is to use the smell of fresh coffee and baking bread, so have lunch before you shop to avoid being influenced by the aroma of chicken roasting at the deli counter. Refuse the tempting 'promotional' tasters of wine and cheese, and don't be fooled by those slices of pre-sliced, shrink-wrapped melon: it's astounding what a bit of clingfilm adds to the price.

Cashing in on the tactics of Las Vegas casinos, supermarkets nearly all have cash machines on the premises. With wads in your wallet, you're even more likely to spend, right? "Well, this isn't something we really do or would be prepared to comment on," says a supermarket spokesperson. It all means that there can be only one rule: buyer beware.

### Questions & Assignments

1. Explain the phrase *'walk off the shelves'*. (Paragraph 1)
2. Where are expensive goods placed? Explain why.
3. Why are goods aimed at children placed on lower shelves?
4. Where else are goods aimed at children placed? Explain why.
5. What do you think the writer means by *'packaging hype'*? (Paragraph 3)
6. Why is fake grass used in the greengrocery section?
7. Why do you think that the colour blue is used in the frozen foods section?
8. How do supermarkets attempt to sell goods approaching their sell-by date?
9. What other tricks are mentioned in the passage? Describe some other methods used by supermarkets to (a) attract customers and (b) sell goods that are not referred to in the passage.

## PERSONAL WRITING

### ASSIGNMENT

Write two or three paragraphs (approx 120 words) offering advice to someone considering shopping in one of the following stores:

(a) a shoes and clothes store
(b) a computer store
(c) a hi-fi and audio shop
(d) a pet shop.

You may write in a style similar to the passage above or else in the form of a series of DOs and DON'Ts.

## WORD PUZZLE

Solve each of the word puzzles below. Some clues are provided to help you. The clues are not in the same order as the anagrams. For example, the first clue 'Holds a letter' refers to puzzle 1 — 'ELNEVOEP'. Can you spot a **similarity** in the spelling patterns of each word?

1. ELNEVOEP
2. NRTEE
3. EYOJN
4. ORNSDEE
5. NYEV
6. AENGNDER
7. CTIEEN
8. EOARNEVDU
9. GGEAEN
10. NREOL
11. EAGELNR
12. SNCOELE
13. NORCEE
14. IEENNG
15. ERENTI

- Holds a letter
- To lure
- Keeps the car going
- To make bigger
- Whole
- To sign a register
- To put at risk
- To try
- To give support
- To shut in
- To occupy oneself
- It means again
- To take pleasure in
- To go in
- Jealousy

# IRELAND - EAST COAST DUBLIN SOUTH

**Walks, Foothills & Mountains**

Some of the most attractive features of the South Dublin area are situated inland, in public parks and the Dublin Mountains. It is unique to have city bus services that run daily to the edge of mountains, which rise to nearly 600m. Signpost walks, in peaceful uncrowded surroundings, are a paradise for nature lovers and those looking for outdoor exercise, whether strollers or energetic hill-walkers.

A linear park along the Dodder River provides a pleasant ramble from Clonskeagh Bridge westwards to the historic Ely Arch on Lower Dodder Rd. This is about 3km long; on the way, birdlife is abundant and there is fishing in the Dodder.

The Wicklow Way, the longest and most varied marked trail in Ireland (132km) starts at Marlay House. The way exits from the south gate of Marlay Park and continues over the Dublin and Wicklow Mountains to Clonegall in County Carlow (a specialised map and a descriptive book are available). Within this county, one can follow the trail from Marlay to Glencullen and, with a short section on road, arrive at Johnny Fox's (the highest pub in Ireland), after a distance of about 13km.

## MONKSTOWN

Situated about half a mile from Dun Laoghaire on the main road to Dublin, Monkstown derives from the Cistercian Monks who arrived in the twelfth century and built Monkstown Castle, which can still be viewed today. In the centre of the village is Monkstown Church (Church of Ireland), built in a unique Moorish Gothic Style. The Church was claimed by John Betjeman as his favourite Victorian Church and is well worth a visit.

Arching away from the church is the very attractive Monkstown Crescent, with charming Edwardian villas on one side and with Gourmet restaurants, fashion boutiques and vintage wines. For the thirsty traveller, Goggins Pub beckons.

The Lambert Puppet Theatre is situated in Clifton Terrace, Monkstown. The theatre incorporates a Puppet Museum and a workshop for teachers and students.

Joyce Tower - Sandycove.

Check the newspapers or Tourist Information Office for details and times of performances.

*Cultúrlann*, 32 Belgrave Square, phone 2800295, Irish Cultural Institute, is the headquarters of Comhaltas Ceoltoiri Éireann, the Association of Irish Traditional Musicians, and has a modern theatre, with facilities for Irish dancing and refreshments. During the summer, various shows are staged every night during the week (except Sunday); throughout the year, there is a Céilí (traditional house dance) on Friday nights, and informal sessions with musicians on Saturday nights.

### SANDYCOVE & GLASTHULE

South of Dun Laoghaire 1km along the seafront is Sandycove, with its Martello tower and its pleasant little harbour. Sandycove Harbour is a popular picnic and bathing spot. The area is best known for its Martello tower, now the James Joyce Museum. The path leading up to the tower passes the famous Forty Foot men's bathing place, with its ambiguous sign FORTY FOOT GENTLEMEN ONLY. It is believed to have been named after the Fortieth Foot Regiment who were stationed in the battery adjoining the tower.

### THE JOYCE TOWER AND MUSEUM

About twenty-six Martello towers were built around Dublin in 1804 to protect the East Coast against a threatened invasion by Napoleon. The tower in Sandycove is a typical example, with massive granite walls thirteen metres high and three metres thick, a single door three meters above the ground, and a circular gun platform on the open roof. In 1904 it was lived in briefly by James Joyce (as the first guest of Oliver St. John Gogarty) and became the setting for the first chapter of his famous novel *Ulysses*.

Opened as the James Joyce Museum in 1962, the Tower is a sacred spot for all lovers of literature. It contains a fascinating collection of items associated with the writer, including his death mask, his letters and manuscript, and his waistcoat, tie and guitar. First and rare editions of most of Joyce's work are on display, in addition to the original *Ulysses*, published by Shakespeare and Company in 1922.

Glasthule is a quaint village situated less than 2km from Dun Laoghaire Harbour. On the 16th June each year it celebrates Bloomsday, an annual 1920s festival featuring a parade of old-fashioned vintage cars, with local people dressed in 1920s costumes.

There are many restaurants and bars to suit everyone's budget and taste. Glasthule is less than 1km from the James Joyce Tower and Museum, and a short walk from Sandycove/ Glasthule Dart Station.

### DUN LAOGHAIRE

Dun Laoghaire is a seapoint with a bustling centre of high fashion and commerce and is the largest sailing and water sports centre in Ireland.

Sailing in Dun Laoghaire.

The harbour was built between 1817 and 1860 and has two massive piers, the East Pier and the West Pier, 1.3km and 1.5km in length respectively. At the end of the East Pier is the famous Kingston Battery built in 1850. It is one of the only two gun saluting stations in the country. There are bands playing on the East Pier on several Sundays throughout the Summer. The new ferry terminal houses a restaurant, shops and the tourist office and is capable of accepting the world's largest high speed ferry, the Stena Line *HSS*. There are four Yacht Clubs along Dun Laoghaire seafront, the Dun Laoghaire Motor Yacht Club, the Royal Irish, the Royal St. George and the National Yacht Club. The Dun Laoghaire Festival is held in July every year.

Dun Laoghaire as a shopping town has an excellent array of shops, pubs and restaurants, including a shopping mall with over thiry outlets and the new Bloomfields shopping centre on Lower George's Street adds to the wonderful collection of shops. Dun Laoghaire Market, open every Saturday and Sunday, has bric-a-brac, arts and crafts, second-hand goods etc.

## Questions & Assignments

1. If you wanted to go sailing where would you go?
2. Where and when would you find an open-air market?
3. If you wanted to see a puppet show what would you do?
4. (a) What is the Forty Foot?
   (b) Where is it situated?
   (c) How did it get its name?
5. List five facts about Martello towers.
6. What is *Ulysses*?
7. (a) If you were interested in literature where would you go?
   (b) What would you find there?
8. What happens at *Cultúrlann*?
9. Explain how the city bus service helps hill-walkers.
10. (a) What is a *'linear park'*?
    (b) Where can river fishing be found?
11. Name the highest pub in Ireland.
12. What is one of the oldest buildings in Monkstown?
13. Where would you find a Victorian Church?
14. Name a good place to have a seaside picnic.
15. What is the Wicklow Way?
16. Bearing in mind that the first Bloomsday took place on 16th June 1904, is there any information in this extract that may be incorrect? Explain your answer.

The following **Spot the Errors** exercise is aimed at sharpening your basic writing skills. Spot the 20 errors in the Passage below and rewrite the passage correctly. (Note: Refer to the Guidelines on pages 1—15.)

## 17   The Upside-Down Turtle

One evening as i was relaxing on the balcony, I become aware of a great commotion on the beach below. I glanced over and saw a crowd of people clustering around something at the water's edge. They're was a narrow fishermans boat pulled up on the sand nearby, and all I could think of was that the fisherman had come in with a lot of fishes and that the crowd was looking at it. A haul of fish is something that has always facinated me.

I picked up my drink and stepped down from the balcony on to the beach. But it wasnt a haul of fish they were stairing at. It was a turtle, an upside-down turtle lying on its back in the sand. But what a turtle it was? It was a giant, a mammoth. I had not thought it possible for a turtle to be as enormous as this. Had it been the right way up, I think a tall man could have sat on it's back without his feet touching the ground. It was perhaps two metres long and one and a half metres across, with a high domed shell of great beauty.

The Fisherman who had caught it had tipped it onto its back to stop it from getting away. Their was also a thick rope tied around the middle of its shell, and one proud fisherman stood a short way off holding the end of the rope with both hands.

Upside down it lay, this magnificent creture, with its four thick flippers waving frantically in the air and its long rinkled neck stretching far out of its shell the flippers had large sharp claws on them.

"Stand back, ladies and gentlemen, please!" cried the Fisherman. Stand well back! Those claws are dangerous, man! they'll rip your arm clear away from your body!

From <u>The Boy Who Could Talk to Animals</u> by Roald Dahl. (Note: Turtles are an endangered species and it is illegal to catch them.)

# FIVE STAR HOSTEL!

### AN ÓIGE puts on a bright new face . . .

- An Óige was founded in 1931 and at the end of that year, it had just 215 members and two hostels but today the organisation has 37 youth hostels located countrywide.
- Its hostels vary in size from a large mansion in 70 acres of lawns and woodland (Aghadoe House, Killarney), a converted Norman castle (Foulksrath Castle, Co. Kilkenny), old coastguard stations and cottages to very modern buildings.
- An Óige hostels cater for between 200,000 and 250,000 visitors every year.
- The Cork hostel – on the Western road, opposite UCC – has also been refurbished and has 102 en-suite rooms.
- The Dublin hostel on Mountjoy Street has had nearly £200,000 spent on refurbishments. It has 350 beds but no en-suite rooms.
- Some £100,000 was spent refurbishing Dunquin hostel in Co. Kerry which is open all year round.
- Another hostel in Aghavannagh, Co. Wicklow, is also to be upgraded. It was formerly owned by the Parnell family and featured in the 1798 rebellion.
- About £750,000 was spent on Cork International Youth Hostel.

### Hikers get chance to stay in the lap of luxury

Ireland's hostels are going up-market. And the first purpose-built hostel opens in Glendalough, Co. Wicklow, today – complete with luxury en-suite bedrooms.

An Óige, the Irish Youth Hostel Association, has invested more than £2.5m in the last 18 months in upgrading hostels. Cheap and cheerful, they used to fill the student and backpacker gap in the market. But now en-suite bedrooms, conference facilities and restaurants have been introduced in a bold upmarket move.

Work on the flagship hostel at Glendalough has just been completed with an estimated £1.34m spent on renovations to upgrade it to international standards. Its capacity has increased from eight rooms and forty-six beds to twenty-six en-suite rooms with two, four and six-bedded rooms and a total of 120 beds.

### Designed

The new doughnut-shaped building was designed by architect Paul Lennon and features a conference room along with a new restaurant and a large games room and common room. Many of the original features of the former 19th century fishing lodge including the magnificent wood-panelled hallway, carved staircase and granite stonework have all been retained. And the lawns are dominated by magnificent Scots Pines and by a rare Manna Ash. But the nightly rates for visitors have been pegged back. They range from £6 for under-18s to £9.50 for adults, prices rising to £7.50 and £13 respectively during the summer.

### Guests

An Óige's old rule that guests have to arrive on foot and not with the aid of 'combustion engines' is long since gone.

Today everyone can avail of the facilities – although walkers are especially welcome and are catered for with a special drying room and laundry.

The rule of 'early to bed' etc has also disappeared with the introduction of the state-of-the-art keycard system which gives modern hostellers 24-hours access.

An Óige's marketing manager, Lucy Kelly, said: 'This is our flagship hostel, it's the best we've got and I think everybody will be thrilled when they stay here. It's comfortable and it has magnificent views.'

There are many local legends about the Lodge which nestles in the valley of Glendalough overlooking St Mary's church and the 6th century monastic ruins and the Lower Lake.

### Haunted

The building is reputed to be haunted and home to a number of ghosts. Locals also believe that there is a secret passage from the basement of the old house leading to the nearby graveyard.

Glendalough hostel was a different place in the 1950s when hill-walking guide Sean Dunne took his first group there. 'It was an old schoolhouse and the dorms were very crowded and dilapidated,' recalls Sean.

## Questions & Assignments

1. Explain the phrases *'going up-market'*, *'purpose-built'* and *'flagship hostel'*.
2. What was the Glendalough Hostel like before it was renovated?
3. Describe the improvements made in the Glendalough Hostel.
4. The Glendalough Hostel was used for two separate purposes before An Óige took it over. What were these?
5. What features of the older building were not changed?
6. What An Óige rules have changed over the years?
7. What buildings can be seen from the Glendalough Hostel?
8. What kind of legends surround the Lodge?
9. What do we learn about Sean Dunne?
10. How old is An Óige?
11. Name some of the different kinds of buildings that are now used as hostels?
12. Is An Óige an expanding organisation? Give reasons for your answer.
13. Is An Óige important for the tourism industry? Explain your answer.
14. (a) Do you think the headline — *Five star hostel!* — is a good one. Give one reason for your answer.
    (b) The feature has two smaller headlines (*An Óige puts on . . .* and *Hikers get chance . . .*). Which one did you prefer? Explain your answer.
    (c) The feature also contains three sub-headings (*Designed, Guests* and *Haunted*). In the case of each one, suggest an alternative.

## ASSIGNMENTS

**PERSONAL WRITING**

1. Write out the text of a radio advertisement for the Glendalough Hostel. Your answer should be around 75-100 words in length.
2. Write a short article for a school magazine encouraging students to join An Óige.

# TROCAIRE CAMPAIGNS FOR CODE OF CONDUCT

## ASIAN WORKERS PAID 7P AN HOUR TO MAKE TOP SELLING TOYS

**ARE you shopping for Tellytubbies and Furbies this Christmas?**

If you are then spare a thought for the workers who are being paid less than 7p an hour in appalling conditions to make the toys. Around £100m will be spent on toys in Ireland this Christmas with on average £116 spent on each child in the country.

But did you know?

- Furbies and Tellytubbies are made by Hasbro but the workers who actually make the toys in China, which supplies 80pc of the world's toy exports, have to work 16-hour days, seven days a week – for £1 a day.
- Workers making Tellytubbies at Dor Lok in China work through the night and are only allowed four hours sleep a day.

### SANTA'S FORGOTTEN HELPERS

Trocaire and the Irish Congress of Trade Unions (ICTU) today asked parents to think before they buy the toys this Christmas. And to highlight the situation Minnie Mouse and one of the Teletubbies will be meeting shoppers on Grafton Street today.

"We want them to look behind the smiling masks of toy companies and think of Santa's forgotten helpers – the toy makers of Asia who work in appalling conditions and are paid a pittance in wages."

Mae Wong, of the Asia Monitor Resource Centre, said: "We are not suggesting a boycott. We suggest that the consumer can write to the big international toy companies in order to show their discontent because working conditions for the toy workers in China are really bad."

"We're not asking people not to buy what they want. But they can use their consumer clout to ensure fair play for workers. We are not being killjoys," a spokesperson for Trocaire added.

### PROTEST

Today's protest coincides with new research, carried out by Trocaire on toy workers in China and their conditions. The research shows they are:

- Exposed to toxic chemicals with no protection while on the factory floors.
- Being beaten up and abused for yawning in work.
- Subjected to beatings from security workers.
- Suffering from breathing problems from chemicals.
- Not entitled to join trade unions.

Trocaire and the ICTU are urging Irish consumers to call on multinational companies to adopt and implement codes of conduct for the companies which supply them with the toys. Mattel, which makes Barbie, Fisher Price and Disney products, has a code but workers on the factory floor are still being mistreated, according to Trocaire.

The total sales for Mattel and Hasbro last year was $8bn (about £6bn). The toy campaign is part of a wider campaign on ethical trade and shopping. And December 8 is National Ethical Shopping Day of Action when people are urged to shop with a conscience.

## Questions & Assignments

1. (a) At what group of people is this passage aimed?
   (b) What are they being asked to do?
2. What do we learn about the toy business (a) in Ireland and (b) worldwide from the passage?
3. How does the passage show us that working conditions in China are appalling?
4. What organisations are trying to bring about changes?
5. Do you think the heading — *Santa's forgotten helpers* — is a good one? Explain your answer.

# SILENT SPRING

There was once a town in the heart of America where all life seemed to live in harmony with its surroundings. The town lay in the midst of a checkerboard of prosperous farms, with fields of grain and hillsides of orchards where in spring white clouds of bloom drifted above the green fields. In autumn, oak and maple and birch set up a blaze of colour that flamed and flickered across a backdrop of pines. Then foxes barked in the hills and deer silently crossed the fields, half hidden in the mists of the autumn mornings.

## SUBHEAD

Along the roads, laurel, viburnum and alder, great ferns and wild flowers delighted the traveller's eye through much of the year . . . Even in winter the roadsides were places of beauty, where countless birds came to feed on the berries and on the seed heads of the dried weeds rising above the snow. The countryside was famous for the abundance and variety of birdlife, and when the flood of migrants was pouring through in spring and autumn, people travelled from great distances to observe them. Others came to fish the streams, which flowed clear and cold out of the hills and contained shady pools where trout lay.

## SUBHEAD

Then a strange blight crept over the land and everything began to change. Some evil spell had settled on the community: mysterious maladies swept the flocks of chickens; the cattle and sheep sickened and died. Everywhere was a shadow of death. The farmers spoke of much illness among their families. In the town the doctors had become more and more puzzled by new kinds of sicknesses appearing among their patients. There had been several sudden and unexplained deaths, not only among the adults but even among children, who would be stricken suddenly while at play and die within a few hours.

## SUBHEAD

There was a strange stillness. The birds — where had they gone? Many people spoke of them, puzzled and disturbed. The feeding stations in the backyards were deserted. The few birds seen anywhere were moribund; they trembled violently and could not fly. It was spring without voice. On the mornings that had once throbbed with the dawn chorus of robins, catbirds, doves, jays, wrens, and scores of other bird voices there was now no sound. Only silence lay over the fields and woods and marsh.

### SUBHEAD

On the farms the hens brooded, but no chicks hatched. The farmers complained that they were unable to raise any pigs — the litters were small and the young survived only a few days. The apple trees were coming into bloom but no bees droned among the blossoms, so there was no pollination and there would be no fruit.

### SUBHEAD

The roadsides, once so attractive, were now lined with browned and withered vegetation as though swept by fire. These too, were silent deserted by all living things. Even the streams were now lifeless. Anglers no longer visited them, for all the fish had died.

### SUBHEAD

In the gutters under the caves and between the shingles of the roofs a granular powder still showed a few patches; some weeks before, it had fallen like snow upon the roofs and the lawns, the fields and streams. No witchcraft, no enemy action had silenced the rebirth of new life in this stricken world. The people had done it themselves.

— *Rachel Carson*

## Questions & Assignments

1. What details in the first two paragraphs give the impression
   (a) that the countryside around the town was very beautiful?
   (b) that it was a healthy environment for wildlife?
2. What seasons are mentioned in the first two paragraphs?
3. Why do you think that the author chose the words *'flamed'* and *'flickered'* in paragraph 1?
4. At what times of year did the migrating birds pass through the countryside?
5. What words in paragraph 3 suggest that nobody understood why the animals and people were dying?
6. How does the writer show that the change to the environment was happening on a very big scale?
7. Do we learn the reason for the frightening change? Explain your answer.
8. Do you agree with the final sentence — *'The people had done it themselves.'* Give a reason for your answer.
9. What is the meaning of each of the following?
   (a) *'The countryside was famous for the abundance and variety of birdlife'* (Paragraph 2)
   (b) *'mysterious maladies swept the flocks of chickens'* (Paragraph 3)
   (c) *'the dawn chorus'*
10. Suggest another title for the passage and a brief one-word or two-word subhead for each paragraph.
11. Would you agree that the events that are to come later in the story will be even more terrifying? Give a reason for your answer.

# SCHOOLDAYS

At the age of eight, in 1924, I was sent away to boarding-school in a town called Weston-super-Mare, on the south-west coast of England. Those were days of horror, of fierce discipline, of no talking in the dormitories, no running in the corridors, no untidiness of any sort, no this or that or the other, just rules and still more rules that had to be obeyed. And the fear of the dreaded cane hung over us like the fear of death all the time.

"The headmaster wants to see you in his study." Words of doom. They sent shivers over the skin of your stomach. But off you went, aged perhaps nine years old, down the long bleak corridors and through an archway that took you into the headmaster's private area where only horrible things happened and the smell of pipe tobacco hung in the air like incense. You stood outside the awful black door . . . You took deep breaths . . . You lifted a hand and knocked softly, once.

"Come in! Ah yes, it's Dahl. Well, Dahl, it's been reported to me that you were talking during study last night."

"Please sir, I broke my pen and I was only asking Jenkins if he had another one to lend me."

"I will not tolerate talking in study. You know that very well . . . Boys who break rules have to be punished."

"Sir . . . I . . . I had a broken pen. . . I . . ."

"That is no excuse. I am going to teach you that it does not pay to talk during prep."

He took a cane . . . that was about three feet long with a little curved handle at one end. It was thin and white and very whippy. "Bend over and touch your toes. Over there by the window."

"But sir . . ."

"Don't argue with me, boy. Do as you're told."

I bent over. Then I waited. He always kept you waiting for about ten seconds, and that was when your knees began to shake.

"Bend lower, boy! Touch your toes!"

I stared at the toecaps of my black shoes and I told myself that any moment now this man was going to bash the cane into me so hard that the whole of my bottom would change colour . . .

Swish! . . . Crack!

Then came the pain. It was unbelievable, unbearable, excruciating. It was as though someone had laid a white hot poker across your backside and pressed hard.

The second stroke would be coming soon and it was as much as you could do to stop putting your hands in the way to ward it off. It was the instinctive reaction. But if you did that, it would break your fingers.

Swish! . . . Crack!

The second one landed right alongside the first and the white-hot poker was pressing deeper and deeper into the skin. Swish! . . . Crack!

The third stroke was where the pain always reached its peak. It could go no further. There was no way it could get any worse. Any more strokes after that simply prolonged the agony. You tried not to cry out. Sometimes you couldn't help it. But whether you were able to remain silent or not, it was impossible to stop the tears. They poured down your cheeks in streams and dripped on to the carpet.

The important thing was never to flinch upwards or straighten up when you were hit. If you did that, you got an extra one.

Slowly, deliberately, taking plenty of time, the headmaster delivered three more strokes, making six in all.

"You may go." The voice came from a cavern miles away, and you straightened up slowly, agonisingly, and grabbed hold of your burning buttocks with both hands and held them as tight as you could and hopped out of the room on the very tips of your toes.

That cruel cane ruled our lives . . . We were caned for talking in the dormitory after lights out, for talking in class, for bad work, for carving our initials on the desk, for climbing over walls, for slovenly appearance, for flicking paper-clips, for forgetting to change into house-shoes in the evenings, for not hanging up our games clothes, and above all for giving the slightest offence to any master. (They weren't called teachers in those days.)

In other words we were caned for doing everything that it was normal for small boys to do.

– *Roald Dahl*

## Questions & Assignments

1. What is your impression of the school from the first paragraph?
2. What things about the journey to the headmaster's office stand out in the author's mind?
3. Why was the author caned?
4. Do you think that the headmaster was a fair man? Give a reason for your answer.
5. How does the writer show us that the beating was very painful?
6. In your view was the author (a) bitter or (b) amused when he wrote this piece? Give a reason for your answer.

PERSONAL WRITING

## ASSIGNMENT

Write about the day you were called to the principal's office.

The following **Spot the Errors** exercise is aimed at sharpening your basic writing skills. Spot the 20 errors in the Passage below and rewrite the passage correctly. (Note: Refer to the Guidelines on pages 1—15.)

## 18  Bad News

The miners wife stood at the door of the cottage and said goodbye to her Husband and three suns. They were going to work at the mine. It was not yet daylight and she sighed as she saw them disappear in the dark.

When daylight came she got busy about the house there was not much to do becuase it was so small. But there were always close to mend, water to be carried from the stream and would to be collected for the fire.

When she had finished that and prepared the evening meal for the men when they came back, she told her two daughters to come with her to meet there father and brothers.

"They will be coming up from the mine soon," she said. "it's a nice day. Well walk to the crossroads to meet them."

They set of slowly, because they have plenty of time and it was warm, being summer. The girls skipped ahead. Before they got to the crossroads they stopped as a man on horseback came riding towards them. He got down from his horse his face was serious and he did not speak at once.

"Mrs jones," he said at last. "I think you should get back home."

The miner's wife looked hard at him.

"They will be bringing your husband and two sons home . . ." He new she understood. It was not the first time he had had to carry messages like this and he knew it would not be the last.

"Two sons?"

"Charles and John."

"And Jeremy?"

The man shook his head. He's still below," he said. "we cannot bring his body back. He's buried there.

# Newspapers in Ireland

In Ireland every day, over half a million newspapers are bought. Some of these are Irish publications and some are British. Newspaper publishing is just as much an industry as making cars or television sets and, like all businesses, newspapers need to earn profits in order to survive.

The free flow of information of all kinds is clearly important in all societies. But even more importantly, it is vital that individual nations profit from healthy, vibrant indigenous media. **Indigenous newspapers**, in particular, serve a critical purpose.

In comparison imported newspapers — including those with the word 'Irish' tagged to their masthead — provide few Irish jobs. They contribute little to our culture and do not provide in-depth coverage of Irish events. Nevertheless, largely because of their ability to sell at lower prices, the sales of British newspapers continue to rise while Irish newspaper sales continue to decline.

> **INDIGENOUS NEWSPAPERS** are newspapers which are produced in Ireland and which are aimed at Irish readers. Such newspapers provide a uniquely Irish viewpoint and are a major contributor to the cultural, social, economic and political life of the nation. They deliver Irish and world news from an Irish point of view. They are an important part of our national culture. No one can accurately describe and comment on a nation's affairs better than those who live there.
> In addition, indigenous newspapers give employment to almost 4,000 people, with many thousands more engaged in related activities.

At the moment the indigenous Irish newspaper industry currently faces a number of very serious challenges which threaten its very future. The growing market share of British titles in Ireland has placed indigenous newspapers under severe commercial pressure. At the simplest level, falling circulation obviously means falling sales revenue. As a result, advertisers — who want to reach the largest possible audience at the lowest possible cost — may be tempted to look elsewhere.

A newspaper with falling circulation becomes more dependent on income from advertising. However, this will quickly begin to fall off as advertisers stop placing advertisements in those papers with dropping circulation figures.

Also, the trend towards British newspapers poses a threat to our our national identity. In many ways, this is a more serious development. In general, standards of journalism in Irish newspapers are very high. Over the years Irish newspapers have, by thorough and fair reporting and balanced comment, made an invaluable contribution to Irish life.

**WHY THE LOWER PRICES?** Firstly, British newspaper publishers have an advantage in that their home market is enormous. In the newspaper publishing business the size of the market is vital. The real cost of producing a newspaper goes into the first copy. Once the first copy has rolled off the presses, there are essentially no more costs except paper, ink and machine time. Clearly, the larger the print run, the more economical the operation. While a print run of 100,000 would be considered large in Ireland, it is tiny by comparison with British print runs. There are around five million copies of The News of the World printed every week.

These large print runs make it possible for the publisher to include glossy magazines and supplements at very little extra costs. With a print run of around 100,000 such extras would add a good deal to the cover price.

Also British newspaper publishers are often part of vast multi-national corporations with immense financial resources. For example, News International, which publishes The Sunday Times and The Irish Sun, is part of News Corporation, Rupert Murdoch's dominant global empire with branches in each media sector.

This enormous wealth brings obvious advantages, one of which is the ability to sustain losses over a prolonged period. Irish newspapers hold the view that British publishers use this advantage to unfairly price their newspapers below cost in the Irish market.

## Questions & Assignments

1. Outline clearly in your own words (a) why it is important that our indigenous newspapers are supported and (b) why imported British newspapers cost less than their Irish equivalents.
2. Compare a copy of a British newspaper with a same-day Irish equivalent and write a report on their respective coverage of news and features relevant to the lives and interests of Irish readers.

## Target Audiences — Tabloids and Broadsheets

What makes people choose *The Irish Times* rather than *The Star*, *The Irish Sun* rather than *The Examiner*? Different people like different types of newspapers. Some people like newspapers that mainly report on and analyse subjects such as politics, business and important home and foreign news.

Other people like newspapers that print a lot of sensational stories and gossip about the private lives of well-known people as well as 'human interest' stories and competitions. These are generally known as popular papers or the tabloid press (because of their size). They often exaggerate stories, sensationalise trivial events and even invent scandals in order to boost sales.

Of course the broadsheets too have been known to devote pages to sensationalism and tabloids often cover serious issues that matter to the lives of their readers.

It would be unfair to regard all news reports in tabloid papers as trivial and sensational. Much of their coverage of events is honest and balanced and presented in a snappy, colourful and chatty style that is easier, for many people, to digest.

---

### Broadsheets and Tabloids — Different Layouts

Layout is a term used to describe how items are arranged on a page.

#### Tabloid Layout
- A variety of typefaces
- Very large headlines — often taking up more space than the story.
- Photographs with many stories.

#### Broadsheet Layout
- Little variety in typefaces.
- Smaller headlines and longer stories on each page.
- Few stories illustrated with photographs.

---

## Style of News Reports

### Broadsheet Style

In general, the broadsheet 'quality' newspapers adhere to a **formal** style in their news reports. The formal style is reflected in word choices such as 'television' instead of 'telly'; 'mother' instead of 'mum'; 'young child' instead of 'toddler'; 'garda' or 'police' instead of 'cops'.

Can you think of other examples?

The broadsheets also aim for a **neutral** approach to news. They set out to give the facts without comment or prejudice, letting the readers form their own opinions. This neutral approach is reflected in word choices such as 'thieves' rather than 'thugs'.

### Tabloid Style

**Descriptive language** rather than neutral language is used in order to add interest and drama to stories, e.g. 'munched' instead of 'ate'; 'smashed' instead of 'broke'; 'wrecked' instead of 'damaged'; 'lashed' instead of 'criticised'.

**Emotive language:** Words and phrases are used which stir the emotions of readers — and give a story a touch of drama, e.g. 'a savage mob'; 'drunken yobs'; 'helpless old-age pensioners'; 'gardai finally rounded up the troublemakers . . . '

**Personal Details** are given, such as age, earnings, marital status, wealth etc, which have no direct relevance to the story but which add to it in terms of human interest.

**Idioms and Slang** (such as '*rip-off*', '*mates*', '*sacked*', '*conned*') give headlines and reports an informal and chatty tone. An idiom is a phrase where the meaning is not immediately clear from the actual words, e.g. 'to bury the hatchet' means to make friends after a quarrel.

Make a list of idioms that you know and explain each one — you should get at least thirty.

## Questions & Assignments

### HEADLINES

Headlines in newspaper pages make it easy for readers to find stories that interest them. A headline tells us what the story following it is about.

Certain words are used again and again in headlines. These words are (a) short and save page space (b) are particularly dramatic and descriptive.

A selection of these words is listed in the exercise below. Use each word in the list to rewrite the headline beside it.

**Test A**

1. **Chief** — Rugby Team Manager is questioned by Gardai   *Cops Quiz Rugby Chief*
2. **Deal** — A new wage agreement with firemen is signed
3. **Bug** — Doctors warn of a flu virus
4. **Rap** — A football manager criticises the behaviour of fans
5. **Haul** — A quantity of drugs is seized by Gardai
6. **Quit** — A radio presenter resigns
7. **Crook** — Thieves rob a jewellery store
8. **Shock** — Surprising and frightening revelations about safety standards on trains
9. **Flee** — A couple leave their home in fear of local gangs
10. **Plea** — A strong request for more assistance for the homeless by a bishop

**Test B**

1. **Boom** — A large increase in tourist traffic
2. **Killing** — An incident which may be manslaughter or murder
3. **Scare** — Alarm over the safety of drinking water
4. **Alert** — A severe weather warning about storms
5. **Held** — A murder suspect is detained by Gardai
6. **Quiz** — A murder suspect is questioned by the Gardai
7. **Drama** — A schoolboy slips into the polar bear enclosure at the Zoo
8. **Axes** — Plans to build a library are abandoned
9. **Looms** — A strike of pilots seems likely to take place
10. **Clash** — A politican disagrees strongly with a farmers' leader

## Test C

1. **Blast** — An explosion which injures two people
2. **Boost** — A plan by Bord Fáilte to increase tourism figures in Mayo
3. **Horror** — A serious motorway accident on the M7
4. **Pledge** — The Minister for Education gives a commitment to build a new school
5. **Mob** — A large group of drunken supporters vandalise a train after a match
6. **Smash** — A cigarette smuggling ring is broken up by Gardai
7. **Curb** — The use of pesticides is restricted
8. **Snubbed** — Social workers were offended when a politican ignored their request for a meeting
9. **Hits** — Commuters are affected by bus strike
10. **Ordeal** — Teenagers are trapped in a lift for three hours

## Test D

1. **Soar** — House prices rise rapidly in Galway
2. **Rise** — An increase in the number of drug related crimes
3. **Riddle** — A puzzling incident of a dog who made his way on to a plane
4. **Link** — A possible connection between a jail escape and a kidnapping
5. **Plunge** — A sharp decrease in the number of American tourists
6. **Drive** — A campaign to cut down on domestic rubbish
7. **Probe** — An investigation into missing documents from the Department of Finance
8. **Chaos** — A taxi-drivers' protest leads to traffic jams, disorder and confusion
9. **Toll** — The number of people killed in an earthquake rises to 50
10. **Dud** — Forged notes discovered in Carlow

## Test E

1. **Weds** — A goalkeeper marries a model
2. **Row** — A violent disagreement between farm leaders
3. **Urge** — A trade union official strongly recommends strikers to stop picketing
4. **Chief** — Managing Director of a bank is injured in sailing accident
5. **Slam** — The actions of taxi-drivers are strongly condemned by shopowners
6. **Seek** — Baggage handlers look for increased overtime payments
7. **Ban** — The law prohibiting smoking on buses is criticised
8. **Bid** — The Air Corps attempt to rescue a yachtsman
9. **Cuts** — Working hours for nurses are decreased
10. **Backs** — Anthony White supports Tony Brown for the position of party leader

*Spectrum 2*

### Hit the Headlines — 1

1. The original headlines of each of the stories opposite have been removed. (All the stories were taken from tabloid newspapers.) Compose your own headline for each story.

   For example: **F** could be **Fighter Frog Falls Ill**

2. All the original headlines are printed in the box below — but the words have been jumbled. Can you match each headline to its original story?

   For example: ①  it may frog Medical croak
   This should read: ① **Medical frog may croak it** (This is story **F**)

   > ①  it may frog Medical croak
   > ②  quiz groan phone David's
   > ③  is Sarge charged
   > ④  terror in jet Drunk
   > ⑤  lesson a bin It's
   > ⑥  yobs Burning train car hit
   > ⑦  do Brainiest battle
   > ⑧  plunge in hurt Two
   > ⑨  Post slams TD An

3. When you have completed Question 2 above pick out one feature of each headline or story which is typical of the style used in tabloid newspapers.

   For example:  ① **Medical frog may croak it**
   The phrase 'croak it' is slang for die. It is used here with a double meaning as frogs also croak when they call out.

### A

**A MAN** must pick up rubbish outside his own door-step as punishment for littering the capital's main street, a judge ordered yesterday.

James Murphy (25) was sentenced to pick up all the litter on Tree's Avenue in Dublin for kicking a glass bottle on the O'Connell Street pavement, causing it to shatter at 2.30am on September 14 last.

The work is to be carried out next Saturday (January 23) and Gardai are to inspect it and report back to court on January 26.

It if is done, a charge of breach of the peace against him will be dismissed, Judge William Early said at Dublin District Court.

The bottle hit a post box outside the Gresham Hotel and smashed but Murphy claimed it had rolled that way.

Judge Early said: "You could just as easily have picked up the bottle."

### B

**A LEADING TD** lashed out at An Post yesterday for failing to mark this year's centenary of the Pioneers Association.

Fine Gael's Theresa Ahearn said the failure to commemorate the anniversary was "a rebuke to an organisation which has had a unique impact on Ireland."

An Post said their stamp programme was based on the recommendations of an independent committee.

### E

**FORTY** passengers had a miracle escape when yobs pushed a burning car into the path of a speeding commuter train.

Travellers screamed as the train hit the stolen Sierra and caught fire at Cwmbach, South Wales.

The driver and conductor led all 40 to safety as flames engulfed a carriage, melting seats inside.

Cops hunting the thugs said: "It's very serious, people could have died."

### C

**TWO INJURED ESB workers** were recovering in hospital last night after falling from a pole while restoring power supplies in gale-hit north Mayo.

### F

**A FROG** hailed as a potential new weapon against cancer is under threat from a fatal skin disease sweeping Australia.

The fungal disease burrows into a frog's skin cells, causing them to thicken.

As a result the animal suffocates and dies. All species are affected.

### D

**AN IRISH** army sergeant is to face a court martial over a duty-free racket. He is accused of re-selling £1·2m worth of tobacco and alcohol bought in Cyprus.

### G

**A CRAZED** drunk aboard a jet had to be subdued and handcuffed after he tried to open a rear exit door at 30,000ft.

Three passengers and a crewman were injured in the struggle on a Continental Airlines flight from Newark, USA, to Gatwick.

Police said: "It's one of the worst air rage incidents we have dealt with." A 31-year-old Scotsman is in custody.

### H

**UNLUCKY** David Hogg missed out on £61,000 on TV's Who Wants To Be A Millionaire – by phoning the wrong pal for help.

David rang Dave Mushet for advice on this £125,000 poser: "Which US firm made Coronet and Charger cars?"

Dave didn't know – so David took £64,000 already in the kitty.

He later found out brother Martin, who was on another line but didn't get the crucial call, knew the answer was Dodge.

David, 34, of Paisley, said: "I was gutted."

### I

IRELAND'S brightest young students will this week unveil their inventions and solutions for the new millennium.

The annual Young Scientists Exhibition kicks off in Dublin's RDS tomorrow.

And hundreds of inventive pupils will do battle to win the Young Scientist of the Year title.

The competition, sponsored for the first time by Esat Telecom, will be officially opened by Taoiseach Bertie Ahern on Friday.

Judges will start evaluating the 480 projects from tomorrow.

One Dublin student has come up with a blueprint for a "Self-Repairing Tyre" while an Ennis entry attempts to answer the question: "Why can't everyone sing?"

*Spectrum 2*

## Questions & Assignments

**Hit the Headlines — 2**

1. The original headlines of each of the stories opposite have been removed. (All the stories were taken from broadsheet newspapers.) Compose your own headline for each story.

2. All the original headlines are printed in the box below — but the words have been jumbled. Can you match each headline to its original story?

   ① by fire damaged College
   ② air suspended Galway route
   ③ supply hits Lightning power
   ④ robbed and Men stripped
   ⑤ post Fermanagh robbed office
   ⑥ in jobs are 28 lost Limerick
   ⑦ retire to Vice-Chancellor

3. When you have completed Question 2 above pick out one feature of each headline or story which is typical of the style used in broadsheet newspapers.

**A**

IT was confirmed yesterday that 28 jobs are to go at the US-owned company Stryker Homedica Osteonics Inc at Raheen Industrial Estate, Limerick. The company employs 400 and manufactures orthopaedic implants. According to a spokesman the redundancies are part of a rationalisation.

**B**

GALWAY Regional Airport has expressed disappointment at the suspension of the Galway-London route after only eight weeks in service. The operator, Air Kilroe, said it was suspending the service between Galway and Luton from Monday, pending a review of flight times, aircraft and fare structures. The company stressed that it was not cancelling the service.

**C**

ARMED raiders held up staff at a Co. Fermanagh post office yesterday. Two armed and masked men made off with an undisclosed sum of cash after threatening staff at the office in the village of Garrison.

**D**

A STRIKE of lightning in Galway city left 15,000 ESB customers without power yesterday. Supplies were restored within an hour. The strike hit the ESB transformer at Salthill shortly after 10am and caused significant damage, according to a board spokeswoman. The areas affected were in the west of the city and from Salthill to Clifden.

**F**

More than £100,000 of damage was caused by a fire at Patrician College in Finglas, Dublin, early yesterday morning. Three rooms in a single-storey section were destroyed.

The Garda Press Office said it would not know if the fire was suspicious until the forensic evidence from the site had been examined.

**E**

THE VICE-CHANCELLOR of the University of Ulster, Lord Smith of Clifton, is to retire in September. Lord Smith (61) is best known for his successful campaign to build the Springvale educational campus on Belfast's 'peace-line'.

Before he came to the University of Ulster in 1991, he was professor of political studies and senior vice-principal at Queen Mary College, University of London. He was also chairman of the Joseph Rowntree Reform Trust, vice-president of the UK Political Studies Association, and former chairman of the Statesman and Nation publishing company.

**G**

TWO young men were accosted in Dublin last night, stripped and had clothing and money stolen. The incident happened in Blanchardstown at 11.20pm when the two were stopped by five adults travelling in a jeep.

In a follow-up operation in Cappagh, two women and three men were arrested and taken to Blanchardstown Garda Station. A jeep was seized and money, clothing and a weapon were recovered.

# DRIVE-IN DRINKER REVS UP

## Booze ban trucker hits a pub

A TRUCK driver pulled a fast one after being refused more drink — by backing his lorry into the pub.

He downed an orange juice and a bag of peanuts when bar staff told him he had had enough booze.

He then left, telling doormen at the Pickled Pig in Bray, Co. Wicklow: "Now I'm going to take my truck for a drink".

"Ten minutes later, a 40ft Scania was being reversed through the front door," pub owner Charlie Pollard said yesterday.

"He hit some railings along the way and only for they slowed him down, he would have driven right into the pub."

Gardai arrested a man for drink driving after the incident around 12.30am last Friday.

"We have a strict rule about people getting sozzled," Mr. Pollard said.

"My manageress told him he'd had enough, so he asked for a Britvic orange and a packet of peanuts and she just thought he wanted to sober up.

"I've had to take off the front door altogether.

"There's a few thousand pounds of damage, but no-one was hurt."

A spokesman for the Irish Road Haulage Association branded the driver's actions "reprehensible".

"To get into any vehicle with excess alcohol is bad but especially a truck," he said.

"Maybe this guy thought it was funny but someone could have been very badly hurt or killed.

"Anyone who would do something like that has a problem and should get themselves seen to."

The truck incident came after six weeks of hell when Mr. Pollard first took over the pub two years ago.

"There had been an unruly element in it before and we decided to clean it up," he said.

"Not everyone was happy – people used to drive by flinging jars of paint at the pub and 36 windows were broken over a four-week period."

**BRAKES ON BOOZE:** Garda at the truck outside the Pickled Pig in Bray, Co. Wicklow

### PINTS GO TO BLAZES!

PUB patrons abandoned their drinks and turned fire-fighters after flames suddenly engulfed the entrance to their 'local'.

It is believed the blaze was started by a disgruntled customer who poured petrol in the doorway.

Regulars at Cleary's pub in Ballycroy, Co. Mayo, used fire extinguishers to put out the blaze.

Gardai questioned a man over the incident and a file was being prepared for the DPP.

# TED WINS THE LOTTO

*Ted and wife Eileen celebrate their win yesterday*

**He nets £1m pot, £11,000 on cards and £34,000 on a TV gameshow**

*By Myles McEntee*

DELIGHTED Ted O'Reilly collected a £1million cheque yesterday – his third big Lotto win.

The dad-of-ten continued an amazing run of luck when he picked up a half share of the weekend jackpot.

He'd already scooped more than £11,000 on scratchcards and another £34,000 from a TV lotto gameshow.

And vet Ted, 60, of Bishopsvale, Co. Louth, revealed how he almost pocketed the jackpot with five winning numbers a year ago.

Amazed bookies said the jovial punter's odds of landing such a winning streak were a whopping 10 million to one.

# HOSPITAL BEDS NOT AVAILABLE

**SPECIAL REPORT By OLIVIA DOYLE**

**PATIENTS on trolleys in a packed hospital say that dedicated staff are being let down by the Health Minister.**

Sick people were being placed two to a cubicle in the crammed casualty ward of Dublin's Beaumont Hospital yesterday.

And they had few kind words for Brian Cowen, who is "away" as the health service copes with its annual winter crisis.

*Heart patient James Ryan (70) faced a night on a trolley after being there for six hours* already when The Star spoke to him at tea-time.

### Disgrace

"I think the lack of beds is a damned disgrace," said the Dublin man.

"Mr. Cowen should be brought in here by the scruff of the neck to see what ordinary people have to go through.

"Being on a trolley is inconvenient and uncomfortable but we're getting the best of care – it's the staff I'm concerned for, they're worn out."

Sharing his cubicle was Mike O'Neill (74), already on a trolley for more than 24 hours with a lung infection.

"They get you onto a trolley and seen to immediately – the problem is getting up in the wards to a bed.

"My experience is that the staff do a wonderful job but it's stressful."

The mother of a 16-year-old, who was brought in with suspected pneumonia and nearing 24 hours on a trolley, was angry that her son was still in casualty.

"He was in the red-alert area where they bring in the crash victims overnight and he didn't sleep a wink," she said.

### Straight

"I bet if Mr. Cowen gets ill, he doesn't have this, he just goes straight into a private bed."

Malachy Potts (70) was looking forward to going home after getting the all-clear for his chest pains.

"The staff are marvellous but it's all these colds and flus – we need a belt of snow to clear the air."

Casualty consultant Mr. Leo Vella said they had 28 people in A & E yesterday morning, just short of the record of 30.

"The rule is that the less sick you are, the longer you wait – we have had people on trolleys for two-and-a-half days," he said.

"But we ARE helping people, a 93-year-old with pneumonia is not left in a bed at home to die, they're brought in and given the highest quality treatment.

"I would trade being on a trolley and treated for being dead any day."

# IT'S BRIT BASHING
## Boyz' boss in awards fury

**By Kathryn Rogers**

LOUIS: *Award anger*

**BOYZONE boss Louis Walsh has lashed out at the Brit Awards – claiming his band weren't nominated because they were "too big".**

"We sell too many records to be included in the Brit Awards," said the hunks' manager.

"If these awards were decided by the general public, then we would win awards across the board. But it's just a few hundred failed musicians-turned-writers who make these nominations," he fumed.

### Failed

Former Take That star Robbie Williams scooped a record six nominations for the awards which take place at London's Dockland Arena on February 16.

*Other acts nominated include Catatonia, Gomez, Massive Attack and George Michael.*

However, top girlband The Spice Girls also failed to be nominated for a gong despite their record-breaking third Christmas No. 1 single.

"We're not considered hip enough or trendy enough. Boyzone never set out to be hip – they are quite happy to sing songs that people like to hear," said Walsh.

### Test

"The best compliment we could have been paid was not to be nominated," he added.

"The Spice Girls – one of the biggest pop acts in the world – weren't nominated either. Make sense of that," he said.

He claimed the real test is when the awards are decided by the fans.

*"More than 250,000 people voted for Boyzone on ITV just weeks ago. The band won The Record of the Year award for* **No Matter What**,*" said Walsh.*

## Questions & Assignments

### Tabloid Style

1. In the case of each of the stories on the previous two pages, pick out at least four features of style or layout that are typical of tabloid newspapers.
2. Rewrite each story (shorter if you want) in a more formal style.
3. In your view, should any of these stories be printed on the front page of a newspaper? Give reasons for your answer.

## Sentence Building

The exercise below contains ten sentences. The sentences have been broken up into a number of parts and the parts have been mixed up. Rearrange the sentences correctly and write them out again, adding the necessary punctuation.

### BATS

1. a large group / bats are classed as mammals, / In the animal kingdom / men, mice, lions, and dogs / that includes

2. bats nurse their young / Like all mammals, / and bear living young / they have hair / on milk, / and like most mammals,

3. from all other mammals / bats are different / But / in one way / Bats can fly

4. is not like / a bird's wing / a bat's wing / However

5. a double layer of skin / The bat's wing is / its arm and fingers, / a little like a kite / the thin bones of / stretched over

6. except a short thumb, / which is left free / The wing / covers all fingers

7. on the end / at the top of the wing / A sharp claw / of the thumb / forms a hook

8. and other rough surfaces / rocky walls / the bat uses its hooks / are folded / to climb tree trunks, / When its wings

9. upside down / perching upright / because it is easier / Bats hang / for them than

10. to the body / Their small legs / in a way / are attached / that makes perching awkward

## How Newspapers Get Their News

Every day a vast number of news stories reaches the offices of the Irish daily papers. This news comes from a variety of sources: reporters, 'stringers', press releases, news agencies, press conferences and public relations agencies.

### How Newspapers Get News

**Reporters**
These are people employed by the papers to cover local and national events. The editor assigns reporters to stories as they 'break' and some reporters have regular spots such as the courts.

**'Stringers'**
These are reporters working on provincial papers who send stories from their regions that they think will have a national interest.

**News Agencies**
Agencies such as Reuters and The Associated Press are large news gathering organisations, employing reporters worldwide. They send bulletins of events happening throughout the world. The newspaper pays the agency a fee for any stories used.

**Press Releases**
Instead of holding a press conference an organisation may simply send details of an announcement directly to the press.

**Press Conferences**
Some news is 'manufactured'. Businesses, political parties and other organisations invite reporters along when important announcements are to be made. A question and answer session usually follows the announcement.

**Public Relations Agencies**
These are organisations that specialise in helping companies and (usually wealthy) individuals deal with the press. Generally staffed by ex-journalists, public relations (PR) agencies understand how the media works. A PR company will help its clients to project a positive image for the press and media in general.

## WHAT IS NEWS?

Of the hundreds of news stories that arrive at a newspaper every day very few make it into print. The editor and staff of the paper must decide which stories will be used and which ones will be discarded. In a nutshell, stories that are **newsworthy** are used and stories that are not newsworthy are discarded.

What makes a story newsworthy depends on the interests of the **target** readership. Of course events such as major crimes or trials, elections, major accidents and other dramatic events will be of interest to everyone. But a story about changes in bank interest rates may not interest the same readership as a story about a fashion model dating a pop star.

The newsworthiness of a story can be measured under the following four headings.
— What? Where? When? Who?

### WHAT HAPPENED?
The nature of the event itself must be of interest or importance to a particular group of readers. Editors, knowing the interests of their particular type of readers, will know if what has happened will be of interest to them or not. A story could be regarded as newsworthy by a tabloid editor but not by a broadsheet editor. Likewise a story could be newsworthy for a local paper but not for a national paper.

### WHERE DID IT HAPPEN?
The place where the event occurred decides whether or not a story is newsworthy. In general the closer the event is to the target readership the more newsworthy the event. 'Flood deaths in China rise to twenty' would not make banner headlines on a Irish daily but substitute *Kerry* for *China* and it would be the lead story.

### WHEN DID IT HAPPEN?
The event must have happened in the recent past — i.e. it must be 'new' news. Old news, as they say, is history. However, an event that happened a long time ago but is only now coming to light may be newsworthy.

### WHO WAS INVOLVED?
The people involved also determine if a story is newsworthy. The more famous — or infamous — they are the more newsworthy the story. Someone who has never been in the public eye will barely merit a few lines if they are convicted of drunken driving. A model or a pop star or a politician convicted of the same offence makes the story newsworthy.

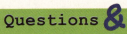

Suggest five news story topics which would be newsworthy to each of the following newspapers.
(a) Your local paper — *The Meath Chronicle, The Sligo Champion* etc.
(b) *The Irish Sun*
(c) *The Irish Times*

Your answer should consist of fifteen topics. Here are three examples:
    (a) Sligo antique shop robbed — nothing valuable taken.
    (b) A Liverpool bus-driver who claims that he taught his parrot to read.
    (c) A reduction in unemployment figures.

## Writing News Stories

Very few people read newspapers from cover to cover. Readers, generally, will have only a slight interest in many news events and will want to find out the bare facts. The first few sentences should supply these facts. Therefore when a reporter is writing a story he or she must arrange the details in order of importance. The opening sentences of a news report must contain the main points of the story — the who? what? when? where? why? and how? The remainder of the story will provide extra details. The less important details of a story come towards the end.

Another reason for this method of writing news stories is that sub-editors, laying out the paper, may not be able to fit the full story into an available space. They need to be able to cut a few paragraphs towards the end without having to check whether they are cutting out the more important details.

## Assignments

### Assignment 1
Write a news story set in your local area about each of the following:
(a) a flood, (b) a fire, (c) a traffic accident, (d) a strike and (e) a robbery. Each answer should be at least ten sentences in length.

### Assignment 2
Write a news report based on each of the following list of 'facts'. You may have to rearrange the order in which you present the facts.
(a) Cat found on ship; cargo vessel *New York Star* arrived in Cork on Wednesday; cat discovered by captain just before the ship docked; ship crossed Atlantic with cat on board; stowaway cat at present in Cats and Dogs Home; kind home wanted.
(b) Peter Jacobs cancels plan to cross pacific by balloon; Jacobs (39) from California said that strong winds forced him to cancel; flight being sponsored by California Soft Drinks Company; co-pilot Sean Breen (32), son of Paddy Breen, emigrated to California from Killarney in 1952; hopes to attempt cross early next week if Met services give the go-ahead.
(c) Molly Smith angry; owns German Shepherd dog; Molly does not want dog muzzled; 'King' name of dog; the law says the dog must be muzzled; Molly writing to Minister for exemption; King is a trained Search and Rescue Dog; regularly helps to find missing persons in the Wicklow Mountains; government officials promise to review the situation; King may get exemption; guide-dogs don't have to wear muzzles; Molly Smith lives in Wicklow town.

## OPINION

As well as reporting the news, newspapers also offer opinions on the events that make the news. Opinions on a wide variety of subjects are found in editorials, features, reviews and in columns by regular writers such as Paddy Murray in <u>The Star</u>. The paper's readers are given an opportunity to express their opinions in the Letters to the Editor page. Opinion pieces can praise or condemn, ask questions or demand action. Good opinion pieces will not only contain opinions but also reasons and facts to support the opinion.

### Questions & Assignments

Here are thirteen extracts from a selection of opinion pieces.
1. What is the topic of each one?
2. What opinion is being expressed? (Consider if it is praising, criticising or demanding some action to be taken.)
3. What facts or reasons are used to support the opinion?
4. Do you agree with the opinion given? Give reasons for your answer.

---

**1**

*IN 1991, when New York's murder rate hit its peak, there were six killings a day and more than 2,200 in the year. Commuters cowered in their cars as menacing beggars ran filthy cloths over windscreens and demanded money.*

Times Square, the heart of the city, was clogged with thugs and crack cocaine addicts. Tourists were warned not to walk around at night.

The streets seethed with violence while police officers were discouraged from making arrests for minor crimes and forbidden from taking drug dealers into custody for fear that, being so poorly paid, they would fall victim to bribery.

The city had surrendered to crime and an annual increase in murder and robbery was thought inevitable.

Criminals were just a few years away from taking over the whole city which, in 1992, was ranked the second most dangerous in America behind Philadelphia. Police said their orders to stay in cars and respond only to major crimes in progress made them feel powerless.

Today New York is not even in the top 100 most dangerous cities in America. There are 137 which have a higher murder rate. This year there will probably be fewer than 600 murders for the first time since 1967.

The solution has been zero tolerance — tolerating no crimes whatsoever. Tolerating minor crimes leads to major ones, tolerating simple assaults leads to more murders and, above all, never let the criminals get any kind of grip on your neighbourhood through graffiti, begging or public drunkenness.

— **Daniel Jefferies** (adapted)

---

**2**

IN many parts of the world, such as some game reserves in Africa, luxury hotels designed to cater for wildlife enthusiasts have a negative impact on the environment and may even deprive local people of scarce resources like drinking water, which ends up being diverted to watering lawns or filling those classic azure swimming pools.

Tourists are to blame for stress-related illness which has caused a 30% fall in the cheetah population of Kenya's Masai Mara National Park since 1993 and for the fact that iguanas in the Galapagos Islands have abandoned their territories and, in some areas, lost the ability to find food for themselves. Wildlife tourism does more harm than good.

— **Frank McDonald** (adapted)

Reading & Media

### 3

THE NEWS that Charlie McCreevy's Budget would include £20 million towards Croke Park's rebuilding costs has annoyed many bodies disappointed with their allocation…

Should the GAA have been given the money? What about all the other things £20 million can be used for…?

It is the GAA which is hauling the kids in, putting jerseys on their backs, hurleys in their hands and teaching them about skills and team spirits and responsibilities and their own possibilities. And it is Croke Park, great and gleaming, which those kids dream about. It might be a Cumann na mBunscoil match in the rain in October or an All-Ireland in the sunshine in September but the GAA is feeding their imaginations and building their muscles.

Go to practically every community throughout the country, from Finglas to Farranfore and the story is the same. It is the GAA which has bought the pitches, provided the club houses, built the dressing rooms. It is the GAA which has scrounged funds by every means possible, from raffles to golf classics, to get their clubs up and running, to provide a sporting outlet for local children.

Back in September, I had the pleasure to stand with my friend, John Keogh, in the new premises and pitches built by the Killarney Crokes club in Killarney. What an astonishing testimony to the resilience and passion of GAA people to stand in that freshly painted building and gaze over the perfect pitches hewn out of a tangled ribbon of wasteland by John and a small army of FÁS workers and volunteers.

They hauled rocks out of there and turned the earth and loaded topsoil and planted grass and put down little trees to break the breeze. They sold raffle tickets and ran dances and made collections and hustled sponsors. Nobody made a penny profit out of any of it.

On Saturdays and Sundays and summer evenings sometime soon, my friend John Keogh will gaze out of the big clubhouse window we stood at in September and see the pitches below teem with local people and local children, playing Irish sports for the sheer pride and enjoyment of it all. That will be his reward and the community's reward.

And when they come to Croke Park and see the sweeping elegance of the new stands, the splendour of the skyline, this confident statement of our cultural renaissance, they will know that they were appreciated.

For their love and passion, for their expressiveness and dedication, for their ability to exist as a crutch before a national sports policy or grants agency had ever been invented, Croke Park shall be part of their just reward too.

— **Tom Humphries** (adapted)

### 4

**AS things stand the English football hooligan is a man to be reckoned with. The attention of the international media and politcans provide a considerable boost to his ego.**

So does the vast security operation created at great expense involving international police forces across the continents. By such means the English hooligan is pleased that he is noticed. Why not simply stop known terror-spreaders travelling?

And those who offend should go to prison for years rather than months when they are caught.

Bearing that in mind, trouble in Toulouse or elsewhere during this tournament, must pose questions about England's future participation in international football.

— **Eamonn Dunphy** (adapted)

**OPINION**

### 5

WE often hear automobiles criticised. Safety experts say they are dangerous. Ecologists tell us they pollute the air. But even if all these accusations are true, the automobile is still an improvement on its principal alternative, the pedestrian. Cars last a hundred thousand miles or so. Just try to take anybody that far on foot. Pedestrians are slow, require complex maintenance procedures and have bewildering fuel requirements.

Most of the time you can predict what an automobile will do. And if you lose control of an automobile you can jump out of it. But pedestrians are completely unpredictable. And when you're a pedestrian it's difficult to jump out of yourself. Clearly cars are better than people in most respects.

— **P.J. O'Rourke** (adapted)

## OPINION

### 6

THIS country may be undergoing a change from an emigrant to an immigrant society. If this is so, it is not at all surprising that refugees should be attracted to our shores in search of sanctuary, welfare and – eventually – work. This, after all has been the experience of many generations of Irish people who left this country to seek more rewarding work elsewhere in the world.

Rather than turning such people away as a matter of course and in a way which gives Ireland an increasingly inhospitable reputation, it would be better to start planning for immigration and forming plans to enable those who come here in search of employment to find a welcome.

— *Irish Times* editorial (adapted)

### 7

ONLY 65% of students on technician courses in our third-level colleges complete their studies. Whatever the causes, the result is unacceptable. Dropping out implies an enormous waste of public money, but more serious is the loss of skills which our economy badly needs. If skills shortages worsen, the onward march of the economy could be gravely impeded.

Schools should look closely at the way they guide young people towards careers. And they should emphasise the value, for the individual and for society, of skilled manual work.

— *Irish Independent* editorial (adapted)

### 8

MAEVE BINCHY is a most remarkable writer. Not only is she the first in the Eason listing of the top 100 Irish best sellers; she is also the third, fourth, eleventh, fifteenth, sixteenth and seventeenth.

Such success must almost be an embarrassment to her. And into the bargain, quite unlike the majority of her competitors, she is a kindly and loving person, who does good to other writers, and to needy friends. She deserves the glory and also the rewards which she has earned from her books.

— **Bruce Arnold** (adapted)

### 9

FROM the city streets bestrewn with takeaway containers to the roadsides featuring fertiliser bags to the beauty spots piled with rubbish, one might call every part of the country a problem area. Monitoring and hefty fines can be at best only part of the solution. The problem derives from our extraordinary lack of civic spirit, and civic spirit cannot be imposed by the Government. It must be taught in the home and in the school. We must clean up our country, but we should not do so just because we fear that tourists will no longer come here.

— *Irish Independent* editorial (adapted)

### 10

*TO overcome congestion in towns like Killarney, Clifden and Dingle, we will soon have to take our cue from some of the small, delicate Italian hill towns which have devised a series of concentric zones setting strict limits on the movement of cars and tour buses, or from towns on the Italian Riviera, where cars are no longer allowed at all.*

And instead of, say, ruining Slea Head by widening its narrow road to cope with increasing volumes of traffic, it would be much more sensible if Kerry County Council introduced a one-way system on the loop which connects Dingle, Dunquin and Ballyferriter. Already, bus tour operators have voluntarily agreed to travel oneway around the Ring of Kerry.
— **Frank McDonald** (adapted)

### 11

**SO do we need channels crammed with re-runs of third-rate shows that no-one bothered watching first time round? Do we need endless coverage of sporting and leisure pursuits such as archery, trampolining and underwater basket-weaving?**

Do we really want the choice of 50 kinds of Fame and Fortune lottery shows, with 50 quizmasters grinning at bewildered panellists while asking them in 50 different languages not to exhibit any talent but merely to push a button guaranteeing them oodles of money?

You only have to flick through the channels available in France or Denmark or Italy or indeed to sample the pay channels available from Sky to realise instantly that more choices are far from better. More is just more.
— **John Boland** (adapted)

**OPINION**

### 12

THE EXTENT of tax evasion in Ireland cannot be unrelated to the lenient manner in which evaders are treated. There has been no high-profile case in which tax defaulters receive the full rigour of the law. Attitudes to such matters are rather more relaxed in this State. In Galway Circuit Court last week, a jail sentence was imposed for the first time in a case in which a local businessman, with a £500,000 Isle of Man account, was convicted on 15 counts of tax evasion. The businessman in question received a two-year suspended sentence.
— *Irish Independent* editorial (adapted)

### 13

PERHAPS the most breathtaking sight in Coney Island is yet another famed rollercoaster — The Thunderbolt. In an overgrown field beside the Riegelmann Boardwalk, this massive structure stands alone, broken, rusted and covered with ivy and weeds. It is an eerie and spectacular ruin, something from a futuristic movie in which you might also expect to find the Statue of Liberty buried sideways on the beach.
— **John Kelly** (adapted)

# Tabloids — American Style

Some American tabloids with impressive-sounding titles such as *Weekly World News*, specialise in printing outlandishly sensational stories that are obviously invented — but are presented as fact. If such stories were true they would run in the face of all scientific knowledge. The stories are usually backed up by the views and findings of 'experts' with important sounding titles. Yet we never learn where these experts can be found. The suggestion behind all the stories is that the government is aware of them but wants them kept secret in order not to cause panic among the general public.

The stories sometimes contain comments from unnamed government 'sources'. The articles never make a claim that can stand up to any examination. Many of them are illustrated by photographs that have been doctored. While many regard these stories as harmless fun, a considerable amount of people take them seriously.

## Questions & Assignments

1. Write an article of your own inspired by the photograph shown here of the Loch Ness monster.

2. The following pages contain three articles from American tabloids.
   (a) In each case give your views on the content of the article.
   (b) Write articles of your own similar in style to the 'reports' shown here.

# 'A SPACE ALIEN ATE MY DOG!'

### Florida Woman's Horrifying Encounter

A 40-YEAR-OLD woman says a space alien attacked and ate her pet dog, Teeny, in one of the most horrifying close encounters ever!

And while Madge Kinston's story might sound ridiculous, consider this: Investigators say that dozens of eyewitnesses have spotted similar animal-eating extraterrestrials at UFO hot spots around the world in the past six months.

"I don't care if people think I'm crazy or not — I know what I saw and my precious dog is gone," said Miss Kinston of Miami, Florida.

"That monster, that thing, snatched him off the ground like he was a worthless stray. Then, as God is my witness, it ate my Teeny alive."

The mind-bending drama reportedly unfolded on the morning of June 13. Miss Kinston said she was in her backyard when she heard an eerie 'whistling noise' and noticed shrubs bending as if they were straining under a strong wind.

A split second later, she said, a strange creature that looked like a cross between a lizard and a human materialised under a saucer-shaped UFO that was hovering at treetop level 35 feet away.

Miss Kinston said she started to run but the extraterrestrial glared at her with glowing yellow eyes — causing her to freeze in her tracks.

"I couldn't scream. I couldn't move. I couldn't do anything but watch," said the woman, who waits tables in a delicatessen.

"At first it just looked around like it was lost. Then it started waving a silver wand that was attached to a satchel strapped to its back."

"The next thing I know Teeny bolted out of the house and ran over to the alien, wagging his tail. I wanted to stop him but I couldn't move a muscle.

"I couldn't even close my eyes to keep from looking when that monster got Teeny. It was a nightmare I'll never forget."

Miss Kinston says the space alien was the size of a grown man with a green, scaly hide and long, thick tail.

It had a head like a lizard or a dinosaur, she claims. "After the alien ate Teeny it just vanished from the face of the Earth," she continued. "The UFO started humming and whistling, then it vanished, too."

Miss Kinston said she alerted authorities, who referred her to the Tallahassee-based UFO researcher Dr. Cal Dent.

He said that independent researchers have investigated "dozens of similar encounters in Argentina, Brazil, Mexico, New Mexico and Texas" since January.

# VAMPIRE MAKES FBI'S MOST WANTED LIST

WASHINGTON, D.C. The FBI made vampire Paul Marriot the Most Wanted Criminal in America in a secret memorandum dated November 14, but you'll never see his picture in a post office — because the agency believes the news will cause "a national panic".

That's the word from an anonymous FBI expert, who quotes highly placed agency insiders as having said that Marriot, 42, made the FBI's list after he attacked 38 people with his fangs — and sucked their blood. "I know it sounds like something out of a horror movie, but Paul Marriot and the threat he presents to us, is real," said Stocken, whose riveting new book, *Criminals The FBI Is Afraid To Talk About*, is due for release in January. "Marriot is a savage predator who will stop at nothing in his unrelenting quest for blood."

According to sources, Marriot has already attacked victims in 11 states. But nobody has a clue to his whereabouts. And the FBI declined to comment "pending official review of Mr. Stocken's new book."

In spite of the official silence, insiders privately confirmed that "Marriot is not on *the* FBI's Most Wanted Criminal lists.

"You won't find him on our standard Most Wanted List," said an agency source, "because that is reserved for ordinary murderers, bank robbers and the like."

"Marriot is on our *secret* Most Wanted List – which is populated by criminals the FBI doesn't want the general public to know anything about."

To say that Marriot is a man without a past is an understatement. The FBI has devoted thousands of hours to the investigation and all they really know is that he tells victims that he hails from Georgia and sleeps in a coffin.

# FIRST-EVER SURGICAL EXORCISM!

## Doc removes demon from man's head!

by KEVIN CREED/
WEEKLY WORLD NEWS

VIENNA, AUSTRIA A brilliant doctor has stunned the world by doing the first-ever "surgical exorcism" — an operation in which a demon was surgically removed from a man's head!

Brain surgeon Klaus Riedler says he consulted priests, demonologists and Bible experts before extracting an evil spirit from the left temporal lobe of factory worker Franz Bauer's brain.

"I've always believed that medicine and religion should work together," Dr. Riedler said. "But people in my profession don't understand demonic possession. Surgery has never been used to remove an unclean spirit.

"Mr. Bauer was clearly possessed. And neither his doctors nor the Church could help him. It was up to me to stop his headaches and violent behaviour."

So Dr. Riedler combined his surgical skills with his painstaking research into exorcism. He opened Bauer's skull and pulled out a vicious, wriggling demon.

"It was terrifying," says attending nurse Monica Luethi.

"When Dr. Riedler made the incision and exposed the brain there was a small red lump on it. When he pulled on it, I suddenly realized the lump was the demon's fingertip.

"He yanked out the demon, screaming and squirming, and the creature slipped from his grasp.

"Then it made a puffing sound and vanished up into the fan vent."

Witnesses say when the demon came out, it was about 2 feet tall.

"It's important to remember evil spirits can change size, form and shape as easily as we humans change our clothes," says Dr. Riedler.

Bauer, who had suffered with the demon for nearly five years, says he owes his life – and his soul – to Dr. Riedler.

# Assignment

## Functional Writing – Writing a Report

A crime has been committed. Three people witnessed it. Here are their statements. Separate the useful bits of information from the useless and write out a report on this crime based on the statements of three witnesses.

### Witness 1 – Jason

I was sitting on my bike, leaning against the bus stop. My friend Darren was to meet me at eleven but, as usual, he didn't show up. I remember looking at my watch to check the time and noticing it was quarter past eleven when I heard the bang. I looked up and saw two blokes at the window of the jewellery shop.

One had a big stick like a hurley and was after smashing the window. He was wearing white runners and blue jeans and had a track-suit top with the hood up.

The other was stuffing all the jewellery from the window into a kind of a sports bag. It was a blue bag. Then the guy with the hurley drops it and starts helping the other guy to fill the sports bag.

A man came out of the shop and started shouting at them. He was an old man with glasses and he looked shocked.

Then there was a squeal of tyres and this car comes speeding up the road and stops opposite the shop. The doors fly open and the two blokes hop in. I remember noticing that the guy who smashed the window seemed to walk in a sort of funny way. It's hard to describe it but I remember noticing it — like he had a cramp or something in his leg.

The car takes off like a flash. It was an Opel, a brown Opel and I'm nearly positive that it had a 97 WX number plate. There was a big puff of exhaust like when my Dad's car broke down. The driver of the car had a thin pointed face and long hair — I think it was black.

### Witness 2 – Maura

I was going to the shops for my mother when I noticed this car parked outside my friend's house. Sharon is my best friend and they were supposed to be getting a new car. Sharon had told me that they were getting a brand new Opel and that it was going to be red. I remember noticing it because this car was not red. It was more like a shade of tan or orange and it certainly was not new. The number was 98 WX but I can't remember the rest.

What made me think that it was Sharon's car was that the man sitting in it was bald just like Sharon's dad. Then when I was close to it the driver seemed to put on a kind of a cap or a scarf over his head and almost

immediately started up the car and sped down the road. I remember the smell of the exhaust as it took off— a puff of smelly black smoke.

I stopped opposite the shops by the bus stop. I could hear the screaming sound of the brakes as it stopped. I heard people shouting but I was too far away to see anything clearly.

I saw two men running across the road towards the car. One of them seemed to be dragging his leg after him as if he was hurt. They jumped into the car and it sped off.

### Witness 3 – Deirdre

I work in the newsagent opposite the jewellers. I can remember clearly the two of them coming into our shop. One had a sports bag and a hurley but he didn't look like a fellow who played hurling if you know what I mean. He was very thin and pale looking and seemed to walk with a limp.

The other guy with him had a scar under his right eye. They went over to the magazines rack but they didn't seem to be looking for any magazine in particular. They just picked up different ones, computer magazines, business magazines, gardening magazines and they kept glancing out the window. They seemed very nervous.

I asked them if they wanted any magazine in particular and the one with the hurley and the sports bag said that they were just looking. He sounded like he was from Wexford. I'd recognise a Wexford accent because I have been going on holidays there for the last twenty years.

I was just about to ask him what part of Wexford he came from when they walked out and the next thing I heard the sound of glass being broken. I was so shocked that I couldn't move.

A few seconds later I saw them getting into a brown car. I can't remember what the driver looked like but I think that he had blond hair.

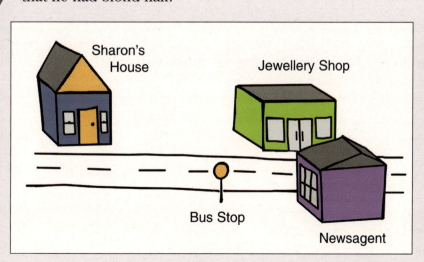

# SPOT THE ERRORS

The following Spot the Errors exercise is aimed at sharpening your basic writing skills. Spot the 20 errors in the Passage below and rewrite the passage correctly. (Note: Refer to the Guidelines on pages 1—15.)

## 19  Mr. Tom's Dog

Willie heard a scrabbling noise. He turned. Sniffing among the leaves at the foot of the tree was a Squirrel. He recognized it's shape from pictures he had seen but he wasn't prepared for one that moved he was teriffied and remained frozen in a crouched position. The squirrel seamed quite unperturbed and carried on scuffling about in the leafs, picking up nuts and tit-bits in its tiny pause. Willie stayed motionless, hardly breeding. The squirrels black eyes darted in a lively manner from place to place. It was tiny, light grey in colour with a bushy tail that stuck wildly in the air as it poked its paws and head into the russet and gold leaves.

After a while Willie relaxed. It seemed as though he had been crouching for hours allthough it couldn't have been more than ten minutes. The little grey fellow didn't seem to scare him as much, and he began to enjoy watching him. A loud sharp barking suddenly disturb the silence. The squirrel leapt and disappeared. Willie sprang to his feet. A small black-and-white collie ran around the tree and into the leaves. It stopped in front of him and jumped up into the air. Willie was more terrified of the dog then he had been of the squirrel. He quickly picked up a thick branch from the ground.

go away he said, feebly. "I'll kill you."

"I wouldn't do that," said a deep voice behind him. He turned to find tom standing by the outer branches."He wont do you any harm"

Tom came towards him, took the branch firmly from his hand and through it to the other end of the garden. The dog scampered after it with a delited bark.

From the novel <u>Goodnight Mr. Tom</u> by Michele Magorian

# Advertising

### Is Advertising Necessary?

The person who has something to sell – whether it is loaves of bread or television sets – must advertise to tell prospective buyers about the products. Advertising is a constant feature of modern life. It is almost impossible to escape from it. We are bombarded with advertisements from television, radio, cinema, newspapers, magazines, outdoor posters – the list is almost endless. Because it plays such an important part in our lives it generates much discussion.

Is advertising a good thing or a bad thing? Without it we would not know what products existed, nor where to buy them. There would be no point in a manufacturer building a factory, installing machinery, buying raw materials, and employing workers if he had no means of telling people about his goods and encouraging them to buy. Without advertising there is unlikely to be a demand for the goods. Advertising leads to competition between manufacturers. As a result, the purchaser benefits by having a greater variety of goods from which to choose, and by having better and better goods – or cheaper goods – offered to him or her.

Advertising is often criticised because of the ways it plays on the feelings of people and persuades them to buy things which they do not really need.

### Which Brand is Best?

Most advertisements set out to persuade people to choose a certain brand from a range of products that differ only slightly – if at all. What makes a certain brand of petrol or shampoo better than its competitors? Are there any significant differences between rival brands of say, heating oil, lemonades, soaps, dishwashers? If so, do the advertisements highlight these differences? Do they show clearly why one brand is different from another?

The answer, in most cases, is "No". The reason is that the differences between rival brands are so slight as to be insignificant. Often rival brands are identical. If there was an important difference – for example a brand of petrol that resulted in 25% more miles per litre than any other brand – then the advertisers would be screaming this fact at us.

An advertisement that makes a plain logical argument in favour of a certain product would probably make very dull reading.

## Advertisements Play on Our Feelings

All people are alike in certain ways. We all share certain feelings – those basic needs, hopes and fears that almost all humans have in common. For example we all like to look good, have friends, stay fit and healthy, care for our family, enjoy a good time and have some of the many goods and luxuries that modern life can offer.

Advertising copywriters – the people who make up advertisements – have a sound understanding of people's inner feelings and how to play on these feelings to get people to buy a particular product.

They know that people generally:
- want to look attractive.
- want to be popular among their friends.
- want to keep up with the neighbours.
- are ambitious to improve their lot in life.
- want the best for their families.
- like to get a bargain.
- like top quality goods.
- are impressed by high technology.
- feel nostalgia for the simple life and traditional values.
- like to be flattered.
- worry about the future.
- enjoy a little adventure and recklessness in life.
- sometimes like to stand out from the crowd.
- value healthy living – but enjoy the occasional spree.

*Most advertisements suggest that by having a particular product, one or more of these needs will be met.*

Many advertisements link the product with things we want from life – friendship, success, popularity and good health. A brand of beer is shown at the heart of a gathering of friends in a pub; a brand of car is driven by a smart and beautiful person; a brand of chocolate is chosen by a pleasant, caring mother for her happy-looking children. For obvious reasons we are never shown the beer being drunk by a group of drunken football hooligans, the car being driven by a drab, awkward-looking individual or a lazy, sloppy-looking mother feeding chocolate to some ill-tempered crying children.

## Techniques of Print Advertising

Most advertisements set out to suggest that one brand is better than its competitors. Print advertisements do it by **words** and **illustrations.** The **illustration** (one or more photographs or drawings) and the **caption** must draw the reader to the **copy** (the paragraph or two of writing which attempts to persuade the reader to buy).

### Illustrations

There is an old saying that a picture is 'worth a thousand words'. In the advertising business, a picture can often say more about a product than a thousand or even ten thousand words can. And it can do so in an instant.

Advertisers take great care in creating illustrations that will tempt people to buy a certain brand or product. All illustrations in advertisements are aimed at showing or suggesting the benefits of the product.

**Illustrations do at least one of the following:**
- Show what the product looks like.
- Show the product in use.
- Show an unpleasant scene caused by not having the product.
- Highlight an important selling point of the product.
- Present a pleasant setting in which readers would like to be.
- Show a 'before and after' scene.
- Present a glamorous and sophisticated setting for the product (e.g. a fashion show, an embassy party, a race meeting etc).
- Present a sentimental or emotional image (e.g. babies, puppies, kittens, grandparents playing with grandchildren etc).
- Provide an unusual image — shocking, amusing, unexpected, interesting — which seems totally unconnected with the product but which catches the attention of the reader. The link will be established by the headline and copy.
- Show people using the product who appear to be happy, confident, successful, glamorous, trendy etc. (Look out for 'props' and background details which symbolise these qualities.)

## The Language of Advertising

The words in most print advertisements divide into two categories – the **headline** (sometimes referred to as the **'slogan'** or **'caption'**) and the **copy** — usually a few paragraphs of printed text.

### Headlines and Captions
The **purpose** of the headline in an advertisement is the same as one in a news report – to get the attention of readers and draw them into reading the entire advertisement. Some advertisements may have more than one headline.

The headlines in advertisements have much in common with newspaper headlines. They may contain a straightforward piece of information they may make use of alliteration, rhymes or other forms of word-play. Many captions can be funny, dramatic or puzzling.

### Copy or Test
The purpose of the text or copy is to back up the headline and illustration by suggesting why the brand being advertised is better than another brand.

## Language and Advertising Techniques

Advertising can provide useful information about new products or show you where to pick up the best bargains. However, it can also lure you into buying what you don't need or persuade you that a particular brand of a product is superior to the rest – when it is virtually identical. You should approach every advertisement with these two basic questions:

- What hard facts about the product are presented in the advertisement?
- How does the advertisement set about making the product appealing?

Answering these two questions about any advertisement may seem easy but advertisers spend a great deal of time and money to make the task difficult.

### MAKE IT DIFFERENT

Some manufacturers take an ingredient or a process that is common to every brand of a particular product, register it under an impressive sounding name and then claim that their product is unique. For example all washing machines have a rinse programme but by simply registering a term such as 'triple action rinse programme' — a meaningless phrase — a manufacturer can now state:

**Novex Washing Machines —
The only machines with the Triple Action Rinse Programme**

Or

**Trident —
The only televisions with Multi-frequency Sound Systems
(i.e. loudspeakers)**

Even a different container is fair game for this method — 'The only washing up liquid in the X-shaped container'. Some consumers then assume that because the product is different it's superior. Sometimes they put in a few letters and numbers to give it a scientific ring.

**Glade —
The only shampoo with pH4 Anti-Dandruff Agent (i.e. soap)**

### THE FAKE COMPARISON

This is where words such as bigger, cleaner, better, best are used without the comparison being completed.

**Sudz Washes Whiter**

This statement is meaningless because the comparison is not finished. If it said **Sudz washes whiter than Persil** then the comparison would be valid.

### THE 'COP OUT' WORD

A word slipped in to a claim for a product which makes the claim meaningless and empty.

**Helps** cure dandruff
Made **with** 100% Irish Beef
**Part** of a healthy diet
**Can** lead to reduced weight

### STRIKE A POSITIVE NOTE

Use words which have positive connotations, i.e. describe things we like.

healthy, new, free, miracle, refreshing, traditional recipe, home-baked, fresh, natural, kind, cares, soft, nourishing, crispy golden…

### OR A NEGATIVE ONE

Use words with negative connotations to suggest a scenario that will come about from not having the product.

weary, germs, greasy, stains, dandruff, dull, ache…

### Get them worried
Make a statement or pose a question which might worry the reader.
**"What if you have an accident while on holiday in Europe...?"**

### Have Figures and Tests to Prove It
Numbers, percentages and test 'results' have an authoritive ring to them.
**Nine out of ten men asked...**
**Tests show that cats prefer...**
**Made with twenty oranges...**

### Aim at the Target
Address a particular target group.
**"Thinking about retirement?"**
**"Mums, have you tried...?"**
**"Farmers..."**

### Get an endorsement
Have a celebrity or an 'expert' to praise a product.
**Ace striker Darren Flash eats Golden Shred.**
**Most vets surveyed recommend Doggy Grub.**

### The Easy Way
Suggest that the product saves time and effort — that it makes life easier in some way.

### Pose a Question
Pose a question which sympathises with the reader's problem.
**"Fed up with dandruff?"**
**"Wouldn't you prefer a simpler way of...?"**

### It's a Fact
Offer an opinion as if it were an undisputed fact.
**"Quite simply the best washing powder ever"**

### Flatter the Buyer
**You deserve the best...**
**You've worked hard so why not treat yourself to...**

### Tempt and Promise
Make a statement which tempts the reader.
**"Send today for your free microwave cookery book"**
Or make a promise.
**"You will be glad that you changed to...."**
Or offer a bargain.
**"The best buy at the price..."**

#### Remember
Not all advertisements set out to trick and deceive. There are many advertisements that communicate worthwhile facts about products in a clear, interesting and often humorous manner.

Spectrum 2

## Questions & Assignments

1. Discuss the language used in the claims made about each of the products in the following advertisements. Identify examples of some of the techniques outlined in the previous pages and explain how they persuade consumers to buy the product. State clearly the product being advertised and the kind of people at whom the advertisement is targeted.

Many of us complain of rheumatic aches and pains – and have found relief with copper. Now the famous Rumaton™ 100% copper bangle adds new power incorporating concealed magnets which sufferers find highly effective. The bangle is styled to look great on anyone and the combined power of copper and magnets can benefit you greatly day and night. It is presented in its own velvet pouch with certification as a genuine Rumaton™ product –
The name you know you can trust.

| Rumaton™ Bangle | 81216 | £12.95 |
|---|---|---|
| 2 or More | 81217 | £11.95 each |

The six-cylinder charisma, the smooth automatic transmission, wheel suspension that straightens out the curves and first-class comfort – they are already enough to make the Volvo 960 a very special car.

As one of the safest cars in the world, it also provides peace of mind – to make your journey all the more uplifting.

The Volvo 960 Series includes estates and saloons, all generously equipped with the very latest in automotive technology. Whichever version you choose, you can combine it with a wide range of options – and have a Volvo 960 to match your very own way of life.

**The Volvo 960**

### Cover Up That Tired Sleepless Look

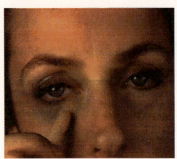

Restore the sparkle to your looks – the same way as professional make-up artists do.
Unique gentle formula goes on as easy as cream in the tender under-eye area, then turns to a smooth unnoticeable powder finish. Easy-to-use stick helps completely cover embarrassing dark circles while preventing eye make-up from creasing and flaking. You won't believe your eyes!

### Herbal Treatment For Arthritis – Could It Help You?

If you suffer from arthritis, spondylitis, gout or muscle disorders this complete herbal remedy might just be able to help you.
No guarantees can be given but, by following the dietary recommendations and taking Arthrem tablets and Herbrem syrup this treatment might be able to help towards your recovery.
Arthrem was developed after Steve Khan, an arthritis sufferer, was given a herbal remedy by an old wise man who lived in the hills of Pakistan. The treatment, together with the diet regime, brought about such an amazing recovery which led to the development and introduction of Arthrem-Herbrem. No drugs or steroids, completely herbal based. Do continue with prescribed treatments and if in doubt consult your doctor.

| Arthrem/Herbrem 25 day course | 81145 | £39.95 |
|---|---|---|

Although average 4 – 5 day treatments usually required, a 30 day money back guarantee is given if after treatment as prescribed your condition has not improved.

## Revealed – The Secret Of That Showroom Shine

**Mer** will really transform your car and restore the 'showroom shine'. Protects against rain, snow, ice, salt, rust and harmful ultra-violet rays and even removes tar and grease – cleaning as it shines!
**Mer** is used by the professionals in the motor, caravan and boat industries. Not readily available in the shops so buy it now direct. Simple to use – twice a year as a neat treatment – during the year as a wash 'n shine – and as well as working wonders on the bodywork of your car, you can use it on many household surfaces.

| Mer Polish | 82720 |
|---|---|
| 500ml | £9.99 |
| 1000ml | £14.99 |
| 3000ml | £29.99 |

## Kill weeds with heat ➤

Take the backache out of weeding with the Weed Wand. This gas-powered heat gun is what many pro gardeners use in preference to poisonous chemical weedkillers. You don't have to burn the weed to a cinder – simply give it a short blast of intense heat that makes the weed's cell walls burst. Within 2 or 3 days the leaves should wilt and die, and all you have to do is sweep away the debris. Small annual weeds die completely after just one treatment, while hardy grasses, dandelions and other perennials may require further treatments. Made in the UK, the Weed Wand is entirely self-contained; it has an integral piezo electric trigger/igniter (no batteries required) and the gas canister fits neatly onto a universal valve. Please note: we cannot send pressurised gas via post. Disposable 185g propane gas canisters are widely available in DIY stores and camping shops. Measures approx. 76.5cm (30")
**Weed Wand £34.95** QA28668

## Learn T'ai Chi With Your Own Personal Instructor

The ancient art of T'ai Chi is becoming increasingly popular with people of all ages throughout the western world. Now thanks to these excellent instructional videos you can learn for yourself in your own time and in perfect privacy. Known as 'meditation in motion' T'ai Chi is a system of smooth slow moving exercises intended to reduce stress, enhance, relaxation and clear the mind of confusing thoughts. Presented by leading teachers, there are 3 videos – Short Form for beginners, Chi Kung for intermediate and the Long Yang Form for advanced.

## Peel potatoes in minutes! ➤

Hand-peeling a family-sized load of spuds is such a soul-destroying chore, so a machine that does it for you automatically is great news. This mainspowered Potato Peeler has a capacity of over 1kg (2lbs) of old or new potatoes.
You load it up, turn it on and sit back . . .
but not for long, because the potatoes should be perfectly peeled in only around 2–4 minutes. The unit has easy-to-clean stainless steel blades and a transparent lid so you can see when the potatoes are ready – and for extra safety, a microswitch on the lid stops operation instantly if it is opened in use. Measures approx. 24cm high × 26cm (9·5" high × 10·25"), with integral cord storage and non-slip rubber feet.
**Electric Potato Peeler £39.95** QA27221

## Fresh Clean Air In Your Car!

We all live in an environment which is becoming increasingly polluted. Now with this handy sized unit (40 × 80 × 110mm) you can have fresh clean air in the car in minutes! The ioniser purifier reduces smoke, dust, pollen, air-borne bacteria and static charge, making your journey a much more pleasant one. Simply plug into the car lighter socket with car plug supplied for clean air on the move!

| Air Ioniser/Purifier | 89504 | £9.99 |
|---|---|---|
| 2 or More | 89505 | £8.99 each |

### Amazing 'On The Spot' Cleaner

New patented odourless **Right-Out** totally outperformed rivals in independent USA tests. It is the only stain remover you are likely to need. Removed virtually ALL stains including coffee, tea, cola, food, blood, make-up, ink etc. from ALL fabrics including silk. Right-Out comes in a convenient pop-top bottle with a Built In Application Brush. NO messy liquids or creams, NO bulky appliators, NO wastage. Brilliant at removing small and large stains from clothing, upholstery, carpets, car interiors etc.

| Right Out | 81249 | £6.95 |
|---|---|---|
| 2 or More | 81250 | £5.95 each |

### A Beam That's Half A Mile Long!

Imagine the brilliance of 500,000 candles and you'll appreciate the remarkable illumination of this tough, impact, and corrosion resistant, halogen lamp.

It features a pistol grip for steady handling, together with a momentary switch for hands-free use. Visible from more than 10 miles away, yet powered by a 6 volt battery.

The Night Tracker is cordless and can be fully re-charged from a car's cigarette lighter or from the mains using the adaptor supplied.

**SPECIAL OFFER!**

| Night Tracker | 82525 | | |
|---|---|---|---|
| Was £69.95 | | SAVE £20! | NOW £49.95 |

### What if it happened to you?

Consider all the problems that you will face if your cards are lost or stolen, and think how quickly you'll have to act to protect yourself.

Among all the emergency telephone numbers which one do you call first? How many can you remember

if your wallet or purse has been stolen? Do you know all your card and account numbers?

You will have to write a letter of confirmation to each card issuer.

And if you are stranded without cash, late at night, or even abroad, your problems are multiplied.

But it needn't happen.

Now there's an easy solution. When you take out a Card Protection Plan policy, you make just one FREE phone call to CPP and everything is done for you.

### Escape Ladder – It Could Save The Lives of You & Your Children

Imagine the horror of being trapped by fire in an upstairs room with no way of escape. Lives can be lost – yet a simple, portable ladder kept in a convenient place could provide a safe means of escape. The Fire Escape ladder can be easily stored under the bed or in a drawer or cupboard, and will fix to a ledge ready to use in just 10 seconds. The incredibly stong yet light steel construction is tested for weights of up to 400 kilos, while adjustable stand-offs allow you to get yourself and your family down to the ground quickly and safely. Available in two sizes 15' and 25', more than long enough for most two-storey houses. For less than £60 it could be a life-saving investment. Order now – for yourself, and perhaps as an especially thoughtful gift.

| Escape Ladder | 89748 | 15ft | £59.99 |
|---|---|---|---|
| | | 25ft | £89.99 |

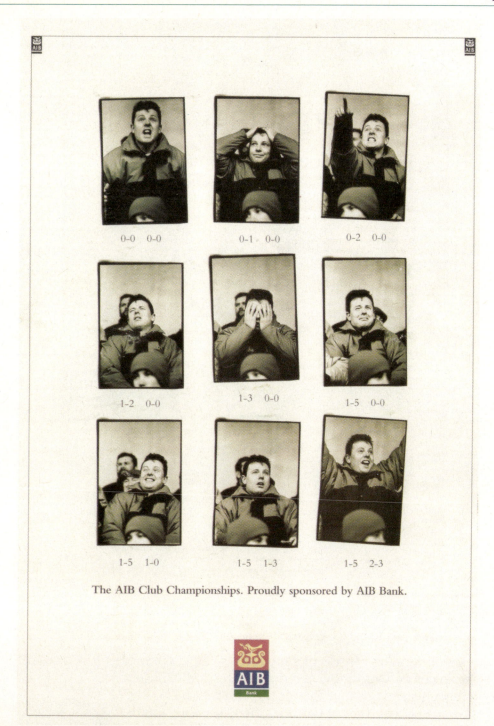

The AIB Club Championships. Proudly sponsored by AIB Bank.

### Questions & Assignments

1. Name the company that placed this advertisement.
2. What is the purpose of the advertisement?
3. Describe each photograph in the advertisement and explain how they are connected.
4. What is your view of the AIB Bank logo? (Part of it represents Noah's Ark.)

## Questions & Assignments

1. (a) The illustration consists of a montage — a picture made up of parts of other pictures. Write a detailed description of the illustration.
   (b) What message, in your view, is the illustration conveying?
2. On what aspect of Natural Gas does the first paragraph of the copy focus?
3. (a) What are the other three paragraphs of the copy persuading people to do?
   (b) What methods of persuasion are used?
4. Why is there an asterisk (*) after the word 'free' in the third paragraph of the copy?
5. Why do you think that the final three lines of copy are printed in very small print?
6. What is your view of the Bord Gáis logo? (Note: Natural gas comes from under the sea-bed off Kinsale in Co. Cork.)
7. Is the caption 'Purity & Efficiency for a Greener Environment' suitable. Explain.
8. What are the two dominant colours used? Suggest why these colours were chosen.
9. Give four reasons why you consider this advertisement is or is not a good one.

# Advertising

## PAUL DANIELS SAYS...

## "I learnt a New Language in 7 days"

"Television viewers were amazed when I spoke Spanish on BBC's 'QED' programme. Nothing special about that you might think... until you realise that just about the only Spanish word I knew seven days before was Ole! A self-confessed 'dunce' in languages at school, I learned to speak Spanish in one week! For once my 'magic' amazed even me!"

"Now you can be amazed too. Because the method was so successful, I decided to perfect it and make it available to everyone.

### IT'S AS EASY AS LEARNING ENGLISH!

"Now you can forget all those old-fashioned courses that teach you useless phrases by boring repetition. With my Method you'll learn each **word** (including its gender) **first**; the grammar and sentence construction come later – it's exactly the same method you used when you learnt ENGLISH – and that wasn't difficult, was it?
Because it's based on simple memory retention techniques that ensure every word you learn becomes part of your personal vocabulary, recalling what you've learnt is that much faster and easier.
IT'S SO STUNNINGLY SIMPLE, IT'S MAGIC! And your very own memory is the key.
Don't worry if you think you have the world's worst memory, you'll soon be amazed when you learn how I can help you expand the hidden capabilities of your own mind.

### A REVOLUTIONARY SYSTEM

"The secret lies in a little known but proven and established technique of word/picture association. Its application to language was developed by Dr. M. M. Gruneberg of the Department of Psychology at the University of Swansea who has evolved a complete system. I had such confidence in the Method I spoke in Spanish on BBC's QED and performed my act in Spanish on Spanish TV in front of an audience of millions. You might not want to impress millions, but you **will** impress all your family and friends.
Now I've mastered the German course, too, and I'm just about to start on French. C'est magnifique! It's the most useful and easiest language-learning system around – and I guarantee you'll learn so fast you won't have time to get bored either!"

ACCESS/VISA/AMEX CREDIT CARDHOLDERS MAY ORDER BY PHONE ON OUR 24HR CREDIT CARD LINE

**0908-319952**

quoting your initials, surname, address, postcode, credit card number and expiry date, together with your telephone number. You may also order by phone on 0908-319767 9.00 a.m. to 5.30 p.m. Monday to Friday. ORDER BY FAX. Credit cardholders can also order by Fax 24 hours a day. Simply fill in the coupon and FAX to 0908-320579.

### LEARN ANYTIME, ANYWHERE

"My Magic Language Memory Method comes on a set of twelve standard audio cassettes which break the language down into easily remembered sections. The course consists of 800 useful everyday words which, experts say, is more than enough to get by.
You can learn in the comfort of your own home, while travelling in a car or even while commuting to work.
Whether you need to learn a foreign language for business, for exams, or merely for the pleasure of conversing in another language, you'll be thrilled with the speed and ease with which you'll be able to accomplish this.

### THE EDUCATIONAL ADVANTAGE

"My Magic Language Memory Method provides a recognised system of self-teach language learning which can also be used as the perfect companion to conventional teaching methods. It's the ideal supplement to your children's education and will give them a valuable head start. And because of its special 'speed-learn' approach I can confidently recommend it as a 'crash course' too. If I can learn a new language in seven days, it is possible that anyone could!

### EVERYTHING YOU NEED

"The presentation pack includes everything you need. There are 12 cassettes each with its own printed cover. And they're all contained in a special case along with an introductory booklet which displays the words for visual recognition and gives valuable instructions, hints and tips on how to use my Magic Memory Method to best advantage!"

Magic Marketing Ltd .(Dept **SCM16**) 39 Alston Drive, Bradwell Abbey, Milton Keynes MK13 9HA.

**ONLY £99.95 POST FREE**

SEND TO: MAGIC MARKETING LTD. (DEPT SCM16) 39 ALSTON DRIVE, BRADWELL ABBEY, MILTON KEYNES MK13 9HA.
14 DAYS 1ST CLASS POST DELIVERY

Language Required (Tick Box)
FRENCH ☐
SPANISH ☐
GERMAN ☐
ITALIAN ☐

Please send me the Paul Daniels Magic Language Memory Method at £99.95 inc p&p
Please indicate whether for Business ☐ Pleasure ☐ Exams ☐
I enclose cheque/P.O. for £ _____ or debit my MASTERCARD/ACCESS/VISA/AMERICAN EXPRESS
CARD NO |__|__|__|__|__|__|__|__|__|__|__|__|__|__|__|__| Expiry Date ___/___
NAME: _____ Signature _____
ADDRESS: _____
_____ Postcode _____
Registered in England No. 2265658

---

## Questions & Assignments

(Paul Daniels is a popular 'magician' who appears frequently on television.)

1. Is there more than one product being advertised here? Give a reason for your answer.
2. Do you regard the main caption – 'Paul Daniels says… "I learnt a new language in 7 days" – effective in grabbing readers' interest in this advertisement? Explain why or why not.
3. The main copy of the advertisement is divided by a number of small headlines. Make a list of these and, in the case of each one, say why you think it is or is not effective. Suggest an alternative for each heading.
4. What techniques are used to persuade people to buy the product? You should identify at least four.
5. At what types of people is the product aimed?

# BRIGHT IDEAS COME CHEAP.

# BRILLIANT ONES COST A LITTLE MORE.

When it comes to quality, innovation and proven reliability, nothing performs like a genuine Mag-Lite.®

Our exclusive features include computer-designed reflectors for a perfectly focused beam at any distance. Switches are made from corrosion-resistant alloys to last a lifetime. And a more durable anodised finish protects components inside and out.

So don't just settle for a bright idea. Make it a brilliant one. Make it a Mag-Lite.® The world's finest torch.™

Mag-Lite®, Mini Maglite® and Solitaire® flashlights.

FROM: OUTDOOR, COUNTRY SPORT, DIY, AUTO, CYCLE, ELECTRICAL, PHOTOGRAPHIC, GIFT SHOPS & SELECTED DEPARTMENT STORES

U.K. Importer/Distributor: Burton McCall Ltd., 163 Parker Drive, Leics. LE4 0JP.
Mag Instrument, Inc 1635 South Sacramento Ave: Ontario, California 91761. www.maglite.com

Made in the U.S.A.

## Questions & Assignments

1. What is being advertised?
2. Describe the top illustration accurately. Do you think it is an effective illustration? Give reasons for your answer.
3. The caption is divided into two parts. Do you think that each part is well-positioned on the page? Give reasons for your answer.
4. What is the main selling point of this advertisement?
5. The caption on its own, tells us nothing about the product being advertised. Show how the copy explains the caption more clearly.
6. Identify a claim made in the advertisement that cannot be proven.
7. Suggest a different illustration and caption for this product.

*Advertising*

### Questions & Assignments

1. Name the product being advertised.
2. Describe the picture in detail, explaining what is happening.
3. In what kind of magazine would you expect to find it – a comic, a teenage magazine, a woman's magazine, a sports magazine? Explain your choice.
4. What message is the advertisement trying to communicate?
5. In your view is this advertisement a good one? Give reasons for your answer.

Spectrum 2

### Questions & Assignments

Write a detailed description of each of these pictures.

*Advertising*

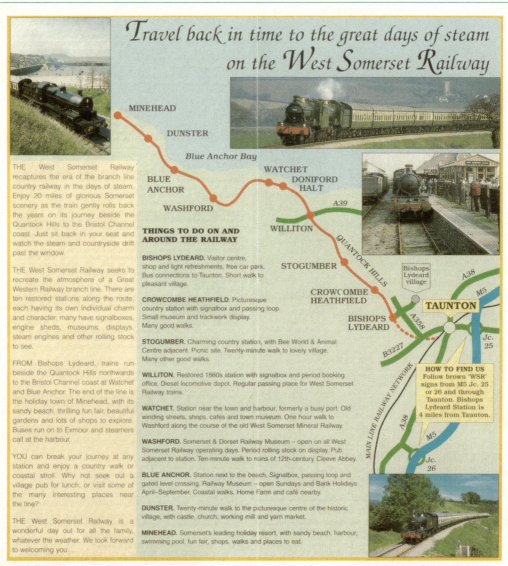

## Questions & Assignments

1. What is being advertised?
2. Explain why the caption uses the phrase *'Travel back in time…'*
3. Write a brief sentence to describe each of the illustrations.
4. What words in the first paragraph of the copy suggests that the train does not travel at high speed?
5. Does the train stop at all the stations? Refer to the text to support your answer.
6. What is the purpose of the map?
7. Imagine that you are working as a guide on the West Somerset Railway. Suggest a destination for each of the following people. Give a reason for your choice in each case.

    Celine   — Interested in farming and bee-keeping.
    Kathy    — Babysitting her nephews aged 12 and 14.
    Eileen   — Wants to paint pictures of an old seaport.
    Gerry    — Interested in old castles and churches.
    Hilary   — Enjoys walking, particularly by the sea.

## The BOOKCLUB of IRELAND™ : how it works

● **SAVE UP TO £97!**
As your special introduction to the club, you can choose any four books from the selection shown within this leaflet from only 99p each, plus £3.99 postage and packing and £3.00 enrolment fee. You could save up to £97 right now!

● **YOUR FIRST PARCEL**
Your introductory package, comprising your books, a membership guide and the latest copy of the club magazine, will be delivered to you promptly.

● **HOME APPROVAL**
You can examine your books for 14 days before deciding whether or not to accept them and become a member of the club. If you are not completely satisfied, simply send them back to us, your membership will be cancelled and you will owe us nothing.

● **JOINING IS EASY**
If you are happy with your introductory package and would like to become a member, return the invoice to us with your payment.

● **YOUR FREE CLUB MAGAZINE**
As a member you will receive a club magazine five times a year. Each issue is packed with bestselling books – all at substantial discounts of up to 50%.

● **ORDERING YOUR BOOKS**
Ordering from the magazine is easy. Just fill in your club order form, pop it in the pre-addressed envelope with your payment and send it off. (To keep costs low a single postage and packing charge of £3.25 is made, however large your order.)

● **ALL WE ASK . . .**
All we ask from you as a member is that you buy at least one book from each magazine. Minimum membership is for just eight magazines. If you wish to cancel your membership after this time, simply give us a month's notice in writing.

● **RETURN THE COUPON TODAY!**
Start saving money on your books right away! Complete the coupon and return it to us – we'll even pay the postage for you. And don't forget – *The Klone and I* is yours FREE, whatever you decide.

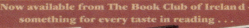
Now available from The Book Club of Ireland – something for every taste in reading . . .

## Questions & Assignments

1. At what month of year do you think this advertisement appeared? Give a reason for your choice.
2. What sentence in the advertisement tells us that the Book Club offers a wide range of books?
3. As a member of the Book Club what is the minimum number of books that you must buy?
4. What is the title of the free book on offer?
5. The introductory offer costs (a) £6·99 (b) £10·95 (c) £97·00? Give a reason for your choice.
6. Write the text for a radio advertisement for the Book Club of Ireland in five sentences.

*Advertising*

Since 1984, Irish farmers have been helping Ethiopian farmers combat the long-term causes of famine.

The Self Help Grow Fund, with the backing of the Irish Farming Organisations, gives you the opportunity to help farmer-to-farmer in a meaningful and practical way.

Your regular contributions have helped to plant over 15 million trees, provide seeds, construct boreholes, flour mills and solar pumps.

In Ethiopia hundreds of thousands of people who depended on food hand-outs are now, with the aid of Self Help, producing a surplus of food. Self Help also works in Eritrea and Malawi.

Help prevent famine. Please complete the coupon and return it to:

Self Help,
Hacketstown,
Co. Carlow.
Tel: 0508 71175

*"ONE OF THE MOST EFFECTIVE AGENCIES I HAVE EVER COME ACCROSS... THEIR WORK IN ETHIOPIA HAS TRANSFORMED WHOLE AREAS FROM FAMINE TO SURPLUS..."*

Matt Dempsey, Editor, Irish Farmer's Journal.

## Questions & Assignments

1. In what kind of magazine did this advertisement appear – a sports magazine, a music magazine, a farming magazine, a religious magazine? Give a reason for your answer.
2. What is the purpose of this advertisement?
3. Do you think that the illustration is a suitable one? Explain your answer.
4. What do we learn about Self Help Grow Fund from the advertisement?

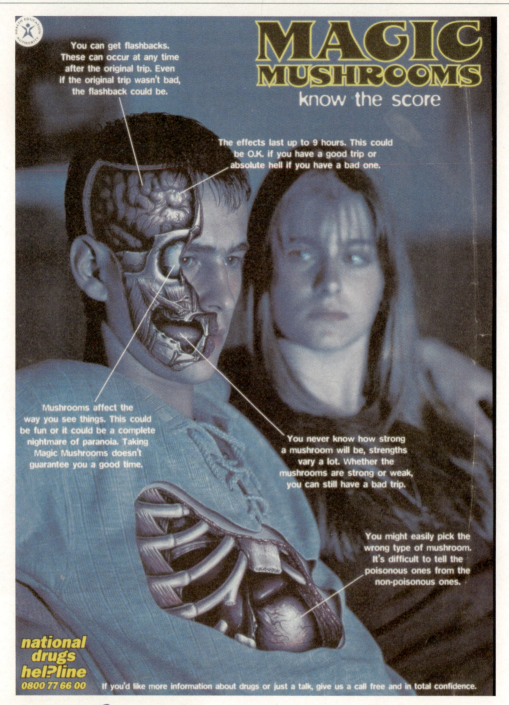

### Questions & Assignments

1. In what kind of magazine did this advertisement appear – a business magazine, a gardening magazine, a farming magazine, a teenage magazine? Give a reason for your answer.
2. What is the purpose of this advertisement?
3. Do you think that the illustration is a suitable one? Explain your answer.
4. What do we learn about '*magic mushrooms*' from the advertisement?
5. Do you think that this advertisement is balanced? Explain your answer.

*Advertising*

### Questions & Assignments

1. What is the purpose of this advertisement?
2. Describe the illustration and explain how it supports the message of the advertisement?
3. What phrases tell us that both companies have been in business for a long time? Why do you think that they include this information?
4. What words are used to describe the food products advertised here?

*Spectrum 2*

# Current Account +

## DO YOU KNOW EXACTLY WHAT YOU'RE GETTING?

## WITH CURRENT ACCOUNT PLUS YOU DO.

Sometimes things aren't always what they're cracked up to be. That's where new Current Account Plus from TSB Bank is different. Because Current Account Plus is a complete banking package that gives you everything you need. This is exactly what you get:

- A Cheque Book
- A '3 in 1' card - that's a Cashcard, a Laser Card and a Cheque Guarantee Card all in one, and, for added security, your photograph and signature is laser-etched onto your card
- Access to over 1,500 ATMs
- Very competitive charges that are easy to understand and when you avail of other TSB Bank services you may qualify for discounts!
- Written notification of any charges and interest sent to you before they are applied to your account
- Overdraft facilities
- Standing Order & Direct Debit facilities

So go on call into TSB Bank today and open a new Current Account Plus - it's the easier way to manage your money.
For further information call 1850 21 11 11

**TSB BANK**

We want what's best for you.

Quarterly Account Charge £10 - this includes a '3 in 1' card, quarterly statements and a minimum of 25 free transactions per quarter. All subsequent transactions (including Laser) are 20p per transaction. Further discounts available. Current Account Plus is available to personal customers only and existing Current Account customers have the option to switch to Current Account Plus. Current Account terms & conditions apply.

## Questions & Assignments

1. What is this advertisement trying to persuade people to do?
2. Describe the illustration and explain how it supports the message of the advertisement.
3. What security measure is included with the '*3 in 1*' card?
4. What 'hard' facts are included about the product being advertised?
5. '. . . *it's the easier way to manage your money*'. Comment on this phrase.

# Advertising

**A**

"I've been tying to get through for an hour!"

*Find out if someone else is trying to ring when your phone is busy.*

**B**

## Introducing Call Waiting

*Another handy service from Telecom Eireann*

With Call Waiting, calls can still get through to you – even if you're already on the phone. So if you're expecting an urgent call or you just don't want to miss another call, you can go ahead and use the phone without worrying. When you're on the phone, you always know if another call is coming in. And you decide what to do. You can take the new call. You can ignore it. Or you can let Call Answering answer it for you. And if you do decide to take the new call, you can do so without hanging up on your first call – you can even switch between the two.

For advice or assistance call us free on 1904.

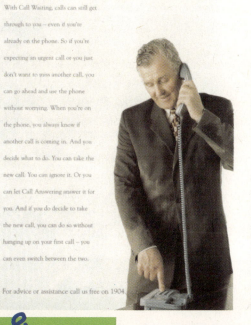

See how easy it is to set up Call Waiting

Lift your receiver and press

It's as simple as that.

### Using Call Waiting

If you're on a call and someone else is trying to get through to you, you will hear a soft 'beep'. (The new caller will hear a normal ringing tone.)

Put the first caller on hold by pressing **R 2** (On some phones, the **R** key is labelled "Recall".) You can now talk to the second caller.

To switch back to the first call, press **R 2** again.

You can switch between these calls as often as you like by pressing **R 2**.

To finish the call you are on and talk to the other caller, press **R 1**.

If you don't want to answer the second call, just ignore the beep. It will stop automatically after 30 seconds. If you have activated Call Answering, the caller will be transferred to your mailbox.

**Switching off Call Waiting**
Pick up your receiver and press

Call Waiting is now turned off. If you're on the phone, a second caller will not be able to get through to you.

Setting up and using Call Waiting is FREE.

## Questions  Assignments

1. What kind of a situation is illustrated in A above?
2. Explain why Call Waiting is a handy service.
3. Imagine that your telephone has Call Waiting set up. You are on the phone to Tracey and your brother phones home.
   (a) What tone will he hear?
   (b) What tone will you hear?
   (c) To find out who is calling, what will you do?
   (d) To finish the call with your brother, what will you do?
   (e) To continue talking to Tracey, what will you do?
4. Comment on the illustration in B.

## Spot the Errors

TThe following Spot the Errors exercise is aimed at sharpening your basic writing skills. Spot the 20 errors in the Passage below and rewrite the passage correctly. (Note: Refer to the Guidelines on pages 1—15.)

### 20  Cereals

Cereals are crops that are members of the grass family and cultivated for there seeds, they are the main source of food throughout the world. The cereals that are most widely grown are wheat, rice, maize (corn), rye, barley, and oats.

The great advantage of serials is that a great deal can be grown on a Small Area of land. Comparatively small areas can feed large numbers of people. The grains are rich in carbohydrates, proteins minerals and vitemins. Because the grains are small and dry, they store well.

Processed brekfast cereals were first produced on a large scale by William Kellogg in michigan, in the united States. Now many diferent sorts are eaten all over the World.

It must have been a grate discovery to early hunters to find special grass seeds that could not only be eaten straightaway, but would store and could be carried easy. The next step forward was taken when nomadic (wandering) people returned to old camping sights to find discarded seeds sprouting and growing. Gradually, people stoped wandering and settled down to grow food.

Wheat was one of the earliest crops to be cultivated. It was first grown in asia around nine thousand years ago. Wheat is largely grown in the temperate regions of the world. There are two types, spring and winter wheat. The spring wheat is grown in the colder regions, sewn in the spring and harvested in the autumn. The winter wheat is sown in the autumn and harvested the following summer.

**Remember, seasons don't take capitals**

# Index of Key Terms

**A**
adjectives 8, 51
advertising 323
advertising techniques 326
alliteration 73
American style tabloid 316
apostrophe 11, 113
assonance 73
author 102, 203

**B**
brand 323
broadsheet style 299

**C**
capital letters 2, 17
characters 112, 227
climax 249
comedy 98
commas 7
conflict 158, 244
copywriter 324

**D**
dialogue 4

**E**
end-stopped lines 44
expectation 180

**F**
film techniques 257-258
first person point of view 102, 113
full stops 17

**G**
ghost stories 165

**H**
headlines 300
hyperbole 51

**I**
illustrations 324-325
image 57
interest 171
irony 237

**M**
metaphor 31

**N**
narrator 102, 203
news 309
news agencies 309
news reports 299
newspapers 297
newsworthy 310

**O**
omniscent point of view 102, 113
opinion 312

**P**
participles 9
pauses 44
plot 158
plurals 6
point of view 102, 113, 146
prepositions 10

press conferences 309
press releases 309
public relations agencies 309

**Q**
quotation marks 4

**R**
report 320
reporters 309
rhyme 35
rhythm 29
run-on lines 44

**S**
science fiction 146
sentences 16, 17, 28, 308
setting 186
simile 31, 57
stringers 309
suspense 202, 203, 249
symbols 75

**T**
tabloid style 299
tension 202, 203, 249
tone 62

**V**
verbs 9, 59, 82

# Alphabetical List of Poems and Short Stories

## POEMS

| | |
|---|---|
| Back in the Playground Blues | 50 |
| Bats | 80 |
| Choosing Shoes | 29 |
| Dover Beach | 70 |
| Evacuee | 63 |
| Happiness | 71 |
| Hedgehog | 78 |
| Holly | 56 |
| Lion | 76 |
| Love Letters of the Dead | 67 |
| Missing You | 46 |
| My Animals | 83 |
| Nora | 54 |
| Parrot | 32 |
| Reported Missing | 66 |
| Spancil Hill | 45 |
| Streets of London | 74 |
| The Band Played Waltzing Matilda | 60 |
| The Battery Hen | 34 |
| The Boys of Barr na Sráide | 48 |
| The Caged Bird in Springtime | 77 |
| The Defence | 79 |
| The Dustbin Men | 30 |
| The Encounter | 78 |
| The Green Fields of France | 64 |
| The Harbour | 72 |
| The Identification | 68 |
| The Intruder | 82 |
| The Pied Piper of Hamelin | 36 |
| The Witnesses | 58 |
| They Will Say | 71 |
| Who Killed Davey Moore? | 52 |

## SHORT STORIES

| | |
|---|---|
| A Break for 3G | 115 |
| Night Train | 159 |
| On My Mother's Life | 189 |
| Smart Ice-Cream | 99 |
| Spit Nolan | 173 |
| Spoil the Child | 193 |
| Strangers | 147 |
| The Anniversary | 153 |
| The Boy Judge | 181 |
| The Goalkeeper's Revenge | 167 |
| The Greatest Gift | 133 |
| The Haunting | 103 |
| The Witch's Fire | 205 |
| Too Many Rabbits | 85 |